COSMIC

Function Points

Theory and Advanced Practices

COSMIC
Function Points

Theory and Advanced Practices

Edited by
Reiner Dumke and Alain Abran

CRC Press
Taylor & Francis Group
Boca Raton   London   New York

CRC Press is an imprint of the
Taylor & Francis Group, an **informa** business
AN AUERBACH BOOK

Auerbach Publications
Taylor & Francis Group
6000 Broken Sound Parkway NW, Suite 300
Boca Raton, FL 33487-2742

Visit the Taylor & Francis Web site at
http://www.taylorandfrancis.com

and the Auerbach Web site at
http://www.auerbach-publications.com

Contents

Foreword

"Plans are nothing. Planning is everything." That's how Dwight D. Eisenhower clearly emphasized the importance of good estimation and planning processes. The real purpose of effective estimation and planning is to set up estimates and plans and also to change the thinking of impacted stakeholders. Estimation and planning facilitate learning. It is neither the precise estimate nor the exact plan, generated with some form of computer support, that counts. Instead, it is the understanding of the direction to go and what risks, obstacles, and dependencies exist that is most important.

Estimation and measurement are means for achieving stated goals, not the end. They are intended to provide directions, not final solutions. Estimation and measurement is a continuous effort because we are living in a world of fast change. An initial estimate and subsequent plan provides guidance in which direction to go. No one would expect this to remain valid without adjustment for a longer period of time. Estimating implies reestimating—based upon measurements.

Over time I have created a simple checklist with ten elements that I walk through with my clients in software management. It applies to this book and to guide you as a reader. Have a brief look at the following list and decide for yourself and for your company how many of the following topics you would mark as "yes" or "true" for your organization:

- Project objectives and contents not aligned with business needs
- Lack of transparency of drivers of estimates and plans
- Estimates are fuzzy and vastly wrong—and nothing improves
- Formalism and lack of commitment dominate pragmatic, agile management processes
- Estimates and plans are not believed and considered unrealistic
- Lack of alignment with many different stakeholders in the project and beyond
- Unclear ownership of management decisions
- Unknown value and impacts of features and releases
- Surprises and ad hoc decisions
- Plans are not followed up, insufficient measurement, estimates are not improved

If you had more than three topics marked, I strongly recommend this book in order to learn best estimation and measurement practices. You might want to select an appropriate chapter and just start reading, or first focus on methodology and then look to concrete case studies.

This book presents methods, practices, and many experiences on software estimation. Estimation is a base practice for project management and for business processes in general. It is closely linked to measurement and planning, because without good measurements, estimates would be vague, and without planning, they would be useless. Like any measurement process, estimates consist of four specific steps, as illustrated in the figure below. First, the baseline has to be established. Why do we estimate, and for what purpose? Then, the estimates are extracted on the basis of estimation methods. COSMIC function points today are state of the practice due to their wide applicability and broad industry experience base. Having extracted a first estimate, it must be evaluated. Is the estimated effort and volume realistic? Have all influencing factors been considered? Do they correspond with past experiences and industry benchmarks? Is the estimate overly conservative, thus endangering the business success of the product or service? Finally, estimates are used to execute decisions. Plans are set up and controlled. If there are deviations, necessary actions have to be taken. Naturally, the process is repeated throughout the project to make sure that plans and decisions are based on a realistic assessment of the situation and progress.

Function points are today the major estimation method in building IT and software-intensive systems. It was thirty years ago when the function point analysis method was introduced to the software development community. It was the first technology-independent way to measure the size of a piece of software. The main reason to develop a size measurement method was the need to better manage software development. Too often software managers had simply no clue where the project stood and how productive it would be. Often software developers those days claimed that software was not measurable. Estimation greats like Charles Symons, Alain Abran, and Reiner Dumke have since improved the method and application of functional size estimation and measurement.

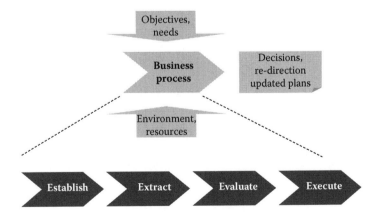

In 1986, the International Function Point Users Group (IFPUG) was formed to foster and promote the evolution of the function point method. It created international standards for function points and educated generations of software managers and developers on the method. In doing so, IFPUG ensured that function points could be used around the world uniformly. Consequently, the IFPUG method would be adapted to other kinds of software systems, such as GUI applications and control systems. It delivered to the ISO/IEC 20926 standard for the IFPUG 4.0 and later the IFPUG 4.1 FSM method. In order to apply function points to all types of IT and software systems, in 1998 the Common Software Measurement International Consortium (COSMIC) was set up. They delivered a modernized software estimation and measurement method, the COSMIC FFP, with the following innovative aspects:

- A functional size measurement method designed to be applicable to all "data movement rich" software, i.e., for business, real-time, and infrastructure software, at any level of abstraction and in any layer of software architecture
- A formal measurement process distinguishing artifacts mapping from measurement per se
- A unit of measure formally defined, based on a few key software engineering principles, independent of any specific software development methods
- The concept that a piece of software has many possible functional sizes, and therefore any measurement needs to be defined by its purpose, the scope, the choice of functional users, and the level of granularity of the software being measured

Honoring the relevance of the COSMIC method based on profound research, the British IT Professional Awards 2006 priced it. It is globally used and has been translated into more languages than any other function point method (including Arabic, Dutch, French, Italian, Japanese, Spanish, and Turkish). Consequently, there are more and more COSMIC FFP certifications around the world.

This book edited by Reiner Dumke and Alain Abran gives an excellent overview about the background of the COSMIC functional size measurement method. The editors have summarized papers from the last five years about the scientific and practical background of this sizing method presented in the international software measurement community. The book is very readable and provides a strong knowledge background for both practitioners and researchers. As such, it will be a useful desktop reference within the software engineering and IT communities.

With its broad background, it is useful for practically implementing and successfully adapting other functional sizing methods. Among its highlights are:

- The consequent division between the functional sizing and the use of this result for cost, effort, or project estimation
- The new level of an FSM method involving the ratio scale type allowing empirical evaluation and exact system comparison

- The demonstration of the practical relevance of the FSM method performing case studies, benchmarking, and analogical conclusions
- The orientation of current software systems such as embedded systems, automotive software, business applications, communication software, and control systems

Estimation with COSMIC function points is useful for various reasons. Better estimates will help project managers deliver according to commitments, and thus to improve business performance. Wrong decisions are hard to reverse afterwards, especially in the early stages of the process, when fundamental business decisions are made. Planning is part of the proactive effort to avoid pitfalls in the later stages. Good estimation, planning, and measurement save 5 to 30% of the software development and IT budget by different levers:

- Visible, committed, and achieved milestones and results
- Basis for measuring hard facts—rather than by table dancing and guessing
- Trust and alignment across software departments, project management, and general management
- Baselined assumptions
- Early removal of inconsistencies
- Simplified monitoring of performance and results
- More effective resource utilization
- Transparent and clear rules for termination or not proceeding
- Increasing accountability for results across the corporation
- Sustainable productivity improvement

The COSMIC full function point techniques presented in this book will help you to implement, master, and improve your estimation process. They will help you as well as your organization to mature your project management. With improved estimation and measurements, always remember the words of one of the leading figures in the field of systems/software engineering and management, Don Reifer: "When the smoke clears, the thing that really matters to senior management is the numbers." For this matter I wish you all the best and good success.

Christof Ebert

Vector
Stuttgart

Preface

The dynamics of the software market lead to a variety of methods for the estimation of product size or development effort in the background of *cost estimation*. The general relationship between different indicators of quality, quantity, effort, and productivity is defined as *quantity = (productivity × effort)/quality*, and could be used in different permutations. Different kinds of effort estimation use the *functional sizing approach*. Some of the project estimation methods are based on the constructive cost model (COCOMO), function point, and software life cycle management (SLIM) approaches. Project estimation could be based on direct effort execution (e.g., SLIM), using and adapting a large set of cost drivers (COCOMO).

One of the main problems of cost estimation leads to the determination of the software size. Different versions of lines of code and more and more function point methods are used to solve this problem. As functional size measurement (FSM) of the *first generation* we can use FSM methods like ISO 20926:2003, Function Point Analysis (FPA); ISO 20968:2002, MKII Function Point Analysis from UKSMA; and ISO 24570:2004, the NESMA FSM Method Version 2.1.

Function point methods should be based on the international generic FSM standard, ISO 14143. It was developed by ISO Working Group 12 (JTC1/SC7/WG12), and is now a six-part project providing an internationally accepted set of standards and technical reports describing the concepts of interest to designers and users of FSM methods:

- ISO 14143-1 (Definition of Concepts) defines the fundamental concepts of FSM, promoting consistent interpretation of FSM principles.
- ISO 14143-2 (Conformity Evaluation of Software Size Measurement Methods) was developed to provide a process for checking whether a candidate FSM method conforms to the provisions of ISO/IEC 14143-1:1998 (the output from this process can assist prospective users of the candidate FSM method in judging whether it is appropriate for their needs).
- ISO TR 14143-3 (Verification of FSM Methods) verifies whether an FSM method meets the quality characteristics of a measurement method, which

are repeatability and reproducibility, accuracy, convertibility, discrimination threshold, and applicability to functional domains.

■ ISO TR 14143-4 (Reference Model) provides standard reference user requirements (RURs).

■ ISO 14143-5 (Determination of Functional Domains for Use with FSM) describes the properties and characteristics of functional domains, and the principal procedures by which characteristics of FURs can be used to determine functional domains.

■ ISO TR 14143-6 is the guide for the use of the ISO/IEC 14143 series and related international standards and is currently under development.

The problems of the first-generation FSM methods are the embroilment of (functional) measurement with (cost) estimation. They start with the estimation aspects from the beginning and don't permit analysis and comparison on the size level only. The COSMIC full function point (FFP) method was designed to measure a functional size of software based on its functional user requirements (FURs). This method was designed to conform to the existing ISO/IEC standard 14143, which sets out the international agreement on the principles of functional size measurement.

COSMIC, the Common Software Measurement International Consortium, is a voluntary initiative of a truly international group of software measurement experts, both practitioners and academics, from Asia/Pacific, Europe, and North America. The principles of the COSMIC FFP method of measuring a functional size of software were laid down in 1999. Field trials were successfully conducted in 2000–2001 with several international companies and academic institutions. The process of developing an international standard for the COSMIC FFP method was started in 2001 and adopted and published by ISO in 2003 as ISO/IEC 19761. This FSM method is designed to be applicable to software from the following domains:

■ Business application software, which is typically needed in support of business administration, such as banking, insurance, accounting, personnel, purchasing, distribution, or manufacturing. Such software is often characterized as data rich, as its complexity is dominated largely by the need to manage large numbers of data about events in the real world.

■ Real-time software, the task of which is to keep up with or control events happening in the real world. Examples are software for telephone exchanges and message switching; software embedded in devices to control machines such as domestic appliances, lifts, and car engines; software for process control and automatic data acquisition; and software within the operating system of computers. Hybrids of the above are used, for example, in real-time reservation systems for airlines or hotels.

It is possible to define extensions to the COSMIC FFP measurement method, such as for software that is characterized by complex mathematical algorithms or other specialized and complex rules (such as may be found in expert systems, simulation software, self-learning software, weather forecasting systems, and so on), and for software processing continuous variables such as audio sounds or video images (such as found, for instance, in computer game software, musical instruments, and the like). The recognition of the COSMIC method can be described by the following characteristics:

- It is recognized and highly visible among FSM experts worldwide.
- It generates significant interest in academia as a new basis for research projects, especially in Europe.
- It is recognized by a fair number of software engineering industry leaders in Europe and Australia.
- It is sufficiently recognized by the industry in Japan to be made a national standard.
- It is quite visible in the software engineering industry in India, and there is some usage in China.
- It is poorly visible and not widely used in the North American market.
- It is poorly visible outside the software engineering market, most probably worldwide.
- The uptake in the real-time world has been noticeably better than in the world of business software, almost certainly due to the fact that the real-time world has not had any acceptable FSM method before the COSMIC method.
- A significant number of consultancies can offer support and training in these markets and tool suppliers are starting to support the method.
- There are demands for our certification examinations in Europe, Canada, and India.

Furthermore, from the software measurement and evaluation point of view, the COSMIC FFP involves the following new quality characteristics:

- The result of the functional counting is a *ratio-scaled measure* using the Cfsu unit for evaluation and consideration.
- COSMIC FFP is *usable for more of the actual kind of systems*, such as embedded and reactive/interactive systems.
- COSMIC FFP can be used for *white box estimation*. (This means that the size *does not include empirical aspects*, and the accuracy of the project estimation depends on the used empirical sources for the adjustment only.)

In 2007, version 3.0 of COSMIC was introduced and led to some extensions and adaptations, such as general principles of approximate sizing by measurement scaling, approximate sizing of changes to functionality, early approximate sizing and scope creep, the evolution of functional user requirements in the early stage of a large software project, methodologies and statistically based conversion formulas for functional size convertibility (between FPA and FFP), and changing the unit from Cfsu (COSMIC functional size unit) to CFP (COSMIC function points).

This book describes the history, intentions, and practical and scientific background of the COSMIC method. The goal is to present general principles for successful innovative (size measurement) methods. Consequently, the book is structured based on the following general experiences:

- One of the main characteristics of sizing of software artifacts leads to *the correct identification of the functionality* itself (shown in Chapter 1).
- One of the further main characteristics of software sizing leads to the *correct identifying of the scale type of the counted functionality* (described in Chapter 2).
- New approaches of software sizing *must satisfy the essential usability requirements*, such as applicability for different kinds of systems, appropriateness for different software processes, and methodologies for different levels of application (demonstrated in Chapter 3).
- A (new) functional size measurement method *must demonstrate the relevance in practice* by using typical methods of validation, such as case studies, benchmarking, or analogical conclusion (given in Chapter 4).
- One of the levels for acceptance of the (new) functional size measurement method *could be its tool support* by using measurement solutions, easy evaluation, and essential experience databases (described in Chapter 5).

Every chapter includes papers chosen from the proceedings of our workshops in the COSMIC community of the past six years, which explain and demonstrate the essential activities in order to comply with the above principles. We thank Shaker Publisher in Aachen, Germany, for agreeing to publish these chosen papers in a summarized book at CRC Press.

Reiner R. Dumke
Magdeburg

Alain Abran
Montréal

The Editors

Reiner R. Dumke is currently working at the Otto-von-Guericke-University of Magdeburg, Germany, as a professor with software engineering as a research field. He is one of the founders of the Software Measurement Laboratory (SML@b) of the Computer Science Department of the University of Magdeburg and coeditor of the *Measurement News Journal*. He is leader of the German interest group on software metrics, and he works as a member of the COSMIC, DASMA, MAIN, IEEE, and ACM communities. He received a diploma-degree (MS) in mathematics in 1970, followed in 1980 by a PhD, with a dissertation in computer science about the efficiency of database projects. He is the author and editor of more than thirty books about programming techniques, software metrics, metrics tools, software engineering foundations, component-based software development, and Web engineering. He can be reached via email: dumke@ivs.cs.uni-magdeburg.de.

Alain Abran holds a PhD in electrical and computer engineering (1994) from École Polytechnique de Montréal (Canada) and master degrees in management sciences (1974) and electrical engineering (1975) from the University of Ottawa. He is a professor and the director of the Software Engineering Research Laboratory at the École de Technologie Supérieure (ETS)–Université du Québec (Montréal, Canada). He has over fifteen years of experience in teaching in a university environment, as well as more than twenty years of industry experience in information systems development and software engineering. His research interests include software productivity and estimation models, software engineering foundations, software quality, software functional size measurement, software risk management, and software maintenance management. Dr. Abran has been a coeditor of the *Guide to the Software Engineering Body of Knowledge (SWEBOK)* (see ISO 19759 and www. swebok.org), and he is the chairman of the Common Software Measurement International Consortium (COSMIC) (www.cosmicon.com).

Contributors

Alain Abran
Software Engineering Management
    Research Laboratory
Université du Québec
Montréal, Canada
abran.alain@uqam.ca

Fatima Aziz
École de Technologie Supérieure—ETS
Montréal, Canada
fatima.aziz.1@ens.etsmtl.ca

Luigi Buglione
Engineering IT
Rome, Italy
luigi.buglione@eng.it

Ton Dekkers
Galorath Technology International
Amsterdam, The Netherlands
tdekkers@Galorath.com

Onur Demirors
Middle East Technical University
Ankara, Turkey
demirors@ii.metu.edu.tr

Jean-Marc Desharnais
Software Engineering Management
    Research Laboratory
Université du Québec
Montréal, Canada
jean-marc.desharnais@etsmtl.ca

Reiner R. Dumke
University of Magdeburg
Department of Computer Science
Magdeburg, Germany
dumke@ivs.cs.uni-magdeburg.de

Pinar Efe
Siemens PSE Turkey
Ankara, Turkey
pinar.efe@siemens.com

Peter Fagg
Software Measurement Service Ltd.
Kent, United Kingdom
md@pentad.co.uk

Thomas Fehlmann
Euro Project Office AG
Zurich, Switzerland
thomas.fehlmann@e-p-o.com

Thomas Fetcke
Otto-von-Guericke-University
Magdeburg, Germany
fetcke@acm.org

Erik Foltin
VW AG
Wolfsburg, Germany
foltin@ivs.cs.uni-magdeburg.de

Pekka Forselius
Software Technology Transfer
Finland Oy, Finland
pekka.forselius@sttf.fi

Cigdem Gencel
Middle East Technical University
Ankara, Turkey
cgencel@ii.metu.edu.tr

Edgar Głowacki
Polish-Japanese Institute of
  Information Technology
Warsaw, Poland
edgar.glowacki@pjwstk.edu.pl

François Gruselin
Facultés Universitaires Notre Dame de
  la Paix
Namur, Belgique
fgruseli@info.fundp.ac.be

Piotr Habela
Polish-Japanese Institute of
  Information Technology
Warsaw, Poland
piotr.habela@pjwstk.edu.pl

Naji Habra
Facultés Universitaires Notre Dame de
  la Paix
Namur, Belgique
nha@info.fundp.ac.be

Malcolm S. Jenner
University of Wolverhampton
Wolverhampton, United Kingdom
M.S.Jenner@wlv.ac.uk

Adel Khelifi
École de Technologie Supérieure—ETS
Montréal, Canada
adel.khelifi.1@ens.etsmtl.ca

Tom Koppenberg
Sogeti Nederland B.V.
Amsterdam, The Netherlands
tom.koppenberg@sogeti.nl

Arlan Lesterhuis
Sogeti Nederland B.V.
The Netherlands
arlan.lesterhuis@sogeti.nl

Mathias Lother
Robert Bosch GmbH
Stuttgart, Germany

Roberto Meli
DPO—Data Processing Organisation
Rome, Italy
roberto.meli@dpo.it

S. Oligny
Software Engineering Management
  Research Laboratory
Université du Québec
Montréal, Canada
serge.oligny@bell.ca

Olga Ormandjieva
Concordia University
Montreal, Canada,
ormandj@cse.concordia.ca

Luca Santillo
GUFPI-ISMA
Rome, Italy
luca.santillo@gmail.com

Ulrich Schweikl
SIEMENS AG Automotive
Regensburg, Germany

Tomasz Serafiński
Łódź University of Technology
Łódź, Poland
tomaszek@kis.p.lodz.pl

Anabel Stambollian
École de Technologie Supérieure—ÉTS
Montréal, Canada
anabel.stambollian@ens.etsmtl.ca

Sophie Stern
Renault Automotive
Guyancourt, France
sophie.stern@renault.com

Kazimierz Subieta
Łódź University of Technology
Łódź, Poland
tomaszek@kis.p.lodz.pl

Charles R. Symons
Software Measurement Service Ltd.
Kent, United Kingdom
charles_symons@compuserve.com

Manar Abu Talib
Concordia University
Montreal, Canada
abutal@cse.concordial.ca

Julien Vilz
Facultés Universitaires Notre Dame de
   la Paix
Namur, Belgique
jvilz@swing.be

Frank Vogelezang
Sogeti Nederland B.V.
Amsterdam, The Netherlands
frank.vogelezang@sogeti.nl

Stefan Weber
SIEMENS AG Automotive
Regensburg, Germany
stefan.weber@at.siemens.de

Chapter 1

Background and Overview of the COSMIC-ISO 19761

Cost estimation, considering the dynamics of the software market, leads to a variety of methods for the calculation of development effort and project duration. Some of the project estimation methods are the constructive cost model (COCOMO), different kinds of point counting methods, and the software life cycle management (SLIM)-based approaches (Bundschuh and Dekkers 2008; Chemuturi 2009; Dumke et al. 2008; Ebert and Dumke 2007; Jones 2007; McConnell 2006).

One of the key problems consists of the "comparable unit" between the different software estimations in practice: this basic unit is the *functional size* (without any empirical meaning). The general methodology of software estimation is shown in Figure 1.1.

This chapter contains essential aspects for software sizing involved in the general field of functional size measurement (FSM). The section by Alain Abran, Serge Oligny, and Charles Symons discusses the key concepts of COSMIC FFP-related FSM design and the structure of its measurement process, as well as the strategy of its worldwide field trials.

The following section by Mathias Lother and Reiner Dumke gives an overview of existing approaches and discussions, and thus deals with problems and opportunities in this area. This study introduces chosen functional size measurement methods and evaluates them with respect to their suitability for certain functional domains and their maturity. Furthermore, general problems of functional size measurement will be discussed as well as alternative approaches presented.

In the section by Pekka Forselius, the hidden development of functional size measurement and other measurement methods are explained. Although no one

1

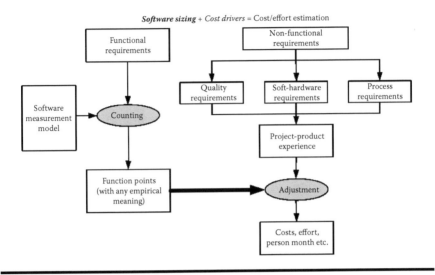

Figure 1.1 General methodology of software estimation.

has invented anything better for size measurement in twenty-five years, the software project management concepts, knowledge databases, and best practices have improved a lot, and finally it's time to adopt them into everyday software development business.

Today, there are many variants of functional size measurement methods in use. In the section by Pinar Efe, Onur Demirors, and Cigdem Gencel, common concepts and common measurement possibilities are investigated for three ISO-certified FSM methods: IFPUG FPA, Mark II FPA, and COSMIC FFP.

The last section in this chapter, by Alain Abran, Peter Fagg, Roberto Meli, and Charles Symons, describes and explains some changes that have been made to the COSMIC FFP method to help improve understanding and consistent use of the method to ensure consistency with existing ISO/IEC 14143 standard terminology and definitions.

1.1 COSMIC FFP and the Worldwide Field Trials Strategy

Alain Abran, S. Oligny, and Charles R. Symons

1.1.1 Origin of Software Functional Size Measurement

Measuring the functional size of software was originally proposed in 1979 by Albrecht in a communication (Albrecht and Gaffney 1983) describing the results of an effort started in the mid-1970s in one IBM business unit. The overall goal of the work described in Albrecht's original paper was to measure the productivity of software development, as viewed from an economic perspective. His method, function points analysis, was proposed as a specific measure of the "output" of the development process, allowing a comparison of projects where software was developed using different programming languages.

The overall approach described in Albrecht's paper to achieve that goal was to select a specific subset of twenty-two software projects, mostly management information system (MIS) software, completed within this one organization. The measurement of the functional size of the software delivered by these projects consisted of a weighted sum of inputs, outputs, inquiries, and master files. The weights assigned to these items "were determined by debate and trial" (Albrecht and Gaffney 1983). Some extra adjustments (±25%) were provided for "extra complicated" (Albrecht and Gaffney 1983) items. In this communication (Albrecht and Gaffney 1983), Albrecht also offered a set of forms and rules to aid in calculating "function points." Many of the rules proposed originally were based on some aspects of the physical implementation of software.

In 1986, the International Function Point Users Group (IFPUG) was formed to foster and promote the evolution of the function point method. The group used Albrecht's revised version of the original method, using a fifth function type ("interface files") and a set of weight tables. Much work went into the subsequent releases of the method to include rules allowing an interpretation of functionality increasingly independent of the particular physical implementation of software. The contribution of IFPUG to the field of functional size measurement has been the documentation of the measurement procedure, which enabled a certain level of uniformity in the application of the method. The basic concepts and implicit model of software, though, remained unchanged from what was proposed by Albrecht in 1984. However, it cannot be postulated that the sample of software used by Albrecht in 1984, which was developed between 1974 and early 1979, is representative of all software developed in the 1980s, 1990s, and 2000s.

1.1.2 A New Generation of Functional Size Measure

A group of experienced software measurers gathered in 1998 to form the Common Software Measurement International Consortium (COSMIC). This group aimed at designing and bringing to market a new generation of software measurement methods. With the support of industrial partners and tapping on the strengths of IFPUG, Mark II (Symons 1991), NESMA (NESMA 1997), and version 1.0 of full function point methods (Abran et al. 2000; Bosch 2003; Büren and Kroll 1999; Kecici et al. 1999; Oligny et al. 1998; Schmietendorf et al. 1999; St.-Pierre et al. 1997a), the group proposed some basic principles on which a new generation of software functional size measurement method could be based (Abran 1999; Synoms 1999; Symons and Rule 1999). In November 1999, the group published version 2.0 of COSMIC FFP, a measurement method implementing these principles. Overall, close to forty people from eight countries participated in the design of this measurement method. Key aspects of the COSMIC FFP measurement method are now highlighted.

1.1.2.1 Allocation of Functional User Requirements

From the perspective proposed by COSMIC, software is part of a product or service designed to satisfy functional user requirements. From this high-level perspective, functional user requirements can be allocated to hardware, to software, or to a combination of both. The functional user requirements allocated to software are not necessarily allocated to a single unit of software. Often these requirements are allocated to pieces of software operating at different levels of abstraction and cooperating to supply the required functionality to the product or service in which they are included.

In the context of the COSMIC FFP measurement method, which is aimed at measuring the functional size of software, only those functional user requirements allocated to software are considered. (The method may be applicable to size functional requirements for information processing that are allocated to hardware, but this needs further research.) For instance, as illustrated in Figure 1.2, the functional user requirements in this example are allocated to three distinct pieces, each exchanging data with another through a specific organization: One piece of the software lies at the application level and exchanges data with the software's users, and the second piece lies at the operating system level. In turn, this second piece of the software exchanges data with a third piece lying at the device driver level. This last piece then exchanges data directly with the hardware. The COSMIC FFP measurement method associates the functional user requirements for each piece with a specific layer. Each layer possesses an intrinsic boundary for which specific users are identified.

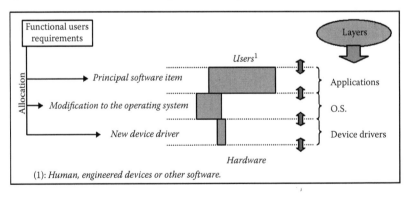

Figure 1.2 Example of functional user requirement allocation to different layers. (From Oligny, S., A. Abran, and D. St.-Pierre. 1999. Improving software functional size measurement. *Proceedings of the 13th International Forum on COCOMO and Software Cost Modeling.* With Permission.)

1.1.2.2 Representation of Functional User Requirements in Software

The functional user requirements allocated to one or more pieces of software are decomposed into and represented by functional processes. In turn, each functional process is represented by subprocesses. A subprocess can either be a data movement type or a data transform type. Version 2.0 of the COSMIC FFP measurement method recognizes only data movement type subprocesses. Further research is deemed necessary to incorporate data transform subprocess types in the measurement method. In the meantime, an approximating assumption is made that each data movement has an associated (small) amount of data transformation. This assumption, which should be valid for most MIS, real-time, and operating system software, is being tested in field trials (see Section 1.1.3), but will clearly not be valid for algorithm-intensive software as used in, e.g., scientific or engineering domains. The approach is illustrated in Figure 1.3.

Given the approximating assumption, a COSMIC FFP functional process is defined as a unique and ordered set of data movements that are triggered by an event outside the software being measured, and which, when complete, leave the software in a coherent state with respect to the external event.

1.1.2.3 COSMIC FFP Software Model

The COSMIC FFP measurement method defines an explicit model of software functionality, derived from the functional user requirements. Based on this explicit

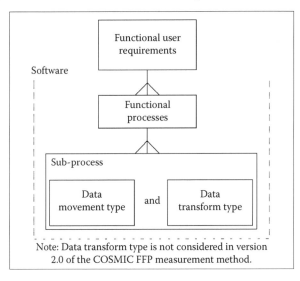

Figure 1.3 COSMIC representation of functional user requirements within a piece of software. (From Symons, C. R. 1999. COSMIC aims, design principles, and progress. *Proceedings of the IWSM'99*. With Permission.)

model of functionality, relevant functional attributes of software are identified. Their extent and limits are defined, and their generic interactions are described. Taken as a whole, these functional attributes form a generic model for any type of software that is not algorithm rich. The model is illustrated in Figure 1.4.

Four types of data movement are defined within this model. They form the basis for defining the standard unit of functional size. The four types of data movement are presented in Table 1.1.

Version 2.0 of the COSMIC FFP measurement method uses only four base functional components: entry, exit, read, and write. Data manipulation subprocesses are not used as base functional components. The method assumes, as an acceptable approximation for many types of software, that the functionality of this type of subprocess is represented among the four types of subprocesses defined earlier.

In COSMIC FFP, the standard unit of measurement, that is, 1 Cfsu, is defined by convention as equivalent to one single data movement at the subprocess level. Another alternative, initially considered by the COSMIC group, was to define the standard unit of measurement based on the number of data element types moved by a data movement type subprocess. The study of such an alternative was one of the field trial aims.

1.1.3 Industrial Field Trials

1.1.3.1 Context

Another key aspect in the development of the COSMIC FFP measurement method is the conduct of a formal field trial period designed to demonstrate that it can withstand being scaled up to industrial software from multiple and varied contexts. The field trial aims were as follows:

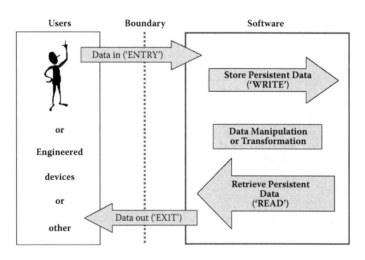

Figure 1.4 COSMIC FFP software model.

Table 1.1   Definition of COSMIC FFP Data Movements

Data Movement Type	Definition
ENTRY	An ENTRY (E) is a movement of the data attributes found in one data group from the user side of the software boundary to the inside of the software boundary. An ENTRY (E) does not update the data it moves. Functionally, an ENTRY sub-process brings data lying on the user's side of the software boundary within reach of the functional process to which it belongs. Note also that in COSMIC FFP, an entry is considered to include certain associated data manipulation (validation) sub-processes.
EXIT	An EXIT (X) is a movement of the data attributes found in one data group from inside the software boundary to the user side of the software boundary. An EXIT (X) does not read the data it moves. Functionally, an EXIT sub-process sends data lying inside the functional process to which it belongs (implicitly inside the software boundary) within reach of the user side of the boundary. Note also that in COSMIC FFP, an exit is considered to include certain associated data manipulation sub-processes.
READ	A READ (R) refers to data attributes found in one data group. Functionally, a READ sub-process brings data from storage, within reach of the functional process to which it belongs. Note also that in COSMIC FFP, a READ is considered to include certain associated data manipulation sub-processes.
WRITE	A WRITE (W) refers to data attributes found in one data group. Functionally, a WRITE sub-process sends data lying inside the functional process to which it belongs to storage. Note also that in COSMIC FFP, a WRITE is considered to include certain associated data manipulation sub-processes.

Source: Abran, A., J.-M. Desharnais, S. Oligny, D. St.-Pierre, and C. Symons. 2003. *COSMIC-FFP Measurement Manual version 2.2.* Common Software Measurement International Consortium. With Permission.

1. To test for a common, repeatable interpretation of version 2.0 of the measurement manual under widely varying conditions: organizations, domains, development methods, and so forth
2. To establish a detailed measurement procedure, where necessary, to ensure repeatable interpretation
3. To test that the measures properly represent functionality
4. To test that the measurement results correlate with development effort
5. To enable a full transfer of technology to the trial "partners"

Starting at the end of 1999, a nine-month period was allocated for conducting formal and organized field trials of the COSMIC FFP measurement method in a significant number of organizations around the world. The data collection was completed in a formal context in a number of organizations: a European aerospace manufacturer, a UK bank with MIS applications, two European telecommunications manufacturers, and an Australian defense software contractor. Additional data were also received from Australia (a defense contractor, a real-time software house, and an aerospace manufacturer) and from Canada (a small software house, a defense contractor, and a public utility organization).

During this period, each participating organization received formal training on the application of the method. Furthermore, multiple items of software were selected from each organization's portfolio and their functional size measured. These results, along with some key data on effort and schedule involved in delivering each software, were registered and centralized for analysis. Once analyzed, a specific report was prepared for each participating organization, offering: (1) guidelines for applying the method based on the organization's software engineering standards, and (2) some preliminary benchmarking information allowing the organization to leverage its investment in the new data and put it to use immediately. Consolidated highlights from the field trials are reported next, at a high level. Further work is required to formally document such observations.

1.1.3.2 Preliminary Results Highlights

The high-level preliminary results highlights are reported here using the structure of the field trials aims.

Common, repeatable interpretation. As can be observed in the number and origin of the field trial participants, COSMIC FFP was used under widely varying conditions: organizations, domains, and development methods. To ensure common implementation of the COSMIC FFP method at the trial partners' sites, training material was developed centrally at UQAM (Université du Québec à Montréal) and reviewed by the COSMIC team; "train the trainers" sessions were organized in three countries to ensure common training. The trainers then delivered the same training material to all trial partners. This training included repeatability exercises during the practical sessions.

Establishing detailed procedures, where necessary, to ensure repeatable interpretation. This was performed by each organization participating in the trials, sometimes with the help of the training and support staff. Some organizations already having significant experience in measurement did not have to ask for support.

Test that the measures properly represent functionality. The following were of interest:

- Can the method be applied equally to MIS and real-time software? Observations and feedback from the field trials indicated that it is easy to interpret the model in both domains. Where some parallel measurements were conducted with the IFPUG method, participants from the domain of real-time software reported significant difficulties at classifying functional processes in only one of the three IFPUG transaction types (inputs, outputs, or inquiries).
- Are the four data movement types of equal size? On very preliminary evidence, using one data set, the answer is yes; of course, such results still have to be formally documented and reported.
- The trials also included a participants' questionnaire to collect their feedback on their assessment of the ability of COSMIC FFP to adequately represent the size of the functionality of their software, reported on a Likert scale. Again, the preliminary analysis confirmed a significant alignment of the measurement results with participants' intuitive assessment of software size.

Correlation of the measurement results with development effort. The field trial participants, from both the formal and informal contexts, provided two sets of projects: development projects and maintenance projects. The development projects included eighteen projects from five organizations (sixteen new developments and two enhancements). They were developed on multiple platforms (seven PC, four DEC, two HP, two IBM mainframe, and one Compaq), and completed between March 1999 and May 2000 with a duration from 5 to 75 months.

The other set of maintenance requests provided twenty-one small functional enhancements completed in a single organization.

For both sets of data, the correlations with effort were significant. Again, these results still have to be consolidated, formally documented, and reported.

Full transfer of technology to the trial partners. The general feedback is very positive, and the project teams were able to grasp the elements of the method easily, and were enthusiastic about the method. It was also reported that the documentation and effort needed are similar to those for applying the IFPUG method, though there is an extra step to identify layers. Also, one of the participating organizations decided early on to continue CFFP (COSMIC Full Function Points) measurements for all new projects and decided to implement this measurement technique as a standard procedure in its development process (a European participant).

Other participants are either preparing or pursuing the deployment of this method within their respective organizations.

From the perspective of the participants in the field trials, the benefit of this approach lies in the availability, at the end of the field trial period, of a database of historical data useful for jump-starting the implementation of the measurement method within their own organizations while respecting the confidentiality of the sources. The benefit to the software engineering community will be the availability of the first functional size measurement method to be developed by an international group of experts and subjected to industrial field trials before finalization.

1.1.4 Summary and Conclusions

Albrecht proposed the function point method, more than twenty years ago, as a new way to measure the size of software. In the past fifteen years, although the method continues to give useful results for much MIS application software, many practitioners have found that Albrecht's measurement method cannot be applied satisfactorily to non-MIS software.

In 1998, building on the strengths of previous methods, the COSMIC group identified the principles on which the next generation of functional size measurement methods were to be built, offering applicability to MIS, real-time, and operating system software. A year later, the group published COSMIC FFP, a functional size measurement method implementing these principles. Key aspects of this method were presented in this paper, and industrial field trials are under way to demonstrate that the method can withstand being scaled up to industrial software environments in multiple and varied contexts.

The COSMIC FFP method has achieved a number of firsts: it is the first functional sizing method to:

- Be designed by an international group of experts on a sound theoretical basis
- Draw on the practical experience of all the main existing FP methods
- Be designed to conform to ISO 14143 Part 1
- Be designed to work across MIS and real-time domains, for software in any layer or peer item
- Be widely tested in field trials before being finalized

Significant progress has been made, and the acceptance from those who have tried the method is good in both MIS and real-time environments. There is strong international interest: The COSMIC FFP measurement manual is already available in three languages (English, French, and Spanish), and translation into three additional languages is progressing well (Italian, Japanese, and German). The measurement manual has been downloaded to date in over thirty countries.

And, planning further ahead, the COSMIC FFP method was proposed in early 2000 to ISO/IEC/JTC1 SC7 (Software Engineering Subcommittee) for a new work item to introduce the COSMIC FFP method through the ISO standardization process. In the July 2000 vote, it received an approval rate of over 90%.

In addition, research activities have been initiated to address the following themes:

■ Convertibility studies with previous methods, such as FFP V1, Mark II, and IFPUG
■ Estimation of functional size with COSMIC FFP, much earlier in the development cycle
■ Mapping of measurement rules in the UML (Unified Modeling Language)-based specifications domain
■ Measurement of functional reuse using COSMIC FFP
■ Development of requirements identification and measurement with the computer-based reasoning (CBR) approach
■ Website (standards and publications): www.lrgl.uqam.ca/ffp
■ Website (generic information): www.cosmicon.com

Acknowledgments

The authors of this paper acknowledge the specific contributions of Jean-Marc Desharnais, Denis St.-Pierre, Pam Morris, Roberto Meli, Grant Rule, and Peter Fagg in the elaboration of the COSMIC FFP measurement method, the support of Risto Nevalainen and Jolijn Onvlee, and the thoughtful and generous comments from all the reviewers of the COSMIC FFP measurement manual (Abran et al. 2003b).

1.2   Point Metrics—Comparison and Analysis

Mathias Lother and Reiner R. Dumke

1.2.1   Introduction

In the area of software measurement, a diversity of methods exist to measure characteristics of software products, processes, and resources. Within the last few years different points metrics, e.g., function points, feature points, object points, and full function points, were developed and introduced. With the help of these measurement methods, functional size measurement is possible, as well as early costs and effort estimations and process-conducting management activities based on functional size measurements. Because of the increasing importance of this topic and the variety of points metrics, the following methods will be introduced, and their basic models as well as their peculiarities will be discussed in Section 1.2.2:

■ DeMarco's bang metric
■ Data points
■ Object points
■ Feature points
■ Three-dimensional function points

- IFPUG function points
- Mark II function points
- Full function points

In Section 1.2.3 the mentioned functional size measurement methods will be evaluated according to:

- The suitability of them for different functional domains
- The degree of penetration and the experience background
- The tool support
- The testing and confirmation
- The standardization status
- The validation

Furthermore, suggestions for the use of a certain method under certain conditions will be given. It is important to take notice of general problems of functional size measurement. The following problems will be discussed in Section 1.2.4:

- Automation
- Objectivity/reliability
- Convertibility
- The meaning of the value adjustment factor
- The inclusion of reuse
- The problems with new technologies
- Possible measurement artifacts

Since the area of functional size measurement is changing continuously, Section 1.2.5 shows some alternative, recently published approaches:

- Predictive object points
- Component reuse method
- Construction points

1.2.2 Overview of Functional Size Measurement Methods

Functional size measurement is of increasing importance for the area of software development, since it adds engineering methods and principles to it. Figure 1.5 shows the general procedure for functional size measurement. As can be seen, there are basically two phases: a mapping phase, where concepts and definitions are applied to the representation of the software, and an evaluation phase, where the extracted elements are counted/measured according to specific rules and procedures.

Further investigations that resulted in the proposal of a generalized structure of functional size measurement were done by Fetcke (1999).

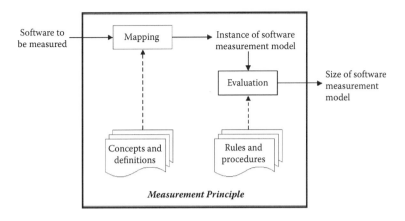

Figure 1.5 **Measurement principle of functional size measurement. (Adapted from ISO. 2003. Software engineering—COSMIC-FFP—A functional size measurement method. ISO/IEC 19761:2003.)**

Since the first worldwide publication of function points in 1979, a lot of changes, extensions, and alternative approaches to the original version have been introduced. In Figure 1.6 important steps of this evolution can be seen in a timetable, including those methods described in detail below. Arrows between the methods indicate influences extensions. The latest method in the figure is the COSMIC full function points approach. Since there are a lot of influences by many previous existing methods, special focus is given to this method in our considerations.

1.2.2.1 Bang Metric of DeMarco

Developer/institution, date

Tom DeMarco, 1982.

Development reason and addressed area

DeMarco's consulting had often taken him to more complex software systems than MIS systems. For that reason, he tried to address the domain of systems and scientific software (DeMarco 1982, 1989).

Basic inputs/model

Basic elements to be measured are (DeMarco 1982):

- Functional primitives
- Modified functional primitives

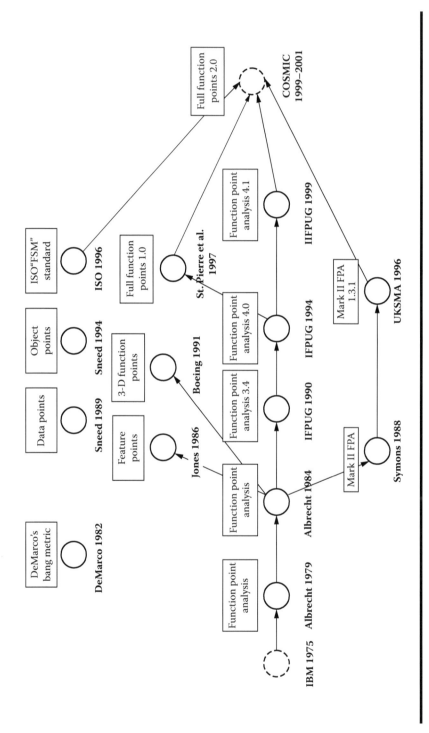

Figure 1.6 Development of functional size methods. (Adapted from Fetcke, T. 1999. *A generalized structure for function point analysis*. Université du Québec à Montréal, Canada.)

- Data elements
- Input data elements
- Output data elements
- Stored data elements
- Objects (entities)
- Relationships
- States in a state transition model
- Transitions in a state transition model
- Data tokens
- Relationships involving retained data models

The measured elements are weighted based on a classification to account for natural differences in the complexity of functions (Winant 2000).

Peculiarities

DeMarco's bang metric is a superset of the Albrecht function point method. Data tokens and state transitions, which are normally associated with more complex software as operating and telecommunication systems, are included. The weights are very subjective (Jones 1991).

Nowadays importance

In spite of a very interesting technical idea, this method has fallen behind the Albrecht function points, caused by better marketing and a larger user community (IFPUG). Thus, the method does not play an important role in nowadays functional size measurement (Jones 1997) but only for a few users (Garmus and Herron 1996).

Suggested further readings

DeMarco (1989).

1.2.2.2   Data Points

Developer/institution, date

Harry Sneed, 1989.

Development reason and addressed area

Data points have been developed to adapt function points to the needs of modern software development. It is aimed to shift the measurement basis from functions to objects of the functions to their data representation (Sneed 1995).

Basic inputs/model

The size of the software is derived with the help of the data model and the graphical user interface. Data points are derived from the weighted quantities of:

- Information objects
- Attributes
- Communication objects
- Input data
- Output data
- Views

The measured elements are weighted with the help of eight quality factors and ten project conditions (Fetcke 2000).

Peculiarities

Data points are a variation of the function points method.

Nowadays importance

There is no statement possible.

1.2.2.3   Object Points

Developer/institution, date

Harry Sneed, 1994.

Development reason and addressed area

Object points are an approach to address object-oriented systems development since, according to the opinion of Sneed, conventional measurement methods were not suitable.

Basic inputs/model

Object points are calculated by the weighted quantities of:

- Object types classes
- Object attributes
- Object relations
- Object methods
- Messages
- Parameters in messages

- Message sources
- Message destinations
- Percentage of reuse

The calculated value is weighted by ten influential factors (Sneed 1995).

Nowadays importance

There is no statement possible.

Peculiarities

Several authors have developed and introduced approaches to address the size of object-oriented systems. Often these approaches have been labeled as or related to object points, for example:

- Object points analysis (from Banker in 1991)
- Function points with OO (from Below in 1995)
- Object points analysis (from Gupta in 1996)
- Use cases and OO (from Fetcke in 1997)
- Object-oriented function points (from Caldiera in 1998)
- Enhanced object points (from Stensrud in 1998)

These methods are not considered in this paper. For detailed information, see the literature review of Abran and Desharnais (1999).

1.2.2.4   Feature Points

Developer/institution, date

Capers Jones/Software Productivity Research, 1986.

Development reason and addressed area

The method aims to gain better measurements for systems and real-time software, since IFPUG function points are originally invented for MIS (Jones 1987).

Basic inputs/model

Compared with the IFPUG method, a new parameter, algorithm, is introduced additionally to:

- Inputs
- Outputs

- Inquiries
- External interface files
- Internal logical files

The weights have been modified, e.g., according to Jones (1987), the logical files have a reduced significance.

Peculiarities

Feature points are a superset of IFPUG 4.0 function points. For MIS applications, feature and IFPUG function points have almost the same results (Jones 1997).

Nowadays importance

The feature points have been experimental for a long time; thus, there is not enough statistical evidence that they can be applied in a consistent fashion, but practitioners who have already applied the method successfully demonstrated this consistency in their environment (Garmus and Herron 1996). The benefit, but also the main problem, is the definition and weighting of the algorithms (Symons 2001; Morris 2000). Today this method is no longer supported by SPR.

1.2.2.5 Three-Dimensional Function Points

Developer/institution, date

Boeing Computer Services, 1991.

Development reason and addressed area

Three-dimensional function points are an approach to cover the area of systems software (Fetcke 2000) to gain a technology-independent metric (including the scientific and the real-time domain) (Garmus and Herron 1996).

Basic inputs/model

To determine three-dimensional function points, the following items are measured:

- Data (according to IFPUG 4.0)
- Number and complexity of functions
- Number of control statements (system states and state transitions) (Fetcke 2000)

Peculiarities

The three-dimensional function point method identifies three dimensions (data, function, control), which express the application problem. Data-strong problems are typical for IS/business software, function-strong problems for scientific/engineering software, and control-strong problems for real-time software (Garmus and Herron 1996). Thus, three-dimensional function points address the mentioned software areas.

Nowadays importance

According to Symons, the method is still used successfully at Boeing, but unfortunately, no details have been published outside Boeing (Whitmire 1995).

Suggested further readings

Symons (1988), Fetcke (2000).

1.2.2.6   IFPUG Function Points

Developer/institution, date

Albrecht/IBM, 1979 → later IFPUG.
Actual version: 4.1, 1999.

Development reason and addressed area

Main goal was to overcome the language-dependent size measurement by lines of code. Target area was MIS.

Basic inputs/model

The following entities are measured and weighted individually according to IFPUG 4.1 (as shown in Figure 1.7):

- External input
- External output
- Internal logical file
- External logical file
- External inquiries

The calculated value is weighted with the help of a value adjustment factor (VAF) that is calculated on the basis of fourteen influential factors (IFPUG 1994).

Peculiarities

The function point method has been developed to address MISs. Although there are some case studies for other software areas (e.g., real-time, object-oriented), there is still a discussion of whether this method meets the needs of these software areas. Aspects of criticism on this sizing method can be found in the following sections of evaluation and the discussion of general problems.

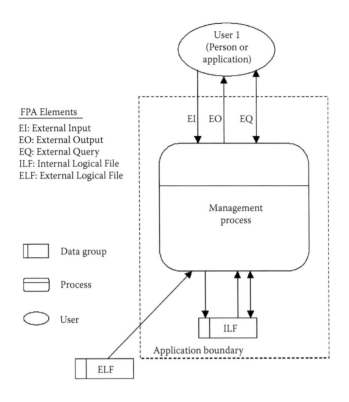

Figure 1.7 Function points analysis elements.

Nowadays importance

Function point analysis is the most widely used functional size measurement technique. IFPUG function points have become a quasi-standard.

Suggested further readings

IFPUG (1999, 2000, 2004).

1.2.2.7 Mark II Function Points

Developer/institution, date

Charles Symons, 1988.
Actual version: 1.3.1, 1998.

Development reason and addressed area

According to Symons (1991), the goal of Mark II function points has been:

- To reduce the subjectivity in dealing with files (compared to IFPUG)
- To ensure that the result is identical if a whole system is measured or the counts for the parts are added
- To focus on the effort required to produce the functionality, rather than on the value of the functionality delivered to the user

Basic inputs/model

The Mark II method measures the following logical transaction types that (see also Figure 1.8) are weighted with certain factors:

- Input
- Processing
- Output

The calculated value can optionally be weighted by nineteen (fourteen IFPUG + five extra) influence factors (Mark II Manual, 2002).

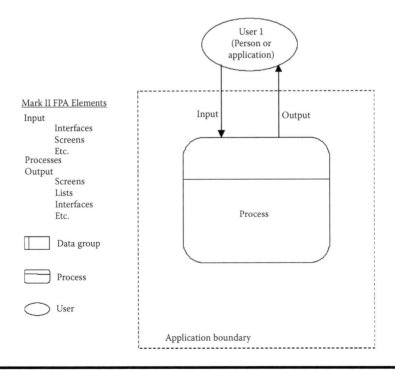

Figure 1.8   Mark II function points elements.

Nowadays importance

The use of Mark II is almost exclusively centered in the UK.

1.2.2.8 Full Function Points

Developer/institution, date

St.-Pierre et al. (1997b)
→ Later modified as COSMIC.
Considered version: 2.1, 2001.

Development reason and addressed area

The full function point analysis aims to cover the area of real-time, technical, and systems software as well as MIS software, thus attempting to overcome the limited band of application types covered by existing functional size measurement methods like IFPUG function point analysis. Priority is given to real-time software.

Based on the approximating assumption that data movements represent the size of a system, this method is suited for most MIS, real-time, and operating system software (Abran et al. 1999; Morris 2000).

Basic inputs/model

The full function point method determines the size of the software by analyzing the functional user requirements.

An important new approach is the integrated layer concept. A software can be divided into several layers, representing different views on the software. Figure 1.9 visualizes a possible variant. Thus, even measurements of distributed and complex systems become possible (Abran et al. 1999).

The functional size is determined by measuring the following data movement types (as shown in Figure 1.10):

- Entries
- Exits
- Reads
- Writes

The standard unit of measurement is 1 Cfsu (COSMIC functional size unit) and is equivalent to one data movement. The size of a system then is the sum of all data movements.

Peculiarities

While version 1 was developed as a superset of IFPUG function points (the basic model is shown in Figure 1.10), version 2 (see Figure 1.11) was developed from

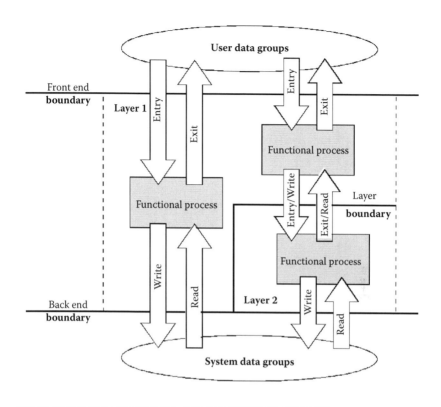

Figure 1.9 COSMIC full function point layer concept. (Adapted from ISO. 2003. Software engineering—COSMIC-FFP—A functional size measurement method. ISO/IEC 19761:2003.)

scratch, taking basic ideas from previous methods (FFP97 1997). This version was developed by the COSMIC, consisting of about forty people from eight countries (Symons 2004).

Nowadays importance

Since the Full Function Points version 2 is relatively new (so-called field trials were finished this year), the future will show if this method will gain more importance or if the IFPUG function points stay predominant.

Suggested further readings

Abran et al. (2003a).

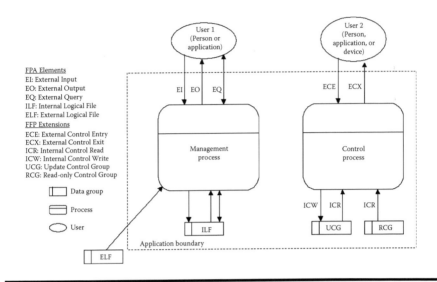

Figure 1.10 **Full function points version 1 elements. (From Abran, A. 1999. An implementation of COSMIC functional size measurement concepts.** *2nd European Software Measurements Conference.* **With Permission.)**

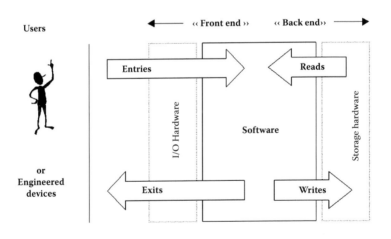

Figure 1.11 **COSMIC full function points version 2 elements. (From Abran, A., J.-M. Deshamais, S. Oligny, D. St-Pierre, and C. Symons. 2003. COSMIC-FFP Measurement Manual. With Permission.)**

1.2.3 *Evaluation of Functional Size Measurement Methods*

This section evaluates the introduced functional size measurement methods according to:

- The suitability for different functional domains
- The degree of penetration and the experience background
- The tool support
- The testing and confirmation
- The standardization status
- The validation

Subsequently, some recommendations for the decision-making process for choosing the right method will be given.

1.2.3.1 *Distribution of Functional Size Measurement Methods per Software Domain*

As could be seen in the overview of functional size measurement methods in the previous section, these methods aim at certain software/functional domains. If there is a need to choose one of these methods, it is important to know if there is a method that fits the functional domains used.

Table 1.2 shows the suitability of the different methods to the functional (software) domains according to Morris and Desharnais (1998). The table shows that data-strong and control-strong systems are covered by the existing methods. Because of the widespread use and long-term experience with function points for MIS, most tools and experiences are in this domain.

Morris (2000) concludes from his investigations that Full Function Points version 1 is the most viable method for real-time embedded and control systems until the Full Function Points version 2 method is released.

The problem of function-strong systems (scientific and algorithmic) has not been satisfactorily solved yet. This is an area where further research is still required.

1.2.3.2 *Degree of Penetration in Functional Size Measurement Users and Experience Background*

Another important criterion for the use of a method is the number of users of this method and the existing experience background. This is important due to the fact that only a community can establish a quasi-standard, and thus enable comparability (also to software outside the company) and repeatability. Furthermore, the probability for training opportunities, consulting, and continuous improvement of the method itself increases, the larger the community is.

Table 1.2 Methods per Functional Domain

Method	A/S	MIS	RT	CS
DeMarco's Bang	X			
Feature Points	X			
Boeing 3-D			X	
IFPUG		X		
Mark II FPA		X	Pot.	
FFPv1			X	X
FFPv2		X	X	X

Legend:	
A/S	Algorithmic/Scientific
MIS	Management Information Systems
RT	Real-time embedded
CS	Control Systems
Pot.	Potentially

An experience database is important to compare one's own measurement data with the measurements of others. In the area of functional size measurement there is the International Software Benchmarking Standards Group (ISBSG) database. Table 1.3 shows the penetration degree of the methods and if there are data in the ISBSG database available (investigations by Morris (2000)).

As can be seen from this table, only IFPUG function points, Mark II function points, and Full Function Points version 1 achieved significant importance. Since the COSMIC is an international group and relies on the concept of Full Function Points version 2, a rapid growth of acceptance and users for this method can be expected.

1.2.3.3 Tool Support for the Different Methods

According to Bundschuh and Fabry (2000) a method without tool support has little chance to survive. Tool support is important for the continuous functional size measurement application because tools help to handle, store, and evaluate the data. Of course, fully automated functional size measurement is desired, but as far as we know, that problem is not solved yet. The reason for this problem is that some items

Table 1.3   Penetration and Experience Background

Method	Degree of Penetration in Users	Data in ISBSG database
DeMarco's Bang	No importance today	No
Feature Points	A few users in the US, mostly SPR clients, not supported anymore	No
Boeing 3-D	Very small, rarely used outside Boeing	No
IFPUG	Most-widely used method	Yes
Mark II FPA	>50% in UK, only a few users outside UK	Yes
FFPv1	Users in Canada, Australia, Japan, Europe, USA	Yes
FFPv2	Users in UK, Australia, Canada, Finland, Japan, India, USA	Planned

that have to be counted/measured cannot be counted/measured automatically, but there are some approaches to this topic. They will be discussed in the general problems section (Section 1.2.4). Thus, tool support and automatic measurement have to be distinguished.

Table 1.4 shows an overview of tools that can support the application of measurements as well as the analysis of results. It can be seen that there is tool support for the existing functional sizing methods. More information about these tools can be found in Dumke et al. (1996) and Fetcke (2000). A new data collection tool, FPC-Analyzer, for Palm computers has recently been developed at the University of Magdeburg. This tool was developed by Reitz (2001) and supports the Full Function Points version 1.

1.2.3.4   Testing and Confirmation of the Functional Size Measurement Methods

An important criterion for the maturity of the methods is if they are tested and confirmed. MacDonnell (1994) has investigated if the complete model has been tested using real-world data (criteria tested) and if it has been evaluated using systems other than those employed in testing the model (criteria confirmed).

Table 1.5 shows that all the functional size methods considered so far have been tested with real-world data. Also, most of the methods have been confirmed

Table 1.4   Tool Support for the Methods

Method	Tool Support
Data Points	PCCALC, SoftCalc
Object Points	SoftCalc
Feature Points	Checkpoint/KnowledgePlan
IFPUG	Checkpoint/KnowledgePlan, PCCALC, ISBSG-Venturi, Function Points Workbench
Mark II FPA	MK II Function Points Analyzer
FFPv1	HierarchyMaster FFP, FPC-Analyzer
FFPv2	HierarchyMaster FFP (support for FFPv2 in development)

Table 1.5   Status of Testing and Confirmation

Method	Tested	Evaluated
Bang Metric	Yes	No
Feature Points	Yes	?
Boeing 3-D	Yes	?
IFPUG	Yes	Yes
Mark II FPA	Yes	Yes
FFPv1	Yes	Yes
FFPv2	Yes	Yes

and thus can be applied. This may be different for other sizing methods, e.g., the alternative approaches introduced in Section 1.2.5, which, e.g., can still be under development and continuous change.

1.2.3.5   Standardization Status

Another motivation for the selection of a certain sizing method is its status of standardization, that is, whether a method is accepted as a standard or not. Methods accepted as international standards will probably have a higher maturity and higher user acceptance.

Currently, four methods are actively going through the ISO process of becoming an international standard:

- Full Function Points version 2.1
- IFPUG function points
- Mark II function points
- NESMA (the Netherlands adaptation of IFPUG function points; this method is not considered in this paper)

1.2.3.6   Validation of Functional Size Measurement Methods

The validation of functional size measurement methods is the check of whether or not the methods measure what they are intended to measure and how well this is done.

According to Kitchenham and Fenton (1995), for the decision of whether a measure is valid or not, it is necessary to confirm the following aspects:

- Attribute validity (e.g., if the entity is representing the attribute of interest)
- Unit validity (e.g., appropriateness of the used measurement unit)
- Instrument validity (e.g., valid underlying model)
- Protocol validity (e.g., acceptable measurement protocol)

Among other things, Kitchenham and Fenton have found some definition problems with Albrecht function points, e.g., that ordinal scale measures are added that violate basic scale type constraints. For Mark II function points, they state that the measure can be valid only if Mark II function points are considered an effort model rather than a sizing model.

Other interesting work in this area has been done by Fetcke (2000), who investigated IFPUG function points, Mark II function points, and full function points with respect to the mathematical properties of dominance and monotonicity. He has found significant differences in the empirical assumptions made by these functional size measurement methods. Among other things, Fetcke's results are:

- While Mark II function points and full function points assume the axiom of dominance, IFPUG function points do not.
- The axiom of monotonicity is assumed by Full Function Points version 2, and by Mark II function points partially. Full Function Points version 1 and IFPUG function points violate this axiom.

As can be seen in this paragraph, the area of validation is very important but also very complex; thus, a more detailed discussion would extend the scope of this paper.

1.2.3.7 Thoughts about the Selection of a Certain Method

It would be ideal if there were a functional size measurement method that would cover all functional domains and would be used everywhere. Furthermore, the method would have been tested and validated, as well as an extensive experience database available.

Unfortunately, this is not the case, and therefore some aspects have to be taken into consideration.

Morris and Desharnais (1998) recommend using full function points if the functional area that is to be measured is not MIS.

A very promising approach is the Full Function Points version 2 method because of its international consortium and the many well-chosen influences from other functional size measurement methods. Possibly at some stage this method will be extended to also cover algorithmic/scientific software.

In the decision-making process to choose the right method, among other things the general problems of functional size measurement should be taken into consideration. This includes, for example, the influence of new technologies on measurements. A detailed discussion about these problems follows in Section 1.2.4.

Important work in the area of selecting the right functional size measurement method has been done with ISO standards 14143-3 (ISO 2002), 14143-4 (ISO 2000), and 14143-5 (ISO 2004). Unfortunately, the final versions of these standards are not published yet.

Part 3 will define verification methods for the following:

- Repeatability and reproducibility
- Accuracy
- Convertibility
- Discrimination thresholds
- Applicability of functional domains

Part 4 will specify a reference model consisting of the following:

- A classification framework for reference user requirements (RURs)
- Guidance on selecting reference FSM methods against which an FSM method can be compared

Part 5 will describe a framework to determine functional domains for use with functional size measurement. For that, characteristics of functional user requirements that contribute to functional size and can be used to define functional domains are specified.

With the help of the given frameworks for the validation methods, the reference model, and the determination of functional domains, the selection of a functional size measurement method can be done on a solid basis.

1.2.4   General Problems of Functional Size Measurement

According to the literature, functional size measurement also means dealing with general problems.

Kemerer (1997, p. 27) quotes Pressmann: "The Function Point metric, like LOC, is relatively controversial…. Opponents claim that the method requires some 'sleight of hand' in that computation is based on subjective, rather than objective, data." Capers Jones found that the "variants in FP counting methodologies can result in variances of up to ±50%" (Jones, 1997, p. 24), and G. Low and D. R. Jeffery published the statement that "within organizations the variation in Function Point counts about the mean appears to be within 30%" (Kemerer, 1997, p. 31).

As can be followed, repeatability and objectivity are core problems in functional size measurement. Other articles, e.g., by Abran et al. (2005), lay the main focus on automation, convertibility etc., for future research. The following important problems will be discussed in this section:

- Automation
- Objectivity/reliability
- Convertibility
- Need of a value adjustment factor
- Inclusion of reuse
- Influence on/of new technologies
- Different measurement artifacts

1.2.4.1   Automation of Measurement

As mentioned in Section 1.2.3, a fully automated measurement estimation tool would be an ideal solution. Corresponding to the actual software life cycle phase, the tool should derive the function points from the actual documents.

Automatic data collection not only reduces the risk of errors being introduced into the extracted data, but also lessens the work effort, and this is important for the acceptance of functional size measurement.

A lot of discussion has occurred about the potential of the methods order to being automatic. Symons (1999), for example, pointed out that the automatic measurement of IFPUG function points can be realized only with great difficulty, but Mark II function points can be automated with the help of CASE tools.

MacDonnell (1994) has investigated whether the product complexity assessment can be totally performed in an automated manner, without requiring input from personnel. The result can be seen in Table 1.6; it shows that in his opinion, a fully automated assessment is not possible.

Several approaches to automate the measurement can be found in the literature. Two of them will be mentioned here.

Table 1.6   Potential of Automatic Measurement

Method	Automatic
Bang Metric	No
IFPUG	No
Mark II FPA	No

A framework approach for automatic function point measurement from source code with the help of program slicing was proposed by Ho and Abran (1999). The proposed framework can be used to build a model for automatic function point measurement in compliance with the IFPUG counting practice manual. Further research has to be done for developing a prototype, since the realization of the model is highly dependent on the ability and efficiency of the slicing tool. The theoretical foundation to this approach was published by Paton (1999). First, an intermediate program representation DF(P), which should contain enough information to count function points, is defined. Second, it is shown that with the help of program slicing (a form of static code analysis) as well as program tracing (a form of dynamic code analysis), this intermediate program representation can be derived. Thus, the automatic function point counting is possible.

Another approach in order to support the automatic measurement of Full Function Points version 1 has been developed by Oppermann (2001) as a diploma thesis in cooperation with Siemens and the University of Magdeburg. After the evaluation of the applicability of full function points at Siemens (Schweikl et al. 2000), it was decided to develop a tool to automate the counting.

Unfortunately, after further investigations it has been found that fully automated counting support is not possible because of the structure and variety of the Siemens specification documents. Thus, a tool has been developed to assist the measurement consisting of two parts. FFPExtract analyzes the Siemens requirements specifications and extracts some artifacts that possibly could be measured. Then FFPCounter shows the specifications and suggests the artifacts in a dialogue. These artifacts then can be accepted by the user, counted, or refused.

Another interesting approach is proposed by Diab et al. (1999, 2001). With the help of a formal definition of IFPUG and full function points, they enable an automation of counting. This approach is specific to the B specification language (for IFPUG) and the ROOM (Real-Time Object-Oriented Modeling) language (for COSMIC full function points).

As no satisfying general solution is available for counting function points automatically (the approaches mentioned here are very specialized), further research has to be done in this area.

1.2.4.2   Objectivity/Reliability

In functional size measurement any subjectivity places too much emphasis on the working methods of particular individual assessors and makes repeatability of the results more difficult.

An example for the inner problems of IFPUG is given by Symons (Mk II Manual 1998): three single systems have individually measured fewer function points than the entire system consisting of these three systems.

Furthermore, in his opinion the weights for the single functional elements as input, output, etc., are chosen arbitrarily and should be adaptable for certain environments.

Kuan Wu (2000) discovered that only about 23% of the companies in a case study (five hundred Hong Kong business firms of different sectors) use function points because this method is too subjective. It is shown that experience in the FPA method is important for repeatability of the results. So, the problem can be overcome by training, but more effort has to be spent. But, in spite of the subjectivity, LOC (Lines of Code) does not seem to be a good alternative for Simon, especially for the domains of scientific applications as data communication and multimedia applications.

MacDonnell (1994) has investigated whether the models as defined always produce the same result for a given system at a given point in time (assuming no counting errors), irrespective of the person requiring or performing the assessment or estimation. The results can be seen in Table 1.7.

Symons (1991) agrees that FPA is partly subjective, but in his opinion Mark II function points are reasonably objective.

According to Abran et al., 1999, for good repeatability with full function points, experience is required in the domain of the functional measurement technique as well as in the functional domain.

As can be seen by the controversial statements, further research has to be done on this topic. Among other things, clear definitions of what and how to count, to estimate what to measure, are necessary for objectivity and repeatability.

To support the evaluation of objectivity/reliability, ISO standard 14143 Part 3 (ISO 2002) will provide a framework for verifying repeatability and reproducibility as well as accuracy.

Table 1.7   Objectivity of Methods

Method	Objective
Bang Metric	No
IFPUG	No
Mark II FPA	No

1.2.4.3 Convertibility

There are a lot of functional size measurement methods that address different functional domains, and thus have different measurement strategies.

If it is planned to introduce a new method or simply to compare results between different methods, the question of convertibility has to be considered. Symons (1999) has mentioned that for the acceptance of a new sizing method, conversion possibilities are necessary.

Analyzing the convertibility, he has found (Symons 1999) that COBOL SLOC and Albrecht function points do not correlate very well; neither do Albrecht function points and Mark II function points.

Capers Jones (1997) said that feature points and function points are developed to be convertible. SPR tools like KnowledgePlan perform these transformations. Because of the different manner of measurement to obtain DeMarco's bang, a conversion between this metric and either function points or feature points is not possible.

Meli (1998) investigated the relation between Mark II and IFPUG function points. Since both measure the same functional aspect, they should be proportional and therefore convertible to one another. But from Meli's point of view, these methods cannot be compared.

The convertibility of full function points is still under investigation. This is one of the most emphasized actual research areas of the COSMIC initiative.

To support the analysis of convertibility, ISO standard 14143 Part 3 (ISO 2002) will provide verification methods for convertibility of a functional size measurement method.

1.2.4.4 Value Adjustment Factors

A very interesting discussion is held about the value adjustment factor. The question is, what is the advantage of it and how should it be used?

Lokan and Abran (1999) share their experience that the general system characteristics and the value adjustment factor are poorly understood. They are generally seen as important, but not as very successful. The attempt to address technical and quality requirements via a value adjustment factor is clearly not valid. According to Symons (2001), one reason for this dilemma is the debate and trial strategy that has led to the set and factors.

In the evolution of function point analysis, the general system characteristics have been modified and extended, and reduced (in their quantity and set).

According to Lokan and Abran (1999), some sizing methods have added characteristics (e.g., Mark II function points have nineteen instead of fourteen general systems characteristics), while several other functional size measurement approaches (including feature points, three-dimensional, etc.) either do not describe their adjustment process or simply adopt the IFPUG recommendations. The ISO standard on functional size measurement excludes the value adjustment factor explicitly.

Later on, Lokan and Abran (1999) state that nobody who has investigated the value adjustment factor could find a higher degree in accuracy of effort estimations by using this factor. Therefore, a growing number of practitioners do not use the general system characteristics or value adjustment factor at all (see also our identical experience at Siemens (Oppermann 2001; Schweikl et al. 2000)). They either ignore it or just take it into account as cost drivers for effort estimation.

As a result, Lokan and Abran (1999) conclude that unadjusted function points and the general systems characteristics measure different aspects of an application. It may be better to regard size as having multiple different dimensions, rather than trying to combine them all into a single number.

The same conclusion comes from Meli (1998). He noticed that we must abandon the use of the value adjustment factor, at least as an element modifying the measurement of the size of an application. Perhaps the value adjustment factor can be used either as a qualifier (e.g., the higher the value adjustment factor, the better the application) or as an element modifying the value of the productivity that will influence production costs.

Symons (1999) suggests that it should be possible to calibrate the general system characteristics and, consequently, the value adjustment factor for different application areas.

In the opinion of Meli (1997a), there are only two possible choices to deal with value adjustment factors. The first choice is to remove the value adjustment factor and use only the unadjusted count. The second one is to use the value adjustment factor in order to "qualify" the number of function points that are delivered for a particular application.

This means that the same number of function points can be counted for a very usable and efficient component and for a less usable and efficient component. Then the qualifier can give an idea of this difference, e.g., the higher the degree of influence (as a calculated number), the better the application.

Further research is necessary to deal with the questions:

■ How many general system characteristics (suggestions are from four to over one hundred) should be defined?
■ Which set is necessary?
■ How should the scale be for the influence (±5, as so far, or other)?

1.2.4.5   Inclusion of Reuse

Functional size measurement traditionally measures the entire functional size of a software product from the user's perspective.

Since new software development methods are introduced that support reuse, e.g., object orientation, COTS, and JavaBeans, for the determination of the self-developed part of the software for business calculation, this measurement is not enough anymore (detailed information can be found in Dumke et al. (1999)).

Meli (1997a) identifies that it becomes necessary to distinguish between function points asked for and released to the user and function points actually developed by the software team. That is why new approaches have to be found and introduced.

Ho et al. (1999) promise a solution for this problem: two different measurements in function points should be defined, one connected to the external user view and the other connected to the administrative and productive needs of the software manufacture.

Ho and Abran (1999) deal with the problem to measure the performance of the software engineering process. Therefore, it is important to identify how much reuse has occurred. To obtain this information, the layer concept of full function points has been used as a means to identify potential sources of functional reuse in the software to be measured.

Meli (1997b) further says that the reuse of existing software, in fact (documents, code, specifications, user manuals, etc.), probably involves savings that can be quantified by using a standard scale of options. This is particularly important for the consideration of the quality of a benchmarking database that can release productivity data "altered" by intensive reuse phenomena, together with newly elaborated software data. Therefore, an average ratio is not useful if it uses projects with a great amount of reuse together with projects realized from scratch. For that reason, there should be a productivity ratio for completely developed function points. Then, for any particular project, with the help of the expected reuse, the effort that is needed can be recalibrated.

1.2.4.6 Impact of New Software Technologies

Traditional functional sizing measurement methods have been developed to meet the needs of traditional software development.

Since several new software development methods and areas have been introduced, it has to be proven if the functional size methods are still suited to measure the new kinds of software. In this context new software areas are:

- Internet and intranet software
- Graphical user interfaces
- Distributed software (e.g., client server)
- Object-oriented systems
- Etc.

According to Longstreet (2001a, 2001b), the main difference for object-oriented systems is the other/different view. The traditional view of software systems is as a composition; in object orientation there is a single entity, the object, that represents both the data and the procedures.

For GUI, Internet, and intranet software, this view is also another consideration of the software. Websites developed utilizing FrontPage or other HTML tools may or may not contain any functionality. The key is to understand where the information resides and how the information is processed. The large majority of websites are nothing more than just menus and text. This has to be taken into consideration for the functional measurement of such systems.

But Longstreet (2001a) has also concluded that IFPUG function points can be applied to an object-oriented environment (since the functional size of the product delivered to the user is independent of the realization), but there must be some normalization factor to compare object orientation to traditional development.

To support his opinion, Longstreet (2001b) has published an extension to IFPUG 4.1 to address the areas of GUI, Internet, intranet, OO, and other new and emerging technologies.

Boehm (1997) has also concluded that the function point analysis is suitable for counting GUI, client/server, and object-oriented systems.

But some problems remain. Of course, with the help of most of the functional size methods, each functional domain can be measured and a value is derived. Then the question is whether this value is the correct representation of a system or just a number without any meaning.

Symons (1999) recognized that one of the difficulties is that the method definition and procedures become increasingly complex, because new rules have been added continuously in order to cope with interpreting an old sizing method in terms of new development methods and technologies. Thus, consistency between these additions is hard to maintain.

Another problem in the area of distributed software is if the view of the user on the functionality is sufficient to characterize the functionality that has to be implemented. A possible solution for this topic is the use of Full Function Points version 2 and the contained layer concept to separate different views on the software.

Future research will show if the new functional size measurement approaches, e.g., full function points, are able to handle these problems completely.

1.2.4.7 Measurement Artifacts

Functional size measurement should be possible in the whole software life cycle. Since the artifacts change in the software life cycle, different considerations are necessary:

- Which artifacts can be used to measure/estimate?
- Which is the earliest point of time for measurement with a certain method?
- Are there methods to estimate?
- Can UML models be used to measure/estimate?
- Are there possibilities to postcalculate from source code?

1.2.4.7.1 Artifacts for Measurement

First, the starting point of time for functional size measurement is discussed. The COSMIC initiative (Abran et al. 1999) identifies pre- and postimplementation functional user requirement models, as can be seen in Figures 1.12 and 1.13.

For all the artifacts shown, there should be the possibility to derive the necessary information for the measurement.

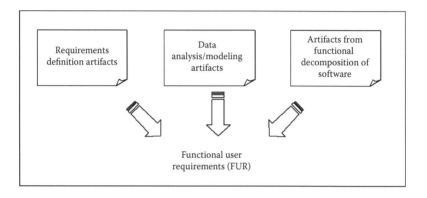

Figure 1.12 Pre-implementation FURs. (Adapted from ISO. 2003. Software engineering—COSMIC-FFP—A functional size measurement method. ISO/IEC 19761:2003. With Permission.)

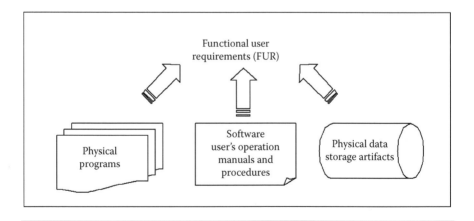

Figure 1.13 Post- implementation FURs. (Adapted from ISO. 2003. Software engineering—COSMIC-FFP—A functional size measurement method. ISO/IEC 19761:2003. With Permission.)

1.2.4.7.2   Earliest Point of Time for Measurement

Garmus and Herron (2002) have stated that DeMarco's bang and three-dimensional function points require detailed knowledge about system processing that is not available early enough for accurate counting (e.g., states and transitions), and this makes it more difficult to count earlier. Thus, it must be measured later in the software life cycle than Mark II function points, feature points, and IFPUG function points, which can be measured at the same time with the same level of detail and with the same precision as function points.

Unfortunately, this required level of detail is only available after 15 to 40% of development time.

1.2.4.7.3   Earlier Estimations

Boehm (1997) points out that the earlier measurements are possible, the earlier the project is under control. Often it has been believed that function point counting is only possible after the design phase, but there are rules (under IFPUG 4.0) that allow us to obtain data earlier. Sometimes heuristics are used. While doing the feasibility study counting is usually impossible, but in the requiring gathering phase, according to the suitability of the generated models, a more or less good estimation is possible. When the business requirements have been completed, an accurate function point count is possible.

To overcome this late point of time, the early function point method has been introduced. The results of applying this method are summarized by Meli (2002; Meli et al. 2000). He found that the early function point method is a very effective way for estimating the function point count of a software project without having all details (functional specifications) needed for a formal standard count.

Important to consider is that the method's effectiveness is guaranteed only by constantly validating the method's coefficients with regard to actual counting cases. But the early function points method has proven quite effective, providing a response within ±10% of the real function points' value in most cases.

Another method for earlier estimation is early full function points. This method is based on the early function points analysis and is under development at this time.

1.2.4.7.4   Measurement Using UML

Several approaches propose and discuss the use of UML elements for estimating functional size.

One approach was introduced by Stutzke (1999) for the estimation of feature points. He refers to a couple of previous works, e.g., Reifer's model (1990), the class points method (by Fischmann/McRitchie), and the South African method (by Meyerson), but he concludes that not all questions are solved. Problematical questions are:

- How much effort is needed to reuse portions of the object models?
- How does the particular analysis method affect effort?
- How much effort is needed to map the design objects into working code?

Longstreet (2001b) shows some examples of how to measure function points with use cases. He stated that each step has to be analyzed to identify if it is a transaction or a data type. He also lists some risks of using use cases for function point counting:

- A necessary transaction was not identified within a use case.
- A transaction was improperly identified within a use case.
- The number of attributes are not defined clearly within a use case.
- The number of attributes cannot be tied to an entity.

But Longstreet (2001a) states that the function point analysis can be applied to the use case method very easily.

Meli and Santillo (1999) mentioned that use cases have become a common method for capturing user requirements. Because use cases describe functionality from the user's point of view, they should be easily converted to function points. But this fact must be validated item by item, since the level of "dissection" of the functional transactions and of use cases may not be the same. Further research should provide some statistical evidence of this potential relationship.

1.2.4.7.5   Postcalculation from Source Code

A last important consideration is the desire to postcalculate function points from source code. Since the functional content to be measured is already implemented, a method to automate this calculation should be possible. An approach for such a method has been described in Section 1.2.4.1.

1.2.5   Alternative Approaches in Functional Size Measurement

In addition to the traditional sizing methods there are some new approaches. Three of these recently introduced suggestions will be discussed in this section:

- Predictive object points
- Component reuse metrics
- Construction points

1.2.5.1   Predictive Object Points

Predictive object points were developed after recognizing that traditional software metrics are inadequate for object-oriented software when used for productivity tracking and effort prediction (Minkiewicz 2000; Teologolu 1999). Predictive object points were designed specifically for object-oriented software and result from measurement of the object-oriented properties of the system.

Predictive object points support the problem of the inclusion of reuse (Section 4.5), means to measure the amount of raw functionality the software delivers, but also to include information about communication between objects and reuse through inheritance. The core of the predictive object points is the weighted methods per class metric of Chidember and Kemerer. But there is also influence by the object-oriented metrics depth of inheritance tree (DIT) and number of children (NOC). The actual status is that research has resulted in a metric and a counting process that, for the data studied, offers a correlation between object-oriented metrics and effort. But, there are still hurdles to be overcome. Additional data have to be collected and the original results have to be refined.

Another point to address is the gap between artifacts available during early analysis and the metrics required for a predictive object points count. Further steps are to look for a direct relationship between use case artifacts and predictive object points and to automate the measurement procedure.

Suggested further readings

Minkiewicz (2000), Teologolu (1999).

1.2.5.2 Component Reuse Metric

Virtanen (2000, 2001) proposes a new method for estimating the software development effort. The component reuse metric combines both the best means of object-oriented component technology and the analysis of human behavior (skill, motivation, team effects) into simple calculation rules. The component reuse metric describes the software size by the number of different kinds of components, considering that these numbers are not additive. Furthermore, risk effects, especially the feature creep effects, are considered. The use of components themselves instead of some size unit is one of its distinguishing properties; the other is the central assessment of the human effects.

Task-based estimation is the most commonly used effort estimation method. The most important metric is the number of windows and database tables. Component reuse metrics can be seen as an extension of that method. Case studies confirmed that the assessment of project and human effects proved to be difficult, at least without experience and historical data. But, according to Virtanen, it has been shown that if these assessments are accurate, the component reuse metric is quite accurate. Further research has to be done on the productivity issues.

Suggested further readings

Virtanen (2000, 2001).

1.2.5.3 Construction Points

Victor and Daily (2001) introduced the SPECTRE approach, which enables estimation of tasks with so-called construction points. The aim is to enable the prediction of the task development time and the module size, which is sensitive to local factors like task content and complexity like individual knowledge and experience.

This approach has similarities to function points analysis in the way both methods are applied, but there are differences in the target entities. Furthermore, function point analysis is a project-oriented metric and construction points are a task-oriented metric.

Construction points are based on accumulated observations over many years of experience and have, according to Victor and Daily, a known and verified accuracy. SPECTRE, with its construction points, is most effective when applied to a task specification that is complete and confirmed. Nevertheless, it can be used to advantage throughout the whole process of developing the task specification.

Suggested further readings

Victor and Daily (2001).

1.2.6 Summary

This paper introduces several chosen and important functional size methods and evaluates them with respect to their applicability and maturity. Furthermore, general problems in the area of functional size measurement have been pointed out and discussed, e.g., the questions of automation, convertibility, etc. Subsequently, alternative, recently published approaches to functional size measurement have been shown.

It can be concluded that functional size measurement is very important for software development, but there are several problems that have to be taken into consideration, e.g., the suitability of the methods for functional domains, the impact of new technologies, etc.

Another conclusion is that still a lot of investigation and research are necessary to deal with general problems in functional size measurement, for example:

- Convertibility between different functional sizing methods
- Mapping between UML and function points
- Measuring in the domain of algorithmic/scientific software
- Measurement of functional reuse
- Automated functional size measurement

Generally, it would be desirable to have one sizing method established as an international standard that can measure domain independence and use artifacts of all software life cycle phases to obtain the input for the measurement.

1.3 Move from Function Point Counting to Better Project Management and Control

Pekka Forselius

1.3.1 Introduction

Most of the business management paradigms emphasize that good management should be based on knowledge and understanding. Knowledge is based on gathered information, and understanding comes from analytical research of that information. Information consists of data, and data collection means different measurements, which are based on methods and metrics. Reliable size measurement is one of the most important parts of data collection at any kind of building industry, because it is impossible to estimate effort of the development project without target size, or to benchmark the productivity of the development team without the actual size. The size information is very important in contract management too.

Allan J. Albrecht published his famous paper introducing a new software size measurement method, function point analysis, in 1979. The original idea is still valid, though several organizations all over the world have developed improved and more sophisticated variations of it. Hundreds of high-quality research papers concerning FPA have been written, and thousands of pages of interpretation rules and counting practices manuals have been published during the last twenty-five years. Capers Jones presented a list of thirty-five different functional size measurement methods at the Experience Forum Conference in Finland in 1997. Some new methods and new versions of old ones have been published every year since then. In addition to 1979, another important year is 1998, when the functional size measurement (FSM) standard, ISO/IEC 14143-1 (ISO 1998), was approved as an international standard. Today functional size measurement is the only standardized (and independent of development tools and technical environment) way to measure the size of a piece of software.

ISO standardization was intended to be the final breakthrough, but unfortunately it wasn't. Still today, there are many more software development projects *not* applying FSM methods than those doing it. There are not very many organizations collecting history data from all their projects, though most of them agree it is one of the most important management best practices of our industry. All around the world there are lots of people in leading positions of software development organizations who have never heard about functional size measurement and its capabilities in assisting management and process improvement. On the other hand, there are hundreds of experienced experts who have been using and promoting these methods for years and years. There must be a link missing between these two groups. Every year we meet FSM experts in several metrics conferences. Unfortunately, we never see top managers there. Experts seem to be mainly talking to each other, which tends to keep the level of conversation very technical. Still, after twenty-five years, their focus is on how to count or which of the methods is best.

However, some movement from a single method and its counting practices to more serious problems has happened already, at least verbally. The FPA users established national function point user groups in several countries in the late 1980s and early 1990s. The United States and Canada established the International Function Point User Group (IFPUG), the Italians had GUFPI, and so on. The European collaboration organization was called EAFPUG. Today we have also JFPUG in Japan and KFPUG in South Korea. Many of these organizations have changed their names and their scope and area of interest from function points to software metrics during the last ten years. The United Kingdom Software Metrics Association (UKSMA) was one of the first to make this move. Today we have DASMA in Germany, NESMA in the Netherlands, and ISMA in Italy, all metrics associations, interested in different software metrics and not only FPA anymore. The next step toward management is a move from metrics to measurement. Instead of the late 1990s' Federation of European Software Metrics Associations (FESMA), today we have the Measurement Associations and International Network (MAIN), and FiSMA changed its name to Finnish Software Measurement Association at the beginning of 2004. Hopefully all this verbal development also means concrete expansion of broader thinking in these countries, among the FSM user community. We expect measurement associations to be much closer to software top management needs than single-method user groups ever were.

1.3.2 Functional Size Measurement Methods Today

If a size measurement method claims to be a functional size measurement method, it should prove its conformance with the ISO/IEC 14143-1 international standard. At least five different methods, all of them widely used somewhere, can be called FSM methods. They are:

- COSMIC FFP functional size measurement method version 2.1 (ISO 2003a)
- IFPUG 4.1 unadjusted (ISO 2003a)
- Mk II function point analysis 1.3.1 unadjusted (ISO 2002)
- NESMA FPA method 2.1 unadjusted (ISO 2005)
- FiSMA FSM 1.1 (Forselius 2004)

All five methods follow definitions and concepts of the international FSM standard. Any of these methods can be used for software size measurement, though they all have different size units. For anyone starting size measurement in his organization, it may be very confusing to have so many standard methods, but this is the reality in 2004. Unfortunately, none of the methods have introduced conversion rules from and to other methods. ISO has published other standards and technical reports in its 14143 series, which should help anyone selecting a FSM method. The last part of this series will be a guide for the use of FSM standards, but it is still under development. However, the guide will neither explain differences between known methods nor recommend any certain method to any functional domain or business area.

Table 1.8 illustrates the main differences between the FSM methods. A common requirement to all FSM methods is that they measure the size only from functional user requirements. The way they manage this varies a lot.

It's quite easy to see from Table 1.8 that terminologies and counting approaches of current FSM methods are different, and none of them are perfectly easy to understand without training. As the IFPUG 4.1 function point counting practices manual says about training requirements: "Reading the Counting Practices Manual alone is not sufficient training to apply function point counting at the optimum level. Training is recommended, particularly for those new to function point counting" (IFPUG. 1999, p. 32). This is true to all of these methods, though usually it's not necessary to count at an "optimum level," whatever that is. The training length varies usually from two to five days, depending on the FSM method and the target level of accuracy. Unfortunately, the training requirement seems to be hard to understand and accept by most IT professionals, and most of the user representatives think that functional size measurement is not their business, but something that requires programming skills. Too often we have seen measurement programs fail for these reasons, when counting has been tried by nontrained IT people alone, without any commitment and involvement from the customer side.

The results of functional size measurement are:

- Functional size of software (in the FSM method specific function points or other units defined by the measurement method)
- Detailed list of functional user requirements categorized to groups defined by the FSM method

The functional size of a piece of software is just a figure. It is important, but far less important than most of the software developers and project managers think. It's essential to understand that the size figure alone, no matter how exact and correct it is, doesn't help in estimating and controlling changes of a development project at all. It is useful in estimating, but only together with other measurement methods and information. For change management and all other communication between the customer and supplier of the software, much more important than the size figure is the list of functional user requirements. If both the customer and supplier representatives agree that all requirements, and nothing else, are included in the list, it is the baseline of the software scope and very helpful in project management. Still, there is no doubt that the size measurement is correct in this case, or at least at a good enough level.

Table 1.8 Comparison of Current FSM Methods

COSMIC FFP	IFPUG 4.1	Mk II	Nesma	FiSMA 1.1
Identify functional processes	Identify data functions and transactional functions	Identify logical transactions and data entity types	Identify and fix the application boundary of the project	Identify business use cases
Identify and make a list of data movements of each functional process: • ENTRY • EXIT • READ • WRITE	Identify and make a list of data functions belonging to each data function type: • ILF • EIF Identify and make a list of transactional functions belonging to each function type: • EI • EO • EQ	Identify and make a list of data element types of each logical transaction: • Input data element types • Data entity types referenced • Output data element types	Identify and make a list of functions belonging to each function type: • ILF • EIF • EI • EO • EQ	Identify and make a list of functional services belonging to each service group: • Navigation and query services • Interactive input services • Non-interactive output services • Data storage services • Interface services to other applications • Interface services from other applications • Algorithmic manipulation services

How accurate are the FSM methods? This is a very common question, probably arising from the bad experiences of trials made by nontrained counters. With all current FSM methods two trained counters will result in ±10% size figures, if the user requirements are reasonably well specified or known. The author has tested this during more than 150 estimating training courses. Another test on his public training courses has proved that if ten project managers from different business areas try to estimate project effort without a systematic approach including FSM methods, the ratio between the smallest and biggest estimates is 1 to 6, sometimes even 1 to 12. In this scope the ±10% result is accurate enough.

As a summary of current FSM methods, the author encourages all customer organizations to demand functional size measurement in their projects. For the software supplier organizations, measurement is recommended too, because it ensures competitive tendering and prevents huge underestimates and big economical losses, especially when the project contract is based on fixed price. Actually, a pricing model based on price/functional size is much better than any other, for both parties (Vogelezang and Lesterhuis 2003), but it doesn't work without functional size measurement. That's why this best practice isn't more common yet. Finally, all the current FSM methods are much better than nothing, and there isn't any type of software development or any functional domain where they wouldn't help. All you need is a decision of FSM use and at least one trained person to make the measurements.

1.3.3 Other Important Measurement Methods

Though FSM methods are good, and functional size measurement is important, too much emphasis is sometimes given to FSM methods and functional size. They are not the silver bullets solving all measurement problems. Size information is essential for effort estimating and productivity benchmarking, but there are other important factors and knowledge items having an impact on software development productivity (ISBSG 2001; Maxwell and Forselius 2000; Wieczorek 2001). In fact, all comprehensive effort and cost estimating models deal with several other factors than just the size of software.

History repositories and project databases include a lot of useful information about delivery rates of old projects. A delivery rate tells how many work hours have been used or will be needed to deliver one function point. Similar information has been published by ISBSG on CDs (ISBSG 2003) and in books (ISBSG 2002, 2003a, 2005). The best-in-class organizations have collected their own databases, which are usually much more reliable than public repositories for estimating purposes. It is easy to calculate an effort estimate, if you have counted the size of your software in function points and have found an applicable delivery rate (h/fp). The accuracy of this estimate may be good, but it still depends on several other factors. If the classification of your project is unambiguous and the data set used to count the delivery rate consists of very similar projects, these things improve the accuracy. Similarity is the key issue when using history repositories (Maxwell and Forselius

2000; Shepperd and Shofield 1997). Another important issue is the robustness of the data collection concept. If we can trust that effort and classification rules are interpreted equally always, the quality of the data will be extremely good, and thus the estimates will be more reliable than otherwise. This should be the case with in-house project databases.

In addition to software size and delivery rate, there are other project-specific productivity factors that shall be determined before calculating the final effort or cost estimate. These factors measure the circumstances of the project compared to an average project. There are several different methods available for this kind of analysis:

- COCOMO I, fifteen productivity factors (Boehm 1984)
- COCOMO II, twenty-three productivity factors (Boehm 2000)
- IFPUG value adjusted factor (VAF), fourteen factors (ISO 2003b)
- FiSMA ND21 situation analysis for new development, twenty-one factors (Forselius 2004)
- FiSMA MT22 situation analysis for maintenance and support, twenty-two factors (Forselius 2004)

All these methods ask the user to determine the most fitting alternative for each of their productivity factors. Based on the selected values, the method gives a coefficient figure, which is a multiplier for the preliminary effort estimate counted from the software size and delivery rate. The basic idea behind all these methods is that the easier and the better circumstances the project has compared to average projects, the less effort will be needed. Table 1.9 shows the lists of productivity factors of the three most commonly used methods.

Some of the methods analyzing project-specific productivity factors try to cover the impacts of reuse, and others ignore it. For example, FiSMA ND21 doesn't cover reuse issues at all. As the software development industry becomes more and more professional, it is believed that the impact of reuse will increase dramatically, and thus the reuse factor should be weighted to be much more influential than any of the other factors. That's why FiSMA has developed and published a separate method for reuse analysis (Forselius 2004). This method considers both the reuse of reusable components in the project and reusability requirements for the components developed in the project, mapping the reuse and functional user requirements and counting the impacts against the functional size. The author has not found any other available reuse analysis methods, except those embedded in productivity measurement methods.

One important additional measurement, which has not yet been discussed, is risk analysis. Based on the definition, risks are not very probable factors, but if they come true, they may have a great impact to the effort and costs of the project. In this paper we don't pay more attention to risk analysis, but the author strongly recommends everybody to remember it as one of the important software development project measurements, especially in the early phases of the development.

Table 1.9 Comparison of the Most Popular Productivity Analysis Methods

COCOMO II	VAF	FiSMA ND21
Project scale factor attributes:	*General system characteristics:*	*Project organizational factors:*
1. Precedentedness	1. Data communications	1. Involvement of the customer representatives
2. Development flexibility	2. Distributed data processing	2. Performance and availability of the development environment
3. Architecture/risk resolution	3. Performance	3. Availability of IT staff
4. Team cohesion	4. Heavily used configuration	4. Number of stakeholders
5. Process maturity	5. Transaction rate	5. Pressure on schedule
		Process factors:
6. Required software reliability	6. Online data entry	6. Impact of standards
7. Data base size	7. End-user efficiency	7. Impact of methods
8. Product complexity	8. Online update	8. Impact of tools
9. Develop for reuse	9. Complex processing	9. Level of change management
10. Documentation match to lifecycle needs	10. Reusability	10. Maturity of software development process
		Product quality factors:
11. Execution time constraint	11. Installation ease	11. Functionality requirements
12. Main storage constraint	12. Operational ease	12. Reliability requirements
13. Platform volatility	13. Multiple sites	13. Usability requirements
14. Analysis personnel capability	14. Facilitate change	14. Efficiency requirements
15. Programmer personnel capability		15. Maintainability requirements

Continued

Table 1.9 Comparison of the Most Popular Productivity Analysis Methods (Continued)

COCOMO II	VAF	FiSMA ND21
16. Personnel continuity		*Product quality factors:* 16. Portability requirements *People factors:* 17. Analysis skills of staff 18. Application knowledge of staff 19. Tool skills of staff 20. Experience of project management 21. Team skills of the project team
17. Applications experience 18. Personnel platform experience 19. Language and tool experience 20. Use of software tools 21. Multi-site development 22. Required development schedule 23. Other		
Ratings: VL/L/N/H/VH/XH The meaning of each choice per factor is explained in the book [42].	Ratings: 0 = not present, or no influence, 1 = incidental influence, 2 = moderate influence, 3 = average influence, 4 = significant influence, 5 = strong influence throughout. The guidelines for how to determine degree of influence are explained in the standard [143].	Ratings: -- = circumstances much worse than in average, - = worse than in average, +/- = normal situation, + = circumstances better than in average, ++ = much better than in average. The meaning of each choice per factor are explained in the method definition document [91].
Coefficient: The exact value of each choice per factor shall be calibrated by the user. The variance of coefficient depends on the calibration.	Coefficient: 0.65, 1.30	Coefficient: 0.5, 2.5 in practice, but theoretically between 0.1 and 15. Exact values of each choice per factor vary between 0.88 and 1.14, based on experience database.

Risks should not be included into the effort and cost estimates, but they should be considered as options in the project contracts.

As a summary of this section, there are several more or less useful and easy-to-use methods available for completing the effort estimates and benchmarking measurements. With a reasonably small amount of training, the project managers and business managers can learn to apply these methods in their own projects. At least they should learn to read the results of these analyses, so that they can use them in decision making and process improvement. The measurements can always be outsourced to external experts, though the cost-effectiveness of that approach may be questionable in the long term. Compared to wasted time and effort in badly managed software development projects, the cost of training these mature methods to all managers involved in software development projects is very small.

1.3.4 Development Management Levels

As discussed in Sections 1.3.2 and 1.3.3, there are plenty of useful software project management and measurement methods available today. One common misconseption is a belief that they will always work, whatever you may develop. The more professional and mature the software development industry has become, the bigger, more complex, and more challenging development endeavors have been. Managers and experts have tried to apply functional size measurement methods and experience databases to large, hybrid ICT (Information and Communication Technology) development programs. The results have not been very encouraging. No better experiences come from very small component programming activities, when there is only one developer. No doubt they are part of software development, but as a whole, this kind of work doesn't meet all different management challenges, which are present in typical projects. Another point considering small development is that individual competences of software developers vary much more than productivity from one project to another. That's why average delivery rates and schedules don't work with product development tasks that are too small.

The Finnish Information Processing Association (FIPA), a network of twenty-five thousand individuals and seven hundred company members, hired two consulting companies and invited ten different member organizations to start a collaborative project to develop new ICT project management models in December 2003. The fundamental work of this project was to define the most important concepts of ICT development management, and particularly project management models for all different ICT project types. The framework for this work was a combination of the Project Management Body of Knowledge (PMBOK 2000), the PMI's standard, and the experiences of all participants coming from different business areas and representing both suppliers and customers. The most important finding from this FIPA endeavor was probably the clear definition of separate management levels. The other breakthrough result was definitions of seven ICT project types. Figure 1.14 illustrates five software development management levels.

Business management level defines the mission and vision of the organization. It may require software development, at least sometimes. If the business management level wants to improve processes and develop new products and services, it usually sets up a permanent development steering committee to manage all kinds of development activities in the organization. This is called portfolio management. If the business of the organization is very multidimensional and the business area is large, the development may be divided into several separate portfolios. Sometimes the ICT development portfolio may be one of those.

A development portfolio consists of one or usually more temporary development programs, which the portfolio steering committee has accepted to be started. These programs include typically several different types of projects. Some of them are ICT projects, and others may be feasibility projects, other business process improvement projects, and rollout projects. Part of the ICT projects is different types of software development projects, which are developing one or more products each. The development program management is done by a program coordinating committee set by the portfolio steering committee. It controls the projects being started and closed in the right order, as early as needed, but not too early. A recommended principle is that the first project of a program should not be started before initiating all its projects. Initiating means that at least the scope statement and critical success factors of the project shall be defined. The product management of software development is all documentation, configuration management, component management, etc., during the development life cycle.

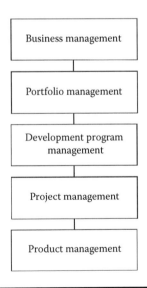

Figure 1.14 Five software development management levels.

Project management is by definition "the application of knowledge, skills, tools and techniques to project activities to meet project requirements. Project management is accomplished through the use of the processes such as: initiating, planning, executing, controlling, and closing" (PMBOK 2000, p. 37). The seven different ICT project types defined by FIPA are:

- Customer-specific new development project
- Software product new development project
- Software version enhancement project
- ICT service development project
- Package software configuration project
- Data conversion project
- Software integration development project

All of these project types require different kinds of management. None of the measurement methods introduced above is applicable to all of these project types. For example, functional size measurement is not very good with ICT service development or package software configuration, where the functional size of the software is not an important factor. Also, the productivity factors and typical risks vary a lot from one project type to another.

When we are using project measurement methods, we have to remember that as such, they are applicable only at the project management level. The situation coefficient is too difficult to measure from an aggregate program of several different projects, because the more different parts we have, the more average all the productivity factors tend to be. Delivery rate information is useful only at the project management level, because the variation and number of outliers increase when the number of exact selection classifiers decrease. Data sets where the development language, project type, and platform type are not defined are not reliable for estimating purposes. Functional size measurement is useful at both the product and project management levels, but useless at higher levels if the program includes other than just software development projects.

Program management and portfolio management need different measurements, parameters, and indicators than project management. The previous sections have introduced useful measurement methods for project management, and the results of using these measurements are essential to all higher management level measurements. There may be some qualitative measurement methods for the higher levels, but they do not give enough input for good benchmarking or development process improvement. All the quantitative metrics at higher management levels are derived from lower-level metrics. For example, the total cost of a development program cannot be counted if we don't know the costs of all its projects. If we want to improve development portfolio management and program management, we have to ensure thorough and reliable application of measurement-driven management processes at the project management level.

1.3.5 Measurement-Driven Software Project Management in Practice

The technical skills of software engineers are reasonably good today. There is more and more evidence of this. Very nice pieces of software have been developed and delivered everywhere. We are talking about ubiquitous information technology, and there are fewer areas of life where any software doesn't exist. We can say proudly that our technical skills are very broadly acknowledged and trusted. But the management skills are another, completely different story. The Standish Group has published several CHAOS reports (Standish Group 1999) during the last decade, all of them telling that the software development projects fail too often. Just reading those results should convince anybody to believe that we have to improve software development project management. On the other hand, we can read any of the published software project risk studies (Honkonen and Lyytinen 1999), in addition to further analysis of CHAOS reports, to see that most of the common reasons to fail are related to scope management. This claims the importance of functional size measurement, or any other good way to catalog the functional user requirements. Project management consists of nine knowledge areas and thirty-nine different processes (PMBOK 2000). These processes construct five process groups, which were already mentioned in the definition of project management. Figure 1.15 illustrates the relationships of the process groups.

The Finnish Software Measurement Association has developed a scope management concept, consisting of five scope management processes. They are largely compatible with PMI's processes. Figure 1.16 introduces the processes of the FiSMA concept.

Developing software is one of the core processes of a software development organization. It is not a scope management process, as all the white boxes in Figure 1.16. When mapped against the process groups in Figure 1.15, initiating project and software is an initiating process, estimating cost and duration is a

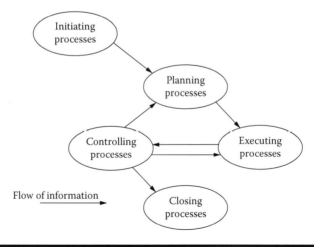

Figure 1.15   Project management process groups.

planning process, developing software is an executing process, controlling progress and managing changes are controlling processes, and finally, closing development is a closing process. So, the FiSMA concept covers scope management over the whole development life cycle.

Initiating is the first step of project management. The key measurement issue, from the viewpoint of scope management, is the classification of the project. If you can't determine all of the most important classifiers (ISBSG 2001; Maxwell and Forselius 2000), you should split the project until the unambiguous classification can be done. Only then can you get a manageable and measurable software development project, where you can apply measurement methods without any tailored interpretations. Selection of measurement methods is one of the subprocesses of initiating process. Believe it or not, it's easier to manage two simple projects and coordinate them at the program level than to manage one hybrid project.

Planning processes provide the project plan, where the most important scope management indicators and deliveries are the total size of software, target delivery rate, situation coefficient, reuse multiplier, list of functional user requirements, definition of the work breakdown structure to be used, productivity profile, and list of top 5 or top 10 risks.

Controlling processes creates improved versions of the estimates. Controlling progress results in the earned value of the software delivered so far. It's based on the list of functional user requirements, work breakdown structure, and FSM. The FiSMA concept tells the earned value in function points, not in money. The change management process covers all kinds of change requests, not only the functional changes. If the quality requirements, people on the team, reusability requirements, or any other factors having influence on the total productivity will be changed, it's better to recalculate the effort and cost estimates.

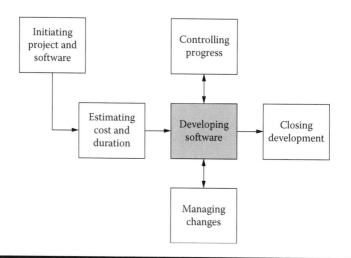

Figure 1.16   Scope management processes of FiSMA scope management concept.

Closing the development is the last phase of a project. In the scope management point of view, it means generating the final—the actual—version of the estimate. In practice, it is collecting actual efforts, actual schedules, costs, and all necessary background information for a thorough postmortem analysis and project benchmarking. It's important to notice that the better the initiating process is, the better project data the organization collects. The data gathering will be faster and more effective, and the repeatability of small projects is much more probable than the repeatability of similar hybrids. Good closing ensures organizational learning.

All the processes above have been developed during the last ten years. The best FiSMA software supplier organizations have fully adopted them since 1999, and the results are amazing. Customer satisfaction has improved on a 5-point scale from 3.1 to 4.1, all software development projects during the last two years have been finished in time and on budget (Männistö 2004), and the overall productivity is at a competitive level.

Very similar results have been reported from the Victorian government, from Austalia, where they have developed and used a southernSCOPE concept since 1997 (Victorian 2002). In their projects, the average cost overrun was soon dropped from 90% to 10% of the original budget (Wright 2000), and customer satisfaction improved remarkably.

The results from Finland and Australia are so good that they should encourage all organizations, both the suppliers and the customers, to stop hesitating and waiting for "better measurement methods." The concepts and methods are already here, but the organizations can't get them without any own work and commitment. At least those organizations where the software development projects are a significant part of their business should take up these concepts and methods as soon as possible.

1.3.6 How to Get Started with Measurement-Driven Management?

Most of you who have read this paper so far have raised the question of the title sometimes. You may wonder about how to get it started in your own organization, or in your country, or worldwide, all over the software development industry. These issues have been discussed a lot in ISBSG, and among all national measurement organizations. Some good ideas have emerged already, but if you invent something new, it will be warmly welcomed by the whole society.

One important way to increase understanding of the importance and usefulness of the measurements in the software development industry is documenting the success stories and publishing them as broadly as possible. One good example of this kind of activity is the public sector report written by ISBSG in 2003 (ISBSG 2003). This report can be downloaded for free from ISBSG's website. The FiSMA and southernSCOPE cases mentioned above are other examples of documenting and telling success stories.

All the measurements should be done because of better management, but the measurement methods have been taught to software developers. It is definitely the wrong audience. They are not very interested in becoming measured. Teaching methods and presenting results should be moved from the technical level to the managerial level. We should be talking to the business managers and customers, who really need measurements. They are the portfolio and program managers, who have power to demand that project managers follow the best project management practices. Moving the measurement conversation to a higher level is a target that should be set in every organization and every country.

One common problem is that the project managers can't apply measurement methods. There are two good solutions. One is to hire external scope managers to help project managers run all measurements needed. There are good experiences of this concept from Australia and Finland. Another solution is, of course, training the project managers. This is probably the better way in the long term, but may be too slow to get started and temporarily too expensive if all project managers will be trained during a very short period.

One more, hopefully helpful, activity to accelerate especially the adoption of functional size measurement methods and all the other methods consequently, is the ISO development project for the guide for use of FSM standards. It should help all the organizations that want to start measurements to select the methods and to understand all the purposes where the use of FSM would be beneficial.

1.3.7 Conclusions

We FSM people have been talking to each other long enough. The current measurement methods and project management concepts are good enough to be used by all people and organizations involved in software development. It is time to make a move, indeed! We have to write and read the success stories of measurement-driven project management; we have to deliver them to the managers and customers; we have to be professional enough to demand good, but not perfect, requirement specifications; and we have to help the program managers split their large development programs into measurable and manageable projects.

1.4 Mapping Concepts of Functional Size Measurement Methods

Pinar Efe, Onur Demirors, and Cigdem Gencel

1.4.1 Introduction

As the quality of size measurement directly influences the effort, cost, and schedule estimates, accurate size measurement is highly critical to reliable planning and effective management of the software development projects.

Functional size is the functionality-based size measure for software. The function point (FP) metric and a related function point analysis (FPA) method were first proposed by Albrecht in the late 1970s (Albrecht 1979; Albrecht and Gaffney 1983). Various FSM methods have been designed since their initial publication.

All FSM methods measure the functional size by quantifying the FURs. However, each method has its own measurement process and metrics. Therefore, when measured by different methods, a software product has several functional sizes. In order to be able to compare functional sizes of software products measured by different methods, we need to convert them to each other.

FSM methods have many similarities in the core concepts. The rules they use in their measurement processes are quite related, even though they categorize these concepts differently, make use of different terminology, and measure functional size with different measurement rules. Each variant of FSM methods defines its own concepts for the measurement of a software system rather than using the concepts and models of a particular development method (Fetcke 2001). Sometimes, they use different attributes of FURs or look at the same concepts from different perspectives or use different abstractions during their measurement processes (Efe 2006; Gencel 2005; Gencel and Dimirors 2004). Concepts and counting rules in different FSM methods do not have one-to-one mapping. Still, most of the concepts and rules utilize the same information.

In this paper, we mainly focus on investigating the similarities and differences between IFPUG FPA (IFPUG 2000), Mark II FPA (ISO 2002), and COSMIC FFP (ISO 2003a) methods. Based on the similarities and differences identified and the concepts defined in ISO/IEC 14143-1 (ISO 1998), we determine the common concepts of these FSM methods and map the terminologies used by them to each other. We present a unification model for IFPUG FPA, Mark II FPA, and COSMIC FFP methods so as to measure a software system simultaneously by applying these methods using a single base of data (Efe 2006). We also discuss the results of a case study that we conducted to evaluate the unification model. This case study involves measuring the functional size of the project by implementing IFPUG FPA, Mark II FPA, and COSMIC FFP methods as defined in their counting guidelines. We also applied the unification model to determine the same metrics and compare the results.

The paper is structured as follows. Section 1.4.2 presents an overview of literature on FSM methods. Section 1.4.3 proposes a unification model, providing common concepts, terminology mapping, and measurement rules for the model. Section 1.4.4 gives the case study for the evaluation of the unification model proposed and the results. Finally, Section 1.4.5 concludes the study.

1.4.2 Literature Survey

Since its first presentation to the public, Albrecht's FPA (Albrecht, 1979) has grown worldwide and has been a basis for several improvements and alternative proposals. These studies result in a number of new metrics and methods to measure functionality. The most significant FSM methods are given in Table 1.10 (Gencel and Dimirors 2004).

Proliferation of metrics resulted in the need for convertibility among metrics. Convertibility studies on FSM metrics mostly aim to develop a statistically based conversion formula. Symons (2001) studied the convertibility of Mark II FP and

Table 1.10 FSM Methods

Year	Method	ISO Approval
1979	Albrecht FPA (by Albrecht, IBM [Albrecht 1979; Albrecht and Gaffney 1983])	
1982	DeMarco's Bang Metrics (DeMarco 1982)	
1986	Feature Points (Jones 1991)	
1988	IFPUG FPA (by International Function Point Users Group (IFPUG 2004))	Yes
1988	Mark II FPA (Symons 1991; Mark II Manual 2002)	Yes
1990	NESMA FPA (by The Netherlands Software Metrics Users Association [NESMA Manual 2005])	Yes
1992	3-D Function Points (by Whitmire, Boeing (Whitmire1992))	
1994	Banker, Kauffman, Kumar (Banker et al. 1994)	
1997	Full Function Points (FFP) (by Software Engineering Laboratory in Applied Metrics of The University of Québec (FFP97 1997))	
1997	Early FPA (by Meli (Meli 1997a; Meli 2002))	
1998	Object Oriented Function Points (by Caldiera, Antoniol, Fiutem, and Lokan [Lokan and Abran 1999])	
1999	COSMIC FFP (COSMIC, (ISO 2003))	Yes
2000	Early&Quick COSMIC FFP (by Meli, Abran, Ho, Oligny [Conte et al. 2004; Meli 2002])	
2004	FiSMA FSM (by Finnish Software Metrics Association [Forselius 2004])	

IFPUG FP to each other, and gave conversion formulas. The convertibility of IFPUG FPA and COSMIC FFP has been studied by Abran et al. (2005) based on the three case study data sets.

It would be ideal that size value obtained by one FSM method could be converted to another by utilizing one mathematical formula. However, there are practical and theoretical reasons why this may not be easy (ISO 2003a). To set up a statistically based conversion formula, a significant number of measurements should be made by applying different methods to measure the functional size of the same project. Such a study requires significant effort as well as expertise in more than one method (ISO 2003a).

Fetcke (2001) proposed an alternative model as a generalized representation for a set of methods: IFPUG FPA, Mark II FPA, and FFP. He used an axiomatic approach based on measurement theory to develop a model for existing FSM methods. He made a representation for transaction types with seven classes of logical activities that manipulate data elements in this model. The generalized representation defines a set of elements to obtain the measurement with any of these FSM methods. This approach enables obtaining measurement results for any of these methods from experience data stored in a form of a generalized representation of different concepts.

1.4.3   Unification Model

1.4.3.1   Overview of Common Concepts

Although the FSM methods differ in some respects when measuring the amount of software functionality, such as in the measurement steps, metrics utilized, or the terminology used, they rely on the same core concepts. Most of these concepts are already defined in ISO/IEC 14143-1 (ISO 1998). We include an extended summary of these concepts below:

- **User:** Any person that specifies FUR, or any person or thing that communicates or interacts with the software at any time.
- **FUR:** A subset of the user requirements. The FURs represent the user practices and procedures that the software must perform to fulfill the user's needs.
- **Boundary:** A conceptual interface between the software under study and its users.
- **Application:** The application is the object of the measurement. Applications provide functions to the users.
- **Type of measurement:** The type of project to be measured. The project can be a development project, enhancement project, etc.
- **Purpose of measurement:** The statement that defines why the measurement is being undertaken, or what the result will be used for (ISO 2003)a.
- **Scope of measurement:** The set of FURs to be included in a specific FSM instance. It is determined by the purpose for measuring the software.

- **Viewpoint:** A form of abstraction, for example, end user viewpoint or developer viewpoint.
- **BFC:** An elementary unit of FURs defined by and used by a FSM method for measurement purposes. They are recognized within the FURs and assign values that are used to calculate the functional size.
- **BFC type:** A defined category of BFCs. ISO/IEC 14143-5:2004 (ISO 2004) decomposes BFC types into four categories: transaction classes, data types recognized, information creation function types, and data retention requirements. Information creation function types correspond to the processing way of a transaction, and range in complexity from very simple Boolean operations to complex mathematical algorithms. The data retention type is the degree of persistency of the data types. Nevertheless, the FSM methods studied in the scope of this study do not recognize any specific information creation function types. Only IFPUG FPA takes types into account in one type of elementary process, the external output. The data retention types are entirely related with data types. Therefore, we have two BFC type concepts in the unification model: data types and transaction. The data retention type is the topic of data concept.
  - **Transaction:** Transactions represent the functionality provided to the user. Transactions are processes of interaction of the user with the application from a logical or functional perspective. They are one of the BFC types of the FSM methods covered.
- **Data types:** Data are stored by the application, and transactions involve groups of data. Data elements represent the smallest data items meaningful to the user. Data elements are structured in logically related groups, data groups, similar to tables in a database (Caldiera et al. 1998). The data concept recognizes data elements as elementary items. They are one of the BFC types of the FSM methods covered.

The terminology used by each FSM method for these core concepts is given in Table 1.11.

1.4.3.2 Constituent Parts of Methods

Although these methods are approved as an ISO FSM standard, they have different constituent parts, different BFC types, and different classifications for different BFC types, i.e., data and transaction concepts. The three variants of FSM methods represent an application by a set of transaction types and a set of groups of data (Fetcke 2001). Even though transaction and data concepts are common to these methods, the detailed definitions, the terminology used for these concepts, identification, and counting procedures differ notably. These differences are summarized in Table 1.12. As depicted in the table, a data concept is contributed to functional size directly by IFPUG FPA. The other FSM methods measure transactions and related data implicitly

Table 1.11   Core Concept of Chosen Functional Size Measurements

	IFPUG FPA 4.1	*Mark II FPA 1.3.1*	*COSMIC FFP 2.2*
User	User	User	User
FURs	FURs	FURs	FURs
Application	Application	Application	Application
Boundary	Boundary	Boundary	Boundary
Type of Measurement	Type of Count	—	—
Purpose of Measurement	Purpose of Count	Purpose of Count	Purpose of Measurement
Scope of Measurement	Counting Scope	—	Scope of Measurement
Viewpoint of Measurement	—	Viewpoint of Count	Viewpoint of Measurement
Transaction	Transactional Process	Logical Transaction	Functional Process
Data Group	Data Function	Data Entity Types	Data Group
Sub-group	Record Element Type (RET)	Sub-type	—
Data Element Type (DET)	DET	DET	Data Attribute

under the transaction concept. Also, COSMIC FFP does not count at the granularity level of a data element type (DET).

The data concept assumes the DETs as elementary items. A data group is a set of data elements stored by the application.

1.4.3.2.1 Data Group Concept

All three FSM methods agree on the data group concept, but each uses different terminology:

- IFPUG FPA defines data function as a "user identifiable group of logically related data or control information referenced by the application" (IFPUG 2004, p. 24).
- Mark II FPA defines entity type as "something (strictly, some type of thing) in the real world about which the business user wants to hold information" (ISO 2002, p. 32).

Table 1.12   Different Constituent Parts of FSM Methods

FSM Method	Data Group Types	Data Group Contribution	Transaction Types	Transaction Parts	Transaction Contribution
IFPUG FPA 4.1	Internal Logical File (ILF)	# of DETs, # of RETs	External Input (EI)	—	# of DETs, # of File Types Referenced
	External Interface File (EIF)		External Inquiry (EQ)		
			External Output (EO)		
Mark II FPA 1.3.1	Primary	Considered in Transaction	—	Input	# of Input DETs
	Non-primary			Process	# of Data Entities Referenced
				Output	# of Output DETs
COSMIC FFP 2.2	Transient	Considered in Transaction	—	Entry	# of Data Movements
	Short			Exit	# of Data Movements
	Indefinite			Read	# of Data Movements
				Write	# of Data Movements

■ COSMIC FFP describes data group as a "distinct, nonempty, nonordered, and nonredundant set of data attributes where each included data attribute describes a complementary aspect of the same object of interest" (FFP97 1997, p. 27).

Each method classifies data groups in its own way:

■ IFPUG FPA has two types of data functions: ILF and EIF.
■ Mark II FPA has two entity types: primary entities and nonprimary entities. There are some variations of primary entity types according to usage of the data entity type in a logical transaction as subentity type and self-referential entity type.
■ COSMIC FFP characterizes data groups by their persistence as transient, short, and indefinite. After identifying the persistence, a data group shall be materialized as a data group on an I/O device, a data group in volatile storage, and a data group on persistent storage.

The ILF type of IFPUG FPA and primary entity type of Mark II FPA are quite similar. IFPUG FPA differentiates data groups that are not maintained inside the application boundary as being EIF, but Mark II FPA does not make such a differentiation. Mark II FPA considers nonprimary entity type, whereas the others do not. COSMIC FFP characterizes data groups by their persistence as transient, volatile, and indefinite. According to COSMIC FFP, materialization of a data group takes three forms, as a data group on an I/O device, a data group in volatile storage, and a data group on persistent storage. Transient, volatile, and indefinite data groups can be present on an I/O device, and transient and volatile data groups can be found on volatile storage for COSMIC FFP. Additionally, COSMIC FFP does not declare any classification of data groups concerning place of storage with respect to application boundary. Moreover, IFPUG FPA and Mark II FPA do not mention the persistence characteristics of data groups. Though these two methods count transient data element types, they do not differentiate transient data groups. ILFs and EIFs of IFPUG FPA and primary entity types and nonprimary entity types of Mark II FPA can be indefinite or volatile data groups.

Based on the different types and findings explained above, we categorized the data groups from two perspectives in the unification model. According to retention characteristics, a data group can be *transient, volatile,* or *indefinite.* According to the place of its storage with respect to application boundary, a data group can be maintained inside the boundary of the application, inside the boundary for a short period of time, or outside the boundary of the application.

In the unification model, the following rules are applied for data group concept:

1. All three methods concur on the data group concept.
2. Data groups contribute to functional size directly only for IFPUG FPA.
3. The default value for retention characteristics of data group is indefinite.

4. The default value for place of storage of the data group is inside the boundary.
5. IFPUG FPA ILF type is the same with the data groups maintained inside the boundary.
6. The IFPUG FPA EIF type is the same with the data groups maintained outside the boundary.
7. Primary data entity types of Mark II FPA are data groups, maintained inside the boundary.
8. Nonprimary data entity types of Mark II FPA are identical to data groups maintained seldom inside the boundary. They are treated as a single entity, system entity, during calculations.
9. According to COSMIC FFP, transient and volatile data groups can be in volatile storage. Volatile and indefinite data groups can be on persistent storage. Transient, volatile, and indefinite data groups can be on an I/O device.

1.4.3.2.2 Data Element Type (DET) Concept

These methods also agree on data element type concept. Moreover, except COSMIC FFP, all use the same terminology, data element type.

- According to IFPUG FPA, a DET is a unique user-recognizable, nonrepeated field (ISO. 2003a).
- Mark II FPA describes DET as a unique user-recognizable, nonrecursive item of information about entity types (ISO 2002).
- COSMIC FFP defines data attribute as the smallest parcel of information, within an identified data group, carrying a meaning from the perspective of the software's FURs (2003).

We can say that there is an exact mapping for the DET concept for all FSM methods covered:

1. The data attributes of COSMIC FFP and DETs of the IFPUG FPA and Mark II FPA address the same concept.
2. IFPUG FPA measures DETs for data types.

1.4.3.2.3 Subgroup Data Concept

Subgroups can be defined on the data elements of a data group. IFPUG FPA defines these subgroups as RETs (Record Element Type), which is a user-recognizable subgroup of data elements within an ILF or EIF. There are two types of RETs: optional and mandatory subgroups. Mark II FPA also considers subgroups in the transaction, but not for the data group. We can define one rule for subgroups in Mark II FPA:

1. The subentity type of Mark II FPA is similar to RET of IFPUG FPA. But, IFPUG FPA considers RETs only once during counting data functions, whereas Mark II FPA counts subentities each time when referred by any transaction. Other methods do not consider subgroups.

1.4.3.2.4 Transaction Concept

All three FSM methods agree on the transaction concept, although each uses different terminology for it. The definitions of the methods for transaction are as follows:

■ IFPUG FPA calls a transaction an elementary process, which is defined as "the smallest unit of activity meaningful to the user, must be self-contained, and leaves the application in a consistent state" (IFPUG 2004, p. 22).

■ Mark II FPA calls a transaction a logical transaction, which is defined as "the lowest level business process triggered by a unique event of interest in the external world, or a request for information and, when wholly complete, leaves the application in a self consistent state in relation to the unique event" (ISO 2002, p. 33).

■ COSMIC FFP calls a transaction a functional process, which is defined as "an elementary component of a set of FURs comprising a unique cohesive and independently executable set of data movements. It is triggered by one or more triggering events and complete when it has executed" (ISO 2003a, p. 21).

Even though the transaction concept is the same for all three methods, transaction types are represented differently in each method.

■ IFPUG FPA defines three types of transactions as EI, EO, and EQ.

■ The others do not have transaction types, but they split transaction into its constituting components.

■ A logical transaction in Mark II FPA contains three components: input component, processing component, and output component.

■ A functional process in COSMIC FFP has four subprocess types, defined as data movement types occurring during the execution of a functional process, as entry, exit, read, and write.

Having defined transaction types and their components, we identify the measurement rules for the transaction in each FSM method before mapping these rules:

■ In IFPUG FPA, the functional size of a transactional function is based on the number of DETs that enter or exit the application boundary, and the number of referenced files, which are ILF(s) read or maintained by that transactional function or EIF(s) read by that transactional function.

- According to Mark II FPA, the functional size is the sum of the size of the input component, the size of the processing component, and the size of the output component. The size of the input element is proportional to the number of uniquely processed DETs crossing into the application boundary. The size of the processing element is proportional to the number of primary entity types referenced during the execution of the transaction. If the system entity is also referenced, the count is incremented by one. Subentity types are counted separately when different processing logic is used in the transaction. The size of the output element is proportional to the number of uniquely processed DETs crossing outside of the application boundary.
- The functional size of a COSMIC FFP transaction is proportional to the number of data movements. COSMIC FFP does not take into account the number of DETs. The functional size is the sum of entry, exit, read, and write data movements.

ISO/IEC 14143-5:2004 (ISO 2004) states that a transaction takes data as input, processes them, and outputs data as a result of the processing. Based on the different transaction types and their components described above, and ISO/IEC 14143-5:2004 (ISO 2004), we split a transaction into three parts in the unification model, as input, processing, and output, and further divide the processing component into one more subtype, as maintained and read.

The *input part* represents the user inputs across an application boundary. The input part has two elements: the input DETs across an application boundary and the input data groups, which hold these input DETs.
1. The number of input DETs of Mark II FPA refers to the number of input DETs.
2. The number of entries of COSMIC FFP is equal to the number of input data groups.

The *output part* represents the outputs across the application boundary. The output part has two elements: the output DETs across an application boundary and the output data groups, which hold these output DETs.
3. The number of output DETs of Mark II FPA refers to the number of output DETs.
4. The number of exits of COSMIC FFP is equal to the number of output data groups.
5. Because the number of DETs of IFPUG FPA is the number of input and output DETs, which enter or exit the application boundary, we can say that it is equal to the number of union of input DETs and output DETs.

The *processing part* holds the processed elements during the execution of the transaction. The processing part has two subtypes: maintained and read. In this part, the methods consider just referenced data groups instead of data element types.

- *Maintained type* involves one element: maintained data group. The maintained data groups shall be of the type indefinite or volatile.
- *Read type* involves one element: read data group. The read data groups shall be of the type indefinite or volatile.

6. IFPUG FPA and Mark II FPA do not differentiate between read or maintained data groups. They just consider referenced data groups. If a data group is both read and written in the same transaction, it is counted only once. Therefore, we count the number of the union of read and maintained data groups for them. For a transaction, the number of referenced entity types of Mark II FPA is equal to the number of file types referenced in IFPUG FPA, and they are the union of these data groups. The EQ transaction type of IFPUG FPA does not write to data functions; it only reads data.

7. The number of reads of COSMIC FFP is equal to the number of the read data groups.

8. The number of writes of COSMIC FFP is equal to the number of the maintained data groups.

The overview of the mappings of the transactional components of the methods to each other in the unification model is presented in Table 1.13.

1.4.4 Case Study

A case study is conducted using the data of a real project to evaluate the proposed unification model. At first, the functional sizes of the project were measured by the conventional approach by applying IFPUG FPA, Mark II FPA, and COSMIC FFP guidelines manually. Then the functional sizes were remeasured using the unification model.

1.4.4.1 Project Characteristics

The case project is a Web-based, military inventory management project integrated with a document management system. It is a data-strong system, which also involves a number of algorithmic operations. The general characteristics are summarized in the following:

- The project staff consisted of six people, one project manager, two senior software engineers, two part-time software engineers, and one part-time software engineer.
- The types of software products and programming language(s) used for the project are Internal Development Framework and Java as programming languages, IBM WebSphere Application Developer as the development

Table 1.13   The Mapping of the Constituent Parts of IFPUG FPA, Mark II FPA, and COSMIC FFP Methods to the Unification Model

	INPUT	OUTPUT	PROCESSING	
			Read	Maintained
	Entry from outside the application boundary	Exit to outside of the application boundary	Read from data groups	Write to data groups
Unification Model	DET_R_IO, DG_R_IO	DET_W_IO, DG_W_IO	DG_R_PS	DG_W_PS
Mark II FPA	# of Input DETs	# of Output DETs	# of references to Data Entity Types	
	DET_R_IO	DET_W_IO	DG_R_PS Union DG_W_PS	
COSMIC FFP	# of Entries	# of Exits	# of Reads	# of Writes
	DG_R_IO	DG_W_IO	DG_R_PS	DG_W_PS
IFPUG FPA	Number of DETs		Number of FTRs	
EI, EO	DET_R_IO Union DET_W_IO		DG_R_PS Union DG_W_PS	
EQ	DET_R_IO Union DET_W_IO		DG_R_PS	–

DET_R_IO: DETs read from I/O device

DET_W_IO: DETs write to I/O device

DG_R_PS: Read data groups of persistent storage

DG_W_PS: Write data groups of persistent storage

DG_R_IO: Data groups of DET_ R_IO

DG_W_IO: Data groups of DET_ W_IO

environment, Rational Rose as the analysis and design tool, Oracle 9i as the database management system, and Tomcat as the application server.

■ The project documents were prepared in compliance with the organizational document standards. The company uses an SRS standard developed by the company itself.

■ The project was started in October 2004 and completed in December 2005.

■ The total effort spent for this project was approximately 7,500 man-hours.

■ Both size estimations presented here are conducted using the Software Requirements Specification (SRS) document of the project, which involves 123 use cases.

1.4.4.2 Case Study Conduct

Two persons performed the functional size measurement together during the conventional measurement. One of them, who is also an author of this study, works for the development organization and is involved in this project. Both of them are experienced in using the methods.

IFPUG FPA, Mark II FPA, and COSMIC FFP methods were implemented separately. The details of the measurement were recorded in Excel sheets.

For each type of count, we first identified the transactions based on the SRS document of the software product. This document involves the detailed information the three FSM methods require. There were 123 use cases in the SRS document, which correspond to 123 transactions.

The functional size measurement of the software product was done by IFPUG FPA, Mark II FPA, and COSMIC FFP, consequently. The functional size measurement of the case project using the unification model was implemented by the same person, who also made the conventional measurement, in order to avoid the subjectivity of the FSM methods, which can affect the measurement results.

As the transactions, data groups, and DETs have already been identified during the conventional measurement, we used these figures during the implementation of the unification model.

The results of conventional measurement and the measurement by the unification model for IFPUG FPA, Mark II FPA, and COSMIC FFP measurements are given in Tables 1.14 to 1.16, respectively.

1.4.4.3 Discussion of the Results

The results of the case study were as expected: the same. The unification model worked properly to measure the functional size of the software product as it was measured in the conventional approach.

Since this case project is a data-strong system, it was rather easy to identify and map the BFC types to unification model. We do not know yet how the unification model would behave for other software systems, which are of different domain types.

Another constraint of this study is that both measurements were performed by the same people relying on the same assumptions when identifying and applying measurement rules. To evaluate the unification model, it is required to replicate the case study by different people.

We also have faced a number of difficulties during the measurements. We observed that we had made some mistakes during the conventional measurement process. We made mistakes in counting DETs and making changes for BFC types whenever needed. In case one of the BFC types changed, we had to identify all these BFC types in all related measurement items of each method and change them. This was very time-consuming and error-prone.

Table 1.14 Case Project—IFPUG FPA Size Measurement Details

	Number of Elementary Processes	Functional Complexities for Function Types					Total Functional Complexity
		ILFs	EIFs	EIs	EOs	EQs	
Traditional Measurement	123	294	0	262	343	26	925
Unification Model Measurement	123	294	0	262	343	26	925

Table 1.15 Case Project—Mark II FPA Size Measurement Details

	Number of Logical Transactions	Number of Input DETs	Number of Output DETs	Number of Data Entity Types Referenced	Functional Size (Mark II FPA)
Traditional Measurement	123	559	1,679	343	1,330.14
Unification Model Measurement	123	559	1,679	343	1,330.14

Table 1.16 Case Project COSMIC FFP Size Measurement Details

	Number of Functional Processes	Number of Entries	Number of Exits	Number of Reads	Number of Writes	Functional Size (Cfsu)
Traditional Measurement	123	206	364	334	156	1,060.0
Unification Model Measurement	123	206	364	334	156	1,060.0

As the unification model contains the largest set of data, the BFC types were stored in a unified way, and we had only one set of data in a unification model format. Therefore, in case one of the BFC types changes, it is enough to identify and change it once in a unified form of data. The unification model allows us to measure this case project from a single base of data simultaneously.

1.4.5   Conclusion

In this study, a unification model for the three selected FSM methods is proposed. The concepts for each method, and the similarities and differences between the concepts are investigated. The common core concepts and BFC types—data types and transaction concepts—are studied. The counting rules in the measurement processes of the methods are studied comparatively. The mapping for the terminologies of the concepts and the mapping for the constituent part of the methods are presented.

In order to evaluate the unification model, a case study was conducted on an industrial MIS project. First, the product was measured based on the SRS document by IFPUG FPA, Mark II FPA, and COSMIC FFP FSM methods separately. Then, the functional sizes were measured by all three methods using the unification model. These case study results confirm that the unification of the methods is possible, and the functional sizes by IFPUG FPA, Mark II FPA, and COSMIC FFP can be obtained by utilizing a single base of data in a form of unification model. The unification model contains the largest set of information needed by these FSM methods. Therefore, it enables us to convert one type of measurement results to another type, providing some additional data required by the unification model.

The validation of the model can be reinforced by implementing more case studies using this model. As this case project is a data-strong system, it would be beneficial to implement the model to measure the size of the projects of different functional domains, such as control-strong systems or algorithmic systems.

Since both measurements were made by the same person, who also was one of the persons proposing the unification model, the same assumptions of measurement rules were taken into consideration. It is planned to replicate the case study for evaluating the model and to improve it.

1.5   ISO Transposition and Clarifications of the COSMIC FFP Method of Functional Sizing

Alain Abran, Peter Fagg, Roberto Meli, and Charles R. Symons

1.5.1   Introduction

The COSMIC FFP method was designed to measure a functional size of software based on its functional user requirements (FURs) for:

- Software from the business (MIS or data rich), real-time and infrastructure domains, and hybrids of these
- Software in any layer of a multilayer architecture, or any peer item within a layer

From the outset, the COSMIC FFP method was designed to conform to the existing ISO/IEC standard 14143-1:1997 (ISO 1997), which sets out the international agreement on the principles of functional size measurement.

The full public definition of the principles and rules and a comprehensive description of the method to help understand and explain the background were first published in a form intended for practical field trials in the measurement manual, version 2.0, in October 1999 (Abran 1999). The experience of the field trials resulted in an improved version (version 2.1) of the measurement manual, published in May 2001 (Abran and Sellami 2002). It is assumed that the reader is familiar with the latter publication.

Over the last year there have been two motivations to further improve the definitions of the method. First, feedback from practical use indicated the need to refine or clarify certain method definitions. Second, the ISO/IEC Joint Technical Committee 1 accepted a new work item to transpose the method definition into an ISO/IEC standard. The process involves a rigorous checking of terminology for consistency with preexisting ISO/IEC terminology on measurement, and several rounds of commenting from the ISO/IEC national bodies. It is an excellent process for testing understanding on a wide scale, and to ensure full coherency over the set of measurement concepts, while using a minimal set of definitions and rules. As an example of the work that had to be done in producing an ISO standard, the rules must be clearly identified within normative clauses, and must be written in a style that specifies compliance criteria using the expression "shall." This standardization in normative clauses then requires that all further informative text be clearly distinguished from compliance text, through notes to the text, or through clearly segregated examples. Hence, these ISO editing standards also led to the elimination of text that had been included in the MM 2.1 for informative purposes and further guidance.

Hence, the resulting ISO/IEC 19761 standard (ISO 2002) will take over as the ultimate authority on the essential principles of the method. The COSMIC measurement manual will continue to give a fuller account with background explanations and examples to facilitate training, but henceforth the aim will be to keep it in step with the international standard. It is constructed to be a guide to the application of the international standard. The ISO/IEC process is now reaching its final stage, so consequently the changes made for the most recent draft of the international standard version (ISO 2003a) have had to be fed back into an updated version (version 2.2) of the COSMIC FFP measurement manual (MM).

The purpose of this paper is to discuss the main areas of debate and consequent changes that have been made in producing the international standard version and in evolving from version 2.1 to 2.2 of the MM. We do not deal with:

■ Minor editorial changes made in producing the international standard
■ Other changes to the MM that are not directly connected to the international standard, or general improvements to the MM that could not be described as corrections

Throughout this process of refinement, it must be emphasized that none of the changes that have been made have altered the principles of the method that the authors defined, or intended to define, since the method was first published.

1.5.2   *The COSMIC FFP Model*

Measurement of the functional size of a piece of software can be carried out whether the software exists only as a statement of FURs, or by inferring its FURs from a piece of software that has already been implemented, or at any stage in between. Regardless, before the measurement can be made, the FURs must be mapped into the COSMIC FFP conceptual model (Abran et al. 2000, 2002, 2003b).

In brief outline, the key concepts proposed in the COSMIC FFP model and in the process of applying it are as follows:

■ It is first necessary to define the *purpose* and *scope* of a measurement, together referred to as the *viewpoint*.
■ The software within the scope may need, depending on the viewpoint, to be broken down into one or more *pieces of software*, in separate *layers*, or *peer items*, within a layer.
■ Each set of FURs for a piece of software whose size has to be measured has one or more *users* that interact with the software across a *boundary*.
■ Any set of FURs can be decomposed into one or more *functional processes*.
■ Any functional process can be decomposed into two or more *data movements*.
■ A data movement is a functional subprocess that moves a *data group* (one or more *data attributes*) about a single *object of interest*, and which may have some associated data manipulation.
■ A data movement can be one of four types:

   – An *entry* moves a data group from a user across the boundary into the software.
   – An *exit* moves a data group from the software across the boundary to a user.
   – A *write* sends a data group from the software to persistent storage.
   – A *read* retrieves a data group from persistent storage for the software.

■ Each data movement is allocated one COSMIC FFP functional size unit (or 1 *Cfsu*).

■ The size of a piece of software is the sum of the sizes of its constituent functional processes; the size of a functional process is the sum of the sizes of its constituent data movements. (A rule is also given for measuring the size of a required change to a set of FURs.)

1.5.3 Clarifications and Refinements of the Model

The definitions of the concepts of any functional size measurement method, and similarly the definitions of concepts of the metastandard of ISO/IEC 14143-1, are inevitably interdependent. It is difficult to discuss any one definition in isolation from related definitions. The same is true for the content of this paper, so the following is an iterative explanation of a series of related clarifications or refinements.

1.5.3.1 The User

In the MM V2.1, *users* are defined as "human beings, software or engineered devices which interact with the measured software" (Abran et al. 1999, p. 26). However, ISO/IEC 14143-1 defines a *user* as "any person that specifies Functional User Requirements and/or any person or thing that communicates with or interacts with the software at any time" ISO. 1998, p. 32. The definition also has a note: "Examples of 'thing' include, but are not limited to software applications, animals, sensors, or other hardware" (ISO. 1998, p. 32).

With hindsight (since the current authors participated in the development of ISO/IEC 14143-1), this ISO/IEC definition clearly embraces two separate concepts in the one term. First, there is what we might call the specifying user (who specifies functional user requirements). This use of *user* is consistent with its use in the expression "functional user requirements." But the second usage, what we might call the physical user (any thing that actually communicates with or interacts with the software), is a different concept. The specifying user need not actually ever use the software in practice. On the other hand, the physical user might be an engineered device that only sends signals to the software, but has nothing to do with its specifications. Unfortunately, the ISO/IEC 14143-1 terms and definitions cannot be changed until a formal revision process is started. In the meantime, the ISO/IEC standard version of the COSMIC FFP method must adopt the term already defined in ISO/IEC 14143-1, and since our goal is to remain compatible and in sync with the international standard, the MM V2.2 must adopt this definition. However, in the latter the COSMIC team is free to add clarifications.

Hence in the MM V2.2, we clarify that when we use the term *user* in the MM, we restrict it to the meaning of "any person or thing that communicates with or interacts with the software at any time." When we mean *specifying user*, we will say so explicitly. This distinction also has implications for the definitions and use of the terms *boundary* and *viewpoint*.

1.5.3.2 The Boundary and (Persistent) Storage

In ISO/IEC 14143-1, *boundary* is defined as "a conceptual interface between the software under study and its users" (ISO. 1998, p. 33). (Note that this definition can only be interpreted correctly if *users* means *physical users*, as we explained above.) The MM V2.1 definition of *boundary* is much longer, but essentially says the same thing. There is no difficulty in the MM V2.2 in adopting the ISO/IEC definition, subject to the correct understanding of *user*. However, again with hindsight, there is considerable potential for confusion, this time in the MM V2.1. This document uses *boundary*, but also uses the terms *I/O boundary*, *storage boundary*, *layer boundary*, and *software boundary* in the text and in various diagrams, without defining them. As an example of the possible confusion, it turns out to be a reasonable inference (but never the intention) from the definition of *user* and the use of the expression "storage boundary" that users could also include storage, and that storage would lie *outside* the boundary. An inconsistency then arises because only entries and exits were defined as moving data across the boundary, whereas writes and reads were not defined as moving data across a boundary.

To rationalize this, the following changes have been made to the ISO/IEC definitions of the COSMIC FFP method and to the MM V2.2. Only the term *boundary* is used, unqualified by any adjective, with the definition of ISO/IEC 14143-1. It is a conceptual boundary, and should not be confused with any other type of boundary that could be envisaged, e.g., the physical boundaries between one layer of software and its adjacent layers.

The term *persistent storage* is introduced, to replace *storage* everywhere it occurs. *Persistent storage* is defined as "storage that is on the software side of the boundary of the software being measured and that is continuously accessible to the software during its execution" (Abran et al. 2003a, p. 23). Furthermore, two notes have been added to this definition, as follows:

> NOTE 1 In the COSMIC FFP model, because Persistent Storage is on the software side of the boundary, it is not considered to be a User of the software being measured.
>
> NOTE 2 Persistent storage enables a functional process to store data beyond the life of the functional process and/or enables a functional process to retrieve data which was
>
> – stored by another functional process
> – or stored by an earlier occurrence of the same functional process
> – or stored by some other process, e.g., in the manufacture of a read-only memory.

The reason for adding the phrase "that is continuously accessible during its execution" (Abran et al. 2003a, p. 28) is to help distinguish persistent storage from storage that is accessed instantaneously, for example, the swiping of a credit card as a means of entering data. The addition of the phrase "storage that is on the software side of the boundary" and of note 1 is needed because this aspect of the definition has always been understood but has not previously been made explicit.

1.5.3.3   Viewpoint (Purpose and Scope)

We have already pointed out that the ISO/IEC 14143-1 standard fails to distinguish *physical user* and *specifying user*. Similarly, in the MM V2.1 the same word *user* is employed, on occasion, for *physical user* and *end user* (e.g., see Section 2.3.1, Case 2).

We will define an *end-user* as a person who uses a business application and sees only the application functionality, being unaware of the functionality provided by the infrastructure software (operating systems, device drivers, utilities, etc.) on which the business application depends. Contrast this with a physical user who only sees the functional processes of the particular piece of software with which he, she, or it interacts.

It has become much clearer, as a result of analyzing the difficulties with the term *user*, that the concept of the "viewpoint" of a measurement is of vital importance. In the new ISO/IEC standard for the COSMIC FFP method and in the MM V2.2, the viewpoint is given much more prominence, and must be reported with any measurement result. *Viewpoint* is at the moment defined as an umbrella term for the purpose and scope of the measurement.

Some other function point methods, such as the IFPUG (IFPUG, 2004) and the Mk II (Mark II Manual, 2002) methods, were designed to measure a functional size from the viewpoint of the end user, as we have defined above. The COSMIC FFP method can be used to measure this size, but can also be used to measure the size from the viewpoint of the specifying user (hopefully the same viewpoint as that of the developer, if they are communicating properly) and from any other viewpoint as long as it is defined. The sizes seen from the end user and from the developer's viewpoints could, of course, be very different. Hence, the emphasis now in both the new ISO/IEC standard for COSMIC FFP and the MM V2.2 is first agreeing on the viewpoint for a measurement and the need to specify the viewpoint whenever a measurement result is reported. The viewpoint has also recently been added as a mandatory parameter for the reporting of COSMIC FFP measurement-based results to the ISBSG database (ISBSG 2005).

Ideally, at some time in the future certain viewpoints should be standardized, so that measurement results from different sources can be safely compared. The end user (for business applications, where the end user is restricted to a human) and developer viewpoints would be the first major candidates to be defined and standardized. Until this stage is reached, one must be very careful in using data from sources where no viewpoint has been defined, and before comparing data to measure convertibility between measurements based on the

COSMIC FFP method and those based on traditional function point methods. It is to be noted that COSMIC FFP can take into account all the viewpoints allowable by the ISO metamodel 14143-1, its user definition including humans, engineering devices, and other software as users of the piece of software being measured. But the viewpoint must always be stated if the measurement is to be understood properly.

1.5.3.4 Definitions of Read and Entry

Certain additions to the rules for these concepts have been made to reduce the possibility of misinterpretation.

First, it had not previously been made explicit that in physical reality, entry and read data movements may involve bidirectional exchanges. Thus, a nontriggering entry may be preceded by a request to receive the entry, and a read must be preceded by a request to read. Nevertheless, in both cases a logical view is taken and only a single data movement is assigned, that is, 1 Cfsu, to any entry or read in the functional process where it is identified.

It is now stated explicitly that any request to receive an entry functionality and any request for a read functionality is not measured separately from the entry and from the read, respectively.

Second, there is a need to eliminate any measurer concluding that it is within the rules to include in the measurement the use of intermediate variables, etc., as reads (or writes). This is addressed now by adding the following to the rules for a read.

> During a functional process, the Read or Write of a data group can only be performed on the data describing an Object of Interest to the user. Constants or variables which are internal to the functional process or intermediate results in a calculation, or data stored by a functional process resulting only from the implementation rather than the FUR, are not data groups, and are not measured.

1.5.3.5 Minor Clarifications

Use of the terms *client* and *server* has been eliminated from the ISO/IEC standard for COSMIC FFP and from the MM V2.2. These terms were used in the description of the relationships between layers and between peer pieces of software within the same layer. But the terms *client* and *server* have connotations beyond those intended in the COSMIC FFP method, and represent a potential source of confusion.

In the rules for identifying functional processes for real-time software, there has always been the statement that a functional process "terminates when a point of asynchronous timing is reached" (Abran et al. 2003a, p. 28). This has not been clear and could have been interpreted as a technical, not a functional, characteristic. Furthermore, if the end user of a business application chooses to take a break partway through entering data for a given functional process, a point of asynchronous timing may be reached, but this was never intended to indicate that the functional process could be complete.

The rule has been clarified by amending it to state that a functional process "terminates when a point of asynchronous timing is reached *according to its FUR*" (ISO. 2003a, p. 30).

1.5.4   Conclusion

Feedback from field experience of using the COSMIC FFP method and the discipline of producing an ISO/IEC standard version of the method has been extremely helpful in discovering areas of weakness in the method's concept definitions.

We believe that the new ISO/IEC 19761 standard for the COSMIC FFP method and the new MM V2.2 will significantly improve the probability of consistent interpretation of the method, and hence of obtaining repeatable functional size measurements.

Acknowledgments

The authors thank the following for their important contributions to the discussions that have led to the clarifications and refinements described in this paper (Moritsugu Araki, Jean-Marc Desharnais, Vihn Ho, Pam Morris, Marie O'Neill, Tony Rollo, Grant Rule, and Denis St.-Pierre). The authors also acknowledge with gratitude the feedback received from users of the COSMIC FFP method in the field, and from the many experts who studied the drafts of the ISO/IEC standard for COSMIC FFP and submitted comments via their national bodies.

References

Abran, A. 1999. An implementation of COSMIC functional size measurement concepts. In *The 2nd European Software Measurement Conferences FESMA 99*, ed. M. Hooft van Huyduynen et al., 29–38. Amsterdam, Netherlands: TVI Publ.

Abran, A., and J.-M. Desharnais. 1999. *Literature review on object points and engineering function points*. Internal report, ETS. Montreal: University Press.

Abran, A., J.-M. Desharnais, and F. Aziz. 2005. Measurement convertibility—From FP to COSMIC-FFP. In *Innovations in software measurement*, ed. A. Abran and R. R. Dumke, 227–40. Aachen, Germany: Shaker Publ.

Abran, A., J.-M. Desharnais, and S. Oligny. 1999. Measuring with full function points. In *Maximising quality and managing risk—Optimising software development and maintenance (ESCOM SCOPE 99)*, ed. R. J. Kusters, 104. Herstmonceux Castle, England: Shaker Publ.

Abran, A., J.-M. Desharnais, S. Oligny, D. St.-Pierre, and C. Symons. 2003a. *Measurement manual COSMIC full function points 2.2, the COSMIC implementation guide for ISO/IEC 19761*. Montréal: École de technologie supérieure, Université du Québec, University Press.

Abran, A., J.-M. Desharnais, S. Oligny, D. St.-Pierre, and C. Symons. 2003b. *COSMIC-FFP measurement manual (COSMIC implementation guide for ISO/IEC 19761: 2003) version 2.2*. Common Software Measurement International Consortium. http://www.lrgl.uqam.ca/cosmic-ffp (accessed January 31, 2010).

Abran, A., and A. Sellami. 2002. Initial modeling of the measurement concepts in the ISO vocabulary of terms in metrology. In *Software measurement and estimation*, ed. R. R. Dumke et al., 9–20. Aachen, Germany: Shaker Publ.

Abran, A., C. Symons, J.-M. Desharnais, P. Fagg, P. Morris, S. Oligny, J. Onvlee, R. Meli, R. Nevalainen, G. Rule, and D. St.-Pierre. 2000. COSMIC FFP field trials aims, progress and interim findings. In *11th European Software Control and Metric Conference (ESCOM SCOPE 2000)*, ed. R. J. Kusters, 31. Herstmonceux Castle, England: Shaker Publ.

Albrecht, A. J. 1979. Measuring application development productivity. In *Proceedings of the IBM Applications Development Symposium*, ed. K. Gibson et al., 34–43. Monterey, CA: IBM Corp. Publ.

Boehm, B. W. 1984. Software engineering economics. *IEEE Transaction on Software Engineering* 10(1):4–21.

Boehm, B. W., et al. 2000. *Software cost estimation with COCOMO II*. Englewood Cliffs, NJ: Prentice-Hall.

Boehm, R. 1997. Function point FAQ. Software Composition Technologies, Inc. www.ourworld.com/homepages/softcomp, (accessed January 31, 2010).

Bosch. 2003. Internet presentation. http://www.bosch.de (accessed January 31, 2010).

Bundschuh, M., and C. Dekkers. 2008. *The IT measurement compendium*. Berlin, NY: Springer Publ.

Bundschuh, M., and A. Fabry. 2000. *Aufwandschätzung von IT-Projekten*. Bonn, Germany: MITP Publ.

Büren, G., and I. Kroll. 1999a. Process improvement by introduction of an effort estimation process. In *Proceedings of the 12th International Conference on Software and System Engineering and Their Applications (ICSSEA)*, ed. J. Printz, 483–95. Paris: CMSL Press.

Caldiera, G., G. Antoniol, R. Fiutem, and C. Lokan. 1998. Definition and experimental evaluation for object oriented systems. In *Proceedings of the 5th International Symposium on Software Metrics*, ed. C. Agresti and M. Zelkowitz, 108–20. Los Alamitos, CA: IEEE Computer Society Press.

Chemuturi, M. 2009. *Software estimation best practices, tools and techniques*. Fort Lauderdale, FL: J. Ross Publ.

Conte, M., T. Iorio, R. Meli, and L. Santillo. 2004. E&Q: An early and quick approach to functional size measurement methods. In *Proceedings of Software Measurement European Forum 2004 (SMEF2004)*, ed. R. Meli et al., 35–43. Rome, Italy: DPO Publ.

DeMarco, T. 1982. *Controlling Software Projects*. New York: Yourdon Press.

DeMarco, T. 1989. *Software Projektmanagement.* Attenkirchen, Germany: Wolfram's Publ.

Diab, H., M. Frappier, and R. St.-Denis. 2001. A formal definition of COSMIC FFP for automated measurement of ROOM specifications. In *Proceedings of FESMA-DASMA,* ed. M. Bundschuh et al., 185–96. Heidelberg, Germany: FESMA Publ.

Diab, H., M. Frappier, R. St.-Denis, and D. Dery. 1999. Counting function points from B specifications. Université du Québec à Montréal, Canada. http://www.lrgl.uqam.ca/ffp.html (accessed January 31, 2010).

Dumke, R. R., R. Braungarten, G. Büren, A. Abran, and J. J. Cuadrado-Gallego. 2008. *Software process and product measurement.* Berlin, NY: Springer Publ.

Dumke, R., E. Foltin, E. Dimitrov, E., M. Wipprecht, and A. Schmietendorf. 1999. *Projekt Softwarewiederverwendung.* Research report. Magdeburg, Germany: University Press.

Dumke, R., E. Foltin, R. Koeppe, and A. Winkler. 1996. *Softwarequalität durch Meßtools— Assessment, Messung und instrumentierte ISO 9000.* Braunschweig, Germany: Vieweg Publ.

Ebert, C., and R. Dumke. 2007. *Software measurement—Establish, extract, evaluate, execute.* Berlin, NY: Springer Publ.

Efe, P. 2006. A unification model and tool support for software functional size measurement methods. Master's thesis, Department of Information Systems, Middle East Technical University, Ankara, Turkey.

Fetcke, T. 1999. *A generalized structure for function point analysis.* Université du Québec à Montréal, Canada. http://www.lrgl.uqam.ca/ffp.html (accessed January 31, 2010).

Fetcke, T. 2000. Two properties of function points analysis. In *Software Metriken-Entwicklungen, Werkzeuge und Anwendungsverfahren,* ed. R. Dumke and F. Lehner, 17–34. Wiesbaden, Germany: DUV Publ.

FFP97. 1997. *Full function points: Counting practices manual.* Technical Report 1997-04. Montréal: Université du Québec à Montréal, University Press.

Forselius, P. 2004. FiSMA functional size measurement method. Version 1.1. FSM Working Group Report. Tampere, Finland: Finnish Software Measurement Association (FiSMA), University Press.

Garmus, D., and D. Herron. 1996. *Measuring the software process—A practical guide to functional measurement.* Englewood Cliffs, NJ: Prentice Hall Publ.

Garmus, D., and D. Herron. 2002. Estimating software earlier and more accurately. *Journal of Defense Software Engineering.* http://www.stsc.hill.af.mil/crosstlk/2002/06/garmush-erron.html (accessed January 31, 2010).

Gencel, C. 2005. An architectural dimension based software functional size measurement method. PhD thesis, Department of Information Systems, Middle East Technical University, Ankara, Turkey.

Gencel, C., and O. Demirors. 2004. Software size estimation: Difficulties and suggestions. In *Proceedings of the First Conference on the Principles of Software Engineering (PriSe 2004),* ed. G. Baum, 22–27. Buenos Aires, Argentina: University Press.

Ho, V. T., and A. Abran. 1999. A framework for automatic function point counting from source code. Université du Québec à Montréal, Canada. http://www.lrgl.uqam.ca/ffp.html (accessed January 31, 2010).

Ho, V. T., A. Abran, and T. Fetcke. 1999. A comparative study case of COSMIC-FFP, full function point and IFPUG methods. Université du Québec à Montréal, Canada. http://www.lrgl.uqam.ca/ffp.html (accessed January 31, 2010).

Honkonen, M., and K. Lyytinen. 1999. *An overview of the use of risk management methods in software projects.* Jyväskylä, Finland: Department of Computer Science and Information Systems, University of Jyväskylä.

IFPUG. 1994. *Function point counting practices manual.* Release 4.0. Westerville, OH: International Function Point User Group (IFPUG) Publ.

IFPUG. 1999. *Function points counting practices manual.* Release 4.1. Westerville, OH: International Function Point User Group (IFPUG) Publ.

IFPUG. 2000. *Function point counting practices manual.* Release 4.1.1. Westerville, OH: International Function Point User Group (IFPUG) Publ.

IFPUG. 2004. *Function point counting practices manual.* Version 4.2. International Function Point Users Group. http://www.ifpug.org (accessed January 31, 2010).

ISBSG. 2001. *Practical project estimation.* International Software Benchmarking Standards Group. www.isbsg.org (accessed January 31, 2010).

ISBSG. 2002. *The software metrics compendium.* International Software Benchmarking Standards Group. www.isbsg.org (accessed January 31, 2010).

ISBSG. 2003a. *Software development projects sector report—Government sector.* International Software Benchmarking Standards Group. www.isbsg.org (accessed January 31, 2010).

ISBSG. 2003b. *ISBSG estimating, benchmarking and research suite.* Release 8. International Software Benchmarking Standards Group. www.isbsg.org (accessed January 31, 2010).

ISBSG. 2004. *ISBSG estimating, benchmarking and research.* Suite R9. Hawthorn, Victoria, Australia: ISBSG Press.

ISBSG. 2005. *Functional sizing methods.* International Software Benchmarking Standards Group. http://www.isbsg.org/isbsg.nsf/weben/Functional%20Sizing %20Methods (accessed January 31, 2010).

ISO. 1993. *International vocabulary of basic and general terms in metrology (VIM).* Geneva, Switzerland: International Organization for Standardization (ISO) Publ.

ISO. 1997. *Software engineering—Software measurement—Functional size measurement—Definition of concepts.* ISO/IEC 14143-1997. Geneva, Switzerland: ISO Publ.

ISO. 1998. *ISO/IEC 14143-1:1998(e)—Information technology—Software measurement—Functional size measurement—Definition of concepts.* Geneva, Switzerland: International Organization for Standardization (ISO) Publ.

ISO. 2000. *Information technology. Software measurement—Functional size measurement: Reference model.* ISO/IEC 14143-4. Geneva, Switzerland: International Organization for Standardization (ISO) Publ.

ISO. 2002a. *Software engineering—Software measurement process.* ISO/IEC IS 15939:2002. Geneva, Switzerland: International Organization for Standardization (ISO) Publ.

ISO. 2002b. *Information technology. Software engineering. Software measurement—Functional size measurement: Verification of functional size measurement.* ISO/IEC 14143-3. Geneva, Switzerland: International Organization for Standardization (ISO) Publ.

ISO. 2002. *Software engineering. COSMIC-FFP. A functional size measurement method.* ISO/IEC 19761. Geneva, Switzerland: ISO Publ.

ISO. 2003a. *Software engineering—COSMIC-FFP—A functional size measurement method.* ISO/IEC 19761:2003. Geneva, Switzerland: International Organization for Standardization (ISO) Publ.

ISO. 2003b. *Software engineering—IFPUG 4.1 Unadjusted functional size measurement method—Counting practices manual.* ISO/IEC 20926:2003. International Organization for Standardization. http://www.iso.org (accessed January 31, 2010).

ISO. 2004. *Information technology. Software measurement—Functional size measurement: Determination of functional domains for use with functional size measurement.* ISO/ IEC 14143-5. Geneva, Switzerland: International Organization for Standardization (ISO) Publ.

Jones, C. 1987. *A short history of FP and feature points.* Internal report. Software Productivity Research, Inc., Burlington, MA: SPR Publ.

Jones, C. 1991. *Applied software measurement—Assuring productivity and quality.* New York: McGraw-Hill.

Jones, C. 1997. *What are function points?* Software Productivity Research, Inc., SPR Publ.

Jones, C. 2007. *Estimating software costs—Bringing realism to estimating.* New York: McGraw-Hill.

Kececi, N., M. Li, and C. Smidts. 1999. Function point analysis: An application to a nuclear reactor protection system. In *Proceedings of the Probabilistic Safety Assessment—PSA '99*, ed. M. Modarres, 963–75. Washington, DC: University Press.

Kemerer, C. F. 1997. Software project management: Readings and cases. Software Engineering@Carnegie Mellon, www.distance.cmu.edu (accessed January 31, 2010).

Kitchenham, B., and N. Fenton. 1995. Towards a framework for software measurement validation. *IEEE Transactions on Software Engineering* 21(12):929–43.

Kuan Wu, S. I. 2000. Using function point analysis method or line of code for software size estimation, project control: The human factor. In *Proceedings of the ESCOM-SCOPE 2000*, ed. K. D. Maxwell et al., 221–28. Munich, Germany: Shaker Publ.

Lokan, C., and A. Abran. 1999. Multiple viewpoints in functional size measurement. In Proceedings of the International Workshop on Software Measurement (IWSM99). http://www.lrgl.uqam.ca/iwsm99/index2.html (accessed January 31, 2010).

Longstreet, D. 2001a. *Use cases and function points.* Longstreet Consulting, Inc. www.softwaremetrics.com (accessed January 31, 2010).

Longstreet, D. 2001b. *OO and function points.* Longstreet Consulting, Inc. www.softwaremetrics.com (accessed January 31, 2010).

MacDonnell, S. G. 1994. Comparative review of functional complexity assessment methods for effort estimation. *Software Engineering Journal* 9(5):107–16.

Männistö, P. 2004. FiSMA ry, prosessien ja projektien johtamisen standardointi- ja kehittämisverkosto. *Sytykery-Systeemityö* 3:23–25. http://www.pcuf.fi/sytyke/lehti/kirj/st20043/st043pdf (accessed January 31, 2010).

Mark II Manual. 2002. *Mark II function point analysis counting practices manual.* Version 1.3.1. London: United Kingdom Software Metrics Association (UKSMA) Publ.

Maxwell, K. D., and P. Forselius. 2000. Benchmarking software development productivity. *IEEE Software* 17(1):80–88.

McConnell, S. 1996. *Rapid development—Taming wild software schedules.* Redmond, WA: Microsoft Press.

McConnell, S. 2006. *Software estimation.* Redmont, WA: Microsoft Press.

Meli, R. 1997a. Early and extended function point: A new method for function points estimation. Paper presented at IFPUG—Fall Conference, Scottsdale, AZ, September 15–19.

Meli, R. 1997b. Early function points: A new estimation method for software projects. In *Proceedings of the ESCOM 97*, ed. A. Gabrielsson, 184–96. Uppsala, Finland: University Press.

Meli, R. 1998. Functional metrics: Problems and possible solutions. In *Proceedings of the FESMA 1998*, ed. H. Coombes et al., 503–14. Antwerpen, Netherlands: TIV Publ.

Meli, R. 2002. Early and quick function point analysis—From summary user requirements to project management. In *IT measurement: Practical advice from the experts*, ed. C. Jones and D. S. Linthinicum, 417–41. Boston: Addison-Wesley.

Meli, R., A. Abran, V. T. Ho, and S. Oligny. 2000. On the applicability of COSMIC FFP for measuring software throughout its life cycle. In *Proceedings of the ESCOM-SCOPE 2000*, ed. K. D. Maxwell et al., 289–97. Munich, Germany: Shaker Publ.

Meli, R., and L. Santillo. 1999. Function point estimation methods—A comparative overview. In *Proceedings of the FESMA 99*, ed. M. Hooft van Huyduynen et al., 271–86. Amsterdam, Netherlands: TIV Publ.

Minkiewicz, A. F. 2000. Measuring object-oriented software with predictive object points. www.pricesystems.com (accessed January 31, 2010).

Mk II Manual. 1998. *Mk II function point analysis counting practices manual*. Version 1.3.1. London: United Kingdom Software Metrics Association (UKSMA) Publ.

Morris, P. 2000. *Total metrics resource—Evaluation of functional size measurements for real-time embedded and control systems*. Working Paper. Total Metrics, Inc. www.totalmetrics.com (accessed January 31, 2010).

Morris, P., and J.-M. Desharnais. 1998. Measuring ALL the software not just what the business uses. In *Proceedings of the IFPUG Fall Conference*, ed. M. Zelkovitz, 1–17. Orlando, FL: IFPUG Publ.

NESMA Manual. 2005. *NESMA functional size measurement method v.2.1—Definitions and counting guidelines for the application of function point analysis*. www.nesma.org (accessed January 31, 2010).

Netherlands Software Metrics Users Association (NESMA). 1997. *Definitions and counting guidelines for the application of function point analysis*. Version 2.0. Amsterdam, Netherlands: NESMA Publ.

Oligny, S., A. Abran, A. J.-M. Desharnais, and P. Morris. 1998. Functional size of real-time software: Overview of field tests. In *Proceedings of the 13th International Forum on COCOMO and Software Cost Modeling*, Los Angeles. http://www.lrgl.uqam.ca (accessed January 31, 2010).

Oligny, S., A. Abran, and D. St.-Pierre. 1999. Improving software functional size measurement. In *Proceedings of the 14th International Forum on COCOMO and Software Cost Modeling*, Los Angeles. http://www.lrgl.uqam.ca (accessed January 31, 2010).

Oppermann, M. 2001. Anwendung und prototypische Implementierung der Full Function Point Methode. Diploma thesis, University of Magdeburg, Magdeburg, Germany.

Paton, K. 1999. Automatic function point counting using static and dynamic code analysis. In *Proceedings of the International Workshop on Software Measurement (IWSM99)*. http://www.lrgl.uqam.ca/iwsm99/index2.html (accessed January 31, 2010).

PMBOK. 2000. *A guide to the Project Management Body of Knowledge*. Newton Square, Pennsylvania: Project Management Institute, PMBOK Publ.

Reitz, D. 2001. Konzeption und Implementation von palmbasierten Werkzeugen zur Unterstützung des Softwareentwicklungsprozesses. Diploma thesis, University of Magdeburg, Magdeburg, Germany.

Schmietendorf, A., R. Dumke, and E. Foltin. 1999. Applicability of full function points for Siemens AT. In *Proceedings of IWSM '99*. http://www.lrgl.uqam.ca/iwsm99/index2.html (accessed January 31, 2010).

Schweikl, U., S. Weber, E. Foltin, and R. Dumke. 2000. Applicability of full function points at Siemens AT. In *Software-Metriken*, ed. F. Lehner and R. Dumke, 171–82. Wiesbaden, Germany: DUV Publ.

Shepperd, M., and C. Schofield. 1997. Estimating software project effort using analogies. *IEEE Transactions on Software Engineering* 23(12):736–43.

Sneed, H. 1995. *SoftCalc 4.1—User manual.* Munich, Germany: SES Press.

Standish Group. 1999. *CHAOS: A recipe for success.* Boston: Standish Group Publ. http://www. standishgroup.com/newsroom/chaos_manifesto.php (accessed January 31, 2010).

St.-Pierre, D., M. Maya, A. Abran, J.-M. Desharnais, and P. Bourque. 1997a. *Full function points: Counting practices manual.* Montreal: University Press.

St.-Pierre, D., M. Maya, A. Abran, A., J.-M. Desharnais, and P. Bourque. 1997b. *Full function points: Function points extension for real-time software—Counting practices manual.* Technical report 1997-04. Software Engineering Management Research Laboratory, Université du Québec à Montréal, Montreal, Canada. http://www.lrgl.uqam.ca/ffp. html (accessed January 31, 2010).

Stutzke, R. D. 1999. Using UML elements to estimate feature points. In *Proceedings of the International Workshop on Software Measurement (IWSM99).* http://www.lrgl.uqam.ca/ iwsm99/index2.html (accessed January 31, 2010).

Symons, C. 1988. Function point analysis: Difficulties and improvements. *IEEE Transactions on Software Engineering* 14(1):2–11.

Symons, C. 1991. *Software sizing and estimation—Mk II FPA (function point analysis).* West Sussex, UK: John Wiley & Sons.

Symons, C. R. 1999. COSMIC aims, design principles and progress. In *Proceedings of the IWSM'99.* http://www.lrgl.uqam.ca/iwsm99/index2.html (accessed January 31, 2010).

Symons, C. 2001. Come back function point analysis (modernized)—All is forgiven! In *Proceedings of the 4th European Conference on Software Measurement and ICT Control, FESMA-DASMA 2001,* ed. M. Bundschuh et al., 413–26. Heidelberg, Germany: TIV Press.

Symons, C. 2004. COSMIC: The Common Software Measurement International Consortium, http://www.cosmicon.com (accessed on January 31, 2010).

Symons, C. R., and P. G. Rule. 1999. One size fits all—COSMIC aims, design principles and progress. In *Maximising quality and managing risk—Optimising software development and maintenance (ESCOM SCOPE 99),* ed. R. J. Kusters, 197–207. Herstmonceux Castle, England: Shaker Publ.

Teologolu, G. 1999. Measuring object-oriented software with predictive object points, project control for software quality. In *Maximising quality and managing risk—Optimising software development and maintenance (ESCOM SCOPE 99),* ed. R. J. Kusters, 136–44. Herstmonceux Castle, England: Shaker Publ.

Victor, D., and K. Daily. 2001. Software estimating at the task level—The Spectre approach. In *Proceedings of the ESCOM-SCOPE 2001,* ed. K. D. Maxwell et al., 215–24. Maastricht, Netherlands: Shaker Publ.

Victorian Government. 2002. southernSCOPE. http://www.mmv.vic.gov.au (accessed January 31, 2010).

Virtanen, P. 2000. Component reuse metrics—Assessing human effects, project control: The human factor. In *Proceedings of the ESCOM-SCOPE 2000,* ed. K. D. Maxwell et al., 171–80. Munich, Germany: Shaker Publ.

Virtanen, P. 2001. Empirical study evaluating component reuse metrics. In *Proceedings of the ESCOM-SCOPE 2001,* ed. K. D. Maxwell et al., 125–36. Maastricht, Netherlands: Shaker Publ.

Vogelezang, F., and A. Lesterhuis. 2003. *Applicability of COSMIC full function points in an administrative environment, experiences of an early adopter.* PW de Meern, Netherlands: Sogeti Netherlands B.V., Sogeti Publ.

Whitmire, S. A. 1992. 3-D function points: Scientific and real-time extensions of function points. In *Proceedings of the 1992 Pacific Northwest Software Quality Conference.* Portland, OR: PNSQC Press.

Whitmire, S. A. 1995. An introduction to 3D function points. *Software Development* 3(4):43–53.

Wieczorek, I. 2001. *Improved software cost estimation - A robust and interpretable modeling method and a comprehensive empirical investigation.* Kaiserslautern, Germany: Fraunhofer Institut IESE, IESE Publ.

Winant, R. 2000. *Management, methods and teamwork.* Esprit Systems Consulting, Inc. http://www.espritinc.com (accessed January 31, 2010).

Wright, T. 2000. Controlling software development, a breakthrough for business. *Software Engineering Australia* 11(1):104–17.

Chapter 2

Measurement, Theoretical Basics, and Aspects of the COSMIC-ISO 19761

Using functional size measurement in project management requires thorough knowledge of the scale characteristics. This means that the counted value would be mapped with the empirical background (such as cost drivers, project characteristics, etc.) in a well-defined statistical manner. The scale type, in particular, decides the application of the measured results.

Figure 2.1 shows the different (function) point approaches and their empirical involvements during the measurement of the functional size.

> One of the other main characteristics of software sizing leads to the *correct identification of the scale type of the measured functionality.*

In the first part of this chapter, Thomas Fetcke, Alain Abran, and Reiner Dumke describe an axiomatic approach based on measurement theory to develop a model for existing FSM methods. This view can be used as a basis for the analysis of FSM methods and for a discussion of their differences.

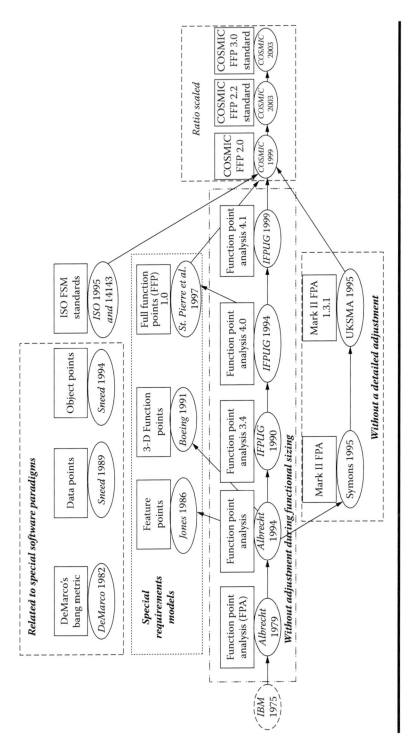

Figure 2.1   Function points method history and their empirical background.

In the next section Luca Santillo presents a method of visualization that can provide significant advantages and make it possible to discover new interpretation and exploitation possibilities over measurement results considering the COSMIC framework.

The third part, by Jean-Marc Desharnais and Alain Abran, proposes an expert-system approach to tackle cognitive issues in order to achieve consistency in the measurement results. The functional size measurement method selected to investigate the feasibility of the approach is COSMIC FFP, and the knowledge system to be used is Help CPR, applying the case-based reasoning methodology.

In software engineering, the functional size measurement (FSM) community was the first to recognize the importance of such quality criteria for measurement, as illustrated in the recently adopted ISO document 14143-3; however, these criteria represent only a subset of the metrology criteria that include, for instance, measurement units and internationally recognized measurement references (e.g., etalons). In the fourth part by Adel Khelfi, Alain Abran, and Luigi Buglione, a design for building a set of normalized baseline measurement references for COSMIC FFP (ISO 19761), the second generation of FSM methods, is proposed.

Finally in this chapter, Manar Abu Talib, Alain Abran, and Olga Ormandjieva present an overview of some measurement concepts across both COSMIC FFP, an ISO standard (ISO/IEC 19761) for functional size measurement, and functional complexity (FC), an entropy-based measure. It investigates in particular three metrological properties (scale, unit, and scale type) in both of these measurement methods.

2.1 A Generalized Representation for Selected Functional Size Measurement Methods

Thomas Fetcke, Alain Abran, and Reiner R.Dumke

2.1.1 Introduction

The management of software cost, development effort, and project planning is a key aspect of software development. Software size is a critical element in these measurement requirements. Various approaches for the measurement of software size have been formulated, among others the number of lines of source code. Functional size measurement (FSM) methods have been proposed to overcome some of the deficiencies of approaches based on source code. It is the goal of these methods to measure the functionality of the software, independent of its implementation. Function point analysis (FPA), published by Albrecht in 1979, can be considered the first FSM method. Based on FPA, several revisions and alternative FSM methods have been formulated (Figure 2.2). These methods differ in their views and definitions of functional size. FPA is an intuitive approach without theoretical foundation. With the lack of a measurement model for FPA, it remains unclear what the method

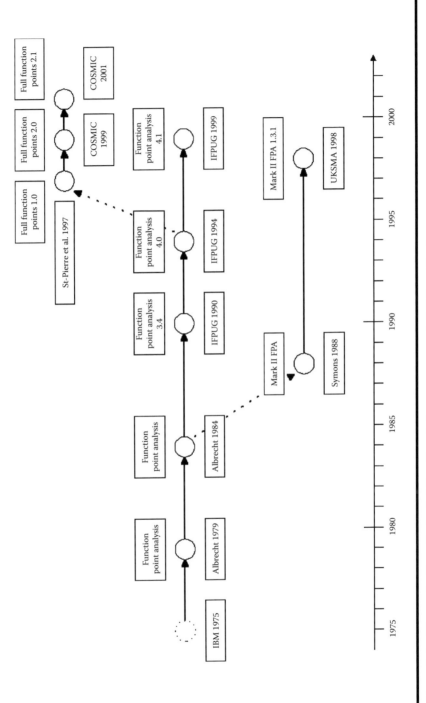

Figure 2.2   The evaluation of selected functional size measurement (FSM) methods.

actually measures. It is therefore difficult to analyze the differences between the different FSM methods.

We propose here a model for existing FSM methods that gives a new view on these methods and will help in understanding the methods. We use an axiomatic approach based on measurement theory to formulate our characterization. Based on the model, assumptions of reality can be formulated as axioms, and the FSM methods can be tested against the assumptions. While FSM methods differ in their views on functional size, a number of methods share a core view and certain core concepts. We propose here a representation for a set of FSM methods. The representation is generalized such that it applies to each of these methods. The representation thus allows a detailed analysis and discussion of differences and common concepts of different FSM methods. Given such a representation, the actual measurement step can be formalized, as we have demonstrated in (Fetcke et al. 2001). In this paper, we give a detailed description of the generalized representation, and we describe how it can be used for the discussion of FSM methods. The following paragraphs give a short overview of the evolution of the FSM methods studied and on related work. Section 2.1.4 describes the approach taken and our view on the measurement process of FSM. The generalized representation is presented and discussed in Section 2.1.7. Section 2.1.8 and following describe the application of the generalization, and Section 2.1.15 gives some conclusions.

2.1.2 Evolution of FSM Methods

Function point analysis (FPA) was developed by Albrecht in the 1970s, with its first presentation to the public in 1979 (Albrecht 1979). The purpose of FPA was to measure the amount of software produced. Albrecht wanted to measure the functionality of software from the user viewpoint, independently of the implementation. He therefore introduced function points as a measure of "functional size." In 1984, the International Function Point Users Group (IFPUG) was formed to maintain Albrecht's FPA. IFPUG has since published counting practices manuals that give standard rules for the application of FPA (IFPUG Manual 1994; IFPUG Manual 1999). IFPUG has thus both clarified the rules and modified Albrecht's original method. Several authors published extensions and alternatives to the FPA versions of Albrecht and IFPUG. Symons (1988) formulated several "concerns and difficulties" with Albrecht's FPA. His critique led him to the proposal of a new variant called Mark II function point analysis. Today, the United Kingdom Metrics Association (UKSMA) maintains Mark II FPA (Mk II Manual 1998). In 1997, St.-Pierre et al. (1997) proposed the full function points (FFPs) approach as an extension to IFPUG FPA 4.0. The purpose of the extension was to capture the functional size of real-time applications. The Common Software Metrics International Consortium (COSMIC) was formed in 1998 to develop an advanced FSM method. COSMIC has taken the FFP approach as a basis and published revisions of this method as COSMIC FFP 2.0

(Abran et al. 1999) and 2.1 (Abran et al. 2002). For this study, we focus on the following FSM methods:

- IFPUG FPA 4.0 and 4.1 (IFPUG Manual 1994; IFPUG Manual 1999)
- Mark II FPA 1.3.1 (ISO 2002c)
- FFP 1.0, COSMIC FFP 2.0 and 2.1 (Abran et al. 1999, 2002; St.-Pierre et al. 1997)

We will see that these methods share a core view of the items that determine functional size. Figure 2.2 presents a view of the evolution of these FSM methods.

2.1.3   Related Studies

Abran and Robillard (1994) analyzed the measurement process of IFPUG FPA. In their view, FPA constructs the function point measure in a hierarchical process of measurements. The counting of data elements, e.g., is considered a measure on the lowest level of the hierarchy. Based on the lowest-level measurements, higher levels are constructed, e.g., the assignment of weights to transaction types. Abran and Robillard then identify scale types for the measurements at each level. We view FSM differently, as a single measurement that assigns numbers to software applications. Based on measurement theory, we can thus discuss conditions or axioms that formulate assumptions of reality (cf. Zuse 1998, Section 4). Hence, we attempt to get a better understanding of existing FSM methods.

2.1.4   FSM Measurement Process

Measurement can be understood as an abstraction that captures certain attributes of the measurement objects. Measurement theory views this abstraction as a mapping that assigns numerical objects to empirical objects. In the context of FSM, the empirical objects are software applications. In terms of ISO 14143-1 (ISO 1998), the software application is characterized by functional user requirements. The FSM methods each define measures that assign numbers to software applications. A goal in the definition of function point analysis was to define the method independent of the technology used for implementation. FSM is therefore formulated without reference to any particular development method. As a consequence, FSM requires two steps of abstraction (Figure 2.3).

2.1.5   Abstraction Steps in FSM

Instead of using the concepts and models of a particular development method, FSM methods define their own concepts for the representation of a software application. The FSM methods thus define an abstraction of software that represents the items deemed relevant for functional size. The abstraction used in the methods covered

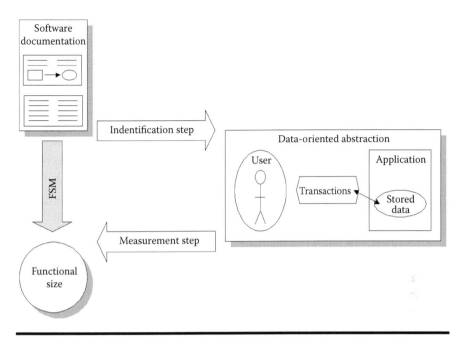

Figure 2.3   Functional size measurement (FSM) requires two steps of abstraction.

in this paper can be characterized as *data oriented*. The FSM methods studied thus define the following two steps of abstraction:

- The software documentation is represented in a data-oriented abstraction.
- The items in the data-oriented representation are mapped into numbers.

The first step of abstraction is applied to the software documentation, regardless of its form. In terms of ISO 14143-1 (ISO 1998), the source of the first step is the documentation of functional user requirements. The standard does, however, not prescribe a format for this documentation. Any FSM method must define how the abstraction has to be obtained, independently of the development method used.

Thus, FSM achieves independence of the technology used for implementation. The result is a representation in the data-oriented abstraction of the particular method that contains the items deemed relevant for functional size. Because of the independence of any formal documentation, this step requires interpretation of rules by humans.

The second step is the actual measurement, the mapping into numbers. Because the source in this step must be in the form of the data-oriented abstraction, this step can in general be automated. Our view on the two steps of abstraction is illustrated in Figure 2.3. Both steps are defined by the rules in the respective documents that define the FSM methods. In these documents, the two steps of abstraction are typically not separated clearly. The abstractions underlying the methods are not presented explicitly in most method definitions. However, COSMIC FFP defines two phases—mapping and measurement—that correspond closely to the two steps of abstraction. In the following section, we give a description of the data-oriented abstraction. The detailed generalized representation is presented in Section 2.1.7.

2.1.6 The Data-Oriented Abstraction

Although not described explicitly, Albrecht's original approach introduces the basic concepts of the data-oriented abstraction. The FSM methods discussed here have been proposed as improvements over the original FPA. These methods differ in both steps of abstraction; i.e., they differ in their representation of software functionality and in the measure functions. However, IFPUG FPA, Mark II FPA, and the FFP approach rely on the same core concepts (Figure 2.4):

- **User concept.** The users interact with an application. Users are not necessarily restricted to human users, but may include software and hardware users.
- **Application concept.** The application is the object of the measurement. Applications provide functions to the users. These functions are the attribute of interest.
- **Transaction concept.** Transactions are processes of interaction of the user with the application from a logical or functional perspective.
- **Data concept.** Data are stored by the application. *Data elements* represent the smallest data items meaningful to the user. Data elements are structured in logically related groups similar to tables in a database.
- **Type concept.** Multiple instances of elements identified by the above concepts are considered a single type.

All FSM methods studied represent an application by a set of transaction types and a set of groups of stored data. The methods differ, however, in the detailed views of these concepts. For example, IFPUG FPA classifies transactions into three classes, while the other methods do not define classes of transactions. Furthermore, the attributes used to characterize transactions differ in detail; e.g., an error message that is displayed to the user may be considered an input in IFPUG FPA 4.0,

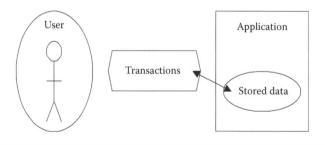

Figure 2.4 The data-oriented abstraction.

while it is considered an output in other methods. The methods also use different names for the core concepts.

As a consequence, it is difficult to analyze and discuss the differences and similarities between the methods. We therefore propose a generalized view of the data-oriented abstraction that allows us to represent each of the methods in a uniform way. The generalized representation is described in the following section.

2.1.7   Generalized Representation

The functionality of an application is represented by a set of transaction types and a set of data group types in the FSM methods studied. We therefore present generalizations for these two core concepts in the following two paragraphs. In the remainder of this section, we demonstrate how the generalization relates to the FSM methods.

2.1.7.1   Generalized Representation of Data Groups

The data concept recognizes data elements as elementary items. A data group type is a set of data elements stored by the application. Subgroups may be defined on the data elements of a data group type. This characterization applies directly to IFPUG FPA and FFP 1.0. In Mark II FPA, the data elements in a data group may be ignored. In COSMIC FFP, subgroups are not considered. Hence, the generalization introduces additional information only for Mark II FPA and COSMIC FFP. The generalized view of a data group type is illustrated in Figure 2.5.

2.1.7.2   Generalized Representation of Transactions

Transaction types are represented very differently in the methods. IFPUG FPA defines three classes of transaction types with up to four attributes, Mark II FPA

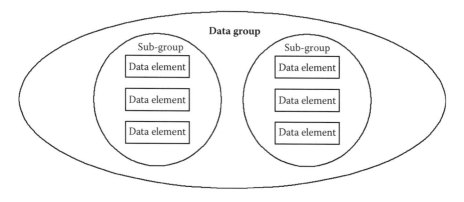

Figure 2.5   A data group type is a set of data elements with optional sub-groups.

uses a single representation with three attributes, and the FFP approach defines a transaction type as a collection of subprocesses. The spectrum of logical activities associated with transaction types, however, is nearly the same in the three variants. Similarly to the subprocess concept in the FFP approach, we represent transaction types here with seven classes of logical activities that manipulate data elements:

- **Entry activity.** The user enters data elements into the application.
- **Exit activity.** Data elements are output to the user.
- **Control activity.** Control information data elements are entered by the user.
- **Confirm activity.** Confirmation data elements are output to the user.
- **Read activity.** Data elements are read from a stored data group type.
- **Write activity.** Data elements are written to a stored data group type.
- **Calculate activity.** New data elements are calculated from some data elements.

The definitions of the logical activity classes are rather brief, because we do not intend to propose a new method for the identification of items here. Nevertheless, these activities can be found in the identification rules of the methods, and we use logical activities to represent the elements identified with those rules.

Given the concept of logical activities, a transaction type can be characterized as a collection of logical activities. The logical activities thus represent the transaction types in more detail than the methods originally do. As a result, the identification rules of each method have to be augmented with rules to map the transactions identified with the original rules onto the generalized transaction types. We describe these mappings in Sections 2.1.11 and 2.1.12. Figure 2.6 illustrates the generalized view on transaction types. Input from the user is indicated by straight arrows that enter the transaction, and lead to

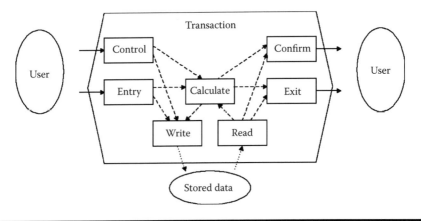

Figure 2.6 Transaction types are represented with logical activities.

entry and control activities. Output, on the other hand, is sent to the user by exit and confirm activities. Dotted arrows depict access to stored data with read and write activities. The data flow internal to the transaction is depicted with dashed arrows.

As mentioned before, the concept of logical activities is very similar to the notion of subprocesses in the FFP approach, and entry, exit, read, and write subprocess classes are used in that FSM method. The generalized representation introduces three additional classes, mainly required for the representation of IFPUG FPA.

IFPUG FPA and FFP 1.0 distinguish between data and control information in regard to input and output. In our generalized view, an input of data is represented by entry activities, while control information input is represented by control activities. On the output side, control information, e.g., error and confirmation messages, is distinguished from data output as well. Therefore, exit activities represent data output and confirm activities represent control information output. Neither Mark II FPA nor COSMIC FFP 2.x makes this distinction between data and control information. In general, these latter methods recognize both types of information as input or output, respectively.

Calculate activities are relevant as a criterion for classification in IFPUG FPA. Neither Mark II FPA nor the FFP approach classifies transactions, and calculate activities are not (yet) recognized in their respective measure functions. The internal data flow depicted by dashed arrows in Figure 2.6 and in the examples below illustrates the interpretation that can be associated with a transaction. It is, however, not taken into account by any of the methods discussed here.

2.1.8 Mapping for IFPUG FPA 4.0

2.1.8.1 Data Groups in IFPUG FPA 4.0

As mentioned in Section 2.1.7.1, mapping the IFPUG FPA 4.0 data group type to the generalized representation of a data group is straightforward: data element types correspond to data elements and record element types correspond to subgroups of data elements.

The class of a data group is not represented as an attribute of the data group; i.e., we do not consider the classification of data groups into internal logical files (ILFs) and external interface files (EIFs) as a part of the first step of abstraction. In fact, this classification can only be made in the context of an application, because IFPUG FPA determines the class of a data group type with the following identification rules (Gaffney and Cruickshank 1997, pp. 5–6):

> ILF Identification Rules … The group of data **is maintained within** the application boundary….
> EIF Identification Rules … The group of data **is not maintained** by the application being counted.

Hence, the class of a data group type in the context of a particular application is ILF, if and only if at least one transaction of that application does write to this particular data group. Otherwise, it must be classified as an EIF.

Therefore, the classification is a part of the second step of abstraction; i.e., the classification can be calculated with the measure function from the application context.

2.1.8.2 Transactions in IFPUG FPA 4.0

In IFPUG FPA, transactions are classified as either external inputs (EIs), external outputs (EOs), or external inquiries (EQs). The identification rules are used to classify the transactions. The rules are also used to identify the attributes that characterize each transaction, i.e., the data element types (DETs) and file types referenced (FTRs). Each class of transactions and the relevant items are identified with a different set of rules. The following paragraphs map these rules to the generalized representation with logical activities. The items relevant for each class are represented by the logical activities.

Note that the class of a transaction is not a part of the generalized representation, but the classification in IFPUG FPA 4.0 can be derived from the logical activities that play a role in a particular transaction. The classification with logical activities is explained in the last paragraph of this section, 2.1.8.2.4.

2.1.8.2.1 External Inputs in IFPUG FPA 4.0

The identification rules for external inputs (EIs), including the rules for the identification of FTR and DET, relate to logical activities as follows:

- Data are received from the outside. This is represented with an entry of data elements from the user.
- Data in an ILF are maintained. This presents a write activity to a data group. The data elements written are identified. More than one data group may be updated, represented by a write activity for each data group.
- Data groups may be read, represented by read activities.
- Error and confirmation messages may be output; these data elements are identified. We represent this with confirm activities.
- The user may specify information that controls the behavior of the application. This information is represented separately from data entry by control activities. The data elements are identified.
- Data elements additional to the data entered may be written to an ILF. The determination of these data elements may be represented with calculate activities.

Output of data elements other than error and confirmation messages are not considered a part of transactions in IFPUG FPA 4.0. Therefore, exit activities do not appear in the representation of EI in IFPUG FPA, although a transaction might include these activities in its requirements.

As an example for a transaction that would be classified as an EI, consider the deposit item transaction depicted in Figure 2.7. A customer deposits an item in a warehouse and the transaction registers attributes of the item, its owner, and storage place (see Fetcke (1999a, 1999b) for a full description of the examples). The following logical activities represent the transaction:

- An entry of the data elements that describe the item: description, pallets, value, owner, and storage place
- A read of the name from the customer data group to verify that the owner is registered
- A read of the location and space from the place data group to verify that the required amount of space is available
- A read of the description from the item data group to prevent storage of an item under an existing name
- A calculate activity that determines the current date, which is stored as the storage date
- A write of description, pallets, value, owner, storage date, and storage place data elements to the item data group
- A confirm to output any error messages

Figure 2.8 presents an illustration of the representation of this transaction with the logical activities described above. IFPUG FPA does not require all the details of these logical activities. Nevertheless, these activities do represent information important for the view in IFPUG FPA:

Deposit item			
Description	Monitors 17"	Owner	ABC Computers
Pallets	2	Storage place	A 21
Value	$3000		
Error message			
	Deposit	Cancel	

Figure 2.7   User interface of the deposit item transaction.

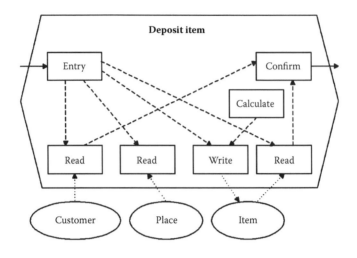

Figure 2.8   Logical activities in the deposit item transaction.

■ The data entry is required by the rules of an EI.
■ The read activities must be considered to correctly determine the file types referenced (FTRs).
■ The write activity and the data elements (DETs) written to the data group are essential for the EI.
■ The confirm activity must be considered to correctly determine the data element types (DETs).

2.1.8.2.2   External Outputs in IFPUG FPA 4.0

As with EI, we relate the identification rules for external outputs (EOs), including the rules for FTR and DET, to logical activities:

■ Data are sent to the outside, represented as an exit of data elements. These data elements are identified.
■ Data elements may be read from data groups, represented as read activities.

User input of data elements is not considered in the rules, although it might be relevant, e.g., as selection criteria for a report EO. Hence, entry or control activities do not appear in this view. Neither do the rules consider confirmation and error messages as output, excluding confirm activities from the representation. Write activities are not permissible for EO. Data elements output may be the result of calculate activities. Derived data are, in fact, the criterion used to distinguish between EO and EQ.

The print bill transaction depicted in Figure 2.9 is an example for an EO. The bill for a customer identified by name is printed. The following logical activities are required for this transaction, illustrated in Figure 2.10:

- The name of the customer is specified with an entry activity by the user.
- A read of name, address, and amount due from the customer data group retrieves data elements for the bill.
- A read of owner names from the item data group is required to obtain the number of items owned by the customer.
- A calculate activity determines the total number of items from the owner data.
- Error messages are output by confirm activities, if necessary.
- An exit activity outputs the data elements name, address, amount due, and total items.

Here, the total items data element is not retrieved by a read activity, but it is calculated from other data elements. Total items is thus derived data, and therefore, print bill cannot be classified as an EQ and must be classified as an EO. Hence,

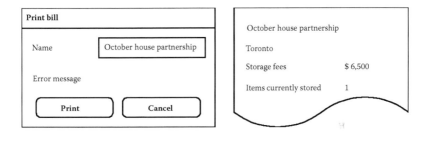

Figure 2.9   User interface of and report produced by the print bill transaction.

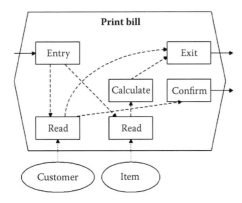

Figure 2.10   Logical activities in the print bill transaction.

the calculate activity in the generalized representation is relevant for classification in IFPUG FPA 4.0. While IFPUG FPA 4.0 ignores the entry of selection criteria, the read activities are necessary to correctly determine the file types referenced by this transaction. Although the error message may be output to the user, it is not considered by the rules for EO. Hence, the distinction of exit and confirm activities is also relevant for the accurate representation of an EO.

2.1.8.2.3 External Inquiries in IFPUG FPA 4.0

The external inquiry (EQ) transaction class is more complex than the two previously discussed classes, as it comprises both an input and an output side. However, the rules allow a distinction to which side of an EQ a logical activity contributes. Hence, in the generalized data-oriented abstraction, the representation of EQ is not different from the representation of EI or EO. The input and output sides appear in the formulation of the measure function in the formalized representation. The identification rules are represented as follows:

- Input data elements enter from the outside. This is represented by an entry activity. The data elements entered are identified.
- Output results exit the application, which is represented with an exit activity. The data elements are identified.
- Data are retrieved from data groups. This presents read activities.
- The retrieved data do not contain derived data. Hence, the data elements output is obtained by read activities, but not with calculate activities.
- Error and confirmation messages may be output. This is represented by confirm activities. Data elements are identified.
- The user may specify information that controls the behavior of the application. This information is represented separately from data entry by control activities. Data elements are identified.

Consider the following example shown in Figure 2.11: the query customer's items transaction. With this transaction, the items owned by a customer are displayed. The logical activities required are the following (Figure 2.12):

- An entry of the customer name by the user is given.
- A read from the customer data group verifies that the customer exists.
- An error message is output with a confirm activity if the customer does not exist.
- A read activity retrieves the description, pallets, value, storage date, and owner from the item data group for the items owned by the customer.
- An exit activity displays the customer name and a list of the items with their values.
- A read activity retrieves the description, pallets, value, and storage date.

For the input side, the entry and confirm activities determine the data element types. On the input side, the customer data group is referenced (read) to verify the name entered. On the output side, the exit activity represents the data element types. To generate the output, the item data group is an additional file type referenced, represented by the second read activity.

2.1.8.2.4   Classification with Logical Activities

As we have seen in the preceding paragraphs, the three classes of transactions can be represented with the seven logical activities of the generalized data-oriented abstraction. However, in a particular transaction class, certain activity classes may be required or prohibited. We observe:

- Write activities may only appear in EI.
- An EI may also receive control input that does not result in data exit.
- Both an EO and an EQ output data via exit activities.

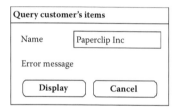

Query customer's items	
Name	Paperclip Inc
Error message	
Display	Cancel

Customer	Paperclip Inc		
Item	Pallets	Value	Storage date
Letter Paper	2	$100	1999-06-16
Paperclips	1	$20	1999-08-04

Figure 2.11   User interface of the query customer's items transaction.

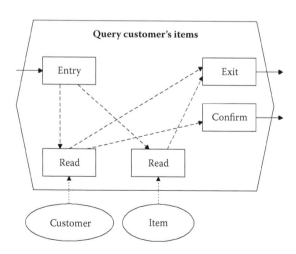

Figure 2.12   Logical activities in the query customer's item transaction.

■ The data sent by exit activities of an EQ must not contain data elements that are derived by calculate activities. Otherwise, the transaction is classified as an EO.

Hence, we can determine the class of a particular transaction from the classes of activities that are used to represent the transaction. This actually does not come as a surprise, because the identification rules used in the classification of transactions are in part represented by logical activities, as we described in the preceding paragraphs. Nevertheless, transactions identified with IFPUG FPA 4.0 can therefore be represented in generalized representation that does not include transaction classes.

As with data groups, classification of transactions is therefore a part of the second step of abstraction; i.e., it is part of the measure function.

2.1.9 Mapping for IFPUG FPA 4.1

The changes in release 4.1 of IFPUG FPA are not fundamental in relation to release 4.0. However, both the identification rules and the measure function have been changed. In respect to transactions, these modifications have a significant impact on the representation in the generalized data-oriented abstraction. We will discuss these changes here.

2.1.9.1 Data Groups in IFPUG FPA 4.1

The concept of a data group type has not been changed in IFPUG FPA 4.1. The formulation of the identification rules has been simplified without change to the notions of an ILF or an EIF. In IFPUG FPA 4.1, the classification of data group types depends on the application context, as it does with IFPUG FPA 4.0. The generalized abstraction therefore applies directly to IFPUG FPA 4.1, as it did apply to IFPUG FPA 4.0 (cf. Section 2.1.3).

2.1.9.2 Transactions in IFPUG FPA 4.1

The overall concept of transaction types has not been changed in release 4.1. IFPUG FPA 4.1 still classifies transactions into the three classes EI, EO, and EQ. The detailed identification rules, however, have been modified. A new concept of *primary intent* has been introduced. The items that contribute to the weights have also been changed in several details.

The representation of transactions with logical activities is principally the same with IFPUG FPA 4.1 as with release 4.0. The changes in the rules have to be reflected mainly in the measure function.

The classification of transactions, however, cannot entirely be derived from the logical activities that represent a transaction, because the logical activities permissible in transaction classes have been extended and classification requires the new concept of primary intent in IFPUG FPA 4.1. The primary intent of a transaction can only be determined as an additional element by the analyst in the first step of abstraction, as either one of:

- Alter the behavior of the system.
- Write to stored data groups.
- Output information to the user.

Hence, the data-oriented abstraction of IFPUG FPA 4.1 is extended by this element for each transaction.

Nevertheless, the generalized representation can still be used to represent the relevant information needed in IFPUG FPA 4.1, provided we add the primary intent for each transaction. We have, however, not included this element in the representation presented in Section 2.1.7.2, because it is not relevant for any of the other methods, and because it is a concept external to the view of transactions shared by all methods studied here.

The examples presented in Section 2.1.8.2 are represented with the same logical activities in IFPUG FPA 4.1. The primary intent of the deposit item transaction is the write to the item data group type. Deposit item would therefore be classified as an EI.

The primary intent of the print bill and query customer's items transactions is output to the user. For these two transactions, classification into EO and EQ has to be derived from the logical activities. The result of the classification here is the same as with IFPUG FPA 4.0.

2.1.10 Mapping for Mark II FPA

2.1.10.1 Data Groups in Mark II FPA

In Mark II FPA, data groups appear as entity types that do not contribute to functional size. Therefore, it is not necessary to identify data elements and subgroups of data elements in Mark II FPA. On the other hand, data elements are used to characterize transactions, and thus data elements are an item of the data-oriented abstraction of Mark II FPA. Hence, data elements are not foreign to Mark II FPA, and the representation of entity types can be extended with data elements and subgroups of data elements. The measure function of Mark II FPA simply assigns a zero value to data groups.

2.1.10.2 Transactions in Mark II FPA

Transactions are called logical transactions in Mark II FPA. A logical transaction is regarded as a unit of input, processing, and output. The input part corresponds to entry and control activities, and output corresponds to exit and confirm activities. The processing part actually represents access to entity types and therefore corresponds to read and write activities. Mark II FPA does not recognize aspects in logical transactions that would correspond to calculate activities.

As an example, let us consider the add place transaction shown in Figure 2.13. The input part of the transaction consists of an entry from the user, comprising the data elements location and space. The processing part includes a read activity that tests whether the place already exists, and a write activity to store the new record. The output part, finally, consists of a confirm activity that outputs an error message to the user if the place already existed. Figure 2.14 illustrates the representation of the add place transaction with logical activities.

2.1.11   Mapping for FFP 1.0

The FFP approach version 1.0 has been formulated as an extension to IFPUG FPA 4.0, where part of an application—designated in FFP 1.0 as "management function types"—is covered by IFPUG FPA, and the remaining part, "control function types," is covered by the FFP approach. Nevertheless, the FFP approach can be regarded as an FSM method in its own right. In this section, we only discuss the FFP concepts. Given an indication which method is to apply to a particular element, it is also possible to represent a mixture of IFPUG FPA and FFP in the generalized representation following the original proposal of FFP 1.0.

2.1.11.1   Data Groups in FFP 1.0

Data group types in FFP 1.0 are defined analogously to IFPUG FPA 4.0. The identification rules are practically identical with IFPUG data group types, in respect to the

Add place	
Location	A 21
Space	6
Error message	
Add	Cancel

Figure 2.13   User interface of the add place transaction.

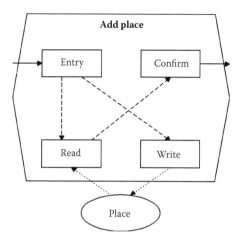

Figure 2.14   Logical activities in the add place transaction.

identification of data elements, and subgroups, in respect to classification. Therefore, the mapping of data groups described in Section 2.1.8.1 applies to FFP 1.0 as well.

However, FFP 1.0 introduces a new class of data groups: single-occurrence groups. These data groups comprise all data elements that only have a single instance in the application. Still, the single-occurrence group can be represented by a generalized data group, as it consists of a set of data elements where no subgroups are defined.

The classification of single-occurrence data groups into read-only and read/write is given by the application context, as with the conventional multiple-occurrence data groups. Hence, there is only one single-occurrence data group in the generalized representation of an application. Of course, the measure function of FFP 1.0 assigns different values to single-occurrence groups than to multiple-occurrence groups.

2.1.11.2   Transactions in FFP 1.0

FFP represents transactions as collections of subprocesses. Four classes of subprocesses are defined for entry and exit of data elements from and to the user, and for read and write from and to stored data groups. The representation of subprocesses with logical activities is quite obvious. However, FFP 1.0 does not have different subprocess classes for data and control information. Even when applied independently from IFPUG FPA, any input would be handled by entry subprocesses, and any output by exits.

The generalized representation with its control and confirm activities thus provides for more detail that is simply ignored in the FFP measure function, where control is equivalent to entries and confirm equivalent to exits. In this sense, the logical activities of the examples presented in the previous sections represent FFP subprocesses.

2.1.12 Mapping for COSMIC FFP 2.x

COSMIC FFP 2.0, as opposed to FFP 1.0, has been published as an FSM method that is applied to all parts of an application, i.e., without reference to IFPUG FPA. In respect to the generalized representation of functional size, there is no difference between versions 2.0 and 2.1 of COSMIC FFP. We therefore present the mapping for both versions here.

2.1.12.1 Data Groups in COSMIC FFP 2.x

In COSMIC FFP, data groups do not contribute to functional size, in contrast to FFP 1.0. Nevertheless, data groups are essential in the identification of subprocesses, because a subprocess may handle only one data group. COSMIC FFP even extends the notion of data groups from stored data that are the subject of read and write activities to "transient" data groups that are used to identify entry and exit subprocesses. However, these transient data groups are not represented in the generalized representation as data group types, because these transient data groups are an attribute in the corresponding input and output activities.

As with Mark II FPA, the measure function of COSMIC FFP assigns a zero value to data groups in the generalized representation.

2.1.12.2 Transactions in COSMIC FFP 2.x

The view on transactions in COSMIC FFP is essentially the same as in FFP 1.0: transactions are represented by subprocesses that are classified as either entry, exit, read, or write. Apart from the naming conventions, the differences lie in the details of the identification rules of the FFP versions. Therefore, subprocesses of COSMIC FFP 2.x can be represented in the generalized representation in the same manner as with FFP 1.0 (cf. Section 2.1.11.2).

Note that COSMIC FFP provides a mechanism for custom extensions that allows, among others, the definition of an equivalent to calculate activities, described as "manipulation subprocesses." Calculate activities are, however, not (yet) a part of the official COSMIC FFP method.

2.1.12.3 Layers in COSMIC FFP 2.x

A concept not present in the other FSM methods discussed has been introduced in COSMIC FFP: software layers. With this concept, the application functionality can be partitioned into layers at different levels of abstraction, e.g., device drivers, graphical user interfaces, and application data management. According to COSMIC FFP, one layer acts as a client of another layer. In terms of the user and application concepts of the data-oriented abstraction (Figure 2.4), a client layer is a user from the point of view of another layer. As a consequence, interfaces that would otherwise be internal to the application can be included in the abstraction of the software. Subprocesses that move data between the layers are included in the abstraction. Hence, the data-oriented abstraction is applied with a higher level of granularity, yet the concepts used to represent the layer functionality are the same as those used to represent application functionality. Therefore, the generalized abstraction applies to COSMIC FFP 2.x, including the layer concept.

2.1.13 Applications of the Generalization

In Section 2.1.7, we have proposed a generalized representation for the first step of abstraction of a number of FSM methods. In our approach, this representation is the basis of a model for the FSM measurement process. Hence, the immediate result of this proposed representation is that we have formulated the basis of a model that allows us to analyze and discuss FSM methods. As the generalization represents the first step of abstraction, we can discuss in detail whether this abstraction is adequate for FSM. With a formalization of the generalized representation, we can also discuss the measure functions. The generalized representation is then necessary to give an interpretation to observations obtained with the formalization. Furthermore, the representation proposed is generalized; i.e., it applies to the abstraction of each of the FSM methods studied. Note that we do not assume that in all cases each method will represent a given application with the same transactions and data groups (although we believe that this is not unusual (cf. Fetcke et al. 2001) for examples). With the layer concept introduced in COSMIC FFP, e.g., transactions can be identified that would not be relevant in other methods. However, we believe that the generalized representation can be used to identify cases where the methods do or do not arrive at the same abstraction, and that this knowledge is relevant for understanding FSM methods. Nevertheless, the generalized representation allows direct comparisons of the methods and analysis of their differences. Obviously, the concepts underlying the different methods are not so different, and one might assume that the effort required for the identification step does not vary dramatically between the methods. As mentioned above, based on the generalized representation, a formalization can be given such that the measurement step has the form of mathematical functions. This approach has two benefits: on the one hand, we can study the measures, and on the other hand, we can use the representation for automation and the representation of experience data. We discuss these aspects in the following two paragraphs.

2.1.13.1 Generalized Function Point Structure

We call the formalization of the generalized representation a generalized function point structure. In the generalized function point structure, an application **a** is a vector of transaction types t_i and stored data group types f_j:

$$\mathbf{a} = (\mathbf{t}_1, \ldots, \mathbf{t}_n, \mathbf{f}_1, \ldots, \mathbf{f}_m)$$

Here, the t_i are each a vector of logical activities and the f_j are sets of data elements with subgroups. In the case of IFPUG FPA 4.1, the t_i also comprise the primary intent of the transactions. Each FSM method defines a measure function FPM such that FPM (**a**) is the functional size of application **a**. With the generalized function point structure, we can formulate assumptions about functional size and test those assumptions with the FSM measures. For example, let us assume that we have two applications **a** and **a'**, and we have a view of functional size that implies that **a** is larger than **a'**. A measure then assumes our view of functional size if FPM (**a**) > FPM(**a'**). With the generalized function point structure, we can formulate such properties of FSM methods axiomatically; i.e., we describe properties of FSM measures in general, instead of by example. In Fetcke (2000), we have demonstrated two such properties that are significant for the use of FSM methods for prediction of other variables.

2.1.14 *Experience Data and Automation*

A practical difficulty with the different FSM methods is that results obtained with one method cannot be compared directly with the results of another method. The practical use of functional size measurement data generally requires experience data from other, previous projects, and such data are coupled with the FSM method used. It is not possible to truly convert measurement values obtained with one method into values that would have been measured with another method. This observation can easily be derived from the measure definitions in the generalized function point structure. Hence, the experience data cannot be used with another method in a meaningful way. However, the generalized representation defines a set of items that are sufficient to obtain the measurement with any of the FSM methods covered. Experience data stored in a form equivalent to the generalized representation can therefore be used to obtain measurement results for any of the methods studied here. Furthermore, the formalized measure functions can be calculated automatically. Under the assumption that for a given application each of the selected FSM methods arrives at the same abstraction regarding transactions and data groups, all measures can be calculated automatically from a single source.

2.1.15 *Conclusions*

In this paper, we have proposed a model for a number of existing FSM methods that gives a new view on these methods. We use an axiomatic approach based on measurement theory that allows us to formulate assumptions of reality based on the model. The basis of our model is a representation of the data-oriented abstraction of the FSM methods. This representation is generalized such that it applies to each of the methods studied. The generalized representation allows direct comparisons of the methods and analysis of their differences. A formalization of the generalized representation in a generalized function point structure allows the formulation of FSM measures as functions. Axioms can be formulated in the generalized function point structure as assumptions of reality. The generalized representation relates these axioms to the elements defined by the FSM methods. The formalization may also be used as a basis for the representation of experience data from previous projects. Furthermore, the mathematical formulation of the measure functions allows automation of the measurement step. The detailed definitions of the generalized function point structure and of the measure functions on this structure have to be presented separately.

2.2   Functional Details Visualization and Classification in the COSMIC FSM Framework

Luca Santillo

2.2.1   Introduction

For software developers, the ability to measure the size of software from its functional requirements or specifications early in the life of a project is a first key step for estimating development effort. Further, as the functional size measure is independent of the technology used, it provides a key component for software project performance measures such as productivity.

The Common Software Metrics Consortium (COSMIC) was founded in late 1998 as a voluntary association of software measurement experts from Australia, Canada, Finland, Germany, Ireland, Italy, Japan, the Netherlands, and the UK. COSMIC's aim is to to develop, test, bring to market, and facilitate acceptance of new software sizing methods to support estimation and performance measurement. The current COSMIC FSM (functional size measurement) method is the COSMIC FFP (full function point) method, version 2.2. This method of sizing the functional requirements of software was approved as an international standard in early 2003 (ISO/IEC 19761:2003) (COSMIC FFP News 2006).

The idea of being able to measure the size of software requirements or specifications, independent of the technology used to build the software, was first proposed by Allan Abrecht of IBM in 1979. His method, known as function point analysis (FPA), has evolved into the IFPUG method, supported by the International Function Point User Group, and other first-generation variants, as the NESMA method from the Netherlands and the Mk II FPA method from the UK. Those other methods have also been approved by ISO, but since they were all designed years ago to work for business application software, or MIS, they cannot adequately handle recent software domains and application types (their domain of applicability is limited).

The second-generation COSMIC FFP method was specifically designed from the outset to measure the functional size of real-time, multilayered software such as used in telecoms, process control, infrastructure software, and operating systems, as well as business application software, all on the same measurement scale. Having been developed in the last few years, the method is compatible with modern specification methods such as UML, and with OO techniques.

2.2.2 COSMIC FSM Framework

The COSMIC FFP measurement method involves applying a set of models, rules, and procedures to a given piece of software as it is perceived from the perspective of its functional user requirements (FURs) (ISO 2003d). The result of the application of these models, rules, and procedures is a numerical "value of a quantity" representing the functional size of the software, expressed by COSMIC functional size units (Cfsu, or shortly CU).

Two phases are involved during the measurement process: the mapping phase and the nominal measurement phase. The mapping phase takes as input a FUR statement and produces a specific software model, by identifying:

- The purpose, scope, and measurement viewpoint
- The software layer(s) under study
- The software boundaries
- The functional processes (FPs)
- The objects of interest (OoIs, or equivalently, the data groups)
- The data attributes

The measurement phase takes as input the instance of software model and, using a defined set of rules and procedures, produces a value of a quantity the magnitude of which is directly proportional to the functional size of the model, based on the current COSMIC FFP measurement principle: the functional size of software is directly proportional to the number of its data movements. By convention, this numerical value of a quantity is then extended to represent the functional size of the software itself—each data movement (DM) is assigned 1 CU.

It is significant to identify and aggregate the data movements by FP, which is defined as an elementary component of a set of FURs, comprising a unique cohesive and independently executable set of data movement types. Data movements are subprocesses and come in four classes: entry (E), exit (X), read (R), and write (W). Therefore, a suggested way to document measures is reported in the COSMIC FFP measurement manual, reproduced here (Figure 2.15).

2.2.3 Remarks

- Mapping phase: Each identified data group is registered in a column; each functional process is registered on a specific line, grouped by identified layer.

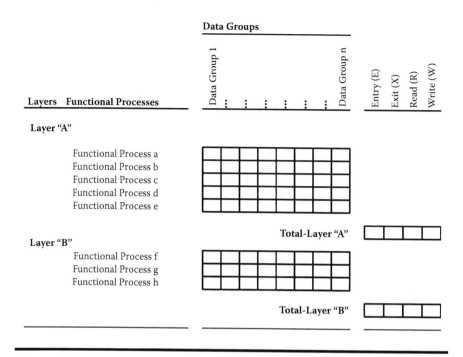

Figure 2.15   COSMIC FFP generic software model matrix—mapping phase.

- Measurement phase: For each identified functional process, the identified data movements are noted in the corresponding cell (E, X, R, W).
- For each identified functional process, the data movements are then summed up by type, and each total is registered in the appropriate column at the far right of the matrix.
- The measurement summary can then be calculated and registered in the boxed cells of each layer, on the "total" line.
- Data groups (or equivalently, OoIs) are not assigned any value in the current measurement method version; still, they must be identified in order to count data movements correctly. The materialization of a data group may take different forms, from a data storage persistent file to a presentation cluster on screen or printed report, usually with transient persistence.
- In the current version of the method, data manipulation subprocesses are not recognized separately, but are considered to be associated with or part of specific data movement subprocesses. Given this approximation, the standard COSMIC FFP method is suitable for sizing movement-rich types of software, but it can be easily extended—as proposed next in this work—for sizing manipulation-rich (or algorithm-rich) software (Figure 2.16).

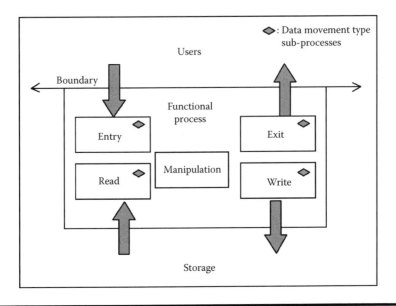

Figure 2.16   The sub-process types and some of their relationships.

2.2.3.1   Representing the Measurement Details

A new visualization diagram (data movement diagram, or DMD) is proposed, as an adaptation of the so-called Hinton diagram (weight matrix, usually used in the neural networks research field to represent the strength of the links between nodes of the network (Saaty 1999)). The data movement diagram provides information about which functional process uses (entries, exits, reads, or writes) which object of interest, or data group, in the measured system (Figure 2.17). FP "a" simply writes data on OoI, given a specific triggering event (the minimum size of any functional process is 2 CU). FP "b" represents an inquiry, where some data are read and shown, or an error message is provided if the required data are not found. The last row, FP "d," represents the case when all the data groups in the system can eventually require to be checked before one of them can be written. Reading the diagram by column, OoI 1 is a case when an object of interest (a data group) is eventually used by each and every functional process in the system, being critical for the system operation. In such a diagram, the box filling design denotes impact/use, while the box size denotes strength (i.e., quantity of the same subprocess type over a single object of interest inside the given functional process scope). Note that in some cases more of one instance of the same data movement type is permitted and measured within the same functional process over the same data group (e.g., FP "c" over OoI 1).

Specific features are provided in case of enhancement projects, where data movements may be added to, changed, or deleted from a functional process (Figure 2.18).

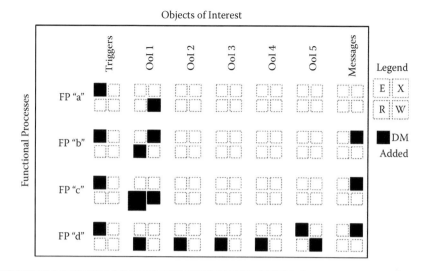

Figure 2.17   DMD example (baseline or development).

FP's "a" and "c" are unchanged; triggers, messages, and OoI's 4 and 5 are not impacted. Remaining processes are modified, due to added, changed, or deleted data movements over one or more OoIs.

Such a DM diagram can be seen as a whole system (layer) profile, or can be examined by perspective:

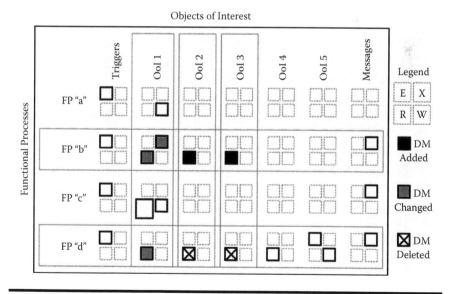

Figure 2.18   DMD example (enhancement with respect to previous example, Figure 2.7).

- By functional process (by row)
- By object of interest (by column)

Data movement diagrams can be seen as a sort of measurement profile to facilitate the visualization of processing operations *density*, or of *impact of enhancement* over an existing system. Within the scope of a single measure, functional processes and objects of interest can be visually compared to identify *similarities* between them, and used as a sort of checklist during the first steps of software analysis (typically, during the requirements analysis).

2.2.3.2 Extending the Measurement Framework and Details

A possibly exhaustive list of thirteen possible action types forming the processing logic of any functional process can be found in IFPUG (2004); such a list has already been proposed within a complexity evaluation framework in Rumelhart et al. (1986) and Santillo (2004). Here, we can classify any action with respect to its coverage in the COSMIC FFP method as a data movement; if so, the action is excluded from further measurement (Table 2.1). The remaining actions form a subset of manipulation classes, which can be used to extend the standard COSMIC FFP method and, within the scope of the current work, enrich the visualization diagram for classification and comparison purposes over measurement results.

However, since the action list should be further reviewed for lack of coverage or functional manipulation overlapping, and for sake of simplicity and readability, only two main classes of data manipulation are considered in the further version of visualization: validation (check) vs. creation. A simple criterion to differentiate those classes could be that whenever an action provides the user with a data content or structure, as requested by the user, which could not be simply retrieved and displayed starting from the database, we identify some kind of data creation.

The previously called data movement diagram (DMD) becomes a functional processing diagram (FPD), with additional representation of such data manipulation classes (Figure 2.19).

Also for validation and creation data manipulation types, a convention can be stated so that the box size represents a sort of count of separate actions, if defined (see Figure 2.19, case of FP "c" over OoI 1). Such a case would require further extension of the measurement method, to clarify how to distinguish separate manipulation subprocesses within a single functional process; such an aim is beyond the scope of the current proposal. Further variations of the diagram conventions could also introduce a way to differentiate validation or creation that occurred associated with a specific data movement within the process (e.g., validation of the entered data vs. validation of data read from a data group, data

Table 2.1   Action list for data manipulation and movement classification

	2.1.10.1 Action	*Measured as Movement*	*Include as Manipulation*
1	Validations are performed		Yes (Validation)
2	Mathematical formulas and calculations are performed		Yes (Creation)
3	Equivalent values are converted		Yes (Validation)
4	Data is filtered and selected by using specified criteria to compare multiple sets of data		Yes (Validation)
5	Conditions are analyzed to determine which are applicable		Yes (Validation)
6	One or more data groups are updated	Yes (W)	
7	One or more data groups are referenced	Yes (R)	
8	Data or control information is retrieved	Yes (R)	
9	Derived data is created by transforming existing data to create additional data		Yes (Creation)
10	Behavior of the system is altered		Yes (Creation)
11	Prepare and present information outside the boundary	Yes (X)	
12	Capability exists to accept data or control information that enters the application boundary	Yes (E)	
13	Data is resorted or rearranged		Yes (Creation)

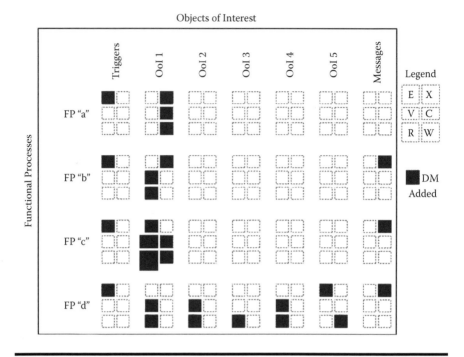

Figure 2.19　FPD example (baseline or new development). Here, "DM" stands for both data movement and/or data manipulation types.

creation in order to update a data group vs. data creation to allow a given exit to be performed, and so on).

Similarly, Figure 2.20 shows an example of a functional processing diagram in the case of changes occurred because of a given enhancement project. Note that functional processing diagrams could correctly express changes that occurred in the data manipulation subprocessing of a process, while the data movement subprocesses might not be affected at all by the required change.

2.2.4　Application Example and Remarks

At first, a trivial case study is offered by the simplest set of functional processes for a single data group management, the CRUDL (create, read, update, delete, and list). Regardless of the specific data group contents, we can easily argue that the base functional processing profile would be as shown in Figure 2.21, case a. Variations are possible, since in real-world CRUDLs the FURs could require some external data update when inserting or deleting an occurrence in the data group being managed (Figure 2.21, case a1), or more validation or creation subprocessing than in the standard case (Figure 2.21, case a2).

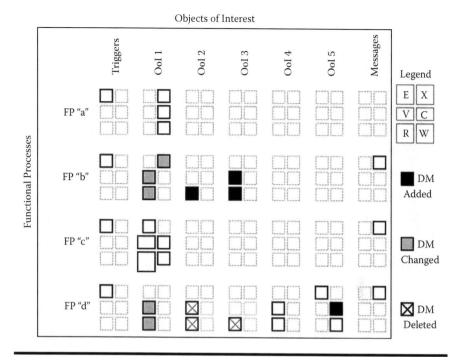

Figure 2.20 FPD example (enhancement with respect to previous example, Figure 2.19). Once again, "DM" stands for both data movement and/or data manipulation types.

We note that the proposed extension (and representation) for data manipulation subprocessing would then clearly distinguish variations in the given cases, which would otherwise be measured and reviewed as identical. Visually, such differences would clearly be expressed when comparing corresponding processes (e.g., the create functional process in cases a and a2, where the REF_DATA might also not be necessary for data to be created by the base process).

2.2.4.1 Remarks

Some remarks are reported, in order to plan potential future improvements of the proposed diagramming technique:

■ Some details of the proposed visualization diagrams should be fixed in further versions whenever accepted by the practitioners' community and validated over a large set of real cases in any possible software domain. For instance, the examples shown above separately list "fake" objects of interest for triggering events and messages. Since any functional process must have a triggering event, and such a triggering event is usually associated with the first (or only)

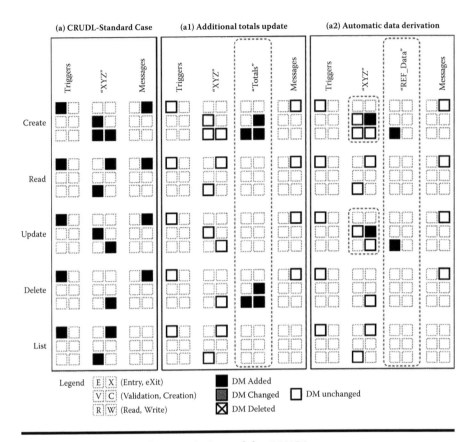

Figure 2.21 FPD's for three variations of the CRUDL case.

part of data entry regarding a real object of interest (in online software types), it could be inferred that such entry data movement, comprising the triggering event, should be assigned to and visualized over a specific object of interest, instead of a generic one.

DM in Figure 2.21 stands for both data movement and data manipulation types. Second and third variations are represented as if enhancements with respect to the first case (a). Dotted frames highlight specific differences between the three cases. In interactive reporting, the three cases could be shown as overlapping one another, highlighting the differences:

a. Standard CRUDL case (in the create FP it is assumed that XYZ is first read to check whether the user-provided key for the new occurrence is not present in the data group.

a1. Whenever an occurrence is inserted or deleted from XYZ, the FURs require that a generic "totals" data group is maintained for further user reference.

a2. When inserting or updating, some attributes are automatically derived by the system, based on some corresponding attribute values read from a distinct OoI REF_DATA.

■ The COSMIC FFP measurement principle has as a consequence the fact that "the smallest theoretical functional size for a piece of software is 2 CU ..., as the smallest functional process must have at least one Entry, and either one Exit or one Write" (ISO, 2003d, p.18). This means that a DMD, or equivalently a FPD, for any functional process must show at least two "filled" boxes, for such data movements.

■ Again, according to the COSMIC FFP measurement principle, "there is no upper limit to the functional size of a piece of software and, notably, there is no upper limit to the functional size of any of its functional processes" (ISO, 2003d, p.19). This means that in theory there's no limit to the size of a DMD, or equivalently of a FPD (although real cases would necessarily be limited in practice).

■ With respect to the previous remark, and for general reasons, automation of the measurement data collection, by means of tool support, and consequently of the visualization of the measurement details would be a great benefit for the practitioners.

■ Automation of measurement data collection and representation would also allow for general pattern recognition techniques to be applied to real-world cases, with subsequent benefits in software assessment and the estimation process.

2.2.5 Conclusions

This work introduced a new way to represent the measurement details and, collaterally, a proposal for extending the current framework to include data manipulation subprocesses type classification in the measurement process. Possible advantages of the proposal would be:

■ Enhanced measurement data collection
■ Added *classification means* for software components
■ Added possibility of *type and structure comparisons* among software systems
■ *Visual traceability* for software development or enhancement requirements

General reasons to take into account such an enhanced visualization/classification tool would then be:

■ To allow *complexity analysis* (from a functional perspective, by diagram comparison)
■ To allow *reuse analysis* (from a functional perspective, by diagram overlapping)
■ To improve cost estimation or value assessment based on effective impact of software size (by component) on project effort (by phase)

Regardless of specific details of the proposed visualization approach, which could be improved after ordinary test and trial, any visual representation tool could help in replacing (or in support to) hard-to-read reporting documents with an overall, instantaneous visual representation of sized systems and enhancement-impacted areas and components for such systems. Especially high-level resources, who are not directly involved in measurement details, could appreciate the proposed visual perspective, for immediate perception of affected areas and components for decision-making purposes or preliminary assessment of interesting software project portions.

2.3   Applying a Functional Measurement Method: Cognitive Issues

Jean-Marc Desharnais and Alain Abran

2.3.1   *Measurement process*

According to Abran et al. (1998; Abran and Khelifi 2004), there are four phases[*] in the measurement process, as follows and as illustrated in Figure 2.22:

1. Design of the measurement method
2. Measurement method application, in a specific context
3. Measurement results analysis
4. Exploitation of the measurement results, for instance, in decision-making models, quality models, and estimation models

Of course, phase 4 (exploitation of results) is the activity of most interest to managers (Desharnais et al. 2001, 2002); however, the quality of decision-making models built and used in this phase depends heavily on the quality of the inputs to such models. Therefore, both the quality of the design of a measurement method (phase 1) and the quality of its application (phases 2 and 3), to ensure that the resulting measures are coherent[†] and of high quality, are important.

The scope of this paper is on phase 2[‡] (measurement method application) and on the related challenges in the context of the measurement of software. To investigate this phase, the application of a specific software measurement method, that is, COSMIC FFP, has been selected as the object of study. In Abran et al. (2003), phase 2 has been broken down into the following three activities (Figure 2.23):

---

[*] We replace the word *step* used in the Abran et al. (2003) article with the word *phase*, in order to avoid confusion with the steps of the COSMIC FFP method.

[†] A measurement is coherent when two measurers with the same documentation (or the same information) obtain the same measurement results.

[‡] To our knowledge, there has been no systematic theoretical search relating to this phase. Nisiyama and Furuyama (1994) tackled this question from the point of view of the quality of the documentation.

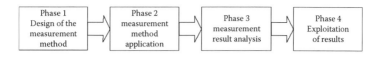

Figure 2.22   Phases in the measurement process.

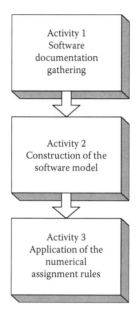

Figure 2.23   Method application activities.

1. Data gathering:* The data gathering activity is specific to an organization, and in general, it is not systematized in measurement methods documentation.† For example, there are generic texts about the type of documentation that the measurer

---

* The Abran and Khelifi (2004) document probably uses the term *data gathering* in the sense of data as opposed to information.

† Documentation is an instance of the word *data*. The interviews constitute another instance of the word "data." For Violaine Prince, data are "tout signifiant susceptible d'être capté, enregistré, transmis ou modifié par un agent cognitif de traitement de l'information, naturel ou artificiel" (Prince 1996, p. 25). In addition, "l'information est un signifié transporté par une donnée" (idem). There may, however, be confusion about what is data and what is information. A document is generally considered information. In the context of functional measurement, it is data, since information is linked to three factors, according to Prince (idem):
- The task or grids through which the data are decoded
- Existing decoding procedures
- The decoding agent and its own cognitive universe

must have, but in practice, this depends on what is available for a specific project in an organization, and the experience and knowledge of the measurer.

2. Model of the software: The software to be measured is modeled using the rules of the measurement method. Several steps[*] are required. In the COSMIC FFP method, these steps are as follows:
   - Identification of the layers of the software
   - Identification of the boundary of each piece of software
   - Identification of the functional processes

3. Application of the rules of numerical assignment: This activity is dependent on the first step of the measurement process and, more particularly, on the definition of the rules of numerical assignment. These rules are applied by the measurer, starting with the identification of functional sub processes (which are recognized as the entities being measured, or as the base functional component (BFC) according to the ISO 14143-1 definitions on functional size measurement), i.e., measurable according to the specific model of the measurement method.

2.3.2 The Measurement Problem

The purpose of phase 2 is to make it possible for measurers to interpret in a coherent way[†] the rules of the measurement method by taking into account the quality and availability of the documentation for the software to measure.

From the point of view of the measurer, applying the rules of measurement ultimately means solving a specific measurement problem. The measurer must address the following cognitive issues: he must understand the software to be measured; then he must interpret its meaning in order to identify what is to be measured; and finally, he must use the rules of the measurement method and the rules of numerical assignment in order to arrive at the measurement solution.

Figure 2.24 shows the cognitive path to be followed by the measurer. By following this path, the measurer can solve a specific problem of the measurement application; i.e., the path connects the measurer's understanding of the software to the measurement rules. For example, when a software project documentation provides an entity/relation model in which the measurer can see ten entities and two relations, the measurer understands that this model can help him determine the number of groups of data in the software that he has to measure. He must then interpret what relations and entities mean in the context of the measurement rules. He must next use the rules[‡] relating to the groups of data. A solution could be that there are eight valid groups of data recognized by the model and rules of the specific measurement method he is using.

---

[*] COSMIC FFP Measurement Guide (Abran et al. 2004) used the word *step*.

[†] From our view, coherence implies repeatability and reproducibility, accuracy, and convertibility (ISO 2000).

[‡] Using rules means using everything that can be useful in the measurement method in connection with the problem to be solved.

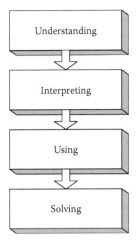

Figure 2.24   The measurer's cognitive path.

The purpose of our research project is provide help for different measurers to arrive at the same solution when using the same set of information as input to a measurement process with the COSMIC FFP method, to ensure the coherence of the measurement results. In the context of software projects, the quality of the input to the measurement process can be impacted by a lack of documentation or by the difficulty in interpreting the documentation (Figure 2.25). The quality of the documentation has a significant impact on the cognitive path of the measurer, mainly on his level of understanding and his interpretation of the documentation. Through practice, we have identified two main factors with an impact on the quality of the documentation:

- Poor documentation or, in some cases, lack of documentation
- Diversity in the representation of software models

Software documentation[*] (which is often expressed via models[†]) is, in practice, frequently incomplete, obsolete, and sometimes even wrong. Documentation

---

[*] The words *application*, *system*, and *information system* are often used as synonyms in business organizations (in banks, government agencies, and insurance companies, for example). The word *software* is used more frequently in other industry sectors. We use the word "software" here for preference, except if the context requires the use of a different word, as this is the word used in ISO standard 14143 (ISO 1998). See also the glossary of the IFPUG Measurement Guide 4.1 (IFPUG Manual 1999).

[†] "Les systèmes d'information d'ores et déjà modélisés font appel à plusieurs modèles de représentation: modèles de données et de traitement, modèles de connaissances, modèles organisationnels et ergonomiques, modèles de communication" (Prince 1996, p. 86). For the purposes of functional measurement, we use mainly the data processes and data models.

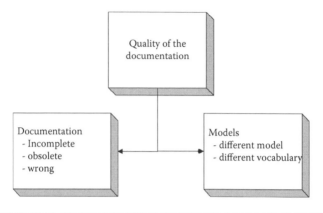

Figure 2.25 Quality factors of the documentation.

problems, during the design and installation of software,[*] affect the way in which the software is understood for the purposes of measurement. Moreover, even when the quality of the documentation is good, it is sometimes difficult to compare the models across organizations or organizational units because each organization tends to use its own methodology,[†] which means that the modes of representation of the models, as well as the vocabulary, have various degrees of differences in the formalisms of models of representation. In situations where the quality of the project documentation is not good enough, the measurer has to rely on the software developers to fill in the information that is lacking. The measurer must therefore either trust the documentation or ask the specialists who developed the software to figure out how to apply the measurement rules. Figure 2.26 presents the mapping of phase 2 of the measurement process to the cognitive path of the measurer. Understanding and interpreting correspond to the data gathering activity, and the use and the solution to the software design activity or to the application of numerical assignment rules activity. In the prior example, the identification of the groups of data belongs to the software modeling activity. By identifying eight groups of data, the measurer has found a solution to his problem of applying the measurement method to a specific context, in this instance the application of the measurement rules to the entity/relation model provided by the documentation.

---

[*] The software itself could be developed in several phases, the name of the phases of which can vary according to the methodology used. There may be one or many phases, some of which address design (e.g., requests, architecture, and functional analysis) and one or more phases that address installation (e.g., coding, test, implementation, and training). Team composition is not necessarily the same (Rivet et al. 2000).

[†] A methodology is "a body of practices, procedures, and rules used by those who work in a discipline or engage in an inquiry; a set of working methods" (see Abran and Symons 2005, p. 26).

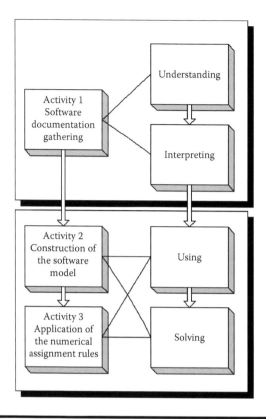

Figure 2.26   The measurer's path and phase 2 activities.

Two additional examples are presented as an illustration of information that the measurer can obtain from the documentation or by interviewing a software developer about the software to be measured:

The first example* describes a request from a user:

> The user wishes to consult a provider's database to obtain a list of the articles purchased during the past month from a specific provider.
>
> The measurement of the functional size of this process involves (based on the data available) a knowledge or understanding of:
>
> - The release process modality
> - The results of the process or the group of data read
> - The validations and the possible results of the validations

---

* A similar example was used in St.-Pierre et al. (1996).

With this information, the measurer applies the measurement rules by progressing through the following cognitive steps:

- Understand what the problem is (release, etc.)
- Interpret the meaning of the user's request
- Use the software design rules (or numerical assignment rules)
- Solve the problem

The second example involves the measurement of a report generator:

The specifications state that the report generator must provide the user with the capacity to define and create screens and reports by using the data available, based on the groups of data of existing software. The parameters are designed, developed, and delivered so that the user can choose:

- Attributes to be displayed or printed
- Selection criteria
- The display or impression format
- Other rules for display or printing

The documentation specifies that the functionalities of the report generator are distinct from the functionalities of a simple report in the following ways:

- The attributes of the report generator are parameters, and not the attributes included in the group of software data.
- What are delivered are not reports, but the capacity to build reports.
- There may be more than one user: a user who is responsible for creating the reports and another who uses the reports; i.e., the type of user is different (the designer vs. the user of a report).
- The architectural environment is different. The design of reports involves choices in terms of the parameters of the report generator and the attributes of the group of software data. There are also the display format and the user of the other display rules.

In this second example, there is more than one problem, or cognitive difficulty, in the execution of a functional measurement. Also, it is possible to uncover a hierarchy of problems; i.e., the solution of one problem can lead to the identification of another problem. This means for any type of cognitive problem a measurer encounters, he could be using the Figure 2.26 path more than once, i.e., one path for each problem identified.

The identification of the functionalities of the report generator (there can be one or more processes to identify) constitutes a distinct problem. A number of questions then arise relating to identification of the report generator processes according to COSMIC

FFP.* The answers to these questions will lead the measurer to the identification of the processes, and then to results, which can in turn lead him to another level of problems, which consist in identifying subprocesses.

The measurer can identify a problem that has a solution that allows direct numerical assignment, or identify a problem that leads him to the identification of a subsequent problem, and so on. Consequently, the measurer must know, that is, he must figure out,[†] the relationships that can be established between the different problems. This could lead to the construction of a decision tree. However, trying to figure out all the possibilities would lead very rapidly to a "computational explosion." For this reason, the expert measurers then turn to heuristics to be sufficiently flexible to accommodate these various possibilities. As pointed out by Dehn and Schank (1982, p. 363), "the heuristics are rules that suggest the way to turn or when to go back and try something different."

To address the measurement problems in a specific instance, there are two types of knowledge that the measurer must have:

■ An understanding of the software (using the documentation, the models,[‡] and other artifacts)
■ A knowledge of the COSMIC FFP method (or any other measurement method) to enable him to apply the method and make connections among the various problems that arise at the time of measurement

2.3.3 Proposal of a Generic Diagnostic Procedure

We propose in this paper a generic diagnostic procedure, as a first step and not the only possible one, to help the measurer solve the various measurement problems he encounters. The description of this diagnostic procedure will be, for illustrative purposes, the COSMIC FFP vocabulary[§] and measurement steps. The various COSMIC FFP steps and substeps that will form the basis of our topology[¶] are described next.

---

* A functional process is a unique set of data movements (entry, exit, read, write) implementing a cohesive set of functional user requirements. It is triggered directly, or indirectly via an "actor," by an event (type) and is complete when it has executed all that is required in response to the triggering event (type) (Abran et al. 2003, p. 8).

† In terms of a cognitive approach, in this case, the measurer must use inference to identify new problems. Rieger (1975) recommends sixteen general classes of inference.

‡ A developer can help the measurer to better understand software models, but for the purposes of measurement, it is still the understanding and interpretation of the measurer that are of primary importance.

§ Its vocabulary and its system of classifying the words used (e.g., the layer is more generic than the boundary, which is more generic than the process).

¶ Topology: The art of, or method for, assisting the memory by associating the thing or subject to be remembered with a place.

Mapping

Step 1a: On the basis of the requirements and specifications relating to the interaction between the equipment and the software, the measurer must detect whether or not there is more than one layer, and he must formally identify it (or them, if more than one).

Step 1b: On the basis of the requirements and specifications relating to the interaction between the equipment and the software, the measurer must identify the users.

Step 2: On the basis of the requirements and specifications relating to the interaction between the equipment and the software, the measurer must identify the boundary of the software.

Step 3a: From the requirements, the measurer must identify all the functional processes of the software.

Step 3b: From the requirements, the measurer must identify all the triggers[*] of the software.

Step 3c: From the requirements, the measurer must identify all the functional groups of software data.

Measuring

Step 4:[†] Subprocesses (4a = input, 4b = output, 4c = read, 4d = write) must be identified for each software functional process.

Step 5: The functional size of the software is derived from the aggregation of the measurement results, e.g., by adding the subprocesses. Because this operation is strictly arithmetic, no particular expertise is required; it is thus not included within the scope of this paper.

Based on these steps, it is possible to create a topology of problems encountered by the measurer (Figure 2.27). There can be multiple types of problems within each block the measurer must seek to solve.

Each type of problem in this topology is referred to as a case problem in CBR terminology. The topology helps to locate the various case problems encountered by the measurer. It should also be noted that there is a hierarchy in the topology of the case problems in Figure 2.28. A case problem at step 1 is more generic than a case problem at step 2, and so on.

This topology, linked to the measurer's path, enables us to propose a diagnostic procedure providing the measurer with typical solutions to different measurement problems, and doing so in a coherent way. It is not the only possible topology, nor

---

[*] The trigger event could also be studied at the subprocess level, because the trigger event could be considered to be at the same level as the other subprocesses. We chose to look at the trigger event at the process level, since it is used specifically to identify the processes.

[†] Step 4 refers to four different problems: identification of entry, exit, read, and write. We grouped them together to simplify our representation in the schema.

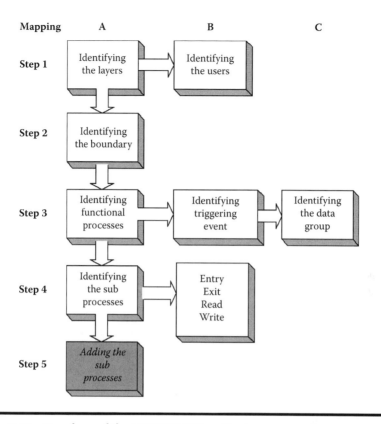

Figure 2.27 Topology of the COSMIC FFP method.

is it necessarily yet a complete one, for the measurer's practice, but rather a starting point. The encounter, and resolution, of new case problems can enrich this topology when there is a feedback mechanism that permits registering the knowledge being built in the problem resolution process.

The proposed diagnostic procedure is as follows:

■ The measurer must identify the nature of the problem. He might also have to identify additional problems related to the nature of the initial problem identified, if there is more than one problem.

■ The diagnostic tool locates case problem(s) using the topology and heuristic formula.

■ For each case problem, the measurer answers the appropriate questions in order to best understand and interpret the problem.

■ The specific answers proposed for the questions will lead to a proposed solution.

■ A proposed solution can lead to another case problem and, with relevant complementary information, contribute to the identification of a typical solution. It can also lead to a new problem and the identification of a relevant solution.

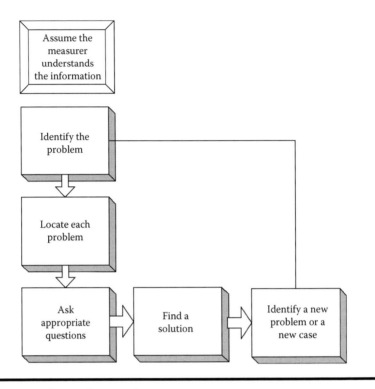

Figure 2.28 Diagnostic procedure.

Research work has begun to implement such a diagnostic procedure by using a cognitive tool, and to demonstrate how it works based on the two examples described earlier. In this initial work, a key difficulty is how to identify what was referred to as an appropriate question in the diagnostic of a measurement problem. Of course, measurers with a lot of experience are better positioned in identifying appropriate questions, while beginners cannot benefit from extensive previous experience. A strategy to help beginners in measurement is to make available to them the expertise of experts through classical expert-based systems, including those referred to as case-based reasoning (CBR) systems (Abran et al. 2004).

2.3.4 Experimentation with a Cognitive Diagnostic Tool (Help CPR)

2.3.4.1 What Is a Case-Based Reasoning (CBR) Tool?

In the cognitive field, a CBR system is referred to as a tool that "is able to utilize the specific knowledge of previously experienced, concrete problem situations (cases). A new problem is solved by finding a similar past case, and reusing it in the new problem situation…. CBR is also an approach to incremental, sustained learning, since a new experience is retained each time a problem has been solved, making it immediately available for future problems" (Aamodt and Plaza 1994, p.34).

The four phases of the CBR cycle are as follows (Figure 2.29):

- *Retrieve* the most similar case or cases that will help solve the problem.
- *Reuse* the information and knowledge from that case to solve the problem.
- *Revise* the proposed solution.
- *Retain* the parts of this case likely to be useful in future problem solving.

A new type of problem is solved by retrieving one or more previously experienced cases, reusing the case in one way or another, revising the solution based on reusing a previous case, and retaining the useful parts of the new case and incorporating them into the existing knowledge base (case base). Unless the retrieved case

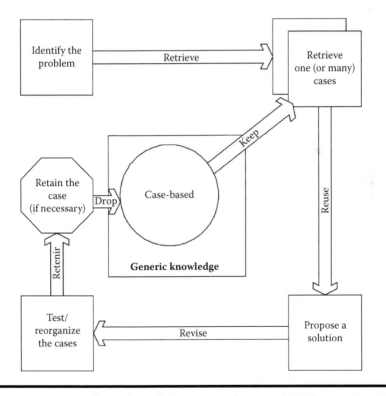

Figure 2.29 CBR cycle. (Adapted from Aamodt, A. and E. Plaza. 1994. Case-based reasoning: Foundational issues, methodological variations, and system approaches. *AI Communications,* **7: 27–34; and Watson, I. 1997.** *Applying Case-Based Reasoning: Techniques for Enterprise Systems.* **UK: University Press.)**

is very close to the solution required, the measurer may wish to repeat the process until a more satisfying solution is found.

Prior to discussing how a CBR tool can be useful to a measurer, the following concepts in CBR terminology are briefly discussed:

■ What is a case?
■ What is the relationship between the measurer's problems and the cases?

For Kolodner (1993), a case in a CBR is a contextualized piece of knowledge representing an experience.

According to our interpretation of several authors' works (Jackson 1998; Knauf et al. 1999; St.-Pierre et al. 1996), a case includes:

■ A description of the situation (the problem encountered) surrounding the case
■ Questions, based on the situation, that describe potential solutions that have already been recorded for the case (generally in the form of probabilities)
■ A result that provides an indication of the solution

In the context of software functional size measurement, the steps and sub-steps in the problem topology constitute the cases for the measurer. When a measurer has a problem with the application of the measurement method in a specific instance, and he is investigating how to solve it, the measurer, using such a proposed diagnostic tool, must answer a number of questions identified as relevant to the nature of the problem he recognized as applicable to his context of measurement. The result proposed then by the diagnostic tool is either a solution or a new case problem.

How can a tool like a CBR be useful for the measurer?

The use of a CBR embodies a number of assumptions, according to Kolodner (1993):[*]

■ Regularity: The world is essentially a regular and predictable place. The same actions performed under the same conditions will normally have the same (or very similar) outcomes.
■ Typicality: Events tend to be repeated. Thus, a CBR system's experiences are likely to be useful in the future.
■ Consistency: Small changes in the world require only small changes to our reasoning, and so correspondingly small changes are needed to our solutions.

---

[*] See also Watson (1997, p. 200).

The application of a measurement method exhibits these characteristics, and by definition, measurement standards require regularity; moreover, the same case problem (or similar ones) recurs on a regular basis in various contexts.

2.3.4.2 The CBR and the Diagnostic Procedure

We present in Figure 2.30 the parallel we have established between the CBR approach (on the left in Figure 2.30) and the diagnostic procedure (on the right-hand side); the links that can be found between the two approaches are also identified in Figure 2.30.

In the context of experimenting with the use of a diagnostic procedure for cognitive issues in software functional size measurement, the CBR-related tool sold by the firm Haley Enterprises, Help CPR, was selected.

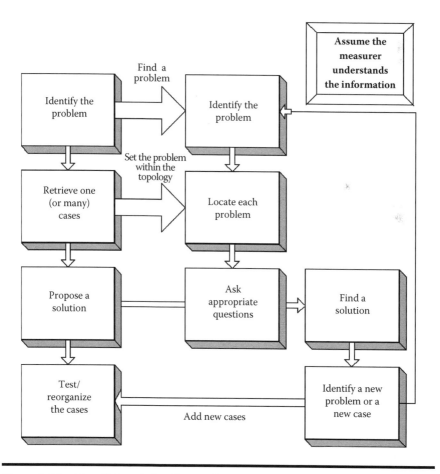

Figure 2.30   The CBR and the diagnostic procedure.

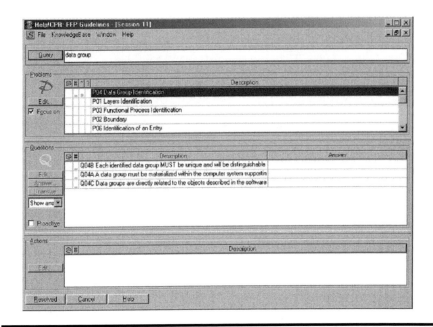

Figure 2.31   Help CPR user interface.

2.3.4.3   *Functional Description of Help CPR, a CBR Tool*

Help CPR has a menu, making it possible to open and back up several databases in Microsoft Access format (Figure 2.31). Help CPR organizes information on the cases into three distinct types of objects: problems, questions, and actions. A fourth type of object is the query. The cases are created by interconnecting these types of objects. It is not necessary to have the object action for the resolution of a case, but all the other objects are essential.

It is possible to assign (via the expert interfaces[*]) information on the problem level (object problems) or action level (object actions), but not on the question level (object questions). This assignment is the equivalent of a hypertext reference.

It is possible to choose a particular problem by using the function or object query, entering a keyword or sentence. Help CPR connects the identified problem and the cases in the case base. It then suggests one or many problems to solve. For example, while entering the term *data group* and the object query, one finds in the object problems the problem relating to the data group.

Automatically, in the object questions, the questions relating to this problem appear. The measurer must then enter a response. The answers provide possible solutions related to the problem to be solved. In this tool, the color green on the left

---

[*] We do not present the Help CPR expert interfaces here. These are described in Desharnais (2000).

indicates a positive answer, while the color red indicates a negative answer. It is also possible to suggest an action according to the nature of the answers to the questions. The action can point to some other keywords to add to the knowledge base.

What is the link between Help CPR and the CBR approach? The object query in Help CPR corresponds to the identification of the problem. The problems in the object problems list correspond to cases found in the topology (Figure 2.32). The result (green or red bar) appears on the screen (left side of the object problems) as the user answers questions (object questions) corresponding to suggestions for a solution. New questions are added and tested manually via the expert interfaces (not described here).

2.3.4.4 Illustration of Help CPR Usage

The use of Help CPR in the implementation of our proposed diagnostic procedure is illustrated using the two examples presented earlier.

The diagnostic procedure can be summarized as follows:

- Identify the nature of the problem.
- Locate case problem using the topology and heuristic formula.
- Use the appropriate questions to probe a problem.
- Find a solution.
- Identify a new problem or a new case, if necessary.

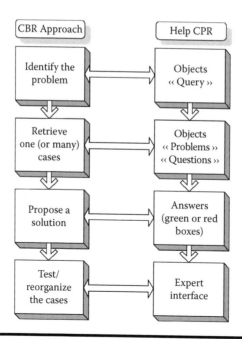

Figure 2.32   Links between Help CPR and the CBR approach.

Example 1 (Reminder)

The user asks for permission to question a provider's database to obtain a list of the articles purchased in the past month from a specific provider. Measurement of the size of this process involves (based on the data available) a knowledge or understanding of:

- The release process modality
- The results of the process or the group of data read
- The validations and possible results of the validations

For this example, the measurer needs to identify the nature of the problem. For each problem identified, the measurer applies the five activities of the diagnostic procedure. For example, the nature of the first problem is the identification of the process, which is step 3a in the topology of the COSMIC FFP method. Appendix A shows seven case problems related to identification of the process, identification of the trigger event, etc. For this particular example, each case problem is at the level of the topology, but in the diagnostic tool the case problem will most probably be at a lower level. The third activity is about answering the questions to determine if what the measurer can understand and interpret from the documentation indeed represents a process. The next activity is coming from the diagnostic tool that suggests a solution, and the proposed solution comes from the heuristics of the tool provided by the expert. Finally, this could lead to the identification of a new problem. For instance, after having identified a process, it is necessary to identify next its first subprocesses or the trigger event.

Example 2 (Reminder)

It is not necessary for the measurer to go through all the various levels of the topology every time. In the first example, the questions were at the level of steps 3 and 4 of the topology. In the second example, however, the questions start at step 1.

In the CBR diagnostic tool used, the questions do not necessarily follow in the same order, and the formulation can be different. This is why they have been numbered differently. There is a distinction, then, between the formulation of the problem by the user and its formulation in the tool. This is because it is possible to use problems in one example for another example. The experts try to generalize the typical problems (e.g., there are a limited number of questions required to identify an entry). This, of course, requires further investigation.

2.3.4.5 Some Limitations of Help CPR and Future Research

The version of the CBR tool used had the following limitations:

- The current system makes it possible to follow, only up to a point, the cognitive path of the user. These limitations will need to be better understood to evaluate the efficiency of the cognitive tool and improve it.

■ The interface explaining the "why" of the answers is not available. If the measurer were to know why the expert provided a specific answer in the diagnostic tool, he could understand himself the cognitive path of the expert when measuring, and he could learn faster and increase his own level of measurement expertise.

Further research: Our purpose was to identify some of the cognitive issues in the measurement of software and the when going from a software documentation, then through all the cognitive steps required to solve the measurement problem to tackle on such a complex intellectual product. In this context, we initiated an investigation on how a CBR approach could help as a diagnostic tool to meet the cognitive needs of the measurer.

We did not tackle in this paper the expert interfaces; several interfaces are already present in Help CPR that we did not describe here for simplicity sake. Further research is required on the cognitive issues relating to these interfaces. There is also a need to analyze the distinction to be made between the formulation of the problem by the user and the formulation of the problem by the expert (as formulated and subsequently structured and recorded in a CBR tool).

The effectiveness of this tool when used by novice measurers also needs to be investigated. More research will be necessary to improve the actual topology and the different concepts related to the concept of topology.

2.3.5   Conclusion

Application of a software functional measurement method is an intellectual process carried out on a complex abstract artifact: this process includes both a mapping phase between the measurement model and the software model, and a measurement phase for the instantiation of the measurement rules to the derived mapping model.

The measurer must go through the following cognitive steps to address this measurement process: he must *understand* the software to be measured, then he must *interpret* its meaning in order to accurately *identify* what is to be measured, and finally, he must *use* the rules of the measurement method and the rules of numerical assignment in order to arrive at the measurement solution.

To tackle these cognitive issues, we proposed a cognitive approach: a diagnostic procedure that follows the case-based reasoning cycle approach linked to a topology based on the measurement method. From there, we illustrated the use of a diagnostic tool to help the measurer solve a specific functional measurement problem. Finally, with a CBR type tool, a measurement expert can enrich this topology, at the time of its use, when there is a feedback mechanism that permits registering the knowledge being built in the problem resolution process.

Appendix A: Problem Diagnostic: Examples

Example 1

Problem 1

A. Identification of the problem: Is this a process?
B. Location of each problem in the topology: Step 3a.
C. Questions: The measurer must ask questions to identify the process and to identify whether or not the function described corresponds to the definition of a process.
D. Result: The trigger event must be identified as being a single one, and conform to the definition of a trigger event. The process must be identified as corresponding to the definition of a process.
E. Identification of a new problem: It will also be necessary to identify the trigger event and subprocess.

Problem 2

A. Identification of the problem: Identification of the trigger event.
B. Locate of each problem in the topology: Step 3b.
C. Questions: The measurer must ask questions to identify the trigger event.
D. Result (or action): The trigger event is identified as being a single one, and conforms to the definition of a trigger event.

Problem 3

A. Identification of the problem: Identification of the group of data.
B. Location of each problem in the topology: Step 3c.
C. Questions: Does each group of identified data conform to the definition of a group of data?
D. Result (or action): The group of data is identified.

Problem 4

A. Identification of the problem: Identification of the entry.
B. Location of each problem in the topology: Step 4.
C. Questions: The measurer must ask questions to identify the entry.
D. Result (or action): Each entry is identified as being a single one, and conforms to the definition of an entry.

Problem 5

A. Identification of the problem: Identification of the group of data read.
B. Location of each problem in the topology: Step 4.

C. Questions: The measurer must ask questions to identify the groups of data read.

D. Result (or action): Each group of data read is identified as being a single one, and conforms to the definition of a group of data read.

Problem 6

A. Identification of the problem: Identification of the groups of data written.

B. Location of each problem in the topology: Step 4.

C. Questions: The measurer must ask questions to identify the groups of data written.

D. Result (or action): Each group of data written is identified as being a single one, and conforms to the definition of a group of data written.

Problem 7

A. Identification of the problem: Identification of the exits.

B. Location of each problem in the topology: Step 4.

C. Questions: The measurer must ask questions to identify the exits.

D. Result (or action): Each exit is identified as being a single one, and conforms to the definition of a group of data exits.

Example 2

The second example involves several levels[*] of problems. The measurer tries to correctly identify a report generator and wishes to apply measurement rules for a report generator.

Problem (Level 1)

A. Identification of the problem: Identification of a report generator.

B. Location of each problem in the topology: Step 1 (or new element in the topology).

C. Question: To determine whether or not this report generator is based on the characteristics of a report generator.

D. Result (or action): An explanation of what a report generator is, and the referencing of another problem that will make it possible to direct the measurer to the report generator measurement. If this is not a report generator, or the probability of it being so is weak, the reasons why it is not a report generator are explained.

---

[*] By level, we simply mean that a more generic problem is at the first level, since a less generic problem is at a lower level. It is possible, in this specific case, to note the relation between the level of the problem and the different steps of the approach.

Problem (Level 2)

A. Identification of the problem: To identify each process of the report generator.
B. Location of each problem in the topology: Step 3.
C. Questions: To help identify the main processes (COSMIC FFP definition) of the report generator.
D. Result (or action): Each process is identified; moreover, to help in checking the results of the a report generator. These processes do not necessarily correspond to the processes identified by the measurer for this particular case, but the reference document serves as a reminder.

2.4 A System of Reference for Software Measurements with ISO 19761 (COSMIC FFP)

Adel Khelifi, Alain Abran, and Luigi Buglione

2.4.1 Introduction

2.4.1.1 Measurement Concepts and Relevance

"Man is the measure of all things" (Protagoras 485 B.C.). Measurement is an integral part of any human activity: social, economic, industrial, academic, environmental, medical, etc. Ubiquitous in our daily activities to provide an objective vision on quality, measurement has become a foundation for industrial, scientific, and social development.

Measurement plays an important part in science and in the engineering disciplines, as well as in our daily lives.

Can we imagine civil engineers constructing buildings and bridges without measurements being taken before and after the construction phase, people buying clothes without measuring their size, spectators attending events without knowing their duration, or more dangerously, pharmacists filling drug prescriptions without measurements? By contrast, no measurement used represents the state of practice in software development, even though there exists a large body of knowledge about software measurement (Buglione and Abran 2004; ISO 2001), notwithstanding the fact that the domain is relatively new and not yet mature.

Nowadays, organizations are in a situation where they must develop or renovate their software. Measurement can be a major analytical tool for better understanding and controlling the development and maintenance of software costs. For implementing changes prudently, measurement is of considerable importance, as it is for controlling expenses, deadlines, and performances. Thirty years ago, software measurement was an area for creative thinking confined to university researchers and industrial engineering, with one of the first papers on the subject probably by Rubey and Hartwick (1968). However, since the end of the 1970s, software measurement has been widely recommended. According to Zuse (1991, 1998), the concept of measurement is discussed or referred to, in one way or another, at a majority of software engineering conferences.

The need for measurement has also been explicitly recognized in the IEEE's own definition of software engineering (IEEE Std. 610.12-1990, p.12): "The application of a systematic, disciplined, quantifiable approach to the development, operation, and maintenance of software; that is, the application of engineering to software." The term *quantifiable* positions measurement as an integral part of software engineering and not simply an add-on.

According to Fenton and Pfleeger (1996; Fenton et al. 1998), software is a physical entity that can be measured by its size, since physical objects are easily measurable. Also according to these authors, the software size measurement operation should be easy. However, software size measurement presents many difficulties, and this is because the concepts of effort, functionality, and complexity related to software measurements have neither agreed upon boundaries nor precise definitions. Fenton and Pfleeger suggest that software size can be described by three attributes: length, complexity, and functionality. In this paper, we focus on the measurement of the functionality attribute of software size, known as software functional size measurement (FSM).

Even though over the past thirty years there has been considerable progress in software engineering, including a large number of proposals for measures and metrics, measurement is still not widely used. Software measurement is still emerging as a field of knowledge, and most often, traditional quality criteria of measurement methods, such as repeatability, reproducibility, accuracy, and convertibility, are not even investigated by software measurement designers.

In software engineering, the FSM community has been the first to recognize the importance of such measurement criteria, as illustrated in the recently adopted ISO/IEC TR 14143-3 (ISO 2002b). These criteria, however, represent only a subset of the metrology criteria, which include, for instance, measurement units and *etalons* (an international material standard used for traceability to internationally recognized measurement references).

There is not yet a system of reference for software measurement, and it is not even discussed in the software engineering literature. Even the FSM methods recognized by the ISO do not yet have such a system, with the exception of a few illustrative case studies.

A system of reference for software FSM would provide a professional framework for software measurers and contribute to the evolution of software engineering measurement. International official recognition of a system of reference for software engineering measurement is of particular interest to both industry and researchers. The goal of this research project is to design, for the first time in software engineering, a system of reference for software FSM results.

In this paper, a design is proposed for building a set of normalized baseline measurement references for one specific FSM method, that is, COSMIC FFP (ISO/

IEC 19761:2003 (ISO 2003d)), the second generation of FSM methods. Such a design could contribute to providing measurement results, the accuracy of which would be directly traceable to it.

2.4.1.2 Research Motivation and Research Issue

The motivation for this research is the need for traceable and widely recognized measurement references in software measurement, as in any other human endeavor with respect to measurement. The following set of simple questions highlight some of the major general measurement-related issues:

- How can you be sure the air temperature is 70°F, by watching the weather bulletin on TV?
- Is this the exact temperature? What temperature is being presented?
- Does it include the wind factor? Was it measured near the coast, or at high altitude?

In mature areas of measurement, the answers to such questions are derived by traceability to widely recognized measurement references with well-documented measurement properties. In mature disciplines of engineering, a result of measurement is accepted if it is traceable to one or more references. We always wonder who is providing this result and to what it is referenced. A measurement result always relates to a system of reference.

A number without a system of reference is not a measurement result, but simply an assertion. Similarly, an evaluation of cost only applies to that which expresses it, at the time when it expresses it, and according to its system of reference. Just look at the endless discussions and debates that cannot come to a mutually agreed upon conclusion if the speakers' systems of reference are different.

That is why, in any discussion, it is necessary to fix the references used; otherwise, it becomes difficult to reach conclusions acceptable to all participants. An example of such a system of measurement references is provided by the International System of Units. Such a measurement system provides a framework of international coherence and provides universal access to knowledge, good practices, feedback from experience, and reference documents.

The development of an international software measurement system of reference documented in a widely recognized system can have a far-reaching impact; for instance, many measurement reference systems within the regulatory and monetary systems contribute to managing some fundamental aspects of our daily lives.

Section 2.4.2 introduces related work about standardization in measurement, including the measurement of software functional size, as well as our research goals and objectives. Section 2.4.3 discusses related metrology concepts, the liaison method for recognizing references, and the design of the research methodology. Section 2.4.4 presents the expected research outcomes in terms of design and verification criteria. Finally, Section 2.4.5 summarizes the industrial impact of such a reference system, as well as suggestions for further work.

2.4.2 Related Work

2.4.2.1 Background on Measurement Standards

Measurement is one of the key concepts contributing to the maturation of engineering disciplines. Measurement, an intellectual construction, is ubiquitous in most human beings' activities. For example, the earliest measurements of distance were derived from the lengths of body members. By 3,000 years ago B.C., there were well-documented standard measurements for the exchange of goods among cities and nations. While there has been a diversity of standards for measuring the concept of distance, it took over 4,800 years following the height of (demise of?) classical Egyptian civilization for the design and acceptance of a standard measurement "for all nations and all times," as defined in the Metre Convention (BNM 2010) and which we now know as the meter.

In the late nineteenth century, other international standards for measures were created:

- The kilogram as the unit of mass. Equal to the mass of the international prototype of the kilogram.
- The second as the unit of time. Currently equal to the duration of 9,192,631,770 periods of radiation corresponding to the transition between the two hyperfine levels of the ground state of the caesium 133 atom.
- The Kelvin as the unit of thermodynamic temperature. Currently equal to the fraction 1/273.16 of the thermodynamic temperature of the triple point of water (BNM 2010).

2.4.2.2 Functional Size Measurement (FSM)

Allan Albrecht (1979) from IBM identified in the 1970s the need for an FSM method independent of the programming languages and techniques used to develop software. Therefore, he designed a method referred to as function point analysis (FPA). Albrecht's design was based on the functionalities delivered to users. From his initial FPA method, subsequent improvements have been proposed over the years, including the one by the Common Software Measurement International Consortium (COSMIC[*]). Indeed, FSMs can be applied early in the life cycle, helping to build estimation models for calculating the effort required to develop the software; of course, they can also be applied at the end of the development phase, helping managers to build software productivity models, as well as to compare the productivity of two software projects using such measurement results.

---

[*] http://www.cosmicon.com.

The initial Albrecht FPA method led, however, to a number of distinct interpretations, as discussed in ISO (2002b), Jones (1991), and Paton and Abran (1995). In addition, researchers have documented a number of theoretical weaknesses (ISO 2001; Jacquet and Abran 1998; Jones 1997), as well as a lack of generalization across functional domains.

2.4.2.3   The ISO 14143 Series of FSM Standards

When FPA was proposed in the mid-1990s as a candidate ISO standard, the ISO experts selected a more encompassing strategy to address some of the fundamental measurement requirements for the acceptance of FSM methods by the international standardization community. ISO 14143 was developed by ISO Working Group 12 (JTC1/SC7/WG12), and is now a six-part project providing an internationally accepted set of standards and technical reports describing the concepts of interest to designers and users of FSM methods:

- ISO 14143-1 Part 1: Definition of Concepts (ISO 1998). This part of ISO/IEC 14143 defines the fundamental concepts of FSM, promoting consistent interpretation of FSM principles.
- ISO 14143-2 Part 2: Conformity Evaluation of Software Size Measurement Methods (ISO, 2001). This part of ISO/IEC 14143 was developed to provide a process for checking whether or not a candidate FSM method conforms to the provisions of ISO/IEC 14143-1:1998. The output from this process can assist prospective users of the candidate FSM method in judging whether or not it is appropriate to their needs.
- ISO TR 14143-3 Part 3: Verification of FSM Methods (ISO 2002b). This part verifies whether or not an FSM method meets the quality characteristics of a measurement method, which are repeatability and reproducibility, accuracy, convertibility, discrimination threshold, and applicability to functional domains. It defines various ways by which the usefulness of a method can be determined.
- ISO TR 14143-4 Part 4: Reference Model (ISO 2000). This part provides standard reference user requirements (RURs). Its purpose is to assess an FSM method against some standard reference points to determine whether or not it yields expected results in a given situation.
- ISO 14143-5 Part 5: Determination of Functional Domains for Use with FSM (ISO 2004). This technical report describes the properties and characteristics of functional domains, and the principle procedures by which characteristics of FURs can be used to determine functional domains.
- ISO TR 14143-6 Part 6: The Guide for the Use of the ISO/IEC 14143 Series and Related International Standards (ISO 2003a). This part is currently under development, at the WD stage.

It must be stressed that the ISO 14143 standard series does not define an FSM method, but presents the characteristics for a measurement method to be recognized as an ISO FSM method.

Once the generic ISO FSM standards had been adopted, four specific FSM methods were submitted to ISO, demonstrating their conformity to the mandatory features expressed in ISO 14143-1, and were recognized as international standards:

- ISO 19761: 2003. COSMIC FFP—An FSM Method (ISO 2003d).
- ISO 20926: 2003. Function Point Analysis (ISO 2003b) (Note: Only the unadjusted portion of FPA is recognized as conforming to ISO 14143-1.)
- ISO 20968: 2002. MK II Function Point Analysis (ISO 2002c), from UKSMA.
- ISO 24570: 2004. NESMA FSM Method Version 2.1 (ISO 2003c, 2005) (to be published, current status DIS*).

2.4.2.4   ISO 19761 Standard (COSMIC FFP)

In this paper, the COSMIC FFP standard (ISO 2003d) has been selected for illustrative purposes; this FSM method is referred to as a second-generation FSM method and addresses some of the major weaknesses found in first-generation FSM methods, such as:

- Practical limitations, such as weak relevance for many software types (e.g., real-time software and multilayered software, as in telecom applications and operating systems)
- Theoretical weaknesses, including, for instance, mathematical operations related to the numerical scale types

The COSMIC FFP method is based on the analysis of software FURs, broken down into subprocesses and data movements. In the COSMIC FFP method, software users include all types of users who exchange data with the software, including human beings, equipment, and other software; first-generation FSM methods, by comparison, which focus on human users, are often not even present in much embedded software that interacts only with engineering devices such as sensors and monitoring equipment. It should be noted that the definition of users in COSMIC conforms to ISO 14143-1.

The COSMIC FFP measurement method involves applying a set of models, rules, and procedures to a given piece of software as it is perceived from the perspective of its FURs. The result of the application of these models, rules, and procedures is a numerical value representing the functional size of the software, as measured

---

* Refer to http://www.iso.ch/iso/en/widepages/stagetable.html, with the codes identifying the approval stage within ISO committees.

from its FURs. In COSMIC FFP, the symbol Cfsu (COSMIC functional size unit) represents the quantitative value of the software functional size.

Last, but not least, the COSMIC FFP method is based on solid theory and decades of international experience. "It has been designed from the outset both to comply with the ISO standard for FSM (ISO 14143) and to be compatible with modern ways of specifying requirements (e.g., use cases and prototyping)" (SMS 2010, p.4). This measurement method is applicable to many software types. It recognizes that modern software development uses components in various layers within software architecture, so it is possible to measure software layers that other methods cannot.

2.4.2.5 Research Goal and Objectives

A system of reference is a major input in decision-making models: it is required to organize, choose, communicate, and evaluate the necessary attributes of software FSMs. This research project is aimed at developing a first generation of a system of reference for FSM methods, on the basis of the metrology body of knowledge.

Two specific objectives are related to this research issue and will be pursued here:

■ How to design a system of reference for software FSM
■ How to make this system of reference available to the practitioner community to develop and implement professional measurement practices in software engineering

2.4.3 Research Methodology

As the design of a system of reference in software engineering had not yet been tackled, a key intermediate deliverable of this research has been the identification, within the domain of metrology knowledge, of the key concepts and techniques required to do so.

For the design of a system of FSM references, the liaison concept is the most relevant for ensuring the traceability of the initial unique universal measurement standards, and then the traceability of individual measurements to these unique standards. This section explains related metrology concepts and how to specify, interpret, and link them, and how to add a measurement reference to the system.

2.4.3.1 Related Metrology Concepts

Metrology and its standards facilitate the exchange of goods, support production automation, increase product quality, increase consumer trust, and improve living standards. The contributions of metrology have been significant to the development of international trade and the reduction of technical barriers to exchanging goods. Metrology is not only a particular discipline of the physical sciences, but it also forms the basis of many of our daily tasks (BNM 2010).

The process model in Figure 2.33 illustrates that measurement results come from a measuring instrument, which is calibrated (or not) with quantities and units, uses a standard of reference, and has some characteristics that limit its field of application.

While these concepts are well known in several fields, they are most often not discussed in software engineering: many of them are not embedded in the practices of software measurement designers, or of software engineering measurers themselves. Metrology-related concepts and terminology have only been introduced recently into the ISO software engineering community; similarly, only a few researchers Abran and Sellami, 2002 have focused on metrology concepts as applied to software engineering standards, including specific methods of measurement. A subset of these metrology-related concepts was first accepted in ISO 14143-3, and then in the ISO 15939 standard for software process measurement (ISO 2002a). More recently, the metrology terminology has been introduced into the development of the next version of the ISO series for the measurement of the quality of software products (ISO series 25000 in JTC1/SC7/WG6).

We investigate next how the use of some of these metrology concepts in the design of software engineering measurements could contribute to developing new measurement-related knowledge for both researchers and practitioners. Particular emphasis is devoted to knowing how to develop etalons for software measures. Of course, software being a complex intellectual construct, it cannot be taken for granted that software-related etalons are simple. Quite the contrary, software as an intellectual product can be quite complex, even within a dimension such as size, and building corresponding measurement standards for such an apparently simple concept can be quite challenging; for instance, it would be expected that a single measurement standard could not yet be achieved, and that most probably it requires a complete system of reference with examples of measurement results from software from many distinct functional domains.

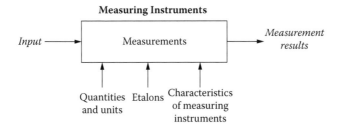

Figure 2.33   Process model of the categories of metrology terms. (From Abran, A. and A. Sellami 2002. Initial modeling of the measurement concepts in the ISO vocabulary of terms in metrology. *Software Measurement and Estimation*, Aachen, Germany: Shaker Publishing. With Permission.)

2.4.3.2   Liaison Method for Recognized References

A key challenge for this project was to figure out how to build measurement standards (e.g., etalons). The International Vocabulary of Metrology (VIM) (ISO 1993) documents a number of different types of measurement standards, ranging from international standards to secondary standards to traveling standards (Table 2.2). The VIM also documents a number of characteristics for the conservation of a measurement standard: traceability, calibration, reference material, and certified reference material. Each of these standards-related concepts can be considered design requirements in the establishment of a system of measurement references.

Once these requirements are identified, an approach must be found to tackle them. The liaison method as documented in (Abran and Sellami 2002) was selected as a relevant approach for the implementation of measurement standards (etalons). More specifically, the liaison of a measurement in a system of reference must allow for the linking of any measurement result to one or more recognized measurement references. The method involves four steps, as presented in Table 2.2. The four steps of the measurement liaison method, as adapted from Baize and Girard (1995), are:

1. Measurement specification. The optimal specification of a software measurement type requires:
   - Descriptions and analyses of existing measurements for this type of software
   - Description of the transitions between measurements
   - Minimal description of the software environment
   - Follow-up allowing better definition of measurement changes

Table 2.2   Detailed Topology of Measurement Standards/Etalons

(Measurement) Standard Etalon	Conservation of a (Measurement) Standard
International (Measurement) Standard	Traceability
National (Measurement) Standard	Calibration
Primary Standard	Reference Material (RM)
Secondary Standard	Certified Reference Material (CRM)
Reference Standard	
Working Standard	
Transfer Standard	
Travelling Standard	

2. Measurement interpretation compared to the system of reference. To interpret measurement results, the measurer draws from the body of knowledge of his professional environment and his personal experience. This interpretation depends on the system of reference and many elements of the measurement process.

3. Liaison with the system. The liaison binds a measurement result to one or more references and then gives the measurement the corresponding name. This is done by technical reasoning, which is in the same order as measurement interpretation. The liaison is a flexible system that requires the study of the resemblance between a measurement and the references. To analyze this resemblance, we can use statistical concepts and methods, such as multidimensional analysis. There exist both simple and multiple liaisons.

4. Addition of a new reference. If a measurement is far from all the references defined previously, we can add it to the system as a new reference. It is always possible to do this, as long as we do not affect system coherence. In the same way, it is possible to announce the existence of new types. However, in order to avoid confusion, any proposal for the creation of a new reference has to go through a preliminary detailed study and be argued in order to maintain general coherence.

2.4.3.3   Research Steps

The following steps were identified as required to design an FSM system of reference:

■ Step 1: We use some of the key outputs derived from the ISO standardization work on FSM, that is, a specific measurement method adopted as ISO 19761(COSMIC FFP).

■ Step 2: We use some of the key outputs derived from the ISO standardization work on FSM, in particular, both the verification procedures from ISO TR 14143-3 and the RURs documented in ISO TR 14143-4, none of which, to our knowledge, have yet been used by industry or by researchers.

■ Step 3: We integrate some of the concepts from three different tracks: metrology concepts, International System of Units definitions, and a methodology described in the field of pedology (the scientific study of the soil), for the definition of a *démarche de rattachement*, which is referred to here as a liaison method. This method will, of course, be transposed and adapted to the software measurement context.

Figure 2.34 presents these steps within our initial approach to the design of a system of reference.

These three sets of inputs are used next for the design of the system of reference itself. The output of this design process will be the integration and synthesis of a system of reference for FSM using COSMIC FFP as a case study.

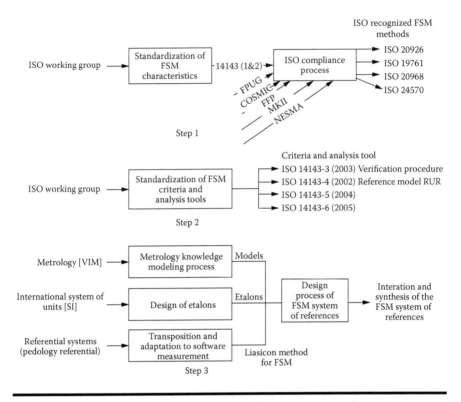

Figure 2.34 Initial approach to the design of an FSM system of references.

2.4.4 Design of the System of Reference

The design process for our FSM system of reference includes both a verification process, to ensure the quality of the measurement results, and a catalog (i.e., repository), to keep track of measurement results and their traceability to the inputs for these measurement results.

2.4.4.1 Verification Process

The application of an FSM method still currently depends on individual measurers' interpretations, either self-learned or derived from particular cases provided by a diversity of trainers. Almost perfect measurement results would require a number of concurrent measurement conditions, such as:

- A perfect measurement method
- A perfect measurement process
- A perfect entry to the measuring process that is not affected by any "noise"*

---

* In a statistical meaning.

If such concurrent conditions existed, then the measurement results under perfect conditions would be the same.

However, in software engineering practices, such ideal measurement conditions are seldom observed, the four main causes for differences in measurement results being:

- Errors in the manual process of measuring
- Imperfections in the automatic measurement tool (Giles and Daich 1995)
- Defects in the measurement method itself
- Imperfect entries to the measurement process

Of course, each of these main causes can be broken down into one or more subcauses, depending on the circumstances or on the context of measurement. To build an optimal system of reference would require that all perfect measurement conditions indicated above be present. The building of a system of reference will necessarily be iterative for the progressive elimination of most of the sources of errors.

Since this has not yet been done in software engineering measurement, it would be unreasonable to expect to produce perfect measurement results at the first attempt: several iterations will be required to eliminate the causes of errors. To populate the catalog initially, some concurrent redundant measurement procedures will be carried out, such as:

- Several people taking several measurements of the same RUR, in order to detect manual errors
- Several automated measurements being carried out with an experimental prototype of the automation of COSMIC FFP in the Rational Rose environment (Azouz and Abran 2004)

In order to analyze and compare the measurement results of the same RUR, results will be verified using the procedure and criteria specified in ISO 14143-3: repeatability and reproducibility, accuracy, convertibility, discrimination threshold, and applicability to functional domains. Figure 2.35 illustrates this verification process.

Of course, it is expected that refinements will be required to the application of these principles and to our initial design of the system of reference for software measurements.

This project will benefit from the direct collaboration of experts from industry. The objective is to define software measurement references and a common language for them.

The participation of some experts from the ISO/IEC JTC1/SC7/WG12 working group will provide greater credibility.

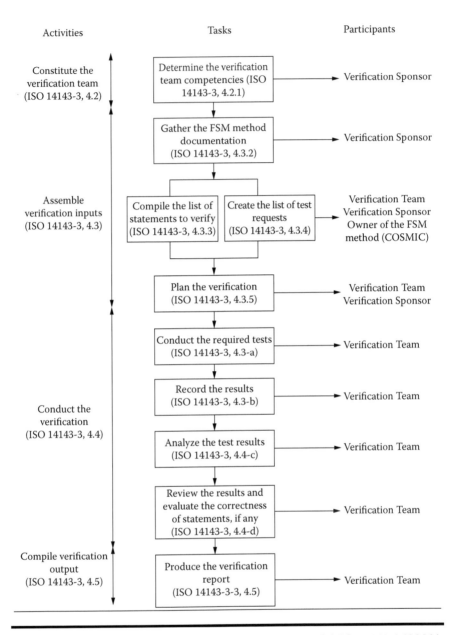

Figure 2.35 Verification Process. (From ISO. 1998. ISO/IEC 14143-1:1998(e). International Organization for Standardization, Geneva, Switzerland: ISO Publication. With Permission.)

2.4.4.2   A Catalog of Measurement Results

The measurement results coming from the application of the COSMIC FFP method to the reference sets of FURs documented in ISO 14143-4 will be cataloged into a computer-based documentation system. Each of these ISO sets contains a number of RURs describing requirements of samples of a management information system and real-time software. These RURs represent the inputs to the measurement process described in Figures 2.35 and 2.36 The catalog for this system of measurement references must include not only the measurement results, but also, for traceability purposes, the inputs to the measurement process. This context of ISO standardization adds relevance and legitimacy to this selection of case studies for our system of reference, the purpose of such a system of reference being to leverage and codify years of international experience.

This design, which includes both a verification process and a catalog, is illustrated in Figure 2.36.

2.4.4.3   Evolution of the System of Reference

Of course, the system of reference will not be perfect initially, and will require an iterative cycle of improvements. Figure 2.37 illustrates the iterative maintenance of the system of reference.

2.4.5   Observations

Software measurement is still emerging as a field of knowledge, and most often, traditional quality criteria of measurement methods, such as repeatability, reproducibility, accuracy, and convertibility, have not even been investigated by software measurement method designers. In software engineering, the FSM community was the first to recognize the importance of such quality criteria for measurement, as illustrated in the recently adopted ISO document 14143-3; however, these criteria represent only a subset of the metrology criteria, which include, for instance, measurement units and internationally recognized measurement references (e.g., etalons). In this paper, we discuss the need, and an approach, for building a system of reference using a specific FSM method, that is, COSMIC FFP (ISO 2003d).

This proposal of a system of reference for software FSM is a real challenge. Such a system of reference has to consider not only the specifications of functional requirements, but also the experts, comments, and current practices in industry with respect to software size measurement. A system of reference for software measurements will allow:

1. Researchers, users, and experts to have independently verified values for reference
2. Measurers to have confidence in the results of measurement
3. The software engineering industry to standardize the design of measurements and to verify the measurement tools

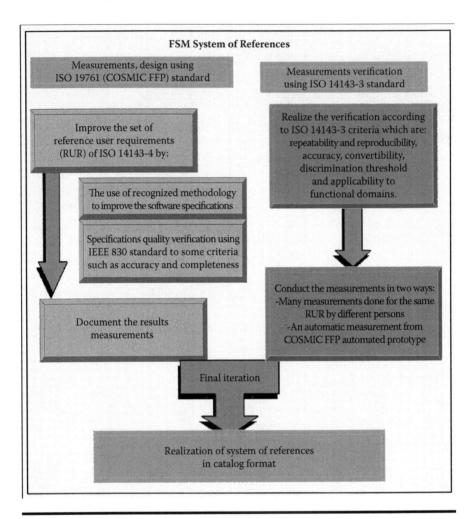

FSM System of References

Measurements, design using ISO 19761 (COSMIC FFP) standard

Measurements verification using ISO 14143-3 standard

Improve the set of reference user requirements (RUR) of ISO 14143-4 by:

Realize the verification according to ISO 14143-3 criteria which are: repeatability and reproducibility, accuracy, convertibility, discrimination threshold and applicability to functional domains.

The use of recognized methodology to improve the software specifications

Specifications quality verification using IEEE 830 standard to some criteria such as accuracy and completeness

Conduct the measurements in two ways:
-Many measurements done for the same RUR by different persons
-An automatic measurement from COSMIC FFP automated prototype

Document the results measurements

Final iteration

Realization of system of references in catalog format

Figure 2.36 Experimental methodology for the FSM COSMIC FFP system of references.

In spite of the seemingly high cost of its construction and exploitation, this system of reference could be quite beneficial if we compare it to the cost of project failures.

The content of this system of reference for software FSM could be used next as input for ISO software engineering working groups tackling the standardization of measurement methods of various types, and not only for FSM. A research result by-product will therefore be a set of suggestions for improving the international standards themselves, thereby contributing to the maturation of the software engineering discipline.

The realization of a system of reference could also contribute to the development of a theoretical analysis of measurement and to laying the foundations for a method of introducing into organizations, whether private or public, traceability of

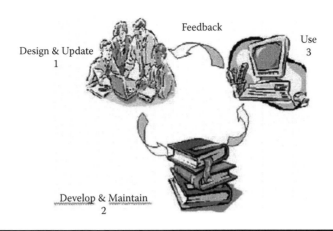

Figure 2.37 The System of References life cycle.

measurement results to international standards as codified in a system of software measurement references.

2.5 COSMIC FFP and Functional Complexity (FC) Measures: A Study of Their Scales, Units, and Scale Types

Manar Abu Talib, Alain Abran, and Olga Ormandjieva

2.5.1 Introduction

The COSMIC FFP (Abran and Symons 2005) functional size measurement method was developed by the Common Software Measurement International Consortium (COSMIC), and it has been adopted as an international ISO standard: ISO 1976 (ISO 2003d). COSMIC FFP measures the software functional user requirements and is applicable throughout the development life cycle, right from the requirements phase to the implementation and maintenance phases. This method has been designed to measure the functional size of management information systems, real-time software, and multilayer systems. Since many of the software systems targeted by the COSMIC FFP method are large-scale and inherently complex, feedback on this complexity would provide additional information to improve its effective management throughout the software life cycle: in Alagar et al. (2000) an entropy-based measure of functional complexity has been proposed.

This paper presents a study of the scales, units, and scale types of both COSMIC FFP and an entropy-based functional complexity measure. Previous studies have analyzed the scale types of many software measures (e.g., Zuse 1991; Fenton and

Pfleeger 1998; Whitmire 1997), but not the concept of scale or how it is used in the design of a measurement method. Well-designed and well-defined measures in sciences and engineering should have most of the many characteristics described in metrology (ISO 1993), including scales, units, and etalons, to which should refer measuring instruments to ensure meaningfulness of the numbers obtained from measurement. However, some of these concepts, such as units, scale, and etalons, are not yet addressed and discussed by researchers on empirical validation approaches (Fenton and Pfleeger 1996) of software measures: for instance, researchers on software measure have, to date, focused on scale types rather than on the scale embedded within the definitions of these measures. This could lead to less than optimally designed software measures. Moreover, when these software measures are analyzed without taking into account these metrological concepts, it can lead to improperly stated conclusions about their strengths.

In this paper, Section 2.5.2 presents the key elements of scale types, Section 2.5.3 the key elements of COSMIC FFP, and Section 2.5.4 the key elements of FC, an entropy-based measure of functional complexity measurement. In Sections 2.5.5 and 2.5.6, the scale, units, and scale types of both measures are investigated, and finally, a discussion and some future next steps are presented in Section 2.5.7.

2.5.2   Scale Types

In measurement theory, the meaning of numbers is characterized by scale types (Zuse 1991), but measurement theory does not address directly the concept of scale, as typically defined in metrology. A scale is defined as a set of ordered values, continuous or discrete, or a set of categories to which the attribute is mapped (ISO 2002a), whereas scale type depends on the nature of the relationship between values on the scale (ISO 2002a).

In a mathematical representation, a scale is defined by <E, N, Φ>, where E is the empirical structure, N is the numerical structure, and Φ is the mapping between them (Zuse 1991). On the other hand, a scale type is always defined by admissible transformations. Relationships between mappings are described in terms of transformations (Whitmire 1997). There are five major scale types: nominal, ordinal, interval, ratio, and absolute, which can be seen describing certain empirical knowledge behind the numbers (Whitmire 1997). Knowing the characteristics of each type helps to interpret the measures (Fenton and Pfleeger 1998). In the following subsections, the scale types are summarized.

2.5.2.1   Nominal Scale Type

The nominal scale measurement places elements in a classification scheme (Fenton and Pfleeger 1998; Whitmire 1997). The classification partitions the set of empirical entities into equivalence classes with respect to a certain attribute. Two entities are considered equivalent, and therefore belonging to the same equivalence class, if and only if they have the same amount of the attribute being measured. The empirical classes are jointly exhaustive and mutually exclusive. The classes are not ordered because of a lack of empirical knowledge about relationships among the classes. In nominal scale measurement, each empirical class might be represented by a unique number or symbol, and the only mathematical operation allowed in the nominal scale type is =. The admissible transformations are one-to-one mapping that preserve the partitioning.

2.5.2.2   Ordinal Scale Type

The ordinal scale type is the basis of software measurement. All other extended measurement structures are based on the ordinal scale (Zuse 1991). The ordinal scale assigns numbers or symbols to the objects so they may be ranked and ordered with respect to an attribute (Whitmire 1997). The characteristic of ordinal scales is that the numbers represent ranking only, so addition, subtraction, and other arithmetic operations have no meaning. Also, any mapping that preserves the ordering is acceptable as an ordinal scale (Fenton and Pfleeger 1998).

2.5.2.3   Interval Scale Type

The interval scale type is useful to augment the ordinal scale with information about the size of the intervals that separate the classes. That is, the difference in units between any two of the ordered classes in the range of the mapping is known, but computing the ratio of two classes in the range does not make sense. This scale type preserves order, as with an ordinal scale; however, in interval scales addition and subtraction are acceptable operations. Multiplication and division are not acceptable operations in this scale type (Fenton and Pfleeger 1998).

2.5.2.4   Ratio Scale Type

A ratio scale type is an interval scale with a ratio on which there exists an absolute zero. This zero element represents the smallest scale value, where an object has a null amount of the attribute. Therefore, the measurement mapping in ratio scale must start at zero and increase at equal intervals, known as units. All arithmetic in ratio scale can be meaningfully applied to the classes in the range of the mapping (Fenton and Pfleeger 1998).

2.5.2.5   Absolute Scale Type

An absolute scale type represents counts of objects in a specific class. There is only one possible measurement mapping, namely, the actual count, and a unique unit. As in ratio scale, all arithmetic analysis of the resulting count is meaningful (Abran and Robillard 1994). More details in these scale types can be found in Fenton and Pfleeger (1998), Whitmire (1997), and Zuse (1991).

2.5.3 COSMIC FFP Measurement Method

2.5.3.1 COSMIC FFP Overview

The COSMIC FFP method has been designed to measure the functional size of management information systems, real-time software, and multilayer systems. Its design conforms to all ISO requirements (ISO 14143-1 (ISO 1998)) for functional size measurement methods, and was developed to address some of the major weaknesses of the earlier method, that is, function points analysis (FPA; Abran 1994), the design of which dates back almost thirty years, when software was much smaller and much less varied. COSMIC FFP focuses on the user view of software functional requirements and is applicable throughout the development life cycle, right from the requirements phase to the implementation and maintenance phases. In the measurement of software functional size using the COSMIC FFP method, the software functional processes and their triggering events must be identified (ISO 2002a, 2003d).

In COSMIC FFP, the unit of measurement is a data movement, which is a base functional component that moves one or more data attributes belonging to a single data group. Data movements can be of four types: entry, exit, read, or write. The functional process is an elementary component of a set of user requirements triggered by one or more triggering events either directly or indirectly via an actor. The triggering event is an event occurring outside the boundary of the measured software and initiates one or more functional processes. The subprocesses of each functional process are sequences of events, and comprise at least two data movement types: an entry plus at least either an exit or a write. An entry moves a data group, which is a set of data attributes, from a user across the boundary into the functional process, while an exit moves a data group from a functional process across the boundary to the user requiring it. A write moves a data group lying inside the functional process to persistent storage, and a read moves a data group from persistent storage to the functional process. See Figure 2.38 for an illustration of the generic flow of data groups through software from a functional perspective.

The COSMIC FFP measurement method has two distinct phases: the mapping of the software to be measured to the COSMIC FFP generic software model and the measurement of specific aspects of this generic software model. The following subsections describe in more details these two phases, and they are summarized from COSMIC FFP manual version 2.2.

2.5.3.2 COSMIC FFP Mapping Phase

In all functional measurement methods, the functional size of software cannot be measured directly from the functional user requirements (FURs): certain rules and procedures are to be applied to FURs of software to produce a specific software model that is suitable for measuring functional size. That technique is referred to as

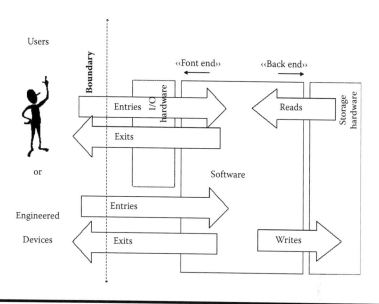

Figure 2.38 Generic flow of data groups through software from a functional perspective. (From ISO. 2003. Software engineering—COSMIC-FFP—A functional size measurement method. ISO/IEC 19761:2003 Geneva, Switzerland: International Organization for Standardization Publication. With Permission.)

a mapping phase in COSMIC FFP. The general method for mapping software to the COSMIC FFP generic model is described in Figure 2.39.

From Figure 2.39, before getting into the mapping phase, the measurer must define why the measurement is being undertaken and what the measurement result will be used for. That is called purpose of a measurement. The measurer also defines the scope of the measurement through the set of FURs to be included in a specific functional size measurement exercise. Finally, it is important for the measurer to identify the measurement view of the FURs of software. More definitions and principles regarding this context are provided in ISO (2002a).

The COSMIC FFP mapping phase takes the FURs of a piece of software as input to produce the COSMIC FFP generic model of that software as output. The question "Is there a need to size subsets of requirements?" will be raised as a first step in the mapping phase. That is because the FURs may apply to software in different layers or peer items. Therefore, the measurer needs to decide if the FUR or the software comprises one or more layers of peer items. A layer is a result of the functional partitioning of the software environment such that all included functional processes perform at the same level of abstraction (ISO 2002a). In a multilayer software environment, software in one layer exchanges data with software in another layer through their respective functional processes. It is to be

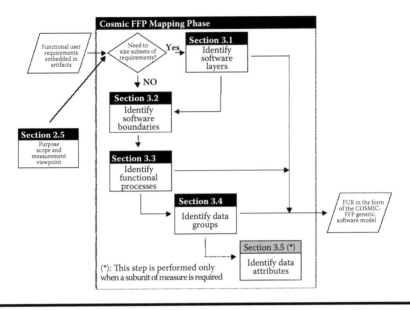

Figure 2.39 COSMIC FFP mapping phase. (From ISO. 2003. Software engineering—COSMIC-FFP—A functional size measurement method. ISO/IEC 19761:2003 Geneva, Switzerland: International Organization for Standardization Publication. With Permission.)

noted that the layer identification is an iterative process. The exact layer will be refined as the mapping process progresses.

After identifying the software layers, the measurer must identify the boundary of each piece of software. According to the COSMIC FFP manual (ISO 2002a), the boundary is defined as a conceptual interface between the software under measurement and its users (human beings, engineered devices, or other software). The boundary allows the measurer to distinguish what is included inside the measured software from what is part of the measured software's operating environment. The third step in the mapping phase is identifying the set of functional processes of the software to be measured from its FUR. A functional process is an elementary component of a set of FURs comprising a unique, cohesive, and independently executable set of data movements. It is triggered by one or more events either directly or indirectly via an actor. It is complete when it has executed all that is required to be done in response to the triggering event (type) (ISO 2002a). Once identified, each functional process can be registered on an individual line, under the appropriate layer, in the generic software model, under the corresponding label. Identifying the data groups referenced by the software to be measured is the fourth step in the mapping phase. A data group is a distinct, nonempty, nonordered, and nonredundant set of data attributes where each included data attribute describes a complementary aspect of the same object of interest (Abran and Symons 2005). A data attribute is the smallest parcel of information, within an identified data group, carrying a meaning from the perspective of the software's FURs (ISO 2002a), and that is what will be identified in the last step of this phase. A data group must contain at least one attribute, and might contain one data attribute if this is sufficient, from the perspective of the functional requirements, to describe the object of interest.

2.5.3.3 COSMIC FFP Measurement Phase

Measurement phase is the second phase considered in the COSMIC FFP method. As described in Figure 2.40, this phase takes the COSMIC FFP generic model of software as input and produces a value of a quantity the magnitude of which is directly proportional to the functional size of the model (ISO 2002a). For each functional process, the measurer needs to identify the data movements' sub-process types (entry, exit, read, and write types). That is the first step in this phase. Next, the measurement method applies the COSMIC FFP measurement

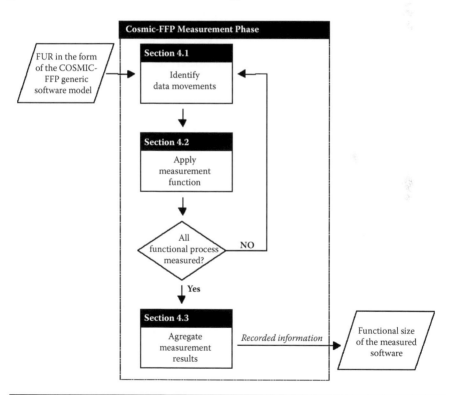

Figure 2.40   COSMIC FFP measurement phase. (From ISO. 2003. Software engineering—COSMIC-FFP—A functional size measurement method. ISO/IEC 19761:2003 Geneva, Switzerland: International Organization for Standardization Publication. With Permission.)

function to each data movement identified in each functional process. According to this measurement function, each instance of a data movement (entry, exit, read, or write) identified in step 1 receives a numerical size of 1 Cfsu. Finally, the measurer aggregates the results of the measurement function, as applied to all identified data movements, into a single functional size value, arithmetically adding them together (Equation 2.1).

$$\text{Size}_{\text{Cfsu}} \text{ (functional process}_i) = \sum \text{size(entries}_i) + \sum \text{size(exits}_i) + \qquad (2.1)$$
$$\sum \text{size(reads}_i) + \sum \text{size(writes}_i)$$

2.5.4 FC—A Measure of Functional Complexity

Information theory-based software measurement was proposed in Khoshgoftaar and Akllen (1995) to quantify functional complexity in terms of an amount of information based on some abstraction of the interactions between software components (Ormandjieva 2002). Entropy is one concept in information theory, and it was introduced by Shannon and Weaver (1969) as a quantitative measurement of the uncertainty associated with random phenomena. It is said that one phenomenon represents less uncertainty than a second one if we are more sure about the result of experimentation associated with the first phenomenon than we are about the result of experimentation associated with the second one.

Considering any set of n events and their probability distribution $\{p_i, \ldots, p_n\}$, the quantification of this uncertainty quantity is calculated using the following entropy formula:

$$H = -\sum_{i=1}^{n} p_i \log_2 p_i \qquad (2.2)$$

In Shannon and Weaver (1969), a new method was proposed for quantifying functional complexity from a software behavior description. The method characterizes the functionality of the system as specified in the scenarios. Functional complexity is quantified in terms of the entropy of an amount of information based on an abstraction of the interactions among software components. Assuming that each message represents an event, entropy-based software measurement is used to quantify the complexity of interactions between the software and its environment, and within the software (between software classes) in terms of the information content of the interactions, based on some abstraction of the interactions (Alagar et al. 2004; Davis and Leblanc 1988; Harrison 1992; Shannon and Weaver 1969). The probability p_i of the i-th event is equal to $p_i = f_i / NE$, where f_i is the number of occurrences of the i-th event and NE is the total number of events in the sequence. The classical entropy calculation quantifies the average amount of information contributed by each event. Therefore, the functional complexity in a time slice is defined in Alagar et al. (2000) as an average amount of information in the corresponding sequence of events and is computed as follows:

$$FC = -\sum_{i=1}^{n} (f_i / NE) \log_2 (f_i / NE) \tag{2.3}$$

where n is the number of different event types in the sequence. We consider the COSMIC FFP generic model of software as an abstraction of the interactions, thus conceptually justifying the applicability of the entropy to quantify the functional complexity in the COSMIC FFP method. Functional complexity (FC) is the quantification for the amount of information interchanged in a given interaction (scenario). The functional complexity in a period of time with higher average information content should, on the whole, be more complex than another with lower average information content. That is, the FC measure is intended to order the usages of the system in a time period in relation to their functional complexity. The scale and scale types of both measurement methods are investigated next in Sections 2.5.5 and 2.5.6.

2.5.5 Identification of COSMIC FFP Scale, Unit, and Scale Type

Measurement with COSMIC FFP is more than counting and adding up the data movements. To identify the types of scales and analyze their uses in the COSMIC FFP measurement process, the procedure of the measurement process must be broken down into substeps, and each substep further analyzed in order to understand the transformation between the steps (Abran and Khelifi 2004). As mentioned previously, two phases (mapping and measurement) are required to measure the functional size of software in COSMIC FFP. Basically, the mapping phase is the process of abstracting a set of FURs, described with whichever methodology, as a COSMIC FFP generic model of the software; this is similar to mapping the distance on water into a meter scale or time into a dial of a mechanical clock. After that only will the measurer be able to read the distance on the scale or read the specific position on the scale of the clock. Therefore, the mapping phase is an important step to map the FUR set into a measurement scale. This, then, gets the measurer into the next phase: the measurement phase. More specifically, the mapping phase is done by identifying software layers (**MAP 1**), and then for each layer the following steps are carried out:

MAP 1.1: Identifying software boundaries
MAP 1.2: Identifying functional processes
MAP 1.3: Identifying data groups
MAP 1.3.1: Identifying data attributes

For **MAP 1**, the concept of software layers in COSMIC FFP is meant as a tool that identifies the separate components that have to be sized and their boundaries (ISO 2003d). In a specific measurement exercise, layers can be distinguished and have an order where, for instance, software in any one layer can be a subordinate to a higher layer for which it provides services. Also, the measurement method defines peer-to-peer exchange as two items of software in the same layer exchanging data (ISO 2003d). From this point on, it can be said that a layer at level 2 is above a layer at level 1, which is used by the above layer, or we can say that two softwares are at the same level or layer. Next, **MAP 1.1** identifies the boundaries between each pair of layers where one layer is the user of another, and the latter is to be measured. In the same layer, there is also a boundary between any two distinct pieces of software if they exchange data in peer-to-peer communications (ISO 2003d). **MAP 1.2** identifies the set of functional processes of software to be measured. In each layer, software delivers functionality to its own users. From at least one identifiable FUR, a functional process can be derived. A functional process comprises at least two data movements, an entry, and either an exit or a write (ISO 2003d). Next, in (**MAP 1.3**) the data groups are identified. A data group is the object of interest that may or may not survive the functional process using it (ISO 2003d). Each data group has a nonempty and nonordered set of data attributes. **MAP 1.3.1** is the last step in the mapping phase. It considers identifying the data attributes for each data group. After this analysis of the steps that are taken in the mapping phase, it is to be noted that steps **MAP 1** to **MAP 1.3.1** by themselves are not taken into account in the measurement of COSMIC FFP functional size; only data movements are considered directly in the measurement, with units of 1 Cfsu, as will be seen later in the measurement phase. Figure 2.41 explains the contribution of the mapping phase to the measurement process. The measurand is basically the textual description of the text within which the functional user requirements are embedded in any kind

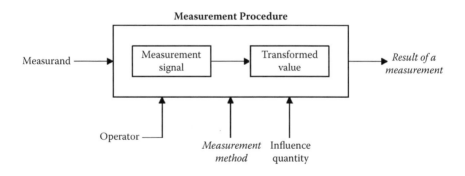

Figure 2.41 Measurement process - detailed topology of sub-concepts. (From Abran, A. and A. Sellami. 2002. Initial modeling of the measurement concepts in the ISO vocabulary of terms in metrology. *Software Measurement* **and** *Estimation,* **ed. R. R. Dumke et al., 9–20. Aachen, Germany: Shaker Publishing. With Permission.)**

of format. Then the measurement signal would be basically the elements within the text that are related to the functional user requirements. Next, the mapping, from whichever format into the generic COSMIC model of software, could be the transformed value. It is to this transformed value (e.g., the identification of all functional processes recognized by COSMIC FFP) that the measurement function would be applied with the corresponding measurement unit.

The second phase is measurement, where the measurer applies the measurement to the required elements of the model produced in the mapping phase. The *measurement* phase is done for each functional process included within the software boundary identified in the mapping phase (**MAP 1.2**), and it is broken into three steps:

MSP1: Identifying data movements
MSP2: Applying the measurement function
MSP3: Aggregating the measurement results

MSP1 identifies the data movements' types (entry, exit, read, and write) of each functional process (ISO 2003d). It is to be noted that it not the subprocesses that are directly taken into account, but the data movements within a subprocess: in COSMIC a subprocess is defined as a combination of a data movement and data manipulation.

Then by convention, only a portion of the subprocess are taken into account in the use of a measurement scale, that is, only the data movement portion.

This could be similar to taking a subprocess, comparing it to a scale of an etalon, and since the scale of the COSMIC etalon (defined by convention at a conceptual rather than material level, as for the meter or kilogram etalons) considers only data movement, taking only this portion as input into the measurement function with its measurement unit, that is, 1 Cfsu.

MSP2 is the next substep in the measurement phase. It applies the measurement function by assigning a numerical value of 1 Cfsu to each instance of a data movement (entry, exit, read, or write). The results of this substep in COSMIC FFP are interpreted in the following way: once the data movements are identified, a measurement scale is used, and it is defined as 1 data movement of whichever type. The measurer assigns to the data movement being measured a measurement unit of 1 with respect to that etalon, and then assigns to it a symbol of 1 Cfsu (COSMIC functional size unit). Therefore, those results are taken as numbers that are counted.

Finally, in the last step, **MSP3**, the results of assigning 1 to each data movement are added together using Equation 2.1, taking for granted that the results of **MSP2** can be ratio numbers to be added.

This measurement of a functional process is closely similar to a classic measurement exercise: a measurement scale of 1 data movement is used, and this is read on the measurement scale as the equivalent of the marks (each mark being 1 data movement = 1 Cfsu). The size is then figured out in terms of the number of marks or units read on the scale.

In conclusion, the COSMIC FFP measure can be considered at least on the ratio scale. Moreover, the zero is meaningful, which means that when size = 0, a software does not have a size according to the measurement unit of COSMIC FFP.

2.5.6 Identification of FC Scale, Unit, and Scale Type

As introduced previously, Equation 2.3 quantifies the amount of information interchanged in a given scenario. That is done through the following steps:

FC1: Calculating f_i for each event in the given scenario.
FC2: Calculating *NE* for the given scenario.
FC3: Calculating f_i/NE for each event in the scenario.
FC4: Calculating $\log_2$ of **FC3** for each event.
FC5: Multiplying **FC3** with **FC4.**
FC6: Adding up **FC5** for all events.
FC7: Multiplying **FC6** with −1.

FC1 is simply counting the frequency of the events' occurrences (that is, identifying an event occurrence, and then adding all of those occurrences identified to get the frequency). Therefore, we may suggest that it's at least on the ratio scale that depends on counting the frequency of events, and as a result, the unit will be the event's occurrence.

FC2 is adding the total number of events' occurrences in a scenario, and it's also suggested to be defined at least on the ratio scale. The unit is the event's occurrence.

FC3 is a derived measure dividing **FC1** (ratio scale) by **FC2** (ratio scale), whose scale type will be the weakest one according to Fenton and Pfleeger (1996). Therefore, it can be on the ratio scale. Division is done through the unified unit event's occurrence and according to the analysis that has been proposed in Al Qutaisch et al. (2005); a ratio of quantities with the same dimensions is itself dimensionless. Therefore, the end result is a dimensionless number that is a percent. It is to be noted that **FC3** is the probability of the *i*-th event happening in the scenario.

FC4 applies the logarithmic function to **FC3**. The ratio value of the logarithmic function $\log_2 n$ is exactly the number of binary digits (bits) required to represent the probability n of the event's occurrences. For instance, the combinations of a three-digit binary number can represent $n = 8$. Thus, this step transforms the dimensionless probability value into the number of digits required to represent it in bits.

In **FC5**, the representation size for probability in bits is multiplied by the probability of occurrences of the same event type. Each bit is a designator of the probability of one event's occurrence. The result is the total number of bits required for representing the probability of all occurrences of one event in the sequence. Therefore, such a multiplication would normally produce a number with bit as a measurement unit. The scale type is suggested to be at least on the ratio scale.

In **FC6**, the representational size for the probability of all occurrences of all events is calculated. The resulting number in **FC6** is negative because of the logarithmic function's nature (it's negative on values less than 1), but the amount of information shall be nonnegative. In **FC7**, multiplication by −1 is required to obtain the nonnegative value for the amount of information. It is a simple transformation that doesn't change the scale type since −1 does not have a unit itself.

In conclusion, the FC measure quantifies the representational size of the probabilities of all events' occurrences in bits, and can be considered at least on the ratio scale. Also, the absolute zero is meaningful since (theoretically) one scenario may have zero functionality, thus requiring zero amount of bits for its representation.

2.5.7 Discussion and Next Steps

In conclusion, it was seen how the scale concept is used in the COSMIC FFP method to ensure meaningfulness of the numbers obtained from its measurement process. We also define the measurement unit for FC measure.

Whenever you do a measurement in day-to-day life, you need a scale. For instance, if you want to measure distance, you need a measuring tape, then you map what you want to measure to the concept of distance, and then you carry out your measurement with a measurement procedure. The mapping phase in COSMIC FFP and **MSP1** (identifying the data movements) is our measurement tape in order to map the set of FURs into a measurement scale. That is exactly Φ, which maps the empirical structure E (FUR set in our case) into the numerical structure N (size in Cfsu unit). Therefore, the number we get as a result of applying **MSP2** and **MSP3** is the functional size for the corresponding set of FURs. We can then say that there is no loss of measurement information from **MSP2** to **MSP3** since both have at least a ratio scale type, as we have analyzed before in Section 2.5.5. Further work is required to investigate whether or not it satisfies all the properties of an absolute scale. Entropy-based functional complexity measure FC has no change of scale types through its steps. This could be interpreted as follows: FC transforms the measurement of the functional complexity of a scenario, based initially on the frequencies for each event, into quantification for the amount of information interchanged in a given interaction. By such study, we also conclude that Equation 2.3 has a measurement unit, which is bit.

In this paper, even though some insights have been gained in the identification and analysis of the scale for the COSMIC FFP measurement method, further analysis might be required to ensure that all metrology-related issues in this measurement method have been adequately identified and analyzed. Among some of the next steps is the investigation on how, in some other software, scales embedded within the definition of these measures are tackled and described. For example, how has the concept of scale been used in the McCabe cyclomatic complexity measure and other object-oriented measures. The metrological concept of etalon presented in the introduction should also be investigated for both of the measurement methods discussed in this section.

References

Aamodt, A., and E. Plaza. 1994. Case-based reasoning: Foundational issues, methodological variations, and system approaches. *AI Communications* 7:27–34.

Abran, A. 1994. Analyse du processus de mesure des points de fonction. Thèse de Doctorat, Département du génie électrique et de génie informatique, Ecole Polytechnique de Montréal, Montréal.

Abran, A., J.-M. Desharnais, S. Oligny, D. St.-Pierre, and C. Symons. 1999. *COSMIC-FFP measurement manual*. Version 2.0. Université du Québec à Montréal, Canada. http://www.lrgl.uqam.ca/ffp.html (accessed Januaryy 31, 2010).

Abran, A., J.-M. Desharnais, S. Oligny, D. St.-Pierre, and C. Symons. 2002. *COSMIC-FFP measurement manual, version 2.1, the COSMIC implementation guide for ISO/IEC 19761: 2002*. ETS Montreal: University Press.

Abran, A., J.-M. Desharnais, S. Oligny, D. St.-Pierre, and C. Symons. 2003. *COSMIC-FFP measurement manual (COSMIC implementation guide for ISO/IEC 19761: 2003)*. Version 2.2. Common Software Measurement International Consortium. http://www.lrgl.uqam.ca/cosmic-ffp (accessed January 31, 2010).

Abran, A., J.-P. Jacquet, and R. Dupuis. 1998. *Une analyse structurée des méthodes de validation des métriques*. Montreal : Laboratoire de recherche en gestion des logiciels, Département d'informatique Montreal, UQAM Press.

Abran, A., and A. Khelifi. 2004. *Software functional size with ISO 19761: 2003 COSMIC-FFP measurement method*. ETS Montreal: Université du Québec.

Abran, A., O. Ormandjieva, and M. Abu Talib. 2004. A functional size and information theory-based functional complexity measures: Exploratory study of related concepts using COSMIC-FFP measurement method as a case study. In *Software measurement—Research and application*, ed. A. Abran et al., 457–71. Aachen, Germany: Shaker Publ.

Abran, A., and P. N. Robillard. 1994. Function points: A study of their measurement processes and scale transformations. *Journal of Systems and Software* 25:171–84.

Abran, A., and A. Sellami. 2002. Initial modeling of the measurement concepts in the ISO vocabulary of terms in metrology. In *Software measurement and estimation*, ed. R. R. Dumke et al., 9–20. Aachen, Germany: Shaker Publ.

Abran, A., and C. Symons. 2005. *About COSMIC-FFP*. École de Technologie Supérieure (ÉTS), Montréal, Canada. http://www.gelog.etsmtl.ca/cosmic-ffp/index.html (accessed January 31, 2010).

Alagar, V. S., O. Ormandjieva, and S. H. Liu. 2004. Scenario-based performance modelling and validation in real-time reactive systems. In *Proceedings of Software Measurement European Forum 2004 (SMEF2004)*, ed. R. Meli et al., 327–39. Rome, Italy: DPO Publ.

Alagar, V. S., O. Ormandjieva, and M. Zheng. 2000. Managing complexity in real-time reactive systems. In *Sixth IEEE International Conference on Engineering of Complex Computer Systems (ICECCS 2000)*, ed. K. Ohmori et al., 12–24. Los Altamitos, CA: IEEE Computer Society Press.

Al Qutaish, R., and A. Abran. 2005. An analysis of the designs and the definitions of the Halstead's metrics. In *Innovations in software measurement*, ed. A. Abran and R. R. Dumke, 337–52. Aachen, Germany: Shaker Publ.

Azouz, S., and A. Abran. 2004. A proposed measurement role in the rational unified process and its implementation with ISO 19761: COSMIC-FFP. In *Proceedings of Software Measurement European Forum 2004 (SMEF2004)*, ed. R. Meli et al., 403–15. Rome: DPO Publ.

Baize, D., and M. C. Girard. 1995. Référentiel Pédologique. Association française d'étude des sols. Internal report. Paris: INRA Publ.

Buglione, L., and A. Abran. 2004. The software measurement body of knowledge. In *Proceedings of Software Measurement European Forum 2004 (SMEF2004)*, ed. R. Meli et al., 84–94. Rome: DPO Publ.

BNM. 2010. Histoire de la mesure. BNM—Bureau National du Métrologie. http://www. bnm.fr/mesuremetrologie/me.histoire1.htm (accessed January 31, 2010).

COSMIC FFP News. 2006. ISBSG database 2(1). http://www.gelog.etsmtl.ca/cosmic-ffp/ newsLetter/COSMICNewsJan2006.pdf (accessed January 31, 2010).

Davis, J. S., and R. J. Leblanc. 1988. A study of the applicability of complexity measures. *IEEE Transactions on Software Engineering* 14(9):1366–72.

Dehn, N., and R. Schank. 1982. Artificial and human intelligence. In *Handbook on human intelligence*, ed. Robert J. Sternberg, 352–91. Cambridge: Cambridge University Press.

Desharnais, J.-M., P. Westwood, and F. Rollo. 2001. The strengths and weaknesses of functional measure as a good negotiation tool for new development projects. In *Proceedings of the ESCOM-SCOPE 2001*, ed. K. D. Maxwell et al., 287–94. Maastricht, Netherlands: Shaker Publ.

Desharnais, J.-M., A. Abran, A. Mayers, L. Buglione, and V. Bevo. 2002. Knowledge modeling for the design of a KBS in the functional size measurement domain. In *Proceedings of the KES 2002*, ed. E. Damiani, 7–12. Crema, Italy: IOS Press.

Fenton, N. E., and S. L. Pfleeger. 1996. *Software metrics: A rigorous approach.* London: Chapman & Hall.

Fetcke, T. 1999a. *The warehouse software portfolio, a case study in functional size measurement.* Technical Report 1999-20. Montréal: Département d'informatique, Université du Quebec à Montréal.

Fetcke, T. 1999b. *The warehouse software portfolio—A case study in functional size measurement.* Berlin: Forschungsbericht des Fachbereichs Informatik, University Press.

Fetcke, T. 2000. Two properties of function points analysis. In *Software Metriken-Entwicklungen, Werkzeuge und Anwendungsverfahren*, ed. R. Dumke and F. Lehner, 17–34. Wiesbaden, Germany: DUV Publ.

Fetcke, T., A. Abran, and R. R. Dumke. 2001. A generalized representation for selected functional size measurement methods. In *Current trends in software measurement*, ed. R. R. Dumke and A. Abran, 1–25. Aachen, Germany: Shaker Publ.

Gaffney, J. E., and R. D. Cruickshank. 1997. How to estimate software system size. In *Software engineering management*, ed. R. H. Thayer, 246–66. Los Alamitos, CA: IEEE Computer Society Press.

Giles, A. E., and G. T. Daich. 1995. Metric tools CROSSTALK. http://www.stsc.hill.af.mil/ crosstalk/1995/02/Metrics.asp (accessed January 31, 2010).

Harrison, W. 1992. An entropy-based measure of software complexity. *IEEE Transactions on Software Engineering* 18(11):91–95.

IEEE. 1990. IEEE standard glossary of software engineering terminology. IEEE Std. 610.12-1990. New York: Institute of Electrical and Electronics Engineers, Inc.

IFPUG Manual. 1994. *Function point counting practices manual.* Release 4.0. Westerville, OH: International Function Point Users Group (IFPUG) Publ.

IFPUG Manual. 1999. *Function point counting practices manual.* Release 4.1. Westerville, OH: International Function Point Users Group (IFPUG) Publ.

IFPUG. 2004. *Function point counting practices manual.* Version 4.2. International Function Point Users Group. http://www.ifpug.org (accessed January 31, 2010).

ISO. 1993. *International vocabulary of basic and general terms in metrology (VIM)*. Geneva, Switzerland: International Organization for Standardization (ISO) Publ.

ISO. 1998. *Information technology—Software measurement—Functional size measurement—Definition of concepts*. ISO/IEC 14143-1:1998(e). Geneva, Switzerland: International Organization for Standardization (ISO) Publ.

ISO. 2000. *ISO/IEC 14143-4 information technology. Software measurement—Functional size measurement: Reference model*. Geneva, Switzerland: International Organization for Standardization Publ.

ISO. 2001. *ISO/IEC 14143-2 information technology. Software measurement. Functional size measurement: Conformity evaluation of software size measurement methods*. Geneva, Switzerland: International Organization for Standardization Publ.

ISO. 2002a. *Software engineering—Software measurement process*. ISO/IEC IS 15939:2002. Geneva, Switzerland: International Organization for Standardization (ISO) Publ.

ISO. 2002b. *Information technology. Software engineering. Software measurement—Functional size measurement: Verification of functional size measurement*. ISO/IEC 14143-3. Geneva, Switzerland: International Organization for Standardization (ISO) Publ.

ISO. 2002c. *Software engineering. MkII function point analysis—Counting practices manual*. ISO/IEC IS 20968. International Organization for Standardization. http://www.iso.org (accessed January 31, 2010).

ISO. 2003a. *Information technology. Software engineering—Software measurement—Functional size measurement: Guide for use of ISO/IEC 14143 series and related international standards*. ISO/IEC 14143-6. Geneva, Switzerland: International Organization for Standardization (ISO) Publ.

ISO. 2003b. *Software engineering—IFPUG 4.1 unadjusted functional size measurement method—Counting practices manual*. ISO/IEC 20926:2003. International Organization for Standardization. http://www.iso.org (accessed January 31, 2010).

ISO. 2003c. *Information technology—Definitions and counting guidelines for the application of function point analysis*. ISO/IEC 24570. Geneva, Switzerland: ISO Publ.

ISO. 2003d. *Software engineering—COSMIC-FFP—A functional size measurement method*. ISO/IEC 19761:2003. Geneva, Switzerland: International Organization for Standardization (ISO) Publ.

ISO. 2004. *Information technology. Software measurement—Functional size measurement: Determination of functional domains for use with functional size measurement*. ISO/IEC 14143-5. Geneva, Switzerland: International Organization for Standardization (ISO) Publ.

ISO. 2005. *Software engineering—NESMA functional size measurement method version 2.1—Definitions and counting guidelines for the application of function point analysis*. ISO/IEC 24570:2005. Geneva, Switzerland: International Standardization Organization (ISO) Publ.

Jackson, P. 1998. *Introduction to expert systems*. Reading, MA: Addison Wesley Publ.

Jacquet, J. P., and A. Abran. 1998. Metrics validation proposals: A structured analysis. In *Software measurement*, ed. R. Dumke and A. Abran, 43–60. Wiesbaden, Germany: DUV Publ.

Jones, C. 1991. *Applied software measurement—Assuring productivity and quality*. New York: McGraw-Hill.

Jones, C. 1997. *What are function points?* Software Productivity Research, Inc., Burlington, MA: SPR Publ.

Khoshgoftaar, T., and E. B. Allen. 1995. Applications of information theory to software engineering measurement. *Software Quality Journal* 3(2):79–103.

Knauf, R., A. J. Gonzalez, and K. P. Jantke. 1999. Validating rule-based systems: A complete methodology. In *IEEE SMC '99 Conference Proceedings*, ed. F. Harashima, 744–49. Los Alamitos, CA: IEEE Computer Society Press.

Kolodner, J. L. 1993. *Case-based reasoning*. San Francisco: Morgan Kaufmann Publ.

Mk II Manual. 1998. *Mk II function point analysis counting practices manual*. Version 1.3.1. London: United Kingdom Software Metrics Association, UKSMA Publ.

Nishiyama, S., and T. Furuyama. 1994. The validity and applicability of function point analysis. In *Proceedings of the EOQ-SC'94*. Basel, Switzerland: SAQ Publ.

Ormandjieva, O. 2002. *Deriving new measurement for real time reactive systems*. Internal report. Montreal: Department of Computer Science and Software Engineering, Concordia University Press.

Paton, K., and A. Abran. 1995. *A formal notation for the rules of function point analysis*. Montreal: Université du Québec à Montréal.

Prince, V. 1996. *Vers une informatique cognitive dans les entreprises: Le rôle central du langage*. Paris: Masson Publ.

Rieger, C. 1975. Conceptual memory. In *Conceptual information processing*, ed. R. C. Schank, 143–50. Amsterdam: North-Holland Publ.

Rivet, M., J.-M. Desharnais, and A. Abran. 2000. A cognitive approach and the implementation of a measurement program. In *Proceedings of the ESCOM-SCOPE 2000*, ed. K. D. Maxwell et al., 151–60. Munich, Germany: Shaker Publ.

Rubey, R. J., and R. D. Hartwick. 1968. Quantitative measurement program quality. In *National computer conference*, ed. K. Maxwell et al., 671–77. Washington, DC: Thomas Book.

Saaty, Th. 1999. Fundamentals of the analytic network process. In *Proceedings of the ISAHP 1999*, ed. E. Kinoshita, 104–18. Kobe, Japan: Meijo University Press.

Santillo, L. 2004. Software complexity evaluation based on functional size components. In *Software measurement—Research and application*, ed. A. Abran et al., 41–56. Aachen, Germany: Shaker Publ.

Shannon, C. E., and W. Weaver. 1969. *The mathematical theory of communication*. Urbana: University of Illinois Press.

SMS. 2010. *Software measurement services. The power of COSMIC FFP*. Software Measurement Services. http://www.gifpa.co.uk/news/8/p2_cosmic.html (accessed January 31, 2010).

St.-Pierre, D., J.-M. Desharnais, A. Abran, and B. Gardner. 1996. *Definition of when requirements should be used to count function points in a project*. Princeton, NJ: International Function Point Users Group.

St.-Pierre, D., M. Maya, A. Abran, J.-M. Desharnais, and P. Bourque. 1997. *Full function points: Counting practices manual*. Montreal: University of Quebec Press.

Symons, C. 1988. Function point analysis: Difficulties and improvements. *IEEE Transactions on Software Engineering* 14(1):2–11.

Watson, I. 1997. *Applying case-based reasoning: Technique for enterprise systems*. Salford, UK: University of Salford, University Press.

Whitmire, S. A. 1997. *Object oriented design measurement*. Chichester, UK: John Wiley & Sons.

Zuse, H. 1991. *Software complexity measures and methods*. Berlin, NY: DeGruyter Publisher.

Zuse, H. 1998. *A framework for software measurement*. Berlin, NY: DeGruyter Publisher.

Chapter 3

Methodologies of the COSMIC Application in Practice

The COSMIC FFP functional sizing method can be applied to several software domains (such as business applications and real-time software). The measurement manual offers a theoretical skeleton, together with examples from those domains. For each specific software domain, a guideline will be developed. Otherwise, software processes can be meant as the development of new products, maintenance of existing solutions and application, or adaptation of acquired systems. For all these kinds of software, production appropriate versions of functional sizing are necessary. Finally, new methods of software sizing must be comparable to other (existing) methods.

Figure 3.1 tries to describe these different requirements for establishing a new approach of FSM methodology.

The first section by Luca Santillo describes the merging of Early and Quick COSMIC FFP with an analytical hierarchy process resulting in a more precise estimation method that is robust to errors in the pairwise comparisons, and self-consistent because of the redundancy and normalization process of the comparisons.

The use of COSMIC FFP for business application software is demonstrated by Arlan Lesterhuis. A guideline aims to describe detailed rules and to provide extensive examples for the sizing of software from that specific domain.

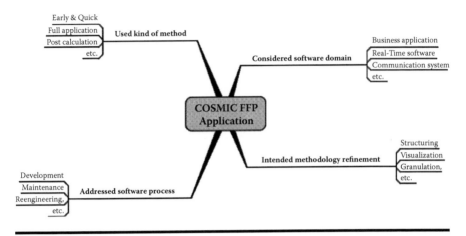

Figure 3.1 Usability requirements for FSM methodologies.

Tom Koppenberg and Ton Dekkers describe the application of COSMIC FFP for enhancement projects of existing software. They believe that COSMIC can be a very good alternative in the very near future.

The use case model seems to be an optimum candidate for serving both general purpose requirement management and measurement input model needs. Piotr Habela, Edgar Glowacki, Tomasz Serafinski, and Kazimierz Subieta demonstrate that use case specification is intended to allow counting the functional size units in a straightforward way for particular scenario specifications.

The last section, by Alain Abran, Jean-Marc Desharnais, and Fatima Aziz, discusses the convertibility ratios between COSMIC FFP (ISO 19761), the second generation of functional size of the software, and function points analysis (FPA) (ISO 20926). The paper presents a survey of previous convertibility studies and reports on findings from an additional data set.

3.1 Early and Quick COSMIC FFP Analysis Using Analytic Hierarchy Process

Luca Santillo

3.1.1 COSMIC Full Function Point Overview

The COSMIC FFP measurement method consists of the application of a set of rules and procedures to a given piece of software in order to measure its functional size. Two distinct and related phases are necessary to perform the measurement: mapping the functional user requirements (FURs) for the software to be measured onto the *COSMIC FFP software model* and measuring the specific elements of this software model (Figure 3.2).

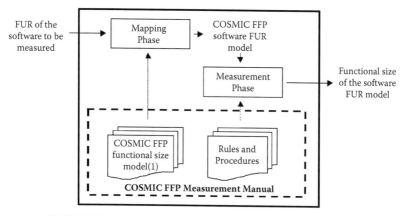

COSMIC FFP functional size model includes concepts, definitions, and relationship of functional size attributes

Figure 3.2   COSMIC FFP measurement process model. (From Abran A., J.-M Desharnis, S. Oligny, D. St-Pierre, and C. Symons. 2003. COSMIC Implementation Guide for ISD/IEC 19761:2003, version 2.2, Common Software Measurement International Consortium. With Permission.)

The COSMIC FFP software model captures the concepts, definitions, and relationships (functional structure) required for a functional size measurement exercise. Depending on how the FURs are allocated, the resulting software might be implemented in a number of pieces. While all the pieces exchange data, they will not necessarily operate at the same level of abstraction. The COSMIC FFP method introduces the concept of the software layer to help differentiate levels of abstraction of the FURs.

The functionality of each layer may be composed of a number of functional processes. A functional process is defined as a unique and ordered set of data movements (entry, exit, read, write) implementing a cohesive set of FURs. The COSMIC FFP software model distinguishes four types of data movement subprocess: in the "front end" direction, two types of movement (entry and exit) allow the exchange of data attributes with the users (or other layers); in the "back end" direction, two types of movement (read and write) allow the exchange of data attributes with the storage hardware (Figure 3.3). These data movements are also referred to as base functional components (BFCs).

The COSMIC FFP measurement rules and procedures are then applied to the software model in order to produce a numerical figure representing the functional size of the software, layer by layer. The unit of measurement is 1 data movement, referred to as 1 COSMIC functional size unit, e.g., 1 Cfsu. Theoretically, functional processes can be assigned any size expressed in Cfsu (from 1 to no theoretical limit—they are not bounded, but in practice they're expected to have some sort of "natural" upper boundary, or *cutoff*).

Conceptually, the mapping phase of the COSMIC FFP method can be considered a process of viewing a software from different levels of functional detail. First,

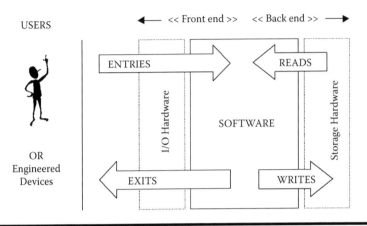

Figure 3.3 COSMIC FFP software model and data movement types. (From Abran A., J.-M Desharnis, S. Oligny, D. St-Pierre, and C. Symons. 2003. COSMIC Implementation Guide for ISD/IEC 19761:2003, version 2.2, Common Software Measurement International Consortium. With Permission.)

the software is viewed at the highest level as composed of software layers, if applicable. Then, each software layer is viewed at a lower level of detail, i.e., functional processes. Finally, each functional process is in turn viewed at the lowest level of detail of interest for measurement with COSMIC FFP, that is, subprocesses (data movement types, or BFCs).

3.1.2   Early and Quick COSMIC FFP Overview

Functional size of software to be developed can be measured precisely after the functional specification stage. However, the functional specification is often completed relatively late in the development process, and a significant portion of the budget has already been spent. If we need the functional size earlier, we must accept a lower level of precision since it can only be obtained from less precise information.

The Early and Quick COSMIC FFP method (E&QCFFP; Meli 1997a) has been designed to provide practitioners with an *early* and *quick* forecast of the functional size, based on the hierarchical system representation cited in the previous section, which can be used for preliminary technical and managerial decisions at early stages of the development cycle. Of course, a precise standard measure must always be carried out in the later phases to confirm the validity of decisions already taken. Here, *early* means that we may obtain this value before having committed a significant amount of resources to a project; *quick* means that we may also use the technique when the software is an existing asset and some constraints (such as costs and time) prevent a precise measurement.

The starting point for an E&QCFFP estimation is the acknowledgment of the hierarchical structure in the functional requirements for the software to be estimated: when we document a software structure, we usually name the root as the application level and then we go down to defining single nodes, each one with a name that is logically correlated to the functions included; we reach the leaf level when we don't think it is useful to proceed to a further decomposition. In the COSMIC FFP model, the leaves are the functional processes.

On the one hand, in the early stages it is not possible to distinguish the single data movements, or BFCs, because the information is not available at this level of detail. On the other hand, however, the preliminary hierarchical structure of the software shows as leaves what are actually nodes in the detailed version. What is required early on in the life cycle, then, is to assign forecasts of average process size, in Cfsu, at the intermediate and top levels in such a way that the final result will be obtained by the aggregation of the intermediate results.

The E&QCFFP technique is based on the capability of the estimator to "recognize" a software item as belonging to a particular functional class; an appropriate table, then, allows the estimator to assign a Cfsu average value for that item (this is applied for each identified layer separately). Each function can be classified, in order of increasing magnitude, as functional process, general process, or macro-process (Figure 3.4):

1. A functional process (FP) is the smallest process, performed with the aid of the software system, with autonomy and significance characteristics. It allows the user to attain a unitary business or logical objective at the operational level. It is not possible, from the user's point of view, to proceed to further useful decomposition of a functional process without violating the principles of significance, autonomy, and consistency of the system. A functional process can be small, medium, or large, depending on its estimated number of BFCs (E, X, R, W).

2. A general process (GP) is a set of medium functional processes and may be likened to an operational subsystem of the application. A GP can be small, medium, or large, based on its estimated number of functional processes.

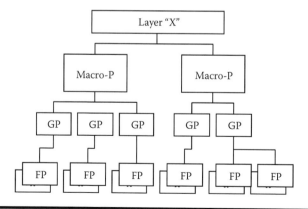

Figure 3.4   Hierarchical process decomposition in E&QCFFP.

3. A macro-process (MP) is a set of medium general processes and may be likened to a relevant subsystem of the overall information system of the user's organization. An MP can be small, medium, or large, based on its estimated number of general processes.

Note that each level is built up on the basis of the previous one. There is a fourth type of process, the typical process (TP), which is offline from the hierarchical structure outlined: it's just the set of the four frequently used functional processes, which are create, retrieve, update, and delete (CRUD) information in a relevant data group.

Each E&QCFFP element is associated with three values in terms of Cfsu (minimum, most likely, and maximum). These numerical assignments are not reported, since they are currently subject to definition and trial on the basis of the data collection activity and statistical analysis for actual projects in the field trial phase of the COSMIC FFP method. Next Table 3.1 reports the ranges to help in classifying the items of the estimation (the quantities n_1, n_2, and n_3 are to be found out empirically during the field trial phase).

One advantage of this technique is that estimates can be based on different and nonhomogeneous levels of detail in the knowledge of the software structure. If a part of the software is known at a detail level, this knowledge may be used to estimate it at the functional process level, and if another part is only superficially known, then a higher level of classification may be used. The overall global uncertainty in the estimate will then be the weighted sum of the individual components' uncertainties. This property is better known as multilevel estimation.

Table 3.1   Scale Ranges and Numerical EFP Assignments

Small Functional Process	n_1 (C_{FSU})
Medium Functional Process	n_2 (C_{FSU})
Large Functional Process	n_3 (C_{FSU})
Small General Process	6–12 FP's
Medium General Process	13–19 FP's
Large General Process	20–25 FP's
Small Macro-Process	2–3 GP's
Medium Macro-Process	4–7 GP's
Large Macro-Process	8–12 GP's

Another characteristic of the E&QCFFP technique is that it mixes both an analytical approach (use of the composition table, Table 3.1) and an analogy-based approach (the analogy can be used with respect to an abstract model or to a concrete set of software objects actually collected and classified, helping to classify the unknown items).

3.1.3 The Analytic Hierarchy Process (AHP)

The analytic hierarchy process (Santillo 2000) provides a means of making decisions or choices among alternatives, particularly where a number of objectives have to be satisfied (*multiple criteria* or *multi-attribute* decision making) (Figure 3.5).

Let's assume that n items are being considered with the goal of providing and quantifying *judgments* on the *relative weight* (*importance*) of each item with respect to all the other items. The first step (*design phase*) set the problem as a hierarchy, where the topmost node is the overall objective of the decision, while subsequent nodes at lower levels consist of the criteria used in arriving at this decision. The bottom level of the hierarchy consists of the *alternatives* from which the choice is to be made, i.e., the n items we wish to compare.

The second step (*evaluation phase*) requires pairwise comparisons to be made between each two items (of the given level of the hierarchy), with respect to their contribution toward the factor from the level immediately above them. The comparisons are made by posing the question: Of two elements i and j, which is *more important (larger)* with respect to the given factor and how much more? The strength of preference is usually expressed on a ratio scale of 1 to 9. A preference of 1 indicates *equality* between two items, while a preference of 9 (*absolute importance*) indicates that one item is nine times larger or more important than the one to which it is being compared. This scale was originally chosen, because

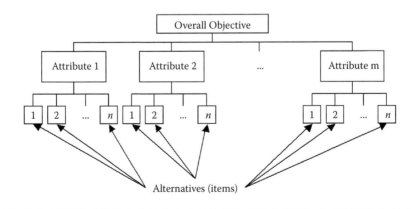

Figure 3.5   Generic hierarchy scheme.

in this way comparisons are being made within a limited range where perception is sensitive enough to make a distinction (Santillo 2000).

These pairwise comparisons result in a *reciprocal n-by-n matrix A*, where $a_{ii} = 1$ (i.e., on the diagonal) and $a_{ji} = 1/a_{ij}$ (*reciprocity property*; i.e., assuming that if element i is x times more important than item j, then necessarily item j is $1/x$ times more important, or equally x times less important than item i).

Suppose, first, that we provide only the first column of the matrix A, i.e., the relative importance of items 2, 3, ..., n, with respect to item 1. If our judgments were completely *consistent*, the remaining columns of the matrix would then be completely determined, because of the transitivity of the relative importance of the items. However, we do not assume consistency other than by setting $a_{ji} = 1/a_{ij}$. Therefore, we repeat the process of comparison for each column of the matrix, making independent judgments over each pair. Suppose that at the end of the comparisons, we have filled the matrix A with the exact relative weights; if we multiply the matrix with the vector of weights $w = (w_1, w_2, ..., w_n)$, we obtain

$$Aw = \begin{bmatrix} a_{11} & a_{12} & \cdots & a_{1n} \\ a_{21} & a_{22} & \cdots & a_{2n} \\ \vdots & \vdots & & \vdots \\ a_{n1} & a_{n2} & \cdots & a_{nn} \end{bmatrix} \begin{pmatrix} w_1 \\ w_2 \\ \vdots \\ w_n \end{pmatrix} = \begin{bmatrix} w_1/w_1 & w_1/w_2 & \cdots & w_1/w_n \\ w_2/w_1 & w_2/w_2 & \cdots & w_2/w_n \\ \vdots & \vdots & & \vdots \\ w_n/w_1 & w_n/w_2 & \cdots & w_n/w_n \end{bmatrix} \begin{pmatrix} w_1 \\ w_2 \\ \vdots \\ w_n \end{pmatrix} = n \begin{pmatrix} w_1 \\ w_2 \\ \vdots \\ w_n \end{pmatrix}$$

So, to recover the (overall) scale from the matrix of ratios, we must solve the problem

$$Aw = nw, \text{ or } (A - nI)w = 0$$

that is, a system of homogenous linear equations (I is the unitary matrix). This system has a nontrivial solution if and only if the determinant of $(A - nI)$ vanishes; i.e., n is an *eigenvalue* of A. Notice that A has *unit rank* since every row is a constant multiple of the first row, and thus all its eigenvalues except one are zero. The sum of the eigenvalues of a matrix is equal to its *trace*, and in this case, the trace of A is equal to n. Thus, n is an eigenvalue of A and we have a nontrivial solution, unique to within a multiplicative constant, with all positive entries. Usually the normalized vector is taken, obtained by dividing all the entries w_i by their sum.

Thus, given the comparison matrix, we can recover the scale. In this *exact* case, the solution is any column of A normalized. Note also that in the *exact* case, A is consistent; i.e., its entries satisfy the condition $a_{jk} = a_{ji}/a_{ki}$ (*transitivity property*). However, in real cases we cannot give the precise values of w_i/w_j but estimates of them, the *judgments*, which in general are different from the actual weights' ratios. From matrix theory we know that a small perturbation of the coefficients implies small perturbation of the eigenvalues. Therefore, we still expect to find an eigenvalue, with a value near to n: this will be the *largest eigenvalue* (λ_{max}), since due to the (small) errors in the judgment, other eigenvalues are also different from zero, but still, the trace of matrix (n) is equal to the sum of eigenvalues (some of which can be complex).

The solution of the largest eigenvalue problem, i.e., the weight eigenvector w corresponding to λ_{max}, when normalized, gives a unique estimate of the underlying ratio scale between the elements of the studied case. Moreover, the matrix whose entries are w_i/w_j is still a consistent matrix, and is a consistent estimate of the actual matrix A. A itself need not be consistent (for example, the judgments could have stated that item 1 is more important than item 2, 2 is more important than 3, but 3 is more important than 1!). It turns out that A is consistent if and only if $\lambda_{max} = n$, and that we always have $\lambda_{max} \geq n$. That's why we take as a consistency index (*CI*) the (negative) average of the remaining eigenvalues, which is exactly the difference between λ_{max} and n, divided by the normalizing factor ($n - 1$):

$$CI \equiv \frac{-\sum_{i=2}^{n} \lambda_i}{n-1} = \frac{\lambda_{max} - n}{n-1}, \qquad \lambda_{max} = \lambda_1$$

To measure the error due to inconsistency, we can compare the *CI* of the studied case with the average *CI* obtained from corresponding random matrices with order n and maximum ratio scale r. Table 3.2 shows the random average consistency indexes $Ci_{n,r}$ for various n and r. Revisions in the pairwise comparisons are recommended if the consistency ratio (*CR*) between the studied *CI* and the corresponding $CI_{n,r}$ is considerably higher than 10%.

This consistency ratio *CR* simply reflects the consistency of the pairwise judgments and shows the degree to which various sets of importance relativities can be reconciled into a single set of weights. In the above example (1 larger than 2, 2 larger than 3, and 3 larger than 1), the consistency score would be poor, and would be considered a violation of the axiom of transitivity. AHP tolerates inconsistency through the amount of redundancy of judgments. For a matrix of dimension n, only ($n - 1$) comparisons are required to establish weights for the n items. The actual number of comparisons that can be performed in AHP is $n(n - 1)/2$. This redundancy is conceptually analogous to estimating a number by calculating the average of repeated observations: the resulting set of weights is less sensitive to errors of judgment.

A quick way to find the weight eigenvector, if one cannot solve exactly the largest eigenvalue problem, is that of normalizing each column in A, and then average the values across the rows: this average column is the normalized vector of weights (or priorities) w. We then obtain an estimate of λ_{max} dividing each component of

Table 3.2 Consistency Indexes ($Ci_{n,r}$)

	R								
n	2	3	4	5	6	7	8	9	10
5	0.07	0.13	0.20	0.26	0.31	0.37	0.41	0.48	0.51
6	0.07	0.14	0.21	0.27	0.34	0.39	0.46	0.50	0.57
7	0.07	0.15	0.22	0.29	0.35	0.42	0.48	0.53	0.60
8	0.07	0.15	0.23	0.30	0.37	0.43	0.49	0.57	0.62
9	0.08	0.15	0.23	0.31	0.38	0.44	0.50	0.57	0.64
10	0.08	0.16	0.23	0.31	0.38	0.45	0.52	0.59	0.65
11	0.08	0.16	0.24	0.31	0.39	0.46	0.53	0.60	0.66
12	0.08	0.16	0.24	0.32	0.39	0.47	0.54	0.61	0.67

Aw ($= \lambda_{max}w$) by the corresponding component of w, and averaging. Finally, we can compute CI (and the corresponding CR) from this estimate of λ_{max} in order to verify the goodness of the judgments.

So far, we have illustrated the process for only one level in the hierarchy: when the model consists of more than one level, then hierarchical composition is used to weight the eigenvectors by the weights of the criteria. The sum is taken over all weighted eigenvector entries corresponding to those in the lower level, and so on, resulting in a global priority vector for the lowest level of the hierarchy. The global priorities are essentially the result of distributing, or propagating, the weights of the hierarchy from one level to the next level below it. For the purpose of applying AHP to E&QCFFP estimation, this multilevel weighting is not required, as shown in the following section.

3.1.4 Merging E&QCFFP and AHP

The analogy between the hierarchical functional decomposition of E&QCFFP and the intrinsic hierarchy of AHP can be quite confusing; we must recall that the nodes in different levels in a AHP hierarchy carry very different meaning (going from the objective level, to the attribute level, to the alternative level), while in the E&QCFFP approach the decomposition is made only in order to separate different ranges (or groups) of functions. This means that the elements of an E&QCFFP hierarchy are indeed all homogenous with respect to the attribute to be estimated, i.e., the functional size. So there is no strict correspondence between the hierarchical structures in the two techniques, but still a strong tie can be found. Although AHP was developed as a mathematical method for prioritizing the alternatives, we can recognize that what we called *importance* is just as extensive a property as many others, as software functional *size* is expected to be, too.

When estimating the software functional size (number of Cfsu), the only criterion is the size itself. Consequently, we can consider a simple AHP hierarchy, with only one level (and the objective estimated size above it); the nodes of this level are the *n* items listed by the estimator, eventually prior to the functional decomposition (this list could even include everything from possible functional processes to macro-processes).

In order to review the possible ways to merge E&QCFFP and AHP, let's recall the intrinsic characteristics of both: AHP makes the subjective comparisons consistent through a mathematical step (the largest eigenvalue solution) and provides the *CR* to evaluate the self-consistency of the estimation, while the E&QCFFP alone provides an estimation together with an uncertainty range (minimum, most likely, and maximum values), permitting us to assign a class to each item based on analogy (eventually with respect to known cases); note that the uncertainty range in the E&QCFFP can be quite large when using mostly the macro-process level.

We could gain better forecasts by combining the two techniques; the possible ways to do the join are basically the following:

1. AHP technique first applied to prioritize the items on a numerical scale, then automatic assignment of the E&QCFFP class from the scale.
2. E&QCFFP technique first applied to allocate the set of items in functional classes, then AHP applied to refine the first estimation.

The first case can be considered a reallocation of a pure AHP estimation on the E&QCFFP classes; here some not-yet-solved problems may arise, as, for example, how to decide which AHP resulting numerical range should be assigned to a given E&QCFFP class. If we manage to solve this and similar problems, we can obtain a hierarchical representation of the estimated system as in a pure E&QCFFP technique, but with more robustness in the input (nonetheless, this may not always result in a more robust output forecast, due to the fact that E&QCFFP categories necessarily blur the exact ratios given by AHP).

The second case is to be considered more significantly, since it requires first an analogical approach, which is usually easier at the beginning for the human estimator, and after that a robust refinement of the estimation in a mathematical way.

Depending on the desired precision or the time at our disposal in doing the estimation, we should decide on which variant to apply to estimate the COSMIC FFP number: only by E&QCFFP, only by AHP, with the case 1, or with case 2. The last approach should result in the most accurate forecast, still saving us from applying an exact (and more time-consuming) COSMIC FFP counting procedure. The next section deals more deeply with the case 2.

3.1.5 Case 2: E&QCFFP + AHP

The case is as follows:

1. E&QCFFP to allocate the items in subsets
2. AHP to revise/refine the estimation

Note that the first step already provides a first estimation, but its uncertainty could be quite wide, if the estimator dealt with one or more high-level class (e.g., general processes or macro-processes). The second step could be an AHP application on the global set of items from the first step, but since the pairwise ratios involved in such a global application would be of magnitude 10^2 and higher, it would be obviously very hard for a human estimator to provide such estimated ratios in the comparisons. An enhancement is to apply AHP separately on homogeneous subsets of the E&QCFFP items, and is shown in Figure 3.6. Only on two contiguous subsets per time (avoiding double sums in the total result) is given in Figure 3.7.

The second variant, mixing and comparing functional processes with general processes, and general processes with macro-processes, would be the more self-consistent and coherent one.

In any case, this approach would maintain the hierarchical representation of the system as first posed by the E&QCFFP estimator, but with a more consistent and robust numerical evaluation of each item compared to the others; the final estimated value is a revision of the first, pure E&QCFFP forecast, but with a lower uncertainty range (the original uncertainty range should be reduced, based on the value of the resulting *CR*). Eventually, some items could be reallocated in terms of their E&QCFFP category, if the AHP step shows some significant change with respect to their original E&QCFFP allocation.

We should not be too scared of the quantity of different comparisons to perform in every AHP step, since we know from Section 3.1.3 that not all the comparisons have to be effectively performed, unless the *CR* is not low enough. So, monitoring the value of the *CR* after several incremental iterations of the AHP step, we could decide to stop them when the *CR* satisfies a predefined accuracy level.

When deriving the final estimation result, two approaches are possible: one or more items should be fixed in their Cfsu value, as landmarks, to propagate the number of assigned Cfsu to the whole set, or the whole set can be mapped in a "fuzzy" way onto an ordered scale of items, as the E&QCFFP classes, with assigned quantities of Cfsu. Future field trials should show which approach is preferable.

The landmarks could be put among the original unknown items to help in both the E&QCFFP and the subsequent AHP step. These landmarks could be taken from a so-called experience database (or catalog of typical elements). This catalog could contain, for example, all the typical processes or functions that can be identified in a generic project, and their average quantities of Cfsu. Once some of these typical elements are identified among the list of items, the comparison matrix (or matrices) would greatly benefit the relative ratios between them. A generic useful case of typical

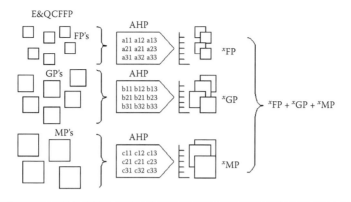

Figure 3.6   AHP application for the E&QCFFP items.

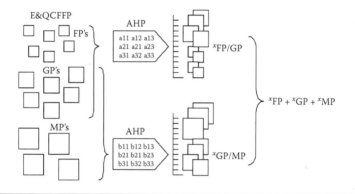

Figure 3.7   AHP application for only two contiguous subsets.

element would be the already cited typical process, or CRUD, which is usually very easy to identify and use as a comparison landmark. In case of more than one landmark, further research is necessary to establish the exact mathematical procedure to fix their values, while propagating the quantities of Cfsu through the unknown items.

A special case of application would be when the E&QCFFP step provides a list of items, all classified at the functional process level. In this case, the whole set would be taken into account for a unique AHP step, in order to compare directly the quantities of data movements contained in each process; this means that it could be significant to compare directly estimated quantities of Cfsu (but still without exactly counting them).

3.1.6   Numerical Examples

Several AHP cases have been studied, as depicted in the following tables. In every case, we have $n = 10$ items, and we assume that the comparisons made between the first item and each of the remaining items (i.e., the first column/row of matrix A) are the best estimates; eventual inconsistency is put in the remaining comparisons (i.e., between second, third, ..., and tenth item). What differentiates each case is the expected ratio between each of the ten items. Since the field trials are still to provide actual numbers of Cfsu for E&QCFFP, for sake of clarity in the examples, we consider the first item always with *unitary size*.

For each case, different inconsistency errors were introduced separately on each pairwise comparison (except for comparisons between the first item and the others, assumed as correct) to simulate the human pairwise comparisons: uniformly random ±10%, ±25%, ±50%, ±75%, ±90%, and ±100% errors. For example, the 100% error means that while the estimator should evaluate "item i is p times item j," the simulation could put "item i is $2p$ times item j" (doubling the expected ratio, i.e., with a 100% error). For each case and each error range, one thousand sample statistics have been generated; all values are approximated at one decimal. The first column of each table denotes the maximum error for single-pair comparison. Table 3.3 shows case A: (1,1,1, 1,1,1, 1,1,1,1), total = 10, $CI_{(n=10, \text{ max ratio}=10)} = 0.65$. Case B, (1,1,1, 1,1,1, 1,1,1,10), total = 19, $CI_{(n=10, \text{ max ratio}=10)}$ = 0.65, is described in Table 3.4. Otherwise, Table 3.5 gives the characteristics of case C: (1,2,3,4,5,6,7,8,9,10), total = 55, $CI_{(n=10, \text{ max ratio}=10)}$ = 0.65. Furthermore, case D, (1,1,1, 1,1,10, 10,10,10,10), total = 55, $CI_{(n=10, \text{ max ratio}=10)}$ = 0.65, is given in Table 3.6. Finally, Table 3.7 shows case E: (1,5,10, 15,20,25, 30,35,40,45), total = 226, $CI_{(n=10, \text{ max ratio}=10)}$ = 2.36.

Note that for uniformly random errors from 10 to 50% we always get acceptable *CR* values, and the final percent deviation between expected and estimated values ($\Delta_\%$) is always no more than three times the *CR* value.

As we stated in Section 3.1.3, the largest eigenvalue λ_{max} is always > n, and increases as the average error in the comparisons increases. Moreover, almost everywhere each item is overestimated with respect to its expected value; exceptions are cases C and E (those with the most widespread values), where the tenth item is underestimated and counterbalances the overestimation of the remaining nine items. However, every estimation is globally *over* the total expected value: this should be taken as a general property; i.e., the AHP estimation is to be taken as an *upper threshold*.

Relevant cases are:

Case A. In this case (all items expected as identical), the more error we put in the simulation, the more error we get in the estimated total. This could be explained as follows: if the set is strongly homogeneous (all items identical), we should not be too easy in estimating wrong ratios between the items.

Case E. This case involves a wide range of items, putting together the first item (unitary size) with a forty-five-times larger item (the tenth). In this case, even a strong (random) error up to 90% on some comparisons is blurred by AHP to give a 11% deviation for the total estimation.

Table 3.3   Case A: (1,1,1, 1,1,1, 1,1,1,1), Total = 10,
$CI_{(n = 10, \text{ max ratio} = 10)} = 0.65$

Error	λmax	CR	Estimates (average)	Total	Δ%
10%	10.0	0.2%	(1.0, 1.0, 1.0, 1.0, 1.0, 1.0, 1.0, 1.0, 1.0, 1.0)	10.3	3%
25%	10.1	1.6%	(1.1, 1.1, 1.1, 1.1, 1.1, 1.1, 1.1, 1.1, 1.1, 1.1)	10.7	7%
50%	10.3	4.8%	(1.1, 1.2, 1.2, 1.2, 1.2, 1.2, 1.1, 1.1, 1.1, 1.1)	11.6	16%
75%	10.8	14.2%	(1.2, 1.5, 1.4, 1.4, 1.4, 1.3, 1.3, 1.2, 1.2, 1.2)	13.1	31%
90%	11.7	28.7%	(1.3, 1.8, 1.7, 1.6, 1.6, 1.5, 1.4, 1.3, 1.3, 1.2)	14.8	48%
100%	15.3	90.3%	(1.5, 3.4, 3.6, 3.1, 2.8, 2.3, 2.2, 1.8, 1.6, 1.4)	23.6	136%

Table 3.4   Case B: (1,1,1, 1,1,1, 1,1,1,10), Total = 19,
$CI_{(n=10, \text{ max ratio}=10)} = 0.65$

Error	λmax	CR	Estimates (average)	Total	Δ%
10%	10.0	0.2%	(1.0, 1.0, 1.0, 1.0, 1.0, 1.0, 1.0, 1.0, 1.0, 10.2)	19.5	3%
25%	10.1	1.2%	(1.1, 1.1, 1.1, 1.1, 1.1, 1.1, 1.1, 1.1, 1.1, 10.6)	20.2	6%
50%	10.3	4.8%	(1.1, 1.2, 1.2, 1.2, 1.2, 1.1, 1.1, 1.1, 1.1, 11.1)	21.4	13%
75%	10.8	14.2%	(1.2, 1.4, 1.4, 1.4, 1.3, 1.3, 1.2, 1.2, 1.2, 11.5)	23.0	21%
90%	11.7	29.1%	(1.2, 1.8, 1.7, 1.6, 1.5, 1.4, 1.4, 1.3, 1.2, 11.8)	25.0	32%
100%	15.3	90.1%	(1.4, 4.0, 4.2, 3.1, 2.7, 2.2, 1.8, 1.8, 1.4, 13.2)	35.8	88%

Table 3.5 Case C: (1,2,3, 4,5,6, 7,8,9,10), Total = 55, $CI_{(n=10,\text{ max ratio}=10)} = 0.65$

Error	λmax	CR	Estimates (average)	Total	Δ%
10%	10.0	0.2%	(1.0, 2.0, 3.0, 4.0, 5.0, 6.0, 7.0, 8.0, 9.0, 10.0)	55.0	0.0%
25%	10.1	1.2%	(1.0, 2.0, 3.0, 4.0, 5.1, 6.0, 7.0, 8.0, 9.0, 10.0)	55.2	0.4%
50%	10.3	4.8%	(1.0, 2.1, 3.2, 4.2, 5.2, 6.2, 7.1, 8.1, 9.0, 9.9)	56.1	2.0%
75%	10.8	14.2%	(1.0, 2.4, 3.5, 4.6, 5.6, 6.5, 7.4, 8.3, 9.1, 9.9)	58.3	6%
90%	11.7	29.6%	(1.0, 2.9, 4.1, 5.2, 6.2, 7.1, 7.9, 8.6, 9.1, 9.6)	61.8	12%
100%	15.3	95.4%	(1.0, 4.6, 6.4, 8.2, 8.5, 10.1, 9.8, 10.0, 10.0, 9.4)	78.0	42%

Table 3.6 Case D: (1,1,1, 1,1,10, 10,10,10,10), Total = 55, $CI_{(n=10,\text{ max ratio}=10)} = 0.65$

Error	λmax	CR	Estimates (average)	Total	Δ%
10%	10.0	0.2%	(1.0, 1.0, 1.0, 1.0, 1.0, 10.2, 10.2, 10.2, 10.2, 10.2)	55.9	1.6%
25%	10.1	1.2%	(1.0, 1.1, 1.1, 1.0, 1.0, 10.5, 10.4, 10.4, 10.4, 10.3)	57.3	4.2%
50%	10.3	4.8%	(1.1, 1.1, 1.1, 1.1, 1.1, 10.9, 10.9, 10.8, 10.6, 10.6)	59.3	8%
75%	10.8	14.2%	(1.1, 1.3, 1.3, 1.2, 1.2, 11.7, 11.3, 11.1, 10.8, 10.5)	61.4	12%
90%	11.7	29.3%	(1.1, 1.5, 1.5, 1.4, 1.3, 12.9, 12.2, 11.7, 10.9, 10.5)	65.0	18%
100%	15.3	90.1%	(1.1, 2.8, 2.5, 2.0, 1.9, 16.5, 15.6, 14.0, 12.3, 10.6)	79.5	45%

Table 3.7 Case E: (1,5,10, 15,20,25, 30,35,40,45), Total = 226,
$CI_{(n=10, \text{ max ratio}=10)} = 2.36$

Error	λmax	CR	Estimates (average)	Total	Δ%
10%	10.0	0.1%	(1.0, 5.0, 10.0, 15.0, 20.0, 25.0, 30.0, 35.1, 40.0, 44.9)	226.0	0.0%
25%	10.1	0.3%	(1.0, 5.1, 10.1, 15.2, 20.2, 25.2, 30.1, 35.2, 40.0, 44.9)	227.0	0.4%
50%	10.3	1.3%	(1.0, 5.4, 10.6, 15.8, 20.7, 25.7, 30.6, 35.6, 40.1, 44.5)	230.0	1.8%
75%	10.8	3.9%	(1.0, 6.1, 11.8, 17.2, 22.4, 27.2, 32.2, 35.9, 40.0, 44.4)	238.2	5%
90%	11.7	8.0%	(1.0, 7.1, 13.7, 19.5, 24.6, 29.3, 33.9, 37.6, 40.9, 44.0)	251.6	11%
100%	15.4	25.6%	(1.0, 12.3, 21.6, 28.7, 32.3, 41.4, 41.2, 43.5, 42.5, 42.6)	307.1	36%

3.1.7 Further Discussion and Conclusion

The examples above are very encouraging, but much investigation still has to be made. For example, very large cases (very high n) introduce difficulties in managing the items. From this perspective, it is noticeable that the original AHP deals only with small n; a suggestion is to try to use homogenous clusters of items, and to make comparisons between these clusters. Of course, further research in realistic field trials is strongly encouraged to test the proposed approach in different situations.

As cited above, the fact that only a single value is to be provided, besides the relative weight estimates, does not mean that more than one true value cannot be used: e.g., if we know the values of items 1, 2, and 3, this means that we have more confidence in fixing several weights in the comparison matrix; *de facto*, in this way we do use the richer information. A further research theme should be on how to make some landmarks "weigh" more than others, if their value is far more accurate.

AHP is a powerful means for several tasks in the estimation and decision-making field. The proposed combination with the E&QCFFP technique can solve those situation in which the use of only E&QCFFP does not provide good results, especially due to atypical or new situations, not collected in the historical statistics, or when it is used for identifying few, high-level items, providing too wide ranges of uncertainty.

3.2 Guideline for the Application of COSMIC FFP for Sizing Business Applications Software

Arlan Lesterhuis

3.2.1 The COSMIC Full Function Points Sizing Method

Like function points analysis (FPA), the COSMIC full function points (COSMIC FFP) sizing method measures the functional size of software. There is, however, a fundamental difference between both methods. FPA is applicable to size business applications software only. It has been used extensively in productivity analysis and estimation. In contrast, COSMIC FFP is not only applicable to size business applications software, but also to technical software, system software, and real-time software.

The basis of COSMIC FFP is the assumption that the size of a function is reflected by the number of its data movements. A data movement is a transfer of a data group (a set of attributes of one object of interest, see below). There are four types of data movements. The data movement types entry and exit transfer a data group from a function's user to a function's user. A user may be a human user as well as another application. The role of the data movement types read and write is obvious: they transfer a data group from permanent storage to permanent storage. Any data movement identified (i.e., any E, X, R, or W) gives 1 COSMIC functional size unit (Cfsu). The size of a functional process or an application is the number of its Cfsu's.

In business applications software, an object of interest is identified for each entity type (or "third normal form" relation) found in the normalized data model of the measured software. In COSMIC FFP, the term *object of interest* is used instead of *entity type* in order to avoid using terms related to specific software engineering methods. Objects of interest can be of a *persistent* or *transient* type. An object of interest is persistent if the software is required to store data about the object of interest concerned. The read and the write data movements always relate to one persistent object of interest. An object of interest is called transient if the object of interest does not survive the functional process using it. Transient objects of interest come into being when analyzing (normalizing) input and output data groups. A data group in input or output of which the key does not correspond to a persistent object of interest defines a transient object of interest.

3.2.2 Why a Guideline for the Business Applications Software Domain

The basic method definitions of COSMIC FFP are contained in the ISO/IEC 19761 COSMIC FFP standard. They are elaborated in the COSMIC FFP measurement manual. This manual contains the definitions, principles, and rules on the measurement method expressed in such a way that they are largely independent of the software domain. It also contains explanations and some examples of these basic concepts of several software domains to help understanding. The COSMIC FFP measurement manual has deliberately avoided many domain-specific examples. For this reason, detailed descriptions of rules and extensive examples for the sizing of software from a specific domain were needed. Another reason is that some methods are relevant for one domain but not for others. Entering these may result in a poorly organized measurement manual. As an example, to apply the COSMIC FFP method to business applications software requires a good understanding of certain data analysis methods. The guidelines are intended to provide these domain-specific examples, each for a specific software domain.

The emphasis in the business applications guideline (hereafter the guideline) is on examples that illustrate the principles and rules of the measurement manual and on material interpreting or translating the COSMIC FFP principles to the business applications domain. There is little duplication of material between the measurement manual and the guideline. The guideline does not contain definitions, principles, and rules. For readers of the guideline, it is therefore necessary to be familiar with the content of the measurement manual and any associated method update bulletins (all obtainable from www.lrgl.uqam.ca).

3.2.3 Structure of the Guideline

The reader should note that, although the concept of the guideline for the business applications software domain is finished, it is now being revised. This means that the final version may differ from the version that has been used for this article.

3.2.3.1 What Is the Business Applications Software Domain?

The guideline starts with a description, in general terms, of what the guideline understands by business applications software domain.

3.2.3.2 Data Analysis and Its Relation to COSMIC FFP

As data analysis is a key element of COSMIC FFP, it assumes knowledge of data analysis. Two main approaches to data analysis, known as entity-relationship analysis and relational data analysis, are succinctly described in a separate section. The background for the need of data analysis lies in the fundamental notion of object of interest of COSMIC FFP. An object of interest may be any physical thing, as well as any conceptual object or parts of a conceptual object in the world of the user (as identified from the point of view of the functional user requirements) about which the software is required to process or store data. In the business applications domain, an object of interest is a synonym for *entity type* on an entity-relationship diagram, and has the same meaning as the subject of a relation in third normal form. As the data movements are coupled to these objects of interest, it is necessary to identify the entities.

Data analysis is important not only to identify the persistent data structures. The principles of data analysis hold when identifying transient data that may appear in the input and output components of functional processes. This is especially the case for transient objects of interest appearing in the output of management reports or ad hoc inquiries. So it is essential to understand and to be able to apply data analysis to the input and to the output of a functional process in order to identify the different data movements that may make up the input and the output.

There is another reason why data analysis is important. The background is an old problem: by data analysis, code tables may emerge as candidates for objects of interest. Code tables are entities with often only two attributes, for instance, country ID and country name. The question is: Do code tables represent objects of interest or not? Recall that an object of interest is a thing in the world of the user about which the software is required to process or store data. The guideline gives the decisive answer: if there is a functional process that *enters* data about the thing or *creates* data about it and exits that data from the software, the thing corresponds with an object of interest. Loosely speaking, only if data about a thing are maintainable by a user does the thing represent an object of interest. The definition does not demand the functional processes that enter or exit data about an object of interest be within the scope of the software being measured.

3.2.4   Identification of Functional Processes

For the identification of functional processes, the guideline gives some valuable hints.

3.2.4.1   CRUDL

First, the idea is not new that each possible transition from one stage to another in the life cycle of every persistent object of interest should correspond to a functional process. This rule is summarized by the acronym CRUDL (create, read, update, delete, and list). Every object of interest must be created, read, updated, deleted, and listed. The guideline states that a separate functional process must be identified for any of these CRUDL transactions, if mentioned in the functional user requirements.

3.2.4.2   What Is a Functional Process?

Often, the functional processes in the functional user requirements (FURs) each fill a paragraph. A point, however, that is often misunderstood is that, conversely, not every paragraph in the FURs describing what looks like a functional process corresponds with a functional process in the COSMIC FFP sense. The guideline gives the decisive answer: for an elementary component of a FUR to be a functional process, it is necessary to be both:

- Independently executable
- Triggered by an event in the world of the users

3.2.4.3 One or More Functional Processes?

Sometimes, the measurer may be in doubt whether a function consists of one or more functional processes. The guideline states that whenever the user has to make a decision (i.e., an event occurs in the realm of the user), this implies a separate trigger, and so a separate functional process is identified.

3.2.4.4 Identification of Data Groups and Data Movements

This part of the guideline is a central section. It presents three steps to identify data groups and data movements. The first step consists of identifying, via the entity types or relations, the persistent object of interest. This is the basis of identifying the read or write data movements in any functional process in which a persistent object of interest is retrieved or made persistent.

In the second step, the objects of interest in the input part of a functional process are identified for the purpose of identifying entries. By identifying the separately keyed data groups of the input whose key corresponds to a persistent object of interest, we identify one entry. For each transient data group in the input, one transient object of interest, and hence one entry, is identified.

In the third and last step, the objects of interest in the output part of a functional process are identified for the purpose of identifying exits. By identifying the separately keyed data groups of the output whose key corresponds to a persistent object of interest, we identify one exit. For each transient data group in the output, one transient object of interest, and hence one exit, is identified.

3.2.4.5 Other Measurement Conventions

In a separate section several measurement problems are treated. They are summarized here, together with their solution. For details, see the guideline:

- Does COSMIC FFP take navigation control data into account, and if so, how? In general, control data are ignored.
- Some functional processes seem to have no triggering entry; how is this considered? A functional process always has a triggering entry. If there is no apparent data group to be transferred, there is a "start function" entry with its associated data manipulation.

■ How does COSMIC FFP measure batch functions? There is no principal difference in measurement between batch and other functions.
■ If a data movement has multiple sources/destinations and formats, is this one or more data movements? In general, if the outputs to two physical devices or destinations are identical, only one data movement is counted. If there are any differences beyond the completely trivial, two outputs are counted.
■ How does COSMIC FFP treat menus, GUI elements, and layouts of lists, screens, and menus? Menu choices, displaying an empty data entry screen, showing header and footer data, are not measured, unless data related to objects of interest are moved.
■ How does COSMIC FFP treat authorization, help, and log functionality? The usual data movements are identified. Calling or exploiting existing functionality is not measured.
■ How does COSMIC FFP consider the different kinds of error messages? One exit for all error messages in any one functional process is measured.

3.2.4.6 Measurement of the Size of Changes to Software

One of the important topics in measuring the functional size of software is to determine the size of a *change* to software. Sizing change is so important because often more than 80% of the time software engineers *change* existing software instead of developing new software.

The measurement manual states that the size of any required functional change to a piece of software is by convention the arithmetic sum of the functional sizes of all the added, changed, and deleted data movements of that piece of software. It is clear what is meant by an added or deleted data movement. But when is a data movement changed? This is answered in the guideline. The measurement manual states that a data movement has two relevant aspects: it moves a single data group, and it may fulfill some specific data manipulation(s). The guideline now defines a change to a data movement as a change to (1) the data group or (2) its data manipulation. If one or more such changes apply to a data movement, one changed Cfsu is measured for this data movement. The guideline concludes by stating that a *data group* is changed if:

■ Attributes are added to this data group
■ Attributes removed from the data group
■ One or more existing attributes are changed, e.g., in meaning or format

or if its *data manipulation* is changed, that is:

- The specific formatting, presentation, or validation of the data are changed
- The data manipulation (i.e., processing or computation) associated with the data movement is changed

3.2.4.7   Developer Measurement Viewpoint

The last big step forward is the specification of measurement with the developer measurement viewpoint. The measurement manual is not very specific about this viewpoint: it contains not much more than the definition of the viewpoint and some examples. In the developer measurement viewpoint *all* functions in the FURs of the software to be developed have to be measured. In the end user measurement viewpoint, only the business applications layer is seen, and any peer item structure of the application is invisible. In the developer measurement viewpoint, multiple layers and peer items within layers become visible. The scope of the measurement will define which software items and their interactions must be considered. Boundaries must now be defined between each item of software within the scope and each of their respective users.

Furthermore, the concept of user is interpreted strictly as defined in the measurement manual ("any person or thing that interacts with the software at any time" [ISO 2003a, p.24]). Hence, in the developer measurement viewpoint, users now become the devices that the application software must interact with, e.g., the keyboard, mouse, screen, printer, etc. And the application software may be divided into peer components, where each component is a user of the components it interacts with. Functional processes of business software must be identified and distinguished exactly as above for the end user measurement viewpoint. But there will be additional functional processes in the developer measurement viewpoint because we now see control and usability functions (for example, a page up/down command) that have to be provided. Also, interactions between the software being measured and any peer items become visible. Rules for identifying objects of interest, data groups, and data movements, and for measuring changes to them, are the same as for the end user measurement viewpoint. But there will be additional objects of interest as a result of considering control and usability functionality.

3.2.5   Conclusion

In the guideline for the business applications software domain, much experience with COSMIC FFP has been collected and many questions answered. It is to be expected that the guideline will be a big step forward to prepare access to the method and unify measurement in the domain.

3.3 Estimating Maintenance Projects Using COSMIC FFP

Tom Koppenberg and Ton Dekkers

3.3.1 Introduction

Nowadays the majority of software projects are projects that enhance and extend existing software. For estimating new projects, acceptance of COSMIC FFP is rapidly growing because it has already proven to be a good alternative for function point analysis (Dekkers and Vogelezang 2003a, 2003b). Estimating enhancements using classic function point analysis has always been somewhat controversial, but we believe that COSMIC FFP can be a very good alternative in the very near future. This article gives an overview of the possibilities of estimating enhancement projects using COSMIC FFP.

3.3.2 What Is Enhancement?

Before we can say anything about the measurement of enhancement, it needs to be clear what kinds of enhancements exist. Two categories of software enhancements can be distinguished: planned enhancements and ad hoc enhancements. Ad hoc enhancements can be explained as solving problems that can't be put off (e.g., bug fixing).

Planned enhancement can be separated into three types:

- Perfective enhancement: Adapting the software to the new requirements of the user, like new functions or better performance.
- Adaptive enhancement: Adapting the software to new circumstances, like new hardware, new middleware, or new legal requirements.
- Corrective planned enhancement: More structured repair of problems or defects solved with ad hoc enhancements.

3.3.3 Estimating Ad Hoc Enhancements

Ad hoc enhancements cannot be addressed in releases by definition. When a problem arises that must be dealt with immediately, planning and estimating are no issues. The problem must be dealt with as soon as possible. Estimating specific ad hoc enhancements is hardly possible, and because of its nature, it has no added value. Resolving the problem always has the highest priority above estimating in these cases. However, for staffing and budgeting purposes, it is important to estimate the yearly costs of ad hoc maintenance. The yearly costs for ad hoc enhancements can be an important trigger to replace the software to be maintained.

The yearly costs for ad hoc enhancement are rather easy to estimate with the existing methods. What is needed are the experience statistics of the number of hours per year per size unit for ad hoc enhancements (reliability). Multiplying this figure with the size of a system leads to the yearly cost for ad hoc enhancements. This method is independent of the method that is used to calculate the size of software.

3.3.4   The Future of Functional Size Measurement

Function point analysis will likely be replaced by next-generation functional size measurement methods like COSMIC FFP in the next decade (Vogelezang 2003, 2004). The main reason for this is that function point analysis does not always works well with a growing number of contemporary software developing environments. COSMIC FFP can be seen as the most important candidate to replace function point analysis.

The next paragraphs will show the difference between the current way to measure software enhancements with function point analysis and the way COSMIC FFP deals with measuring enhancements.

3.3.5   Estimating Planned Enhancement

From a functional point of view, planned enhancement projects can be split into:

■ Adding new functionality
■ Changing existing functionality
■ Deleting existing obsolete functionality
■ Replacing existing functionality (= delete + new)

The measurement of new functionality is identical with the regular measurement of functional size. The others are more difficult and more controversial because there are different ways of dealing with those enhancements within function point analysis.

3.3.5.1   Enhancement and IFPUG Function Point Analysis

For understanding the advantages of COSMIC FFP over function point analysis, it is useful to explain the principles of maintenance function point analysis.

According to IFPUG, enhancements will be measured by measuring all concerned functions. Instead of using the productivity ratio for new development, a different productivity rate will be used for enhancements. In general, this rate will be lower. A disadvantage of using this method is that empirical productivity facts found during developing new software can't be reused, because different productivity ratios will be used.

3.3.5.2 Enhancement and NESMA Function Point Analysis

In 1992 Sogeti (at that time named Interprogram) proposed a method for maintenance function point analysis in which the change of the way data element types and record types are used in a function is measured. Later the NESMA Workgroup FPA and Enhancement published a document describing an approach based on the same principles (Engelhart et al. 2001).

The first step in this approach is to make an inventory of all the (elementary) functions involved in a new release of the software. Some of the functionality will be new, but usually a lot of the functionality of a release will be a change to existing functionality. The effort to deliver these changes depends on the impact on the existing functionality.

The next step is to weight the impact and categorize the function in one of the maintenance classes. Each class has its own impact factor. The size of the functions in each class will be multiplied with the impact factor of that class to get the size of the enhancement in maintenance function points.

There are five different classes:

- Low-impact change
- Average-impact change
- High-impact change
- New functionality
- Deleted functionality

Usually there is not much discussion about the last two classes. For the first three classes this is different: low, average, and high impact tends to be a subjective classification.

Function point analysis for software enhancement is based on the assumption that the way in which a function changes is related to the change of the way data element types (DETs) and file types (FTRs) are used in a function. The number of changes can be defined as follows:

Number of additions + number of deletions + number of changes

The valuation as mentioned in Tables 3.8 and 3.9 is based on absolute number of changes. This method is used by Sogeti. NESMA bases the valuation on relative changes.

The Sogeti approach is pretty straightforward. Three impact factors must be matched to three maintenance classes:

Low-impact change: 0.25
Average-impact change: 0.50
High-impact change: 0.75

Table 3.8   Impact Factors for Changed Functions

ΔDET / ΔFTR	0–1	2–5	>5
0	L	L	A
1–2	L	A	H
>2	A	H	H

Table 3.9   Impact Factors for Changed Data

Δ DET	0–1	2–5	>5
–	L	L	A

The impact factors are empirical factors based on estimation of projects. The impact factor is the ratio between the effort for building functionality and the effort needed to change the functionality in a particular maintenance class.

For deleting functionality, Sogeti works with an impact factor of 0.10. NESMA advises using a factor of 0.40.

The advantage of using the described approach is that the experiences from developing new software can be reused. A disadvantage is that the statistical evidence of the used factors is weak. However, in the years this approach has been used, the factors have not been questioned, and no research is known about calibrating these factors.

3.3.5.3   Enhancement and COSMIC FFP

Applying this approach for measuring maintenance when using COSMIC FFP is just a small step. The only difference is related to the sizing in itself. The size of the functional process (almost equals the elementary function) in COSMIC FFP is measured based on the number of data movements, where in function point analysis the size is derived from function type and complexity classification (Vogelezang 2005).

In COSMIC FFP for any functional process, the functional size of changes to the functional user requirements is aggregated from the sizes of the corresponding modified data movements according to the following formula:

$$\Sigma \text{ size(added data movements)} + \Sigma \text{ size(modified data movements)} + \Sigma \text{ size(deleted data movements)}$$

Sizing enhancement is an integral part of the measurement manual. According to the measurement manual, all new, changed, or deleted data movements should be counted (ISO 2003a, p.22). The impact of enhancement is expressed in the number of data movements that are impacted by the enhancement in any way. For new functionality this approach doesn't differ from function point analysis; the functional process will be measured the same way as it will be measured for new development. For changed functionality only the data movements will be measured that are changed, added, or deleted. The guideline for business application software defines when a data movement is considered to be functionally changed (Lesterhuis and Symons 2004).

This is when:

1. the data group or
2. its data manipulation

is changed in any way. To be more precise:

1. A data group is changed if:
   - Attributes are added to this data group
   - Attributes are removed from the data group
   - One or more existing attributes are changed, e.g., in meaning or format
2. The data manipulation is changed if:
   - The specific formatting, presentation, or validation of the data are changed
   - The data manipulation (i.e., processing or computation) associated with the data movement is changed in any way

The functional size of deleted functions will be determined by the sum of all deleted data movements. For the replacement of a function, only the data movements of the new function will be measured.

3.3.6 Estimating Software Enhancements Using COSMIC FFP

For estimating software enhancements, the product delivery rate for new development can be used for new and changed functionality. For deleting complete functional processes, this will lead to an overestimation of the necessary effort. COSMIC FFP measures the size of the software enhancement in the number of impacted data movements. The deletion of a complete functional process results in the same size as a new functional process. COSMIC FFP does not make use of enhancement classes and impact factors.

When using a product delivery rate for new software, the effort for deleting functionality will be overestimated in comparison to new development. This can be solved by using another productivity rate for deleting functionality. Then there still is the problem that the ratio for effort between the separated functions will not be correct (for example, new functions and deleted functions), so another rate will only work when the ratio between the number of new, changed, and removed functions will be around the same. A second disadvantage when separated experience data are collected for new and enhanced projects is that groups of statistics will be smaller, because new and enhanced projects can't be compared anymore. A solution can be found in using different productivity rates for the different kinds of enhanced functions. For new functions we can use the same productivity ratio as we use for new development. For changed functions we can use this productivity ratio as well. Depending on the weight of the enhancements, the rate *changed Cfsu/original Cfsu* will increase. When all data movements of a function will be changed, the expected effort for the enhancements will be the same as the effort for new development of the original function. When half of the data movements will be changed, the expected effort will be half of the effort for new development. For deleted functions a lower productivity per Cfsu can be expected. The easiest way to determine the productivity for deleting functions is to multiply the productivity rate for new development by an impact factor. Sogeti uses an impact factor of 0.10 in line with estimating enhancements with function point analysis. Experiences within the organization can be used to calibrate the impact factor.

Retesting is not mentioned in the measurement manual. The number of functions that have to be retested can be much larger than the number of enhanced functions. Retesting can be estimated by multiplying the unchanged functions that have to be retested by a productivity rate. Analogously to the removal of functions, Sogeti has determined this productivity rate to be that for new development multiplied by an impact factor of 0.10. Based on my own experiences, this factor can be calibrated. NESMA doesn't explicitly estimate retesting of unchanged functions. The effects of applying the approach with the default values are shown in Table 3.10.

The advantage of using COSMIC for measuring enhancements is that the productivity rate for new development can be reused, and so it's possible to compare the productivity rate of new development and enhancements. A disadvantage is that the right impact factor for deleting functions and retesting has to be found. The advantages of having a calibrated impact factor are obvious: the estimates will be more accurate, and the productivity is in balance with the effort of removal and testing. There are also disadvantages in regard to calibrated impact factors: calibration takes time for research and analysis, and above that creates different "sizes" for each organization. The last complicates benchmarking. Among the disadvantages are that managers take the usually minor effects of a methodical fixed-impact factor for granted and no calibration is done.

3.3.7 Conclusion

COSMIC FFP is already successful for new development. Since the major part of all software development consists of enhancement, COSMIC FFP can only be

Table 3.10 Example Estimating Enhancement Project with COSMIC FFP

Funct. Process	Before	New	Change	Remove	Test	Total	After
FP-1	5						5
FP-2	10				10		10
FP-3	5		2				5
FP-4	8		4				8
FP-5	6		4				7
FP-6	5						0
FP-7	0	9					9
Cfsu	39	9	10	5	10		44
Prod Rate (h/ Cfsu)		8	8	8	8		
Impact		1.00	1.00	0.10	0.10		
Hours		72	80	4	8	164	

successful if there's a reliable method to estimate maintenance projects. In this paper we've described a method that provides opportunities for consistent measurement of maintenance with COSMIC FFP.

3.4 Adapting the Use Case Model for COSMIC FFP-Based Measurement

Piotr Habela, Edgar Głowacki, Tomasz Serafinski, and Kazimierz Subieta

3.4.1 Introduction

Functional size measurement can be perceived as the most promising method of software development effort estimation. The efficiency of such an approach comes from the following features potentially available with it:

■ Applicable early in the software life cycle. Software requirements specification may provide the necessary input data.

- Independent of software development technology (in contrast to, e.g., lines of code-based methods).
- Based on objective criteria. Appropriate precision of functional elements counting rules allows us to expect measure repetitiveness.
- Universality. The properties being the subject of counting are generic enough to cover very different software domains (e.g., not only information systems—the original area of functional measurement application).
- Neutral concerning software development methods.

To realize the above-mentioned features, especially the last one, the function point analysis methods usually introduce their specific functionality modeling notions. This may lead to the need of mapping the development method-specific model of a system's functionality onto the one prescribed by the measurement method. We argue, however, that this would be very problematic for overall software development productivity.

It would be very desirable so that we could apply a measure directly to general purpose requirement documentation. Since the genericity of measurement rules is valuable, it would be necessary to provide a precise interpretation of particular common requirement model forms to perform counting directly on them. However, such an approach is not feasible without ensuring the presence of necessary features of requirements models used. In fact, their adjustment to the measurement method needs may constitute the main effort of introducing functional software measurement. Fortunately, as has been observed, the adjustments dictated by measurement method contribute to overall requirements quality.

Apart from the measurement productivity problem, there are a number of issues inherent to functional size methods. They include, among others, dealing with nonfunctional requirements, internal processing complexity, and functional model redundancy or underestimation. Their satisfactory solution depends on both the suitability of the measurement rules of a given method and the quality of requirements modeling.

In this paper we describe our observations on initial experiences in adopting the COSMIC FFP method to measure software documented using the use case model. As a requirements model we chose to adapt a use case approach that we perceived to be the most promising and universal considering the various kinds of software to be modeled. The paper is organized as follows. In Section 3.4.2 we summarize the functional method's development and describe our motivation behind choosing COSMIC FFP. Section 3.4.3 provides an overview of the use case approach to requirement specification, its standardization scope, flavors, and applications. In Section 3.4.4 we describe the synergetic potential between those two methods and present our approach to adopting them. Section 3.4.5 is our conclusion.

3.4.2 Functional Methods: Needs, Issues, and Advantages

Functional measurement methods offer a big advantage due to the level of abstraction they use. However, as already mentioned, this approach is also prone to several issues that need to be solved to achieve measurement objectiveness and adequacy. Some of them strongly depend on the modeling and measuring principles applied. The evolution of functional point analysis methods shows interesting trends to this extent.

3.4.2.1 Common Issues

Looking for unambiguous determinants of functional size, measurement methods suggest counting the data flows to and from external users, as well as persistent data-related manipulation. Abstracting from particular methods, this approach raises the following problems that method rules should be specific about:

- *Granularity of data.* In order to count a proper number of data flows, granularity of data units need to be precisely defined.
- *Data flow uniqueness criteria.* If functionality contains a number of similar data flows, it should be possible to determine which of them should be treated as unique and in what cases they should be identified as the same functionality and thus counted once.
- *Functional units' uniqueness criteria.* Apart from proper identification and counting of data flows within a given functional unit, it is necessary to verify if the model introduces no redundancy on an interunit basis.

Popular function point analysis methods, such as IFPUG FPA (IFPUG 2004) or Mk II FPA (Symons 1991), attempt to address those issues to remove potential ambiguities. The task is easier when only a particular domain of software systems is considered. This is the case for those methods, as they are primarily oriented toward the information systems area. Note that although user interface design belongs to the later phases of software development, the measurement guidelines referring to its constructs as found in Mk II FPA are useful to properly count the functionality. Concerning the possibility of redundancy, the counting principles tend to extract the common denominators, thus promoting software reuse.

Other key issues are nonfunctional requirements and other environmental factors that could increase the development effort. Taking into account that the effort estimation remains the main purpose of functional measurement, considering those factors is fully understandable. Typically, measurement methods take the following approach:

1. Counting purely functional size
2. Assessment of method-specified factors—a grade from a prescribed range is assigned to each of them
3. Multiplying the functional size by the grades assigned using method-prescribed weights

However, the approach is problematic for at least two main reasons:

■ In comparison to functional size counting, it is not possible to provide equally precise criteria for weighting the nonfunctional factors.
■ Proper weight (that is, impact) of particular factors may be technology dependent and may change over time. Thus, one of the main benefits of functional measurement—technology independence—is undermined.

Those problems are reflected in the evolution of the approach to the issue of nonfunctional factors represented by the most popular functional size methods. IFPUG FPA assumes a regular usage of technical complexity factors to be applied to the counted purely functional size. The newer Mk II FPA method includes a different set of nonfunctional factors, but does not recommend using them (the usage of unadjusted size is preferred). Finally, the newest COSMIC FFP method completely gives up the nonfunctional aspects, focusing on the formulation of precise rules for objective, purely functional sizing.

The last of the main shortcomings of functional size-based effort estimation is the algorithmic complexity of internal processing. Namely, the functionality similar in the sense of external data flows may differ significantly in terms of internal processing, and thus development complexity and effort. The assumption that the processing complexity is proportional to external data manipulations is acceptable only among similar kinds of software. Thus, to make the measurements universally comparable, some additional means of representing the algorithmic complexity need to be employed. However, assignment of additional values (multiplicative or—more suitable—additive to the functional size counted) raises the same questions as discussed above, concerning the objectiveness of such assessment.

3.4.2.2 Use Case Points

In contrast to other measurement methods, use case points (Karner 1993) directly refer to the notions we assume to use for requirements modeling (that is, use case model and class model). This makes the method potentially the most straightforward to apply in our case. However, as will be shown, some drawbacks may suggest considering an adaptation of another functional measurement method.

The method assumes classification of use cases into three groups, based on their roughly determined size or complexity. The criteria are either the number of interaction steps in the use case scenario or the number of (domain model) classes involved in its processing. Based on that classification, each use case is assigned a number of 5, 10, or 15 use case points. Interestingly, the method suggests that the use cases connected through uses or extends* (that is, not connected directly with the actor) should not be counted (Anda et al. 2001). Also, actor count contributes

---

* Newer versions of UML offer a modified organization of relationships among use cases. The uses and extends relationships are replaced with include, extend, and generalization.

to the functional size, though its impact is smaller. Actors are assigned 1, 2, or 3 points, depending on whether they access the system through local API (1), textual interface or network (2), or a graphical user interface (3). Note that in effect, already at this stage a rather nonfunctional aspect (actor's complexity) was introduced.

The use case points method also puts a lot of attention on the nonfunctional factors. It adopts (with minor changes) the set of technical complexity factors (TCFs) of the IFPUG FPA method. In addition, it also introduces a set of so-called environmental factors (EFs), potentially influencing a given organization's productivity. Note that the TCFs may be considered as related to the developed software itself (i.e., influencing its market price). The EFs, in turn, are rather internal to the software developing organization. This remark may be important for a subtle distinction between assessing software price and effort and estimating productivity. The factors, using method-prescribed weights, are applied to the counted number of use case points, transforming the so-called unadjusted use case points into the result expressed in use case points.

In our case there could be two benefits of applying the use case points approach. First, it is directly applicable to the assumed form of requirements document. Second, the way functional size is counted does not enforce full refinement of use case scenarios (it is only necessary to provide enough detail to classify each use case as simple, medium, or complex).

However, we have identified three issues that speak against the application of use case points in the target environment:

■ *Lack of official standard status.* The standardization of a measurement method, e.g., as an ISO specification (like in the case of IFPUG FPA (ISO 2003a), Mk II FPA (ISO 2002), and COSMIC FFP (ISO 2003a)), provides it with an authority, which is desirable, e.g., if the measure is to provide criteria for contract statements.

■ *Potentially inadequate technical complexity factors.* Those factors were identified for the oldest of main functional measurement methods. Their influence today may differ significantly and further evolve. The same concerns actor complexity (e.g., taking into account the progress in the area of graphical user interface development tools or productivity of Web user interfaces).

■ *Use case style impact on measured size.* There is a potential threat of under- or overestimation, due to appropriately locating a significant part of functionality in extending and included use cases, or because of not factoring out a common functionality from several use cases.

3.4.2.3 COSMIC FFP

COSMIC FFP (Common Software Measurement International Consortium full function points) (Abran et al. 2003) is the most recent of mainstream methods. It is based on experiences of earlier common methods, especially Mk II and FFP.

It assumes a broader area of applications, attempting to cover with adequate rules both real-time and information systems domains. That assumption results in a rather generic terminology used. Thus, it is necessary to map the method rules to concrete notions used in the domain of applications (in our case, information systems).

The counting principles are rather simple. The method specifies a data unit called a data group. In the area of information systems, this is equivalent to a normalized entity. Alternatively, a finer data granularity may be used: in that case, the intuitive notion of data attribute is suggested. The functionality is modeled in the form of functional processes that, in turn, are divided into subprocesses. The latter are divided into data movement and data manipulation. The main subjects of counting are data movement subprocesses, classified into four kinds:

- *Entry*: A movement of data from a user into the functional process that needs it.
- *Exit*: A movement of data from a functional process to the user that needs it.[*]
- *Read*: A movement of data from persistent storage (internal to the modeled system unit) to the functional process that requires it.
- *Write*: A movement of data from a functional process to persistent storage (internal to the modeled system unit).

The above-mentioned subprocesses are counted accordingly to the number of data groups being moved within a given functional process (each unique data group movement is counted as 1 Cfsu—COSMIC functional size unit). For algorithmically complex functionality, the method allows for additional counting for data manipulation subprocesses. However, no precise instructions are given on how to objectively elicit the size of the manipulation subprocesses so that it does not upset the whole estimation.

An important feature of COSMIC FFP is the explicit support for partitioning and heterogeneity of modeled systems. The method introduces the notion of layer to handle different levels of abstraction within a model (e.g., application functionality vs. database repository development). What is even more important, the method also explicitly deals with partitioning of functionality at the same level of abstraction. It addresses the complexity of multitier architecture by representing the communication of each distinguished component with its environment separately.

The method's scope of interest includes functional requirements only. Thus, the method can be classified as purely functional. It was developed to be compliant with the respective ISO standard (ISO 1998).

As can be seen, the method principles are quite simple and intuitive; however, they assume a detailed functionality specification. To deal with early functional

---

[*] The definition of *user* is rather broad and includes any external actors directly communicated with the modeled system.

size estimation, it is suggested that we count the functional processes identified, classify them into few categories according to their complexity, and assign them an experimentally determined average functional size. This variant resembles the use case points approach, except the mean values assigned to functional processes are not prescribed.

3.4.3   Use Cases

Use case modeling gained huge popularity within the software industry as the software functional requirements, as well as the business modeling mean. The fact that the approach does not enforce particular development methodology made it easier to adopt. There are several significant advantages over traditional, narrative requirements specifications:

- *Intuitiveness*: The model shows the software user's point of view.
- *Testability*: In contrast to narrative requirements specification, the functionality is described in a uniform way, from which the test scenarios can be easily derived.
- *Goal orientedness*: Interactions of each use case realize some actor's goal. This makes it easier to identify stakeholders, verify requirement completeness with them, and assign priorities.
- *Reuse mechanisms*: The notions of use case model encourage identification and extraction of multiple-use functionality elements.

The versatility of the notion resulted in the development of various flavors of use case specifications. This situation was reflected in the fact that, e.g., the UML standard leaves many aspects of the use case model open. Just the basic visual notations and the definitions of main terms are the subject of the standard's specification.

The main criterion of distinction is the purpose of a use case model. This affects modeled system's boundaries, specification's style, and level of detail. The model may be oriented toward business logic representation or toward strict software functionality specification. Also, within the latter area itself, the model may be more abstract or more design oriented (appropriately essential or system use cases, using the terminology from Ambler (2004)).

The common association for the use case model is the diagram. However, in fact, any of the mentioned applications requires structured specifications of each use case as the core of the model. The style of those specifications is a subject of large variability. The goal-oriented approach described in Cockburn (2000) suggests a popular and useful form of those specifications. The main course of interaction is provided as a numbered list of steps, each of them qualified by their performer. An intuitive and compact specification of alternative flows is realized through separate numbered lists referencing the main scenario steps.

This style of definitions encourages encapsulating simple variants within a single use case definition, and thus prevents to a large extent the abuse of the extend relationship.

Relationships between use cases are often considered a secondary feature, not recommended for inexperienced use case modelers due to the risk of obscuring the definition. However, due to their important functionality reuse potential, the use of those relationships needs to be carefully considered from the functional measurement point of view. It is worth mentioning that originally the uses and extends relationships were variants of the OO inheritance relationship among use cases. However, they were often used in another way. The former relationship was applied to include a reusable interaction fragment (in a procedure-call style). The latter was often applied to define more complex exceptional flows of events. Therefore, the later versions of UML (Anda et al. 2001) reorganized the model, introducing include, extend, and generalization relationships. This legitimizes the mentioned use of the include relationship. However, concerning the extend relationship, some authors (Armour and Miller 2000) argue that it should be used only for adding the steps into the existing base scenario—not for adjusting it.

3.4.4 Applying COSMIC to Use Cases

In this section we present our observations and choices concerning the integration of the approaches described above. We start from formulating our needs concerning the measurement method, and then adjust the use case specifications to serve it. Finally, we tune the counting principles to be intuitively applied to such a requirements model.

3.4.4.1 Choosing the Optimum COSMIC Perspective

Although the area of interest of our project was limited to information systems, we need to deal with very different kinds of software in terms of its purpose and architecture. First, significant differences of complexity were observed depending on the required system's architecture. The COSMIC tier notion helps us to overcome this issue. Modeling functionality that spans through more than one tier results in specifying tiers' boundaries and counting additional entry and exit flows when data need to cross them in a given functional process. It is just necessary to provide precise criteria on when separating a tier is allowed and when it would be an unjustified raise of measured size. The most general assumption is to partition the analyzed system according to different implementation technologies of particular components and to development organization (e.g., different teams/companies).

The second issue concerned the various complexities of data groups (i.e., entities) processed in the analyzed systems. This led us to the decision to base counting on data attributes rather than data group units. The potential problems are the (1) bigger precision of requirement specification needed and (2) lack of straightforward size comparability with measurements based on the standard Cfsu. Our decision was dictated mainly by the specificity of the environment for which we developed our approach. The main aim of our measurement approach was to address the requirements of a department responsible for the development of software, which in most cases integrate various solutions supporting essential business activities of a big corporation. The characteristic of such an environment is the fact that attributes composing a given entity are often distributed among many software systems. In addition, for the future users of the planned solution, it is easier to point out the attributes than name data groups such attributes are part of. Therefore, eliciting entities would entail an extra effort without any justification for the inception stage, whose main aim is to give the answer whether to continue or cease further development. In this particular environment, the business users of the software solutions are able to formulate their expectations quite precisely, and so enumerate the attributes required to satisfy their needs. Taking into account the above circumstances, we came to the conclusion that founding the measurement on data groups would result in constructing a data model that unnecessarily will be reflected in the future solution. In addition, the elicited model would have bigger granularity than the one based on attribute flows, which in turn would produce bigger estimation error—if the estimation model is not transferred into the implementation model. Grouping attributes into entities would lead to unnecessary setbacks in communication with the future users. Specifying the requirements in terms of attributes rather than data groups motivates the users to consider their real needs more deeply, which speeds up the requirements capture. Another reason we decided to found the measurement on attributes is the fact we are just beginning to gather the statistical data required for translation from the functional size to the assessment of labor intensity. More exact measurement data will simply give us more information about the inherent dependencies between development effort and the functional size.

3.4.4.2 Required Features of the Use Case Model

To provide the data movement information needed for measurement, in the use case model we need to take a rather system- or design-oriented perspective. That is, technical realization of functionality needs to be clearly specified, perhaps at the cost of losing some of model flexibility and robustness. Note however, we do not need to delve into, e.g., UI design or programmer's interface signature details. We need to identify all the data that are logically needed to perform a given functionality, but being aware of architectural constraints and external actor requirements.

In order not to lose a general picture, we keep in our use case template some business-oriented specification elements. They include a use case goal formulation, references to a business rules catalog, preconditions, and postconditions. They allow us, e.g., to verify the completeness of modeled functionality from the business logic point of view. For measurement, the central parts of use case specification are the main scenario and alternative scenarios. We assume keeping them detailed enough to easily assign the number of functional size units to a particular scenario step. Thus, a step must specify its performer and a set of data attributes being moved. The scenario cannot be limited to external communications, since persistent data reads and writes performed locally must also be explicitly identified. If some step may be performed by different actors, we need to be aware of communication channels they use. This is because the respective data flows should be counted separately only when the communication method differs technically.

The key problem for measurement objectiveness is ensuring true uniqueness of functional processes. Since we attempt to make the functional counting straightforward,* the main responsibility lies on the model organization side. While in typical, general purpose use case modeling the use of relationships among use cases is optional, here special emphasis for avoiding redundancies is necessary. Thus, an iterative approach to use case modeling should be applied, to identify the repeating elements (whenever it is really feasible to implement them identically) and factor them out using the include, extend, or generalization relationship.

3.4.4.3 Interpreting COSMIC Rules on Use Cases

The way a use case model is prepared and used for measurement needs to respect the standardized rules of the COSMIC method. Thus, we assume that a use case consists of one or more functional processes as defined by the method. However, some variation is introduced by the use of relationships among use cases, as it usually results in a number of use cases that are not self-dependent when considered separately from cases they are attached to. An intuitive rule of the method is that a functional process must at least consist of two data movements to provide functionality to its user. Namely, some triggering input (entry) and at least output (exit) or registration (write) of information should be present. This needs to be revised for any kind of abstract use cases (e.g., responsible for only a fragment of user goal). Therefore, the above-mentioned rule should be applied to verify complete use case instances (joining the functionality of related use cases) rather than to separate use cases. The only place where we diverted from the cosmic rules is the treatment of the triggering event. Since there is a difference of complexity between a flow that just triggers a functionality and an initial flow that provides some input data attribute, we assume counting it only in the latter case. Thus, when counting we may depend on just the steps of the use case scenario.

To keep the method conceptually clean, we avoid any extensions for handling nonfunctional factors. However, as their impact on development effort is in many cases unquestionable, we suggest analyzing those requirements using an aspect-oriented approach (Ambler 2004). This is where the COSMIC FFP layer notion

---

* That is, we assume that counting should be possible within particular use cases independently.

becomes especially useful. Namely, some important nonfunctional requirements can be refined as a functional, cross-cutting concern, located on a lower level of abstraction. If this is the case, such an aspect may be uniformly modeled using use cases, and its data exchange with the main functionality should be counted according to the COSMIC FFP principles.

3.4.5 Conclusions

In this paper we have provided our motivation behind adopting a COSMIC FFP-based purely functional measurement. The approach is to be used for management purposes in an organization developing various kinds of software in the information systems area. When analyzing input data needs of the COSMIC FFP method, we found them to be very demanding concerning the requirements of document completeness, precision, and redundancy identification. However, the additional effort of their construction and refinement seems to also be justified by benefits other than measurement-related ones. Namely, the quality enforced by measurement needs makes the later steps of development easier and promotes code reuse. Thus, a synergy between measurement method and general development process needs can be observed. The most original of the formulated postulates is the avoiding of problematic nonfunctional factors by modeling those requirements functionally in the spirit of aspect-oriented programming.

Our future research will include experimental application of the measurement method to a full-size software development project. This will require refinement of the method's rules. The most prominent issues here include:

- Detailed criteria of partitioning the system into separately counted units
- Architecture-specific templates for modeling multitiered software
- Patterns for modeling of various nonfunctional requirements as aspects

The adequacy and universality of our proposed use case specification template will be also verified.

3.5 Measurement Convertibility—From Function Points to COSMIC FFP

Alain Abran, Jean-Marc Desharnais, and Fatima Aziz

3.5.1 Introduction

Since the late 1970s, function points have been used as a measure of software size to calculate project productivity and project estimates. Even though a large number of variants of the function point analysis (FPA) method have been proposed over the years to tackle some weaknesses in the design of the original FPA method, only four methods have finally achieved recognition as ISO measurement standards:

ISO 19761: COSMIC FFP (ISO 2003a)
ISO 20926: Function Point Analysis (e.g., IFPUG 4.1, unadjusted function points only) (ISO 2003b)
ISO 20968: Mk II (ISO 2002)
ISO 24570: NESMA (ISO 2005)

NESMA (ISO 2005) is a Dutch interpretation of FPA version 4.1 that produces similar results (NESMA 2004). The FPA, Mark II, and NESMA methods were primarily designed to measure business application software. COSMIC FFP, the newest method, was designed to handle other types of software as well, such as real-time, telecommunications, and infrastructure software (Figure 3.8).

Organizations interested in converting to the newest COSMIC FFP measurement method have expressed interest in a convertibility ratio that would allow them to leverage their investments in historical data measured with FPA. The goal of this paper is to provide industry with insights into this issue of convertibility between FPA and COSMIC FFP. The convertibility studies reported here have been carried out with duplicate measurements using both COSMIC FFP and FPA (or NESMA equivalent) on the same set of functional user requirements (FURs). The specific versions of methods used in each convertibility study are documented for each study.

In this paper, the results of the convertibility study from the COSMIC field trials (Abran et al. 2003 and ISO 2003a) are not included: version 1.0 of FFP (Full Function Points) was used in that study, and since major changes to the measurement rules were introduced between versions 1.0 and 2.0, results from this earlier study are not relevant for our purposes, which is convertibility with current versions of these ISO standards.

Business	Business Application Software		Embedded or Control Software
Infrastructure	Utility Software	Users Tools Software	Developers Tools Software
	Systems Software		

Figure 3.8 Software types. (From ISO. 1998. ISO/IEC. 14143-1: 1998(c). International Organization for Standardization. Geneva, Switzerland: ISO Publication. With Permission.)

The following preconditions exist in all studies reported here:

- All functionalities inside the boundary of the software being measured are included in the measurement.
- Measurements have been taken from the human user viewpoint.
- FPA is considered not to include the value adjustment factor (VAF), in conformity with ISO 14143-1 (ISO 1998) and ISO 20926, that is, unadjusted function points (UFPs).

Data from both the Fetcke (1999) study and the Vogelezang and Letherthuis (2004) study were included in the discussion on convertibility in the COSMIC implementation guide to ISO 19761 (ISO 2003a, Section 8). They are discussed as individual data sets in this study.

This paper is organized as follows: an analysis of the Fetcke study is presented in Section 3.5.2, of the Vogelezang and Lethertuis study in Section 3.5.3, and of the Desharnais 2005 data set in Section 3.5.4. A discussion is presented in Section 3.5.5.

3.5.2   Fetcke (1999)

3.5.2.1 Context

In the Fetcke (1999a) study, four software applications of a data storage system were measured. These are business applications with few data entities; all four applications handle three entities or fewer, and these entities are all referred to in the elementary processes being measured by the FPA method. In this Fetcke study, all details of the measurement process are reported for both methods (Fetcke 1999b). It is to be noted that while the Fetcke study used version 2.0 of COSMIC FFP, the results reported are valid for the current version of COSMIC FFP (2.2), the changes not having impacted the related rules applied in the Fetcke study.

3.5.2.2   Measurement Results

The results of the duplicate measurements of the four software applications are reported in the first two columns of Table 3.11: column 1 contains the FPA measurements in UFP units, and column 2 contains the COSMIC FFP measurements in Cfsu units. The measurement results for both methods are presented graphically in Figure 3.9, with the FPA data on the x-axis and the COSMIC data on the y-axis. In this study, the FPA size range is limited (between 40 and 77), and with the software measured being similar, this makes the sample fairly homogeneous.

Table 3.11   Fetcke Data Set

Software	FPA (1)	COSMIC FFP (2)	With convertibility formula in Cfsu (3)	Convertibility Delta (4) = (3) − (2)	% Delta (5) = (4)/ (3)
Warehouse	77	81	79	−2	2%
Large Warehouse Customer Business	56	52	56	4	8%
Customer Management	49	51	48	−3	6%
Manufacturer's Warehouse	40	38	38	0	0%

Source: FEtcke, T. 1999. The warehouse software portfolio, a case study in functional size measurement. Techinical Report No. 1999–20. Université du Quebec à Montréal. University Press.

3.5.2.3   Analysis and Interpretation

The linear regression model of the data in Figure 3.9 provides the following convertibility formula, where Cfsu represents COSMIC FFP functional size units and UFP represents unadjusted function points, with a very high coefficient of determination (R^2) of 0.97:

$$Y(Cfsu) = 1.1 * (UFP) - 7.6 \tag{3.1}$$

The constant in the regression model represents the error term, Of course, with the number of data points being small (that is, only four in the data set), care must be exercised in the extrapolation of these results to larger data sets, and to data sets from different contexts.

The application of the convertibility formula to the FPA data is reported in column 3 of Table 3.11, and the delta between the data from the convertibility formula and the COSMIC FFP data from measurement is reported in absolute numbers in column 4 and in percent in column 5. For this data set, column 5 indicates that there is little variation (0 to 8%) between the number of converted COSMIC FFP units (column 3) and the duplicate COSMIC FFP measurements (column 2).

In summary, the duplicate measurement of software containing few data files and from the human end user viewpoint gave very similar results and a convertibility formula with a slope fairly close to 1.

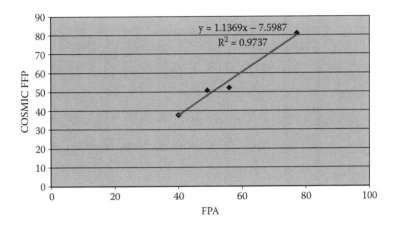

Figure 3.9 Fetcke data graph.

3.5.3   *Vogelezang and Leterthuis (2003)*

3.5.3.1   *Context*

In the Vogelezang and Leterthuis (2003) study, the COSMIC FFP measurements were carried out by Sogeti on eleven projects already measured with the NESMA FPA (ISO 24570) at the Rabobank financial services organization. An earlier version of this data set had previously been reported in (Lesterhuis and Symons 2004) with fewer data points.

3.5.3.2 *Measurement Results*

The results of the duplicate measurements of the four applications are reported in Table 3.12, columns 1 and 2. These data points are also presented graphically in Figure 3.10, with the NESMA data on the x-axis and the COSMIC data on the y-axis.

3.5.3.3 *Analysis and Interpretation*

The linear regression model of the data in Figure 3.10 provides the following convertibility formula, with a coefficient of determination (R^2) of 0.99:

$$Y(Cfsu) = 1.2 * (UFP) - 87 \tag{3.2}$$

Vogelezang and Lesterhuis postulate that the constant 87 probably owes its existence to the counting of the logical files of data ILFs and EIFs in FPA (Vogelezang 2004), which are not directly included in COSMIC FFP; this

Table 3.12   Vogelezang and Leterthuis Data Set

Software	NESMA (1)	COSMIC FFP (2)	With Convertibility formula in Cfsu (3)	Convertibility Delta (4) = (3) – (2)	% Delta (5) = (4)/ (2)
1	39	23	–40	–63	–274%
2	52	29	–25	–54	–186%
3	120	115	57	–58	–50%
4	170	109	117	8	8%
5	218	181	135	46	25%
6	224	182	182	0	0%
7	249	173	212	39	23%
8	260	81	226	145	179%
9	380	368	369	1	0%
10	766	810	832	22	1%
11	1,424	1,662	1,613	53	3%

Source: Vogelezang, F. W. 2005. Early estimating using COSMIC FFP. *Proceedings of the 2nd Software Metrics European Forum* (SMEF05), Rome, Italy.

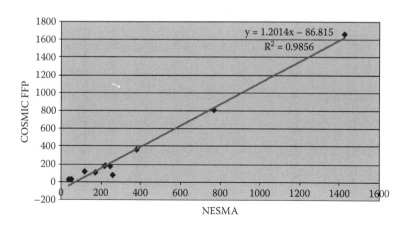

Figure 3.10   Vogelezang and Leterthuis 2003 data graph.

interpretation indicates that the high value of 87 might not be due entirely to the error term alone in this model.

With this specific data set, the two largest projects have a significant influence on the regression model: it can therefore be observed that the conversion formula does not work well for small projects with less than two hundred NESMA points, providing even negative numbers, which is not possible in practice. This means that for small projects in this environment, distinct regression models should be built using only data within a relatively similar range. For instance, this data set could be split into two ranges: from 39 to 170 UFP (Table 3.13 and Figure 3.11), and from 218 to 1424 UFP (Table 3.14 and Figure 3.12).

The linear regression model of the data in Figure 3.11 for projects with less than two hundred 200 NESMA points provides the following convertibility formula, with a coefficient of determination (R^2) of 0.85:

$$Y(Cfsu) = 0.75 * (UFP) - 2.6 \tag{3.3}$$

The convertibility formula from Equation 3.3 with a slope of 0.75 and a much smaller error term of −2.6 is more relevant for representing small-size projects in this data set: this formula leads to a much smaller convertibility delta, in both absolute and relative terms (columns 4 and 5 of Table 3.14 compared to the corresponding columns in Table 3.13 for the same projects).

Next, the linear regression model of the data in Figure 3.12 for projects greater than two hundred NESMA points provides the following convertibility formula, with a coefficient of determination (R^2) of 0.99:

$$Y(Cfsu) = 1.2 * (UFP) - 108 \tag{3.4}$$

The models for the full data set and for the data set of projects over two hundred NESMA points are fairly similar in terms of both their slope and error terms. However, there is still a large difference in convertibility results for project 8 at 260 NESMA points, in both absolute and relative terms. This means

Table 3.13 Vogelezang and Leterthuis—Less Than 200 NESMA Points

Software	NESMA (1)	COSMIC FFP (2)	With Convertibility formula in Cfsu (3)	Convertibility Delta (4) = (3) − (2)	% Delta (5) = (4)/(2)
1	39	23	27	4	16%
2	52	29	36	7	26%
3	120	115	88	−27	−24%
4	170	109	125	16	15%

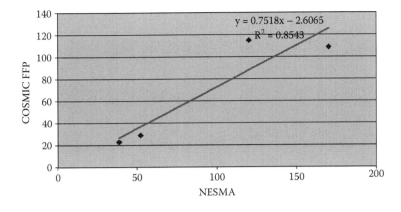

Figure 3.11 Vogelezang and Leterthuis data graph (less than 200 NESMA points).

that there must be some peculiarities in the way that functionality is measured that lead to nonstraightforward convertibility.

3.5.4 Desharnais 2005

3.5.4.1 Context

The duplicate measurement results reported next were collected in 2005 by one of the authors (Desharnais) using FPA 4.1 and COSMIC FFP 2.2. This data set comes from one governmental organization and was measured using the documentation of completed projects.

Table 3.14 Vogelezang and Leterthuis—Greater Than 200 NESMA Points

Software	NESMA (1)	COSMIC FFP (2)	With Convertibility formula in Cfsu (3)	Convertibility Delta (4) = (3) – (2)	% Delta (5) = (4)/ (2)
5	218	181	138	–43	–24%
6	224	182	145	–37	–20%
7	249	173	176	3	2%
8	260	81	190	109	134%
9	380	368	337	–31	–8%
10	766	810	811	1	0%
11	1,424	1,662	1,620	–42	–3%

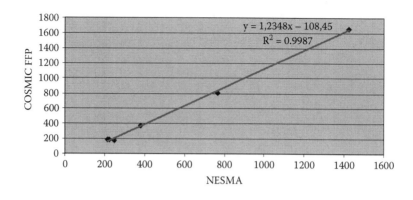

Figure 3.12   Vogelezang and Leterthuis data graph (more than 200 NESMA points).

3.5.4.2   Measurement Results

The measurement results of the duplicate measurement of the four applications are reported in Table 3.15. These data points are also presented graphically in Figure 3.13, with the FPA data on the x-axis and the COSMIC data on the y-axis.

3.5.4.3   Analysis and Interpretation

The linear regression model of the data in Figure 3.13 provides the following convertibility formula, with a coefficient of determination (R^2) of 0.91:

$$Y(Cfsu) = 0.84 * (UFP) + 18 \tag{3.5a}$$

Table 3.15   Desharnais 2005 Data Set

Software	FPA (1)	COSMIC 2.2 (2)	With Convertibility formula (3)	Convertibility Delta (4) = (3) – (2)	% Delta (5) = (4)/(2)
1	103	75	105	30	39%
2	362	209	322	113	54%
3	124	170	122	–48	–28%
4	263	203	239	36	18%
5	1146	934	981	47	5%
6	570	675	497	–178	–26%

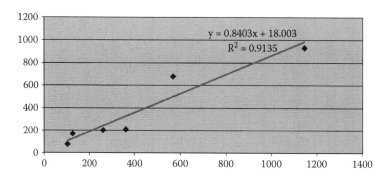

Figure 3.13   Desharnais 2005 data graph.

Again, there is a large difference in convertibility results for project 2 at 362 FPA points, in both absolute and relative terms. This means again that there must be some peculiarities in the way that functionality is measured that lead to non-straightforward convertibility.

In the FPA measurement method, the data are taken into account from multiple perspectives, once as logical data files (ILF = internal logical file, EIF = external interface file) and once again whenever that are references in FPA transactions (input, output, inquiries transaction types). This has already been noted in (Desharnais 2004), where it is reported that in FPA-like methods 30 to 40% of functional size comes from the data files. By taking into account only the FPA data file points from the FPA transaction types points, it is investigated next whether a better convertibility ratio could be derived by excluding the FPA data files, that is, by taking only the NESMA points coming from the transactions (TX).

The FPA points for the transactions only are presented in Table 3.16, and the linear regression model of the data in Figure 3.14, which provides the following convertibility formula, with a coefficient of determination (R^2) of 0.98:

$$Y(Cfsu) = 1,35 * (UFP) + 5.5 \tag{3.5b}$$

There is then a slight improvement in the R^2 for the convertibility formula when using only the results of the transactions for FPA instead of the total number of points that include both data and transactions; again, with such a small data set, this should be taken as indicative only and should be investigated with larger data sets. It can be observed that while the convertibility results of project 2 have improved in terms of converging to the correct COSMIC size, this convergence has decreased for project 3. Not enough information about the detailed measurement is available for investigating such convertibility behavior.

Table 3.16   Desharnais 2005 Data—Transactions Size Only

Software	FPA TX (1)	COSMIC 2.2 (2)	With Convertibility formula (3)	Convertibility Delta (4) = (3) – (2)	% Delta (5) = (4)/ (2)
1	60	75	87	12	16%
2	196	209	271	62	29%
3	60	170	87	–83	–49%
4	179	203	248	45	22%
5	688	934	936	2	0%
6	468	675	638	–37	–5%

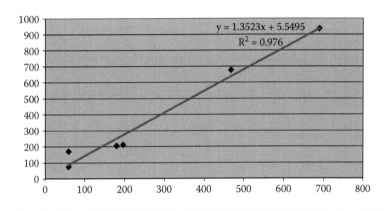

Figure 3.14   Desharnais 2005 data graph — transactions size only.

3.5.5   Discussion

This paper has presented a convertibility analysis from function points to COSMIC FFP for three data sets. In all reported data sets, measurements were taken from the human user viewpoint, that is, taking into account the functionality of the software interacting with a human, and the measured applications were all business software applications.

In summary, these analyses indicate that a relatively simple convertibility formula can be obtained for each data set, and that there are some variations in the convertibility formulas across organizations: thus, these analyses have not come up with a unique conversion formula, and the convertibility formula will vary across organizations. These variations across organizations could be caused by various extraneous factors, such as nonhomogeneity of software types across the organizations where the measurements were derived.

These analyses also provide an indication that convertibility can be fairly accurate for the majority of the projects within a data set, but on the other hand, there are some larger variations for a few projects. This means that convertibility of a full portfolio could be reasonably accurate overall, but that some individual projects would show some larger dispersion from the values predicted by the convertibility models. Further research is required to investigate factors that could explain such larger individual project variations.

This study has not investigated more complex contexts, such as projects with more complex processes or when there are software users other than software or engineered devices, as in real-time software. Under these latter conditions, of course, backward convertibility (from COSMIC FFP to FPA) is not of interest or an issue since such functionality related to nonhuman users (such as interactions with sensors or controllers in embedded software, or in multilayered software) is not usually taken into account in first-generation measurement methods.

References

Abran, A., J.-M. Desharnais, S. Oligny, D. St.-Pierre, and C. Symons. 2003. *COSMIC-FFP measurement manual (COSMIC implementation guide for ISO/IEC 19761: 2003) version 2.2.* Common Software Measurement International Consortium. http://www.lrgl. uqam.ca/cosmic-ffp (accessed January 31, 2010).

Ambler, S. W. 2004. *The object primer.* 3rd ed. Cambridge: Cambridge University Press.

Anda, B., H. Dreiem, D. I. K. Sjøberg, and M. Jørgensen. 2001. Estimating software development effort based on use cases—Experiences from industry. In *Proceedings of the 4th International Conference on the Unified Modeling Language (UML 2001),* ed. M. Gogolla and C. Kobryn, 487–502. Berlin, NY: Springer Publ.

Armour, F., and G. Miller. 2000. *Advanced use case modeling: Software systems.* Reading, MA: Addison-Wesley.

Cockburn, A. 2000. *Writing effective use cases.* Reading, MA: Addison-Wesley.

Dekkers, T., and F. Vogelezang. 2003a. *COSMIC full function points: Additional to or replacing FPA.* PM de Meern, Netherlands: Sogeti Netherlands B. V., Sogeti Publ.

Dekkers, T., and F. Vogelezang. 2003b. COSMIC full function points: Additional to or replacing FPA. In *Proceedings of the 8th European Systems and Software Engineering Process Group Conference (ESEPG 2003).* London: University Press.

Desharnais, J.-M. 2004. *Application de la Mesure Fonctionnelle COSMICFFP: Une Approche Cognitive.* Internal report. Montréal: Université du Québec à Montréal, University Press.

Engelhart, J. T., P. L. Langbroek, A. J. E. Dekkers, H. J. G. Peters, and P. H. J. Reijnders. 2001. *Function point analysis for software enhancement.* A professional guide of the Netherlands Software Metric Users Association. Amsterdam, Netherlands: NESMA Publ.

Fetcke, T. 1999a. *The warehouse software portfolio, a case study in functional size measurement.* Technical Report 1999-20. Montréal: Département d'informatique, Université du Quebec à Montréal, University Press.

Fetcke, T. 1999b. *The warehouse software portfolio—A case study in functional size measurement*. Berlin: Forschungsbericht des Fachbereichs Informatik, Universität Berlin, University Press.

IFPUG. 2004. *Function point counting practices manual*. Version 4.2. International Function Point Users Group. http://www.ifpug.org (accessed January 31, 2010).

ISO. 1998. *Information technology—Software measurement—Functional size measurement—Definition of concepts*. ISO/IEC 14143-1:1998(e). Geneva, Switzerland: International Organization for Standardization (ISO) Publ.

ISO. 2002. *Software engineering. MkII function point analysis—Counting practices manual*. ISO/IEC IS 20968. International Organization for Standardization. http://www.iso.org (accessed January 31, 2010).

ISO. 2003a. *Software engineering—COSMIC-FFP—A functional size measurement method*. ISO/IEC 19761:2003. Geneva, Switzerland: International Organization for Standardization (ISO) Publ.

ISO. 2003b. *Software engineering—IFPUG 4.1 unadjusted functional size measurement method—Counting practices manual*. ISO/IEC 20926:2003. International Organization for Standardization. http://www.iso.org (accessed January 31, 2010).

Karner, G. 1993. Metrics for objectory. No. LiTHIDA-Ex-9344:21. Diploma thesis, University of Linköping, Sweden.

Lesterhuis, A., and C. Symons. 2004. *Guideline for the application of COSMIC-FFP for sizing business/MIS application software*. Working paper. London: COSMIC Publ.

Meli, R. 1997. Early and extended function point: A new method for function points estimation. Paper presented at the IFPUG-Fall Conference, Scottsdale, AZ, September 15–19.

NESMA. 2004. Netherlands Software Measurement Association website: www.nesma.org (accessed January 31, 2010).

Santillo, L. 2000. Early FP estimation and the analytic hierarchy process. In *Proceedings of the ESCOM-SCOPE 2000*, ed. K. D. Maxwell et al., 249–58. Munich, Germany: Shaker Publ.

Santillo, L. 2004. Software complexity evaluation based on functional size components. In *Software measurement—Research and application*, ed. A. Abran et al., 41–56. Aachen, Germany: Shaker Publ.

Symons, C. 1991. *Software sizing and estimation—Mk II FPA (function point analysis)*. West Sussex, UK: John Wiley & Sons.

Vogelezang, F. 2003. *Implementing COSMIC-FFP as a replacement for FPA*. PW de Meern, Netherlands: Sogeti Nederland B. V., Sogeti Publ.

Vogelezang, F., and A. Lesterhuis. 2003. *Applicability of COSMIC full function points in an administrative environment, experiences of an early adopter*. PW de Meern, Netherlands: Sogeti Netherlands B. V., Sogeti Publ.

Vogelezang, F. W. 2004. *COSMIC full function points—The next generation of functional sizing*. Amsterdam, Netherlands: NESMA Jubilee Book, NESMA Publ.

Vogelezang, F. W. 2005. Early estimating using COSMIC-FFP. In *Proceedings of the 2nd Software Metrics European Forum (SMEF05)*, Roma, Italy. http://www.iir-italy.it/smef2005 (accessed January 31, 2010).

Chapter 4

Case Studies of COSMIC Usage and Benefits in Industry

New or next generations of functional size measurement methods must validate their appropriateness and applicability in practice. The user should identify the benefits using the new approaches.

Figure 4.1 shows the general methodologies available to validate (new or innovative) functional size measurement methods.

The first part of this chapter by Ulrich Schweikl, Stefan Weber, Erik Foltin, and Reiner Dumke is based on experience gained in the Siemens AT powertrain environment. It is shown that the FFP technique is applicable to other Siemens applications with a similar mixture of control, state-driven, and network functionality (or a subset), and similar maturity of the specification structure. Note that this case study is based on the first FFP version from 1998.

In the area of software development, software measurement gains increasing importance in order to manage and improve the underlying processes. Especially in the automotive industry with their embedded control software there is the need for high-quality software development processes to ensure the delivery of the software on time and on budget, as well as to meet predefined resources requirements. Sophie Stern discusses the applicability of COSMIC in the Renault IT area for embedded systems.

Frank Vogelezang describes, for the implementation of new regulations and the redesign of existing ones, a software factory set up with three production

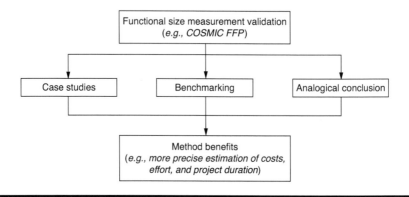

Figure 4.1 Variants of FSM method validation.

lines implementing process chains. Because of the nature of the documentation, COSMIC was used to size the process chains to be implemented. This experience shows that COSMIC can be used to size, estimate, and plan an ERP (Enterprise Resource Planning) implementation with a high degree of parameterization.

Six Sigma has become a major drive in industry and is rapidly gaining interest in software development and maintenance as well. In the last part of this chapter, Thomas Feldmann discusses which measurement method better suits Six Sigma, the well-established IFPUG 4.2 function points analysis or the more modern ISO standard ISO/IEC 19761, known as COSMIC FFP.

4.1 Applicability of Full Function Points at Siemens AT

Ulrich Schweikl, Stefan Weber, Erik Foltin, and Reiner R. Dumke

4.1.1 Management Summary

It is widely acknowledged that software metrics is a useful tool to support the decision-making process in the IT industry. There are thousands of metrics proposed in literature aimed at different artifacts and aspects of software development, namely, product metrics (i.e., size of a program), process metrics (i.e., CMM [Capability Maturity Model] level assessment), and resource metrics (i.e., experience of staff in a specific application area). From a management point of view, productivity metrics are of particular interest to:

- Control the expenses
- Analyze the performance of the resources allocated to software development
- Benchmark against other organizations

In most software cost estimation and productivity models, software size is the key cost driver. Software size can be described from different perspectives. There are either:

- Technical measures, which are dependent upon technical development and implementation decisions (the measure "lines of code" is a typical example)
- Functional measures, which assess or measure the size of a product or service from a user's (or functional) perspective

Such a functional measurement technique, function point analysis (FPA), has been (and still is) used extensively in productivity analysis and estimation in the management information system (MIS) area. FPA, however, works best only in this area; it falls short to account for the additional level of complexity introduced by real-time requirements.

The full function point technique is a recent attempt to fix this problem and to expand the applicability of FPA to other areas of software development. Full function point is a functional measurement technique based on the standard function point analysis. The (rather small) set of function point rules dealing with control concepts has been expanded considerably.

The following report will give an overview of core concepts and definitions of the FFP technique and first experiences in applying the FFP technique to a typical Siemens AT product. A set of rules will be given to illustrate the feasibility of a mapping from the requirement specification document onto the FFP model. The report concludes with an estimation of the impact of FFP on the software development process at Siemens AT.

The full function point technique combines the proven concepts of function points analysis with real-time extensions: first industrial experience has demonstrated that it is a promising tool to capture the size of embedded or real-time software.

4.1.2 FFP Overview

FFP was designed to measure the functional size of both MIS and real-time software. Since FFP is an extension of the FPA measurement method, most FPA rules are included as a subset for the measurement of the MIS functions within a measured software product. In the following, we will concentrate on the real-time extensions; for an overview of FPA concepts, see, for instance, IFPUG (1994, 1999, 2000). The following summarizes the measurement concepts of the real-time extensions of FFP (Abran et al. 1997; FFP97 1997):

- FFP measures the functional size from a functional perspective instead of from a (narrower) perspective of an external user.
- FFP introduces the concept of control processes constituting the embedded system. Each control process is self-contained from a functional perspective and controls, directly or indirectly.

- A control process delivers functionality not only to human users but also to mechanical devices (e.g., sensors, actors, controller networks).
- Each control process is decomposed into subprocesses responsible to read and write data to and from control data groups and to exchange data with the external users of the application.
- Each individual subprocess is measured; therefore, there is no limit to the size of a specific process.

Figure 4.2 shows all elements of the FFP technique. For the sake of completeness, the standard FPA elements are included as well. New function types address the control aspect of real-time software: two new control data function types (UCG and RCG) and four new control transaction function types addressing the subprocesses of real-time software (ECE, ECX, ICR, and ICW).

An *update control group* (UCG) is a group of control data updated by the application being counted. It is identified from a functional perspective. This means that the group of data appears in the (completed) requirement specification. The control data live for more than one transaction, which means they are stored for later use (by either the process creating the data or other processes of the application) and do not comprise intermediate processing results.

A *read-only control group* (RCG) is a group of control data used, but not updated, by the application being counted. It is identified from a functional perspective; the control

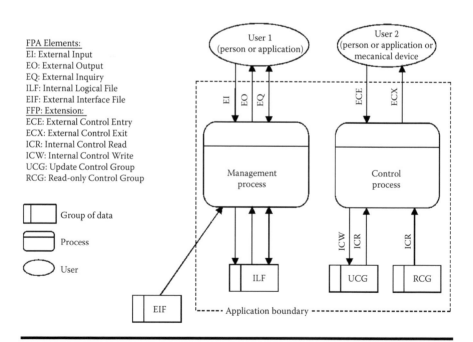

Figure 4.2 Diagram of FFP elements.

data live for more than one transaction. Each control process is decomposed in subprocesses responsible for entering and exiting control data into or from the process.

An *external control entry* (ECE) reads a group of logically related control data originating outside the application boundary.

An *external control exit* (ECX) sends a group of control data outside the application boundary to a human user or a mechanical device.

An *internal control read* (ICR) reads a logically related group of control data from either control data group (UCG or RCG).

An *internal control write* (ICW) writes a logically related group of control data to an update control data group.

4.1.3 First Application of FFP in the Siemens at PT Environment

4.1.3.1 Requirements for Counting

For a successful (and repeatable) FFP count, the following conditions have to be met (ISO 2003):

1. An adequate source of functional information must be available for the counter.
2. The counter should be familiar with the FFP (FPA) concepts and definitions.
3. (Preferably) the counter should either have some experience in the application area or application experts available for consultation.

The following will demonstrate how to map a typical AT powertrain (PT) requirement specification to FFP concepts.

4.1.3.2 0 Guideline for Mapping of FFP Concepts to the Requirements Specification

4.1.3.2.1 Overall Counting Procedure

As the requirement specification contains a series of functional process descriptions, the following order should be used to conduct a FFP count:

1. Identify processes.
2. Process evaluation for every identified control process:
   a. Identify the subprocesses.
   b. Identify the ordering of subprocesses.
   c. Count the subprocesses to determine their contribution to the overall function point count using the FFP rules.
   d. Determine the UCG/RCG data elements defined or used by this process that have not been accounted for yet.

3. Determine the contribution of the identified UCG/RCG control data groups to the overall function point count using the FFP rules.

In general, the FFP method uses a functional perspective. This perspective may be biased by the counter's experience with the application area. Therefore, the following should not be treated as strict rules (this would require a formal specification), but to demonstrate a possible mapping of the Siemens AT requirement specifications to FFP concepts (see also Bootsma 1999).

4.1.3.2.2 Identification of Processes

- Every (sub)section of the specification documentation, including a description of delivered functionality, is a potential candidate for a process.
- A process consists of a series of transactions. It generally processes input data and produces some output data. Each subsection starting, with a table of output data followed by a table of input data, is very likely to be a process definition.
- After the identification of process candidates, check if the candidates are indeed distinct, self-contained processes, or instead a succession of subordinated processes. If the latter is the case, merge all subordinated processes into one process.
- For each identified process, check whether it is a management or a control process. For management processes, the FPA counting rules have to be used. For control processes, the FFP counting rules have to be used.

4.1.3.2.3 Control Process Evaluation

Once a control process has been identified, its subprocesses must be identified. The following elements of the process description in the PT requirement specification help to identify the subprocesses:

- *The table "output data."* The table of output data contains control data that are either used for further processing by processes of the application or used to control devices outside the applications boundary. To distinguish whether other processes use the control data, the index reference of the requirement specification should be consulted. If the output data item in question is used by other processes, it is definitively written to the UCG of the application by an internal control write subprocess.

  If the data item in question is never used by this or any other process of the application, it is possibly sent (by an external control write subprocess) outside the application boundary. These data definitions are usually to be found in Section 4.1.2 (basic SW (Software) inputs and outputs) of the requirement specification.

If the data item in question is not used by other processes and it also does not exit the application boundary, check whether the data item comprises an inconsistency in the requirement specification or is generated for debugging or diagnosis. If the latter is the case, treat the data item as written to the UCG by an ICR subprocess, only if the debugging or diagnosis feature is an explicit functional requirement.

■ *The table "input data."* The table of input data contains control data items that either are read by the process from a group of control data (UCG or RCG) via an internal control read subprocess or enter the process from outside the application boundary via an external control entry subprocess. To distinguish between internal control read and external control entry, the index reference of the requirement specification can be used.

■ *The tables "configuration data" and "calibration data."* These tables contain data that control the behavior of a process. Configuration data and calibration data items remain constant and are not updated throughout the application execution.

The "functional description" section of the process description has to be examined to identify the order in which (groups of) control data enter or exit the process. The FFP model is closely related to the concept of signal flow. In case a signal flow diagram is contained in the functional description, the groups of data entering or leaving the process can be derived directly from this diagram. Figure 4.3 shows a (simplified) process signal flow diagram.

The input data for this process are not coming from outside the application boundary; the subprocesses entering them into the process are therefore internal control reads. For FFP counting purposes, there is no distinction between data items that are calibration data and data items that are intermediate results from other processes. The internal processing logic of a process is only considered insofar as it is necessary to identify groups of logically related (input and output) data. In this example, four groups of logically related input data (with one to four data items) entering the process via four distinct internal control read subprocesses can be identified.*

The output of this process is identified as an intermediate result: it will be stored for use by other processes and is not sent outside the application boundary. The subprocess that writes the output data is therefore an internal control write.

If the signal flow diagram is not provided for a process, an implicit signal flow model has to be derived from the (verbal) algorithm description or the formula section. Depending on the accuracy of the documentation, more or less application knowledge is required.

---

* Subprocesses dealing with rather small groups of data are typical for real-time/embedded systems.

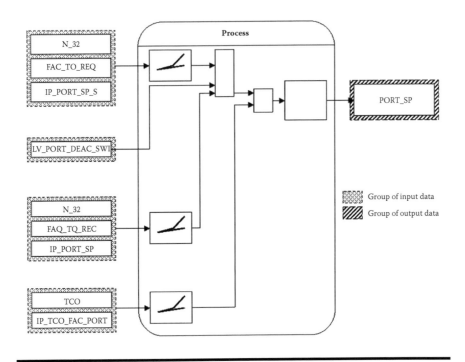

Figure 4.3 Sample signal flow diagram.

4.1.3.3 Actual Counting Experience

Using the mapping above, a sample count has been conducted. The basis of the counting was the specification document SIM98 (1998). From this specification Section 4.1.4 (system variables) has been counted.

Within this section, twenty-five functional processes have been counted, amounting for a total of approximately[*] 130 FFP. All processes were identified as control processes. The processes contributed forty items of updated control data and used another sixty items of read-only control data. The counting took about 4.5 hours, with the counter having only little insight into the application area.[†] The following (positive) findings can be stated after this first application of FFP:

- In general, the Siemens AT PT specification document structure is very well suited to the FFP technique: the section structure is almost unambiguously identical to the FFP concept of processes.

---

[*] Some ambiguity in the specification prevented a reliable, exact number.
[†] This time does not include the time to become acquainted with the specification document. There was also no report created.

■ Using a few rules of thumb to map the specification to the FFP concepts allowed a count with almost no insight into the application area.*

■ In fact, using these rules allowed detecting inconsistencies within the specification documentation.

■ All elements of the FFP real-time concept are identifiable within the specification documentation.

■ On the other hand, the specification documentation contained little information that seemed to introduce some complexity that could not be mapped to FFP concepts (besides algorithmic details; the algorithms are simplified and mapped to a sequence of subprocesses).

■ Most problems with counting details could be identified (with the help of application experts) as a result of ambiguity in the specification documentation.

■ Therefore, a more consistent documentation or more application experience should increase both the counting speed and accuracy.

It must be noted, however, that the above statements are the result of a first judgment and should be treated as hypotheses. Some more counting experiments have to be carried out in order to:

■ See whether there are still unclear counting details when using a more mature specification documentation (a brief inspection of Section 4.1.2 of the SIM99 (1999) specification looks promising)

■ Verify if the above counting guidelines are applicable to all sections of the requirement specification documentation

It must be further noted that this judgment of the suitability of the FFP method for Siemens AT purposes is a mere technical one. A crucial issue is to discuss the results of the counting experiment(s) with application experts to see whether the FFP counts derived from the specification match their (perceived) idea of size for real-time software.

4.1.4   Conclusions

4.1.4.1   General

■ FFP is dependent on the quality of the functional information. Based on the counting experiment carried out, the quality of the functional information available for this experiment was adequate.

---

* It must be noted, however, that most of the evaluated processes were rather small (based on both documentation length and FFP count).

- The FFP count should be treated as estimates. The FFP concepts allow for some degree of interpretation to deal with uncertain and fuzzy information that is typical for early development stages.[*]
- Identifying the groups of data is very crucial for a repeatable count. Signal flow diagrams are a very helpful tool to support the FFP counter to identify logically related groups of data. Verbal (informal) functional descriptions are likely to introduce ambiguity.
- Application experts have to be consulted to see if their perception of size correlates with the FFP count.
- The FFP count is one sole number, which promises to capture the functional size well. It cannot be expected, however, to be "the magical number" to control all aspects of the software development process.

The main aims of the full function points technique are to provide a size indicator for real-time and embedded software systems and to provide a consistent guideline to obtain the function point count. The mere FFP count has to be put into perspective. It can be used to:

- Compare the size of different applications/versions
- Trace the requirement growth throughout the software development cycle
- Act as an indicator for specification maturity
- Serve as the basic input (key cost driver) in software cost estimation/productivity models; this embedding allows it to:

  1. Assess the functional size of requirements delivered to software organizations
  2. Assess the performance of software organizations

There should be little additional effort required to obtain the FFP count. One possibility is to include the FFP counting in the inspection process. The FFP technique requires some structured way to look at the requirement definition, which actually seems to ease the review process. The following strategy should be pursued to implement FFP at Siemens AT:

  1. Conduct a few more counting experiments to:
     a. Gain experience in FFP application
     b. Detail the counting guidelines
     c. Provide sample counts for discussion

---

[*] Experiments with function point analysis have shown that the deviation in counting results based on the same information is in the range of 5% for counters with similar experience. As FFP concepts are comparable, the same should be expected for FFP counts.

2. Discuss the counting results with application experts to check whether their expectations are met
3. Identify milestones for conducting FFP counts within the development project
4. Identify candidates for pilot projects
5. Provide training and tools to assist FFP counting
6. Collect FFP and performance data to establish cost and productivity models

4.1.4.2 Transferability to Other AT Applications

This report is based on experience gained in the Siemens AT powertrain environment. It should be expected that the FFP technique is applicable to other Siemens AT GGs/GZs, providing (compared to PT):

■ A similar mixture of control, state-driven, and network functionality (or a subset)
■ A similar maturity of the specification structure

Some more effort has to be spent to evaluate the applicability of FFP for systems containing not only embedded functionality but also classical MIS functionality (e.g., database handling, graphical user interfaces) like driver information systems.

Appendix: Counting Example

Table 4.1 shows the process of brake servo unit function (File 1F402601.00A, Simtec 81) where means the DET contribution to UCG: 7 (LV_BRAKE_REQ, PBSU, PBSU_DIF, LV_PBSU_EXC, LV_PBSU_AVL, LV_BRAKE_REQ_PRS, MAP_HOM_ESTIM) and the DET contribution to RCG: 9 (C_AMP_BRAKE_TOL, C_PBSU_DIF_BOL, C_PBSU_DIF_HYS, C_PBSU_MAP_HYS, IP_PBSU__V_PBSU_BAS,LDP_V_PBSU_BAS,IP_MAP_HOM_ESTIM__TQI_REQ__N_32, LDP_TQI_REQ_SLOW__MAP_HOM_ESTIM, LDP_N_32__MAP_HOM_ESTIM).

4.2 Practical Experimentations with the COSMIC Method in the Automotive Embedded Software Field

Sophie Stern

4.2.1 Introduction

More and more functionalities are available in cars (to increase security, to reduce CO_2 emissions, to improve the connectivity with the outside world, and so on), and the most part of these new features is realized by software. The automotive industry

Table 4.1 FFP Counting of the Brake Servo Unit Function

Sub-processes		
Type	DET's	FFP
ICR	2 (V_PBSU_BAS, IP_PBSU_V_PBSU)	1
ICR	2 (AMP_AD, C_AMP_BRAKE_TOL)	1
ICR	3 (TQI_REQ_SLOW, N_32, IP_MAP_HOME_ESTIM__TQI_N_32)	1
ICR	1 (LV_BLS)	1
ICR	1 (LV_ERR_PBSU)	1
ICR	2 (C_PBSU_DIF_HYS,C_PBSU_DIF_BOL)	1
ICW	1 (PBSU)	1
ICW	1 (PBSU_DIF)	1
ICW	1 (LV_PBSU_AVL)	1
ICW	1 (LV_PBSU_EXC)	1
ICW	1 (LV_BRAKE_REQ_PRS)	1
ICW	1 (LV_BRAKE_REQ)	1
	Unadjusted FFP for all sub-processes	12

is used to managing very accurately the physical parts costs with its suppliers and now has to face software parts development costs management too. For that, it is necessary to construct effort estimation models based on a standard functional size measurement method that must be explicable, factual, simple, and reproducible.

The major goal of this paper is to give feedback on the Renault practical experimentations with the COSMIC method (ISO 2003) on the embedded software field.

During the last ten years, as the functionalities available for customers are more and more numerous, the car's complexity has evolved increasingly. This complexity is mainly supported by calculators (airbag, ABS, etc.) that we call ECU for electronic control unit.

Historically, Renault subcontracts the development and manufacturing of its ECU to many suppliers. An ECU presents the particularity to be part of hardware and part of embedded software. For several years, Renault has been used to pay each ECU as a whole. But with the increase of the software complexity, and at the same time the decrease of the electronic parts costs, the software development cost is less and less marginal and may be higher than the hardware one for major ECU.

As were the other car manufacturers, Renault was very used to estimating the development cost of physical parts, such as harness or electronic components, and was quite lacking in software development cost estimation.

Several departments, but especially the Renault purchasing one, asked the Renault embedded software group to find a method to estimate the embedded software development cost.

The main goal of this short industry paper is to show how the COSMIC method has been used in the Renault experimentation and the learned lessons.

After the presentation of the reasons why Renault chose to evaluate the COSMIC method for embedded software development effort management, I will present the goals assigned to the experimentation, first results, and best practices, and will conclude on what next.

4.2.2 Why Had Renault Chosen to Evaluate the COSMIC Method for Embedded Software Development Effort Management?

In 2008, the Renault purchasing department requested from the embedded software group a method to estimate the embedded software development cost in order to manage it more accurately.

The first point was to find a standard method to estimate the development effort that could be converted later in development cost with applying the suppliers' rates. As everybody knows, it is not possible to measure a piece of software with a meter or a balance, and it appears that it is not possible anymore to measure one with the number of written lines of code, because it would make no sense with automatic coding. So we decided to interest ourselves in the functional size measurement (FSM) methods (Abran 2001).

The Renault embedded software group started with state-of-the-art FSM methods; two were studied particularly at first because of their past in Renault: the IFPUG and COCOMO methods.

The COCOMO method had been experimented with a few years prior in the ECU diagnostic department, but with unsuccessful results.

The IFPUG method has been used for several years in the Renault information system department, and no new information system can be launched without its cost first being evaluated by the IFPUG software effort estimation cell.

Nevertheless, the possible application of IFPUG on embedded software had to be checked with an evaluation.

In order to benchmark at least two FSM methods, we chose the COSMIC method, as it was announced to be well adapted to real-time software as the embedded software in ECU is.

Our first experiments started on the engine control unit in mid-2008 with the IFPUG and COSMIC methods. The engine control unit is modular, and each of its modules is a set of specifications under the Matlab/Simulink tool, with textual requirements also. The effort supplier invoice is available for each module.

Functional size measurements were realized on the same nine modules with the two studied methods, and then results were compared.

In the Renault experimentation, the IFPUG functional size measurements were always higher than the COSMIC ones; the COSMIC method was well suited for embedded software, whereas the IFPUG method appeared to not be pertinent, especially when the functional software size increased. Furthermore, measurements with the COSMIC method seemed to us easier than the ones with the IFPUG method (Abran et al. 2005).

So we decided to pursue the experimentation for embedded software with the COSMIC method in a project way.

4.2.3   The Renault COSMIC Project

In 2009, we decided to pursue, in a project way, and to take into account another ECU, the body control module (BCM). The BCM is specified by Renault with the Statemate tool and textual requirements. The BCM is specified in software functions; the supplier effort invoice is available for each of them.

The first step was to measure functional sizes on BCM functions and on engine control unit modules and to try to find linear regressions with the supplier effort invoices. For the engine control module, it was on software evolutions; for the BCM, it was on software evolutions and new developments.

In each case, we found one or several linear regressions. At this moment, as the Renault implicated actors and managers were numerous, from different departments and with different interests in the COSMIC method, it appeared to me that it was necessary to define very clearly the goals of the COSMIC method application evaluation on Renault ECU.

We defined four major goals with purchasing departments, departments in charge of specifications, and ECU project management.

4.2.3.1   The Four Major Goals of the COSMIC Method Application Evaluation on Renault ECU

1. Have indicators to manage the supplier productivity year after year.
2. Predict the cost of the software functions development in order to negotiate the right price with suppliers.
3. Be able to estimate a function software development cost as soon as its specification is written to decide whether to implement the function.
4. Benchmark the productivity of the different suppliers.

This objective is a first milestone. The final goal is to be able to contract the price of a functional size in CFP (COSMIC Function Points) with suppliers. Notice that this process has been applied for several years for information systems. These major goals are then divided into smaller goals for each.

I put in place steering committees for each ECU development sector to check regularly the goals, and of course to check the advancement on work packages and usual indicators on projects: problems resolution, risks, and planning.

4.2.3.2 A Cell of Measurers, COSMIC Measurement Textual Guides

Because the software functional size measurements are performed by several measurers, it is mandatory to define very clearly and without any ambiguity the way of measuring functional sizes. We wrote COSMIC measurements textual guides. Several functional size measurements were performed independently by different persons; these experiments showed that even manual measurements are very reproducible, with at most a 1% difference.

4.2.3.3 The Way of Constructing COSMIC Models

We made the choice to have one different COSMIC model for each ECU. We also constructed different models for each supplier. It is interesting to have standards of comparison and to benchmark suppliers.

Until now, we made the choice to split models when influent factors were different, but I intend to pursue our statistics studies with multifactor approaches.

4.2.3.4 Obtained COSMIC Results

We followed the COSMIC method and constructed regression models with only one variable: the functional size in CFP.

After our experimentations, my opinion is that it is necessary to find the balance between too many models and models easily understood by many actors, such as the ECU development project, the purchasing, and suppliers. The split of one COSMIC model into several models must always have a meaning.

4.2.3.4.1 BCM COSMIC Models

The BCM COSMIC model was first split between new developments and function evolutions. Then these two BCM models were split again between manual developments and automatic ones. Four reference COSMIC models are defined at the moment for the Renault BCM (Figure 4.4).

On this raw model, there is one point very close to the confidence interval limit. This BCM function was developed by an expert in the supplier team, so we decided to remove this point from the regression curve and to capitalize on a checklist of particular functions. After this correction, we had the reference model shown in Figure 4.5.

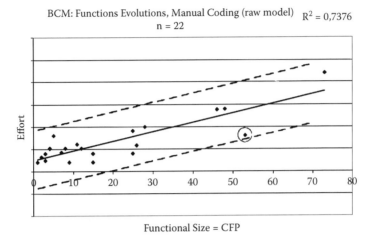

Figure 4.4   Raw COSMIC models for the Renault BCM.

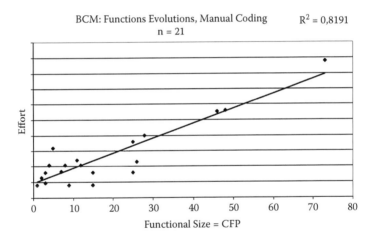

Figure 4.5   Corrected COSMIC model for the Renault BCM.

The number of points for the two BCM COSMIC models for new developments were low, but the coefficients of determination are correct, and these two models have been very helpful for us to realize predictions during a request for quotation (RFQ) with suppliers for a new BCM development (Figures 4.6 and 4.7).

An important point will be to complete the reference COSMIC models with new data when available.

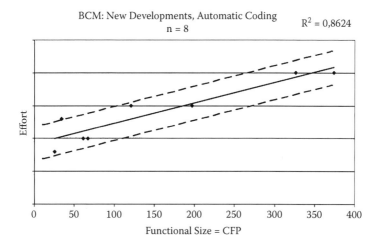

Figure 4.6 COSMIC model for the new automatic BCM development.

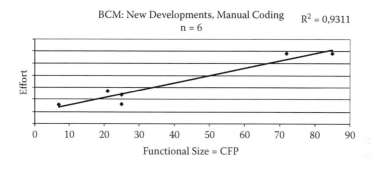

Figure 4.7 COSMIC model for the new manual BCM development.

4.2.3.4.2 Engine Control Unit COSMIC Models

For the engine control unit, the COSMIC model was only split between the different suppliers; all considered developments are module evolutions. One COSMIC model for one supplier is shown in Figure 4.8).

The two points in squares correspond to modules that are very different by their nature from the other ones. They have been removed from the COSMIC model and capitalized in a checklist until we can construct a COSMIC model for this kind of modules. After this correction, we have the reference model given in Figure 4.9.

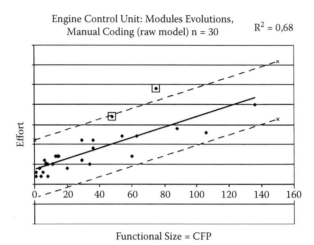

Figure 4.8 One COSMIC model for one supplier.

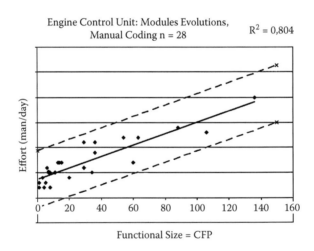

Figure 4.9 COSMIC model for module evolution.

4.2.3.4.3 A Real Experimentation on BCM: COSMIC Predictions in an RFQ Phase

We applied our BCM COSMIC new development models during a request for quotation with suppliers for a new BCM in order to have a target software development cost on the applicative software. As soon as the specifications were written, we predicted the development effort for each BCM function within a prediction interval, and we also predicted the development effort and the associated prediction interval for the whole applicative software. Then we negotiated the estimations with the supplier.

Figure 4.10 shows the comparison between our COSMIC predictions and the supplier's estimations after the first and second rounds with the supplier.

The negotiation is not finished, but this example shows that factual measures realized with a standard method is a good lever to negotiate.

4.2.3.4.4 Predictions for the Engine Control Module

For the engine control module, as there are regular software development invoices for module evolutions, we did predictions on two modules. Each supplier invoice was in our prediction interval.

We have to pursue such experiments to make everybody, inside and outside the company, confident in the predictability of the COSMIC method.

4.2.3.5 *The Success Keys for Applying the COSMIC Models*

4.2.3.5.1 Capitalization

As we are not fortune-tellers, it is not possible to predict software development effort or cost without capitalization on ECU projects from the past. The storage must be precise and complete; in our case, we need to store software specifications and the development cost for each specification. For some ECU, the first step will be to change the process of costs negotiation with the supplier to obtain the detailed software costs.

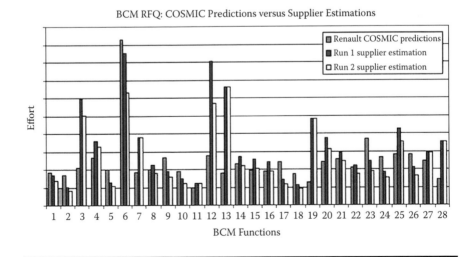

Figure 4.10 Comparison between COSMIC predictions and the supplier estimations.

4.2.3.5.2 The Implication of the ECU Purchasers

The goals of the ECU purchasers are in line with the COSMIC method possibilities. It is important to explain the method and to show some successful experiments in order to have their support, because they may be a very good lever of change inside the company and outside with suppliers.

4.2.3.5.3 The Help of the ECU Project Team

The COSMIC measurers are often embarrassed to explain the points outside the COSMIC regression curves; the help of the ECU project team is mandatory to interpret the module's intrinsic particularities or the ECU development process specificities.

Furthermore, the implication of the ECU project team is that it is very important to deploy the method with the supplier.

4.2.3.5.4 Meeting Points with the Supplier

The final goal of using the COSMIC method is often to share it with suppliers and to contract agreements on the basis of factual software functional measures.

It is important to explain step by step the COSMIC method to suppliers, to make experiments with them to show the accuracy of the method.

4.2.3.5.5 Multidisciplinary Team

The COSMIC core team needs people with knowledge and capabilities in computer science and statistics. As it is very difficult to find people with these two competencies, the best way is first to mix people with different profiles in the same team and train them.

4.2.3.5.6 Process Change

To improve the way suppliers buy software, it is necessary to conduct a process change in the organization with a road map.

4.2.4 Conclusions and Future Directions

As the Renault experimentations with COSMIC are very encouraging for embedded software cost management, we intend to continue with the major following actions:

- Pursue COSMIC experimentations on other ECU
- Experiment with statistical multifactor models
- Find one method to work upstream when simulation models are not available
- Estimate software development efforts other than applicable basic software development effort, ECU functional validation effort, etc.
- Automate the whole measurement process

4.3 Using COSMIC FFP for Sizing, Estimating, and Planning in an ERP Environment

Frank Vogelezang

4.3.1 Introduction: Changing Environments

4.3.1.1 Political Change

In early 2003 the Commission of the European Communities proposed a reform of the common agricultural policy (COM 2003). The main aims of this reform were to cut the link between production and direct payments (decoupling), to make those payments conditional on environmental, food safety, animal welfare, health, and occupational safety standards (cross-compliance), and to increase EU support for rural development by a modulation of direct payments (from which small farmers would be exempted).

The proposed reform came into force in 2006, which means that the information systems for financial support for the agricultural sector have been revised drastically. In the Netherlands, the Office for Regulations (*Dienst Regelingen*) of the Ministry of Agriculture, Nature, and Food Quality is responsible for carrying out all regulations with respect to the agricultural sector.

4.3.1.2 Technology Change

Given the drastic revision of the financial support regulations, combined with the fact that a number of the current systems were at or near the end of their life cycle, the Office for Regulations decided to build a new software environment to support the execution of financial regulations. This new environment had to be based on packaged software. In this way, the Office for Regulations expects to be able to implement new or changed business processes quicker than with custom-built software.

The Oracle E-Business Suite (EBS) has been chosen to be the basis for the new software environment. The EBS is a fully integrated, comprehensive suite of business applications, which can be implemented one at a time, as a predefined set for a special kind of business or as the complete suite (Oracle 2000). The implementation of EBS is further described in Section 4.3.7. Next to the EBS basis, specialized software and custom-built extensions to EBS are still being used.

4.3.1.3 Organizational Change

It is expected that the reform of the common agricultural policy will be followed by other changes in regulations for the agricultural sector. Implementing

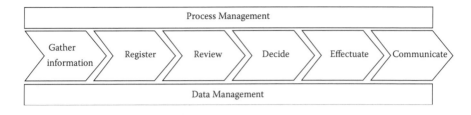

Figure 4.11   Business process model (BPM).

an ERP system was more than an IT project. To achieve maximum flexibility for change, the Office for Regulations decided to use not only one generic software environment, but also one generic working process for all regulations under the jurisdiction of the Ministry of Agriculture, Nature, and Food Quality. What started as system renewal became a journey of change for the whole organization with a far-reaching impact. The new working process was described in a business process model (BPM). The highest level of the BPM is presented in Figure 4.11.

The Oracle E-Business Suite has been preconfigured to support the BPM so that new business processes—based on the BPM—could be implemented easily.

4.3.1.4   Design Change

The new working process called for a different strategy for the design. Usually the design focuses on the functionality, but in this environment the design should have a very strong focus on the working process rather than the automated functionality. This design strategy also had consequences for the applicability of sizing metrics (see Section 4.3.3).

4.3.1.5   Production Change

Many regulations will have to be implemented in the new environment over time. To do this in an economically efficient manner, the implementation of new regulations has not been delegated to different projects. For software development projects, it is not unusual that the project teams are dismantled straight after the delivery of the developed software. The knowledge the project team has acquired fans out over the organization(s) that formed the team. If the software requires a new release or maintenance, all the knowledge has to be reestablished and fans out again. In this situation, it was more economic to set up a software factory (Kranenburg et al. 1999).

The critical success factors of a software factory are productivity and predictability. All other possible targets of a software factory (like price performance, reducing errors, shortening the time to market, reducing cost, and less dependency on "heroes") are derived from the two success factors. A software factory consists of four key elements:

- System engineers (all-round IT knowledge workers)
- Standard working method
- Development and maintenance tools
- Supporting processes and management

A software factory can be split up into a number of production lines, either to be able to split up the workload or to facilitate different development environments. The Office for Regulations has a single development environment, so its software factory is split up into three production lines to balance the workload (see Section 4.3.6.1).

Regulations are implemented as sets of process chains. A process chain is a set of business functions that handles a certain event using all the steps of the BPM. By splitting up regulations into sets of process chains, the workload can be balanced between the production lines.

4.3.2   COSMIC FFP as Sizing Metric

All new regulations are designed to fit the BPM. One of the first design documents that is delivered is the process model. This document describes all process steps in terms of the BPM and gives an indication of whether this is a manual process or a process that will be supported by the E-Business Suite. In this stage, some general information is known about the processes, but little is known about the data interaction. For planning purposes in this stage, estimates were required about the expected size of the software support of the new regulation.

This posed a problem for the project management. The software support for a new regulation or a process chain could not be estimated per EBS component, like a regular ERP implementation, because this implementation does not implement EBS components, but process chains based on EBS components (see Section 4.3.7). The lack of knowledge about data interaction and how process chains relate to functions in this stage of the implementation meant the software support could not be estimated like a traditional custom-built software project by means of EQFPA (Meli 2002). But a program of this magnitude without a way of forecasting the costs and managing the planning schedule was highly undesirable.

The project management decided to use COSMIC FFP as a sizing technique for the process chains that had to be implemented.

4.3.2.1   About COSMIC FFP

COSMIC FFP is a functional size measurement method that has been designed to be equally applicable to business application software, real-time software, and infrastructure software. It is the first functional size measurement method that is designed to meet the principles of the ISO/IEC 14143 standard for functional size measurement (Abran et al. 2003a).

The basic principle of COSMIC FFP is that the functional user requirements of a piece of software can be broken down into a number of functional processes that are independently executable sets of elementary actions that the software should perform in response to a triggering event. The elementary actions that software can perform are either data movements or data manipulations. COSMIC FFP assumes that each data movement has an associated constant average amount of data manipulation. With this approximation, the functional processes can be broken down into a number of data movements. A data movement moves a unique set of data attributes (data group), where each included data attribute describes a complementary aspect of the same, single thing or concept (object of interest), about which the software is required to store or process data.

COSMIC FFP distinguishes four different types of data movements:

- *Entry*: An entry is a data movement that moves a data group from a user across the software boundary into the functional process where it is required.
- *Write*: A write is a data movement that moves a data group from inside a functional process to persistent storage.
- *Read*: A read is a data movement that moves a data group from persistent storage to within the functional process that requires it.
- *Exit*: An exit is a data movement that moves a data group from a functional process across the software boundary to the user that requires it.

The relation between the data movements is graphically represented in Figure 4.12. The value of a functional process is determined by the sum of the constituting data movements. The smallest functional process consists of two data movements: an entry (containing the triggering event) and either a write or an exit

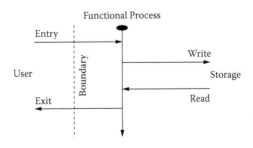

Figure 4.12   The relation between data movements in COSMIC FFP.

(containing the action the functional process has to perform). Every identified data movement receives the value of 1 Cfsu (COSMIC functional sizing unit). The size of the smallest functional process is 2 Cfsu and increases with 1 Cfsu per additional data movement to an unlimited number.

4.3.2.2 Size Measurement in Early Stages of Development with COSMIC FFP

To be able to make a functional size measurement in an early stage of development, an approximation method has been developed: approximate COSMIC FFP. This method counts the number of functional processes to obtain an estimate for the expected software size (ISO 2003). Because of the nature of the design process in this environment (see Section 4.3.4), this approximation method is far more useful than FPA-based methods that rely on early knowledge of the data model (Meli 2002).

The expectation was that the size obtained using COSMIC FFP would reflect the effort needed to implement the process chains, although a lot of the functionality was not actually built, but parameterized from existing functionality (see Section 4.3.7). If there is enough information about the processes to classify them into categories, they can be classified as:

- Small, e.g., retrieval of information about a single object of interest
- Medium, e.g., storage of a single object of interest with some checks
- Large, e.g., retrieval of information about multiple objects of interest
- Complex

This method is called refined approximate COSMIC FFP. The values that are used for each category are:

- Small: 4 Cfsu
- Medium: 7 Cfsu
- Large: 11 Cfsu
- Complex: 24 Cfsu

These values are taken from the measurement manual, although there are indications that these values are environment dependent (Abran and Desarnais 1999; Abran et al. 2005). The precision of the refined approximate COSMIC FFP is about 20 to 30% (Vogelezang 2005). Given the fact that it takes quite a lot of experience data to calibrate the method for a given environment, it was decided that using the values from the measurement manual without a local calibration would be precise enough for planning and estimating purposes until enough data would be available for local calibration.

4.3.3 The Advantage of COSMIC FFP in This Environment

In the first version of the process model, not all data interaction is known. But the description of the process is detailed enough to classify a process into one of the four categories of the refined approximate COSMIC FFP. Based on only the process model, it is possible to get an early estimate of the size of a process chain with an uncertainty of 20 to 30%.

Most early sizing techniques are based on information about the data (Meli 2002). In this environment the process model was designed before the data model, which means that FPA-based techniques can only be used in a later stage.

The EBS contains its own data model. The process chains make use of the EBS data model and a specific data model for the Office for Regulations. The contribution of the specific data model to the functional size can be determined with FPA-based techniques—for the EBS data model this is quite difficult.

The exact structure and the way modules make use of the EBS data model are proprietary information and cannot be determined for sizing purposes. There are no counting rules when and how the data model must be taken into account for FPA-based techniques. With COSMIC FFP the sizing is more or less independent of the structure of the data model. So with COSMIC FFP, the fact that a part of the data model is not known does not influence the quality of the functional size measurement.

4.3.4 Functional Size Measurement with COSMIC FFP

In an early stage of development, the size of a process chain is estimated by classifying each automated process in the process model into one of the four categories of the refined approximate COSMIC FFP and adding together the sizes of all the processes (see Section 4.3.2).

When the process description contains enough information about the data interaction, a detailed COSMIC FFP functional size measurement can be made. As stated in Section 4.3.2, the functional size is determined by the number of data movements. Each data movement moves one data group. The ability to recognize data groups determines the ability to determine the functional size in detail.

> A *data group* is defined as
> a distinct, nonempty, nonordered and nonredundant set of data attributes where each included data attribute describes a complementary aspect of the same object of interest. (ISO 2003, p. 26)
> An *object of interest* is defined as
> identified from the point of view of the Functional User Requirements and may be any physical thing, as well as any conceptual objects or parts of conceptual objects in the world of the user about which the software is required to process and/or store data. (ISO 2003, p. 27)

These definitions show that the ability to recognize data groups is not dependent on the data model, but on characteristics that can be determined without knowledge about the structure in which the data groups are stored. A detailed process model is sufficient to make a detailed functional size measurement.

4.3.5 Planning

The first step in using size estimates for planning the production of process chains was to verify whether a relation can be determined between the measured size and the expended effort. It appeared that for the software factory we had to make a clear distinction between the direct effort and the support effort. The main components of the direct and support effort are given in Table 4.2.

The support effort has a linear relation with time and has no dependency on the size of the process chain(s) to be produced. This can be explained from the fact that these activities are mainly related to the processes with which the software is produced rather than with the (size of the) software itself.

4.3.5.1 Time to Delivery

The time to delivery of a process chain has an exponential relation with the size of the software (Abran et al. 1999, 2003b). The power is a function of the number of production lines that are used:

$$\text{Time}_{\text{Delivery}} = \frac{\text{Size}^{\text{Power}}}{\text{PL}}$$

where:

Time = time to delivery of the process chain in months

Size = functional size in Cfsu

Power = 0.20 for a single production line and 0.37 for two production lines

PL = number of deployed production lines (1 or 2)

The exponent values have been empirically calculated based on the figures of two releases of EBS functionality. No exponent values have been calculated for three production lines, because this would mean that the total software factory should be dedicated to one single process chain, which is a nondesirable situation. A process chain that is so large that it requires more than two production lines is too large to control efficiently and must be cut into smaller process chains.

Table 4.2 Main Components of Direct Effort and Support Effort

Direct Effort	Support Effort
Design administrative organization	Architecture
Design custom—built software	Project Management
Set-up design	ERP set-up
Build custom software	Process improvement
System test	Quality Control
Integration test	Metrics office

4.3.5.2 Working Method of the Software Factory

The working method of the software factory is based on Oracle's Application Implementation Method (AIM Advantage™) for implementing packaged applications.

This method consists of six project phases (Oracle 1999):

- Definition
- Operations analysis
- Solution design
- Build
- Transition
- Production

In each of the phases, the project team will execute tasks in several processes. The full model contains eleven processes. For the tasks of the software factory that affect the direct effort, three major processes are relevant:

- Design (including business requirements definition and mapping)
- Build (including module design and build and documentation)
- Test (including business system testing and performance testing)

In Figure 4.13, these major processes are mapped to the AIM Advantage™ phases.

4.3.5.3 Planning Production

The manpower buildup for the three major processes differs in time. This means that the production of a new process chain can start before the production of a previous chain is completed. The production process can be planned in tiles, where the length of a tile is determined by the size of the process chain to be produced.

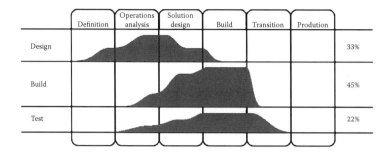

	Definition	Operations analysis	Solution design	Build	Transition	Prodution	
Design							33%
Build							45%
Test							22%

Figure 4.13   The working method of the software factory related to direct effort.

4.3.5.4   *Planning Production Line Staffing Size*

A factor that is essential for the planning is the staffing size of the production line. This size is scaled up or down according to the size and complexity of the process chain to be produced. The size of a production line varies between four and fourteen system engineers. This is consistent with general industry experiences for package customizations (Vogelezang 2005), in which a maximum team size for package customization is reported to be 5 (median value) to 12.8 (75th percentile value).

The main factors that influence the staffing size of a production line are:

- The *size* of the process chain(s) to be produced
- The estimated amount of *reuse*
- The *complexity* of the process chain(s) to be produced
- The relative *autonomy* of the process chain(s) to be produced

The *size* of the process chain(s) is based on early estimates of the functional size from the first design of the process model. This documentation is produced before the design activities of the software factory start.

The amount of *reuse* is currently determined as an expert estimate. The Office for Regulations is setting up a process chain component library. This library will contain the components and their functional size. When this library is in effect, the amount of reuse can be determined more objectively.

The *complexity* is determined by an expert estimate of the number of quality plans[*] that must be developed to produce the necessary user interaction.

The *autonomy* of a process chain is determined by the dependency on other process chains that make use of the same process chain components.

At this moment we are not able to quantify all of these factors with enough precision to derive a formula to predict the required staffing size.

---

[*] A quality plan is a way to parameterize the quality module for the required man–machine interaction.

4.3.5.5   Client Expectations

The early size estimates are very useful to manage client expectations. The implementation of the new regulations in the EBS environment not only is a system renewal, but also contains a lot of business process redesign. The Office for Regulations has to deal with both aspects at the same time. Some of the clients of the software factory do not have a good idea of the impact of the new processes in terms of EBS functionality. For these clients, the size estimates proved to be a very effective tool in communicating that different process chains can have a different software size.

4.3.6   Control

The functional size measurement is relevant not only for planning purposes, but also to provide management with information to control several aspects of the production process. At this point in time, the functional size measurement is used to control:

- Stability rate
- Direct cost (productivity)
- Scope creep
- Change management

4.3.6.1   Stability Rate

The stability rate is the rate between the functional sizes to be produced per unit of time per production line. The target of the software factory is to produce at a level stability rate.

The stability rate can incline due to scope creep, which causes more production with the same staffing size (see Section 4.3.6.3), and corrective maintenance on previous releases, which causes a decrease of the effectively available staffing size. A small incline can be corrected by increasing the staffing of a production line. If the expectation is that the stability rate will remain at a high level for a longer period of time, an extra production line can be added. It takes approximately two months before a production line can produce at a regular stability rate.

The stability rate can decline due to late availability of new process models for process chains. A small decline can be corrected by decreasing the staffing of a production line. If the expectation is that the stability rate will remain at a low level for a longer period of time, a production line can be dismantled.

4.3.6.2   Direct Cost

The cost model for the direct cost within the Office for Regulations is on a fixed price per Cfsu to stimulate the software factory to improve productivity. With the formula for the time to delivery from Section 4.3.5.1, the total cost formula can be described as a function of size and the number of production lines:

$$Cost = \frac{Size^{Power}}{PL} * Constant_{Support} + Size * Constant_{Direct}$$

where:

Size = functional size in Cfsu

Power = 0.20 for a single production line and 0.37 for two production lines

Constant$_{Support}$ = daily support cost per production line in €

Constant$_{Direct}$ = direct cost per Cfsu in €

The direct cost per Cfsu has a target that is based on the productivity the software factory expects to reach after the working process is stable. If the productivity improves, the cost per Cfsu decreases. The first process chain was delivered early this year, and the expectation is that the set productivity goal will be reached at the end of this year. Figure 4.14 gives an indication of the progress toward the productivity goal.

In this environment, the support cost is a substantial part of the development cost of a process chain. The support cost cannot be related to functional size, because there is no relation between the support cost and the functional size. The main factors influencing the support cost are:

- **Architecture:** In parallel with the development of the process chains, the working processes have to be redesigned. To support the business process redesign, there is a heavy architectural support.
- **Project management:** Because of the parallel process redesign and system renewal, each production line has its own project manager. This means a relatively high cost for project management in relation to the delivered functional size.
- **Promotion management:** The EBS environment has no tool support to promote parameterized components from one OTAP* environment to the next. This calls for a lot of manual labor to promote the components.

4.3.6.3 Scope Creep

By comparing the early size estimate with the final functional size when the design is finished, the scope creep can be determined. Scope creep is a measure for the stability of the requirements. Because of the fact that parallel to the system

---

* OTAP = separate environments for build (Ontwikkeling), test, acceptance, and production.

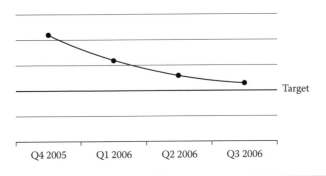

Figure 4.14   Cost per Cfsu versus the set target.

development there is also business process redesign, a high percentage scope creep can be expected, due to information latency between the parallel streams. At this moment, only the scope creep due to change requests is being measured (see next section). This scope creep is around 13%. The total scope creep between the first functional size measurement and the delivered functionality is expected to be somewhat over 20%.

4.3.6.4   Change Management

With COSMIC FFP, changes can be measured easily (ISO 2003). A substantial number of the process chains implement new legislation that evolves after the first stage of design and generates a number of requests for change. To facilitate change management, a simplified procedure has been developed so that each request for change can be sized by the developer that does the impact analysis:

- Substantial change: 100% of the size of the functional process.
- Minor change: 50% of the size of the functional process.
- Deletion: 100% of the size of the functional process to delete.
- New functionality: the size of a comparable functional process.

The functional size that is determined by this procedure is used to evaluate the expert estimate of the impact of a request for change on the development of a process chain. This procedure is now in a pilot stage.

4.3.6.5   Technology Choice

The early size estimate is independent of the chosen technology. With the cost formula introduced in Section 4.3.6.2, the cost of a process chain produced with EBS technology can be calculated at an early stage. This cost can be compared with the cost of producing the same process chain with another technology. This is only relevant for process chains that will be used for a short period of time and are not obliged to comply with the strategic choice for the EBS environment (see Section 4.3.1.2).

4.3.7 Deviation from Average Packaged Software Implementations

Usually ERP projects implement one or more modules from a suite to support the primary business process of the customer. These kinds of implementations are usually estimated based on the relative weight of the module in relation to a core module that is used in most implementations. For ERP implementations, this core module is usually the general ledger.

For the Office for Regulations, not only secondary business processes would be implemented, but also the primary business process. The workflow module is pre-configured to support the BPM. The quality module is used to combine the workflow tasks with other used modules, like trading community architecture, install base, service contract, and advanced pricing (Oracle 2000).

This experience shows that COSMIC FFP can be used for sizing and estimating this kind of ERP project where the EBS modules are used as the development environment instead of implementing them to support secondary processes.

4.3.8 Conclusions

The main reason to choose COSMIC FFP as the sizing metric was based on the kind of documentation that is produced in the early stages of development. When only process information is available, (approximate) COSMIC FFP has an advantage over other sizing metrics, like function points.

This experience shows that functional size measurement can be used for sizing and estimating this kind of ERP implementation, which requires a lot of customization. This knowledge is mainly important for large-scale implementations for multinational companies that cannot change all their processes to the processes required by the ERP modules as they are, and for special implementations that require a lot of nonstandard functionality. Examples of this kind of implementation are typically found in the military.

4.3.9 Proposed Further Research

Further work on mapping the COSMIC FFP concepts to ERP concepts would be beneficial for both fields. Based on this experience, it cannot be concluded that COSMIC FFP or any other kind of functional size measurement is suitable for estimating, planning, and controlling regular ERP implementations. This experience only shows the applicability for a special kind of ERP implementation.

Further research should concentrate on the possibility of using functional size measurement to support the current practice of estimating ERP implementations based on the relation with a core module-like general ledger.

Affiliation

The author has been working as a practitioner and consultant within the area of software metrics since 1999. Within this area, he specialized in sizing and performance measurement programs within client organizations. He is a metrics consultant and scope manager for the center of expertise in Sizing, Estimating, and Control of Sogeti Nederland B.V. He is a member of the Measurement Practices Committee of COSMIC and a member of the COSMIC working group of NESMA.

4.4 When to Use COSMIC FFP? When to Use IFPUG FPA? A Six Sigma View

Thomas Fehlmann

4.4.1 The Six Sigma Approach

Six Sigma is about eliminating defects in the value chain processes. A defect is a mistake or wrong behavior of the product, or in the service, that affects customers' needs. The process orientation of Six Sigma mandates that not only the end customers are regarded, but those that use a process's results can cut costs when they receive error-free input for their process. A software testing group that receives error-free code can concentrate on detecting application errors, ergonomic failures (all B defects), or even late requirements errors (A defects), rather than helping developers in fixing bugs.

However, writing software is a knowledge acquisition process. Since not everything is known from the beginning, knowledge acquisition is ongoing throughout software development and makes requirements volatile and growing. Thus, software cannot be completely free of all sorts of defects. However, its statistical defect density in a given moment in its life cycle is computable. For density measurements, we need functional sizing information.

Six Sigma endorses the define-measure-analyze-improve-control cycle as its approach to process improvement; in other words, it measures process results and their defect density for each process step. This well-established management method also works well for software. Since all software metrics somehow relate to software size, this means that functional sizing measurements are a must for every Black or Green Belt who wants to address software development or maintenance. However, which sizing method should we choose?

4.4.1.1 The Choice of Software Metrics

Functional size measurements are necessary to calculate defect density for both A defects and B defects. There are several ISO standards for functional size measurements: among them are ISO standard ISO/IEC 20926, which corresponds to IFPUG 4.1 Unadjusted Function Points Analysis (FPA), and ISO standard ISO/IEC 19761, known as COSMIC 2.2 Full Function Points (FFP) (Abran et al. 2003a). IFPUG has meanwhile issued the measurement manual V4.2 (IFPUG 2004). Other sizing methods, such as use case points (UCPs) (Clemmons 2006), were also investigated.

4.4.1.2 The Criteria for Evaluation

One important criterion was the previous inability of the organization to estimate efforts for enhancing their software or writing new software for customers. In Six Sigma terms, this is a B defect, since due dates are usually known, and if not met, this affects customers. Functional sizing as a base for effort estimation is well established, and this organization—having no statistical data from the past—used the ISBSG project repository (ISBSG 2003) for sizing.

Another criterion was the ability for early estimation. Very often projects are decided almost on the fly, and important investment decisions cannot wait until a sophisticated estimation process finishes. Such estimation must necessarily include all aspects of the project under investigation.

Furthermore, sizing must cope with the multitier Web service architecture. The predominant applications are not data centric. They involve quite a number of complicated functional processes. All that gives FFP a head start over FPA, at least for the engineering people. How will FPA ever be able to correctly estimate the organization's engineering work?

4.4.1.3 The Base Count

Counting existing applications was not much of a problem. On the contrary, both measurement approaches, FPA and FFP, proved capable and could be used to calibrate against each other and, if available, against actuals. Many applications were services, accessible over browsers or from other applications. As expected, FPA modeled a user-centric view on the applications, and FFP identified the functional processes behind it. Much of the contribution to the count came from the persistent configuration data of the services, managed by transactions in the application and used by its functional processes. Thus, there was little systematic difference between the two counting approaches; however, with FPP it was much easier to identify the application boundaries.

The problem was a different kind: it was very difficult to get good requirements to count when doing early estimation. In many cases, important aspects are not seen early enough. And the biggest problem was that early estimation almost never could be based on a use case analysis, or similar.

4.4.2   A Sample Sizing

Rather than the said company, we use for this paper a well-known example to demonstrate the issues encountered with the sizing approaches. All details of the counts are available on the website of the author (Web 2010).

4.4.2.1   The Wylie College Case Study

We use the Wylie College course registration system case study, documented in the Rational Unified Process (RUP Version 2003.06.00.65) as an example of a website project, which was counted in Web (2010) by Khelifi and Abran. All references are citations from Web (2010). The new system will enable all professors and students to access it through PCs connected to the Wylie College computer network and through any personal computer connected through the Internet. Furthermore, the new system will bring Wylie College to the leading edge in course registration systems, thus improving the image of the college, attracting more students, and streamlining administrative functions.

4.4.2.2   Count according to COSMIC FFP

The *measurement viewpoint* in the Wylie College case study is that of the software developer who is interested in quantifying the functionality of the software he has to develop (Figure 4.15). The *measurement purpose* is to measure all of the software requirements documented in the vision document, Release Notes version 1.0, and use cases specification of this case study. The *measurement scope* is all of the software functional processes, and only these. The count according to COSMIC FFP (Web 2010) identified the following use cases:

Administrative:
   1.1 Logon
   1.2 Close registration
Maintain professor information:
   2.1 Add a professor
   2.2 Modify a professor
   2.3 Delete a professor
Register for courses:
   3.1 Create a schedule
   3.2 Modify a schedule
   3.3 Delete a schedule
   3.4 Save a schedule
Maintain student information:
   4.1 Add a student
   4.2 Modify a student
   4.3 Delete a student

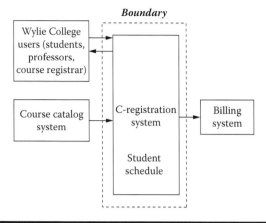

Figure 4.15 Application boundary for C- registration system.

4.4 Select courses to teach
4.5 Submit grades
4.6 View report card
4.7 Monitor for full course

The count yields 137 Cfsu COSMIC functional sizing units). There is not yet a well-established PDR (= project delivery rate) available for benchmarks. The median for new MIS applications taken from ISBSG Repository R9 (ISBSG 2004) suggests a PDR of 10.2 hours/Cfsu. This corresponds to 1,397 hours total effort (PWE = project work effort).

Note that the counter found the following ambiguities:

■ In the close registration use case specifications there is an issue stated by the authors: "Need to resolve what to do if too few students registered for a course."

For this measurement, the following assumptions were made:

■ We add the "Monitor for full course" functional process in order to resolve it and have a more accurate measure.

Thus, the count added an important technical requirement. However, how will we know that we have all functional processes identified when we count?

4.4.2.3   Count with IFPUG FPA

For the business people with our customer, a count based on IFPUG FPA looks more attractive because the input and output requirements are known much earlier than the use cases and functional processes, which require analysis. However, for the engineering people, it is difficult to believe that such a measurement ever yields a sizing comparable to a COSMIC FFP count from the developer's viewpoint, because creating the GUI is seldom the major cost driver for development. Other architectural or technical difficulties to solve may matter much more for cost.

For the Wylie case, we identified 3 ILF with 24 UFP (unadjusted function point), 3 EIF with 15 UFP, 13 EI with 43 UFP, 10 EO with 45 UFP, and 8 EQ with 25 UFP. This yields a total of 152 UFP. For a value adjustment factor (VAF) of 1.01, the total function point count according IFPUG 4.2 is 152 FP as well.

Based on the ISBSG benchmarking database R9 (ISBSG 2004), a likely PDR is 10.1; thus, the PWE estimation yields 1,528 hours—a little more than the COSMIC estimation.

A side effect of the count is to clarify the business requirements. For the count, we have to decide whether we take one ILF, "registered users," with three RETs, or three separate ILFs for students, professors, and registrars.

- Without separate ILFs, a professor would not be able to register for a course. From the available sources of requirements, this is not specified, but that requirement affects the overall count!
- Furthermore, the user's addresses are not specified either. We decided there must be an EIF for this, since neither use cases nor functional processes are provided to address maintenance, which is a significant application of its own.

These are two typical A defects. Thus, we conclude that functional sizing is essential when pursuing Six Sigma for software, regardless of the counting approach.

4.4.2.4 Count with Use Case Points

Although use case points (Clemmons 2006) are no benchmarking standard, we also compared them with this method. With a technical complexity factor of 1.01, an environmental complexity factor of 0.83, unadjusted use case points of 100, and a productivity factor of 20, we got a total expected effort of 1,668 hours. This is still in the same range, although the productivity factor is an assumption.

The use case count did not give any additional insight into requirements and therefore was not really helpful.

4.4.3 The Six Sigma Approach

Combinatory metrics is a technique that links business requirements to technical requirements—could it be used to combine the two measurements methods as well? FPA for the business requirements and the users' perception of business functionality required, to get early estimations, and FFP for sizing the technical requirements, to incorporate the technical concerns that often enough make an impact on the actual efforts used. In a recent study, the ISBSG compared those projects in its data set that include estimations with the actual numbers at the end of the project. While about 20% had reasonable estimates, for the balance of the projects, there were significant underestimates or significant overestimates.

Moreover, it is well known that all functional size measurements methods are good at uncovering missing business requirements (such as data element types that are never queried, or data kept and managed in an application). FPA, in particular, is completely independent from the solution approach or architecture, and thus helps to keep the focus on the business needs. But it cannot help in detecting missing requirements in architecture or technology. On the contrary, FFP is able to use developer's viewpoints as well, and therefore is capable of detecting missing technical specifications, and sometimes even analyzing the suitability for the purpose of the selected architecture. Thus, if we could combine the two counting methods, we could possibly get the best from both to reduce our A defects count.

4.4.3.1   Combinatory Metrics—QFD Plus Metrics

Combinatory metrics connects two functional topics. Functional topics describe the knowledge about the functionality of the system under consideration. Business and technical requirements are the two most important functional topics that can be combined using combinatory metrics.

Combinatory metrics is based on the method of quality function deployment (QFD) (Akao et al. 1990). QFD is widely used as the vital part of design for Six Sigma; see, for instance, Fehlmann (2005) and Töpfer (2004). According to a communication from Professor Akao, the matrices of QFD were invented originally as a convenient form to combine several Ishikawa (fishbone) diagrams. QFD is a cause-effect analysis in the form of a matrix.

Note that QFD for services—and software—is slightly different from QFD for physical entities. Cause-effect relationships do not describe physical forces, but rather the usefulness of certain solution approaches, whether they are suitable means for reaching a goal. You can select which relationships to use; they are not given by physics.

4.4.3.2   The Cause-Effect Matrix—Describing Knowledge

Knowledge about two functional topics, G and X, is the set of cause-effect relationships, which characterize how X relates to G. Formally, we write $X \rightarrow G$.

The functional topics consist of requirements. A functional topic may have a potentially unlimited number of requirements. Usually, we limit our attention to only a selected few of those requirements.

Requirements are bound to functional topics. User requirements and the many kind of technical requirements are different. The failure to understand that difference is the main reason why software development processes are difficult to manage (Humphrey 1989; Preece 2001; Preece and Decker 2002).

A technical solution supports a business requirement, if that solution is part of the requirements in the functional topic one step below. Thus we say: "The technical solution is why (the cause) your software supports the said business requirement."

For instance, a certain number of use cases supports a required business scenario. Each use case, in turn, depends on the classes that implement the functionality required in the use case (Figure 4.16).

The solution requirements are not equally weighted, because they do provide specific contributions to the goal. It is a common practice to distinguish three different levels of cause-effect relationship: *weak*, *medium*, and *strong*. A strong relationship means that the respective solution requirement is a strong influence factor for the respective goal requirement; this corresponds to a weight of 9. A medium relationship means that it is an indispensable service but might be used in other contexts too; this gives a weight of 3. Weak means useful but not vital,

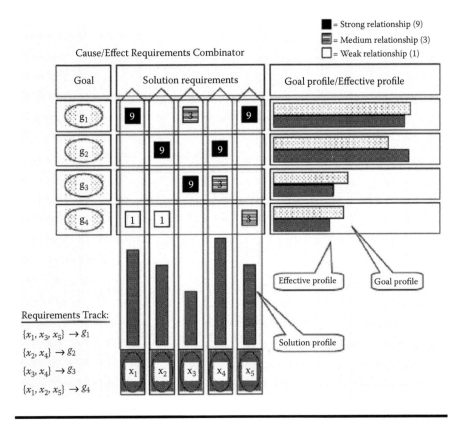

Figure 4.16 Combinator relating requirements <g1, ..., g4> with solution <x1, ..., x4>.

and we assign a weight of 1. No cause-effect relationship corresponds to a weight of zero.

Well-established techniques exist for characterizing functional topics with only a few requirements (Herzwurm et al. 1997; Saati et al. 1981). By choosing comprehensive requirements for functional topic G, you can keep the number of requirements low for that functional topic, and thus describe the relationship between topics by just a few characteristic requirements on both the input and the output side.

4.4.3.3   Topic Profiles—Measuring Knowledge

QFD measures knowledge acquisition. This constitutes the basic idea behind design for Six Sigma. We do not need to size knowledge by some absolute scale. It is sufficient to compare the functional topics, assigning them weights. These weights yield a profile. The peaks in the profile correspond to high priorities among the requirements; the lows in the profile are the less important requirements.

Usually, business requirements constitute the goal, and technical requirements are the means, or the solution approach, to reach the goal. The profile of the business requirements we call the *goal profile.*

The solution requirements have equal weights. Their respective importance weights also yield a profile for them: we call it the *solution profile.*

It is natural to ask whether the chosen solution profile characterizes a technical solution that yields desired results. The profile of such a result, which can be achieved with the chosen solution, we call *effective profile.*

Thus, if we had a way to compute the effects of a solution profile, we could predict the effective profile for a given solution profile. Comparing the effective solution profile with the goal profile then allows us to find an optimum solution with an optimum solution profile, optimizing the solution profile accordingly. With a little statistical analysis, we can say how stable the found solution is. Thus, we relate technical requirements that describe the solution to business requirements.

The QFD technique is widely used for design for Six Sigma. The metrics aspect comes from using the 1-3-9 valuations of the cause-effect relationships. In this view, the QFD matrix becomes a linear mapping.

Let $<g> = <\gamma_1, \ldots, \gamma_n>$ be the goal profile, and let $<x> = <\xi_1, \ldots, \xi_m>$ be the solution profile. Compute the vector formula:

$$\varphi(\langle x \rangle) = \langle \varphi_1, \ldots, \varphi_n \rangle = \left\langle \sum_{j=1}^{m} \alpha_{1,j} * \xi_j, \ldots, \sum_{j=1}^{m} \alpha_{n,j} * \xi_j \right\rangle$$

Then $\phi(<x>) = <\phi_1, \ldots, \phi_n>$ is the effective profile.

4.4.3.4 Comparing Profiles—Analyzing Knowledge

However, how do we know whether our requirements combinators are accurate enough to allow for such backtracking? We need a metric that tells us how well our knowledge terms model the software development processes. For this, we need statistical process control for the requirement profiles.

To compare vectors, it is not sufficient to compare their difference. Although you can compute the difference vector as soon as you have the same amount of components, the result may be useless unless the components of the two vectors are of comparable size. In order to achieve that, we need normalization.

The requirement profiles, as normalized vectors, show the direction our project has to go on our quest for knowledge acquisition in the vector space of our functional topics. It is possible to eliminate requirements that are not contributing to the desired effect, or change our solution approach. This simply means to find a better solution.

4.4.3.5 The Convergence Factor—Improve the Cause-Effect Relationship

We need a metric to measure how well our choice of solution profile matches the goal. This metric we call the *convergence factor*. It is the length of the profile difference between goal profile and effective profile, divided by the number of profile coefficients.

Let $<g> = <\gamma_1, ..., \gamma_n>$ be the goal profile, $<x> = <\xi_1, ..., \xi_m>$ be the solution profile, and $\phi(<x>) = <\phi_1, ..., \phi_n>$ be the effective profile, computed by the vector formula as before. Then the convergence factor is the square root of the length of its profile difference $<g>-\phi(<x>)$ divided by the number of goal coefficients n:

$$\kappa = \sqrt{\frac{\sum\limits_{i=1-n}(\gamma_i - \phi_i)^2}{n}}$$

(convergence factor)

A convergence factor (κ) of zero means complete match between goal and effective profiles. $\kappa = 0.2$ is generally considered good; $\kappa = 0.5$ is at limits, as this a deviation of direction in the underlying vector space by 10%. κ greater than 1 indicates a significant difference between the goal profile and the effective profile achieved with the chosen solution approach, meaning that such a solution may cause it go in a totally different direction. The convergence factor is a quality indicator for a cause-effect analysis.

When we have a matrix with a bad convergence factor, there are two resolutions:

1. Add better requirements to the solution profile that better supports the goal profile (e.g., better fit customer's needs), until the convergence factor decreases. This is the preferred way experienced by QFD practitioners.
2. Use the convergence factor as the minimum target for linear optimization. There are standard mathematical algorithms that reliably decrease the convergence factor by optimizing the solution profile.

Linear optimization finds a local optimum but does not detect all possible solutions. Moreover, it may give zero solutions where real solutions exist indeed. It cannot replace the search for better solution requirements. For more details regarding linear optimization with QFD, see Fehlmann (2004).

4.4.4 Using the Convergence Factor to Get Functional Processes Early

We use the convergence factor to complete the choice of functional processes.

4.4.4.1 Identifying Customer's Needs

The key is in Section 4.4.2.1 of this paper, where—very briefly—the customer's needs are listed for the Wylie College project: "The new system will enable all professors and students to access it through PCs connected to the Wylie College computer network and through any personal computer connected through the Internet. Furthermore, the new system will bring Wylie College to the leading edge in course registration systems, thus improving the image of the college, attracting more students, and streamlining administrative functions" (Figure 4.17).

This statement can be converted into business objectives, constituting customer's needs in our case. The priorities may have come from a Six Sigma workshop in the Wylie College IT department. This yields the goal profile.

4.4.4.2 Mapping Customer's Needs to Functional Processes

It is quite straightforward to map the business objectives to functional processes, and it is no surprise that the convergence factor is excellent, almost ideal (Figure 4.18).

The solution profile is almost a perfect match for the business objectives. The functional processes selected for this solution approach exactly match the objectives. Their solution profile reflects what the software engineering manager should invest into the software. The grading of students and the report card provide the highest value; he should concentrate efforts there to get the most out of the resources allocated for implementing the project, and to get the highest possible satisfaction among its users. So far, this is pure QFD.

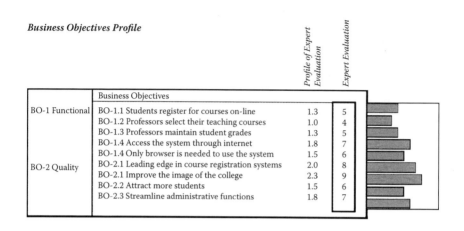

Figure 4.17   Prioritizing customer's needs.

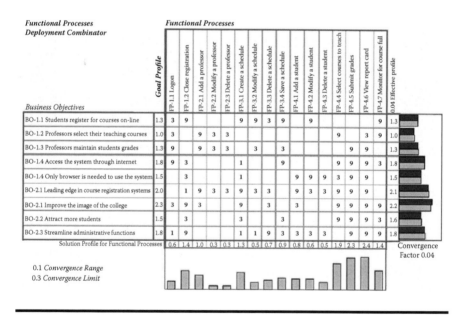

Figure 4.18   A QFD deployment of business objectives into functional processes.

4.4.4.3   How to Detect Missing Requirements

Indeed, if we go back to the early stages of the project, when the use case analysis was not yet available, what could have happened? We investigated two likely possibilities to forget some of the functional processes.

In the first example, we forget to include the functional processes for modifying and deleting entries. We only count input functions. The resulting convergence factor immediately degrades (Figure 4.19).

Even worse is the effect when a student's grades had been left out. This has been found in the QFD analysis to be the most important technical requirement, but it may not be immediate, because it extends the scope of the old mainframe solution. You may even be temped to postpone that to phase 2: it is obvious that the resulting solution profile is not able to fulfill the business objective BO-1.3: "Professors maintain student grades." The technical requirement needed to meet stated business objectives is missing. This may seem easily detectable in this sample case, but in reality such statements like BO-1.3 are often overlooked. Thus, using the COSMIC FFP counting approach also helps us to avoid A defects, and on the other hand, using a Six Sigma approach to software development helps identify the functional processes needed for early functional sizing using the COSMIC FFP counting approach (Figure 4.20).

4.4.5 Results

The combinatory metrics profile connects both functional sizing measurements, suggesting that there cannot be a single conversion factor that holds for all kinds of FFP or FPA counts within an application area. Conversion between FFP and FPA is rather a linear mapping function hat that depends on the relationship matrix

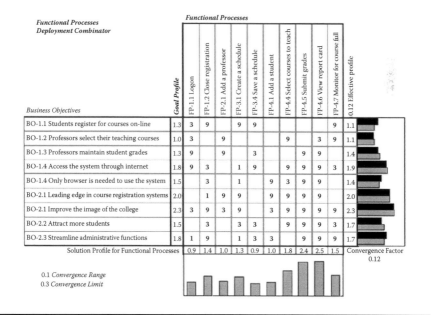

Figure 4.19 Effect on convergence factor when omitting input flexibility.

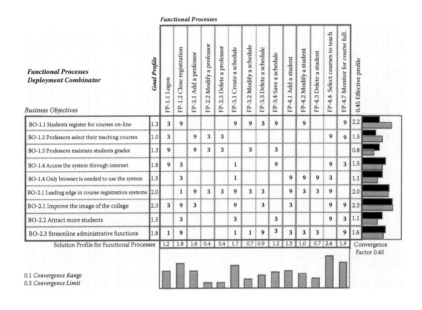

Figure 4.20 Effect on convergence factor when student's grading had been left out.

between business and technical requirements. The quality function deployment method generates that linear mapping between business requirements and technical requirements.

The Six Sigma approach gives interesting new insights into old problems. Combining quality function deployment with FPA and FFP addresses both kind of problems usually encountered when developing software: the late deliveries (B defects) and the wrong functionalities (A defects). FPA is better in business, and FFP in technical requirements. The key for success is always measurements.

Acknowledgment

Sincere thanks are given to all who have contributed with discussions and suggestions, especially in the session of the Swiss Metrics Association (SwiSMA), an expert group of SwissICT.

References

Abran, A. 2001. *COSMIC—Deployment of the second generation of FSM methods.* Presentation at JFPUG 2001. www.gelog.etsmtl.ca (accessed January 31, 2010).

Abran, A., and J.-M. Desharnais, 1999. *Literature review on object points and engineering function points.* Internal report. ETS Montreal, Canada: University Press.

Abran, A., J.-M. Desharnais, and F. Aziz. 2005. Measurement convertibility—From FP to COSMIC-FFP. In *Innovations in software measurement*, ed. A. Abran and R. R. Dumke, 227–40. Aachen, Germany: Shaker Publ.

Abran, A., J.-M. Desharnais, and S. Oligny. 1999. Measuring with full function points. In *Maximising quality and managing risk—Optimising software development and maintenance (ESCOM SCOPE 99)*, ed. R. J. Kusters, 104. Herstmonceux Castle, England: Shaker Publ.

Abran, A., J.-M. Desharnais, S. Oligny, D. St.-Pierre, and C. Symons. 2003a. *Measurement manual COSMIC Full Function Points 2.2, the COSMIC implementation guide for ISO/IEC 19761*. Montréal: École de technologie supérieure, Université du Québec, University Press.

Abran, A., J.-M. Desharnais, S. Oligny, D. St.-Pierre, and C. Symons. 2003b. *COSMIC-FFP measurement manual (COSMIC implementation guide for ISO/IEC 19761: 2003)*. Version 2.2. Common Software Measurement International Consortium. http://www.lrgl.uqam.ca/cosmic-ffp (accessed January 31, 2010).

Abran, A., M. Maya, J.-M. Desharnais, and D. St.-Pierre. 1997. Adapting function points to real-time software. *American Programmer* 10(11):32–43.

Akao, Y., et al. 1990. *Quality function deployment (QFD)*. University Park, IL: Productivity Press.

Bootsma, F. 1999. Applying full function points to drive strategic business improvement within the real-time software environment. In *Proceedings of the 1999 Annual IFPUG Conference*, ed. M. Zelkowitz, 159–218. Los Alamitos, CA: IEEE Computer Society Press.

Clemmons, R. K. 2006. Project estimation with use case points, CrossTalk. *Journal of Defense Software Engineering*. http://www.stsc.hill.af.mil/crosstalk/2006/02/0602Clemmons.html (accessed January 31, 2010).

COM. 2003. Explanatory memorandum: A long-term policy perspective for sustainable agriculture. 23 final. Commission of the European Communities, Brussels. http://ec.europa.eu/agriculture/capreform/memo_en.pdf (accessed January 31, 2010).

Fehlmann, Th. 2004. The impact of linear algebra on QFD. *International Journal of Quality and Reliability Management* 21(9):83–96.

Fehlmann, Th. 2005. *Six Sigma in der SW–Entwicklung*. Braunschweig/Wiesbaden, Germany: Vieweg Publ.

FFP97. 1997. *Full function points: Counting practices manual*. Technical Report 1997-04. Montréal: Université du Québec à Montréal, University Press.

Herzwurm G., W. Mellis, and S. Schockert. 1997. *Qualitätssoftware durch Kundenorientierung. Die Methode Quality Function Deployment (QFD)*. Grundlagen, Praxisleitfaden, SAP R/3 Fallbeispiel. Braunschweig/Wiesbaden, Germany: Vieweg Publ.

Humphrey, W. S. 1989. *Managing the software process*. Boston: Addison-Wesley Publ.

IFPUG. 1994. *Function point counting practices manual*. Release 4.0. Westerville, OH: International Function Point User Group (IFPUG) Publ.

IFPUG. 1999. *Function points counting practices manual*. Release 4.1. Princeton, NJ: International Function Point Users Group (IFPUG) Publ.

IFPUG. 2000. *Function point counting practices manual*. Release 4.1.1. Westerville, OH: International Function Point Users Group (IFPUG) Publ.

IFPUG. 2004. *Function point counting practices manual*. Version 4.2. International Function Point Users Group. http://www.ifpug.org (accessed January 31, 2010).

ISBSG. 2003. *ISBSG estimating, benchmarking and research suite*. Release 8. International Software Benchmarking Standards Group. www.isbsg.org (accessed January 31, 2010).

ISBSG. 2004. *ISBSG estimating, benchmarking and research*. Suite R9. Hawthorn, Victoria, Australia: ISBSG Press.

ISO. 2003. *Software engineering—COSMIC-FFP—A functional size measurement method*. ISO/IEC 19761:2003. Geneva, Switzerland: International Organization for Standardization (ISO) Publ.

Kranenburg, K., F. Nelissen, and J. Brouwer. 1999. *De moderne softwarefabriek: De organisatie en werking van een software development and maintenance center*. Internal report. Ten Hagen en Stam, Netherland: Den Haag Publ.

Meli, R. 2002. Early and quick function point analysis—From summary user requirements to project management. In *IT measurement: Practical advice from the experts*, ed. C. Jones and D. S. Linthinicum, 417–41. Boston: Addison-Wesley.

Oracle. 1999. *AIM Advantage™: A comprehensive method and toolkit for implementing Oracle's packaged applications*. Oracle White Paper, Revision 1.0. http://www.oracle.com/consulting/collateral/AIMadvantage.pdf (accessed January 31, 2010).

Oracle. 2000. *Oracle E-Business Suite*. http://www.oracle.com/applications/e-business-suite.html (accessed January 31, 2010).

Preece, A. 2001. Evaluating verification and validation methods in knowledge engineering. In *Micro-level knowledge management*, ed. R. Roy, 123–45. San Francisco: Morgan Kaufman Publ.

Preece, A., and S. Decker. 2002. Intelligent web services. *IEEE Intelligent Systems* 17(1):15–17.

Saaty, T. L., and J.M. Alexander. 1981. *Thinking with models*. Oxford: Pergamon Press.

SIM98. 1998. *Engine management system SIMTEC 70*. SW version 710SB000. Reegensburg, Germany: SIEMENS Automotive System Group, Siemens Press.

SIM99. 1999. *Engine management system SIMTEC 81/82*. SW version 0203001A. Reegensburg, Germany: SIEMENS Automotive System Group, Siemens Press.

Töpfer, A. 2004. *Six Sigma—Konzepte und Erfolgsbeispiele für praktizierte Null–Fehler Qualität*. Berlin: Springer Publ.

Vogelezang, F. W. 2005. Early estimating using COSMIC-FFP. In *Proceedings of the 2nd Software Metrics European Forum (SMEF05)*, Roma, Italy. http://www.iir-italy.it/smef2005 (accessed January 31, 2010).

Web. 2010. Website for this paper: www.e-p-o.com/WhichSizingMethod.htm (accessed January 31, 2010).

Chapter 5

Foundations of Measurement Tools with COSMIC

One of the main aspects of acceptance of new FSM methods consists in the level of tool support and existing experience data. Note that tools can only support the counting process. Usually it is not possible for automation for such measurement processes.

Figure 5.1 shows the general components involved in a tool-based application of functional size measurement methods.

The part of this chapter by Malcolm Jenner shows a method for estimating the functional size, in COSMIC *functional size units*, of a software system specified using UML. It is demonstrated how this can be automated when the model is developed using a suitable CASE tool.

In the real world, a knowledge-based system (KBS) must often accommodate a considerable number of references that support the particular knowledge domain. The size of such a knowledge repository makes its detailed verification challenging and subsequent maintenance onerous. New technology can help improve both the verification and maintenance of these knowledge repositories. To investigate the effectiveness of new technologies for verification and maintenance, Jean-Marc Desharnais, Alain Abran, Julien Vilz, Francois Gruselin, and Naji Habra developed two subsequent versions of a KBS designed to improve the consistency of software measurement using ISO 19761 and the COSMIC FFP guide.

Many software tools have been developed to support the implementation of the ISO 19761 COSMIC FFP standard on functional size measurement. The part by

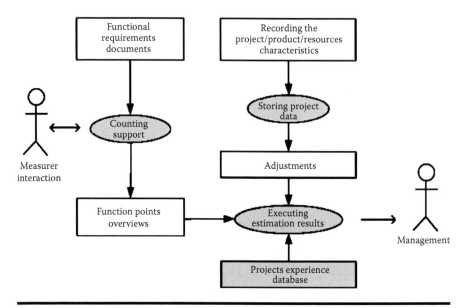

Figure 5.1 Components of FSM method tool support.

Anabel Stambollian and Alain Abran presents a reference framework for the set of functions that is of interest to practitioners who implement ISO functional size measurement standards. It also includes a 2006 survey of COSMIC-related tools available in the market and in the research community. Finally, a gap analysis is presented in which the functions that still need to be addressed by tool vendors are identified.

5.1 Automation of Counting of Functional Size Using COSMIC FFP in UML

Malcolm S. Jenner

5.1.1 Introduction

In a previous paper (Jenner 2001), building on earlier works by Bévo et al. (1999, 2003), I showed a way of mapping the concepts of the COSMIC FFP method into UML. Bévo et al. proposed equating use cases with COSMIC functional processes, but their research indicated problems with apparently different estimates of size, depending on how the system was partitioned into use cases. Further consideration led to my suggestion that these disparities could be removed if the use cases were fully specified, so that the same total functionality was apparent whatever the level of partitioning. Specifically, this involved the recognition of a use case as comprising a number of functional processes. Provided that these are well defined, this seems to be a more practical method than that suggested by Grant Rule (2001), in which use cases must be broken down to the smallest level, each consisting only of one interaction. Practical considerations indicate that larger use cases, comprising a relatively small number of discrete interactions performed in sequence, are more useful for describing and specifying software systems. This relationship between use cases and COSMIC functional processes is represented by Figure 5.2 (derived from the COSMIC model). Representing each use case by its sequence diagram then leads to a simple method of counting the size of the use case in COSMIC functional size units (Cfsu).

5.1.2   Method

The method can best be shown by considering a simple example. Figure 5.3 is a sequence diagram for a use case taken from the example originally used by Bévo et al. (1999) (taken from Muller 1997). This is a system for controlling access to various doors in a building. The system boundary is indicated by the broken vertical line. An arrow crossing this boundary from left to right corresponds to a COSMIC entry. An arrow crossing this boundary from right to left corresponds to a COSMIC exit. An arrow going into an object (representing a message or a function call) corresponds either to a COSMIC read or to a COSMIC write. Usually in object-oriented systems each method in a class will only be a read or write operation and not a more complex operation involving both read and write activities. If we are simply concerned with the total size, then it is not important to try to distinguish between read and write messages. So in this case we get a total size of 8 Cfsu for this use case (three entries, two exits, two reads, and one write).

Figure 5.4 shows the sequence diagram for a more complex use case from the same case study. In this we note that the arrow from right to left between the

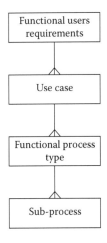

Figure 5.2   COSMIC FFP functional processes.

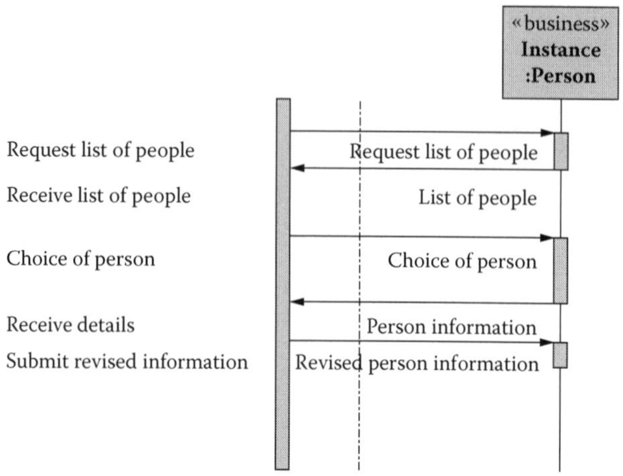

Figure 5.3 Sequence diagram from Bevo for doors access controlling.

access object and the group of doors object represents a write. The other right-to-left arrows between objects simply represent return of data on a read, and are optional within UML. Following the same rules as in the previous case, we get a total size for 16 Cfsu for this use case (four entries, three exits, five reads, and four writes).

Another way of showing the interaction between an actor and the system involves the use of an interface object. An example of this is shown in Figure 5.6 (the sequence diagram for the use case "return of item" from the use case diagram in Figure 5.5). These are taken from the case study of a library system in Eriksson and Penker (1998). In this case the arrows from the actor to the interface object correspond to entries. Arrows from the interface object to the actor correspond to exits (there are none in this case). Arrows between objects correspond to reads or writes. There are no return arrows from reads in this diagram to worry about. Counting the arrows gives us a size of 8 Cfsu (three entries, four reads, and one write).

5.1.3 Automation of the Counting Process

Provided that:

1. the sequence diagram for a use case is complete, and
2. the optional return arrows are omitted,

then it would seem to be a relatively simple matter to automate the counting process if the arrows on a sequence diagram can be identified within the model stored by a CASE tool.

In Select Enterprise (which was used for Figures 5.3 and 5.4), the model appears to be stored in a set of binary files that can only be read by the CASE tool. In

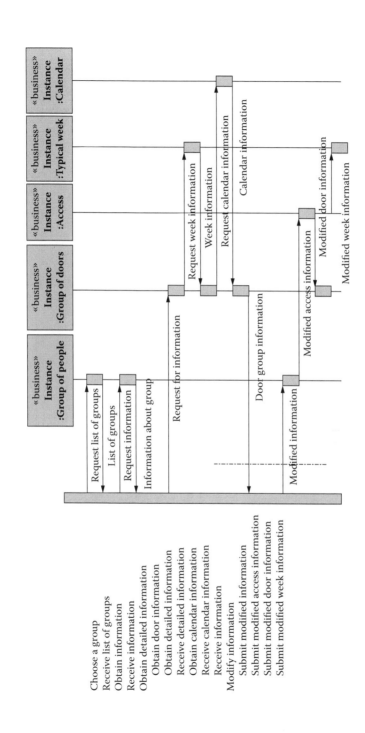

Figure 5.4 Sequence diagram for doors access controlling with more details.

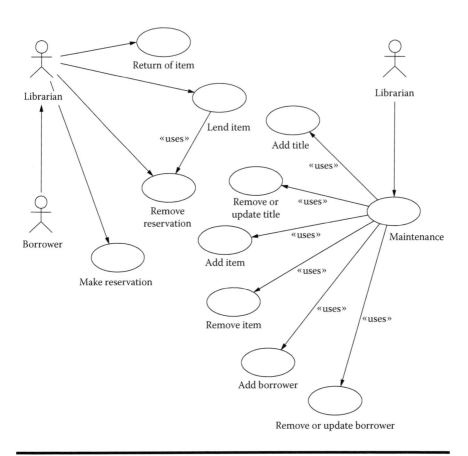

Figure 5.5 Use case diagram of a library system.

Rational Rose (which was used for Figures 5.5 and 5.6), the model is stored in a text file within which one can identify the arrows in the sequence diagram for any use case, as they are simply stored as the coordinates of their ends. Other CASE tools and diagramming tools have yet to be investigated.

5.1.4 Problems

The case study from Eriksson and Penker shows some of the problems of getting the specification in a form where the size can be easily estimated. The use case "lend item" uses the use case "remove reservation." Eriksson and Penker, however, provide two sequence diagrams for the use case "lend item," entitled, confusingly, "lend item" and "lend a reserved title" (Figures 5.7 and 5.8, respectively). The latter of these overlaps in functionality with the "remove reservation" use case (Figure 5.9). Neither of them actually calls the "remove reservation" use case. This clearly needs

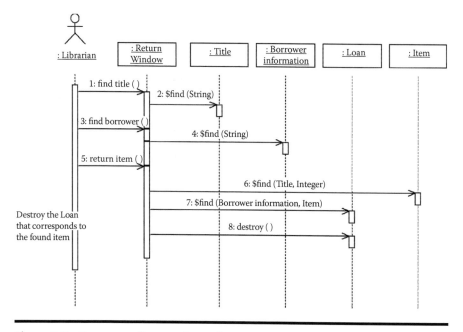

Figure 5.6 Sequence diagram for a chosen use case.

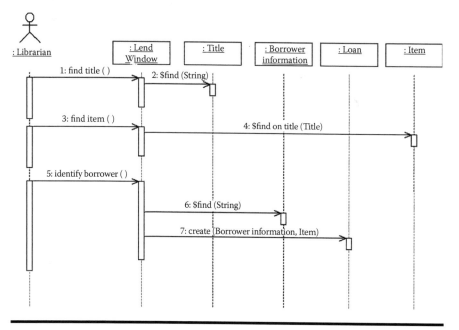

Figure 5.7 Sequence diagram for lended titles.

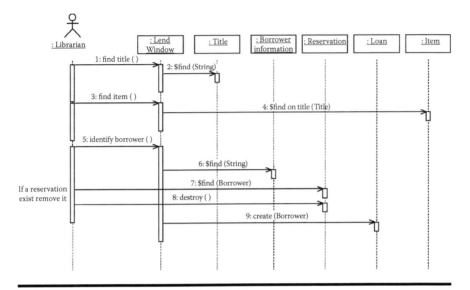

Figure 5.8   Sequence diagram for lending of reserved titles.

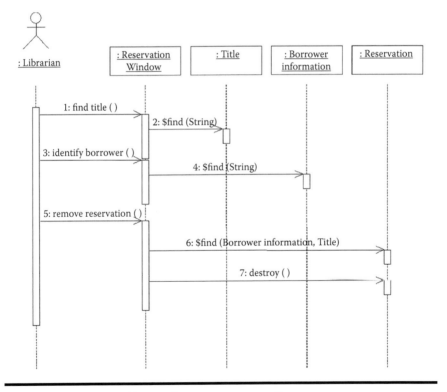

Figure 5.9   Sequence diagram for remove reservation.

tidying up to provide a consistent description of the system. This has the benefit of not only allowing for an accurate estimation of size, but also giving a more precise and unambiguous specification of the system.

5.1.5 Benefits of Automation

Many software systems are developed in an iterative manner, adding detail as required. In object-oriented systems this is particularly common, and applies to all stages of development, from analysis of requirements to final detailed design. This allows feedback from decisions as to precisely what will be implemented, choice of programming language, etc. Automated counting of the size in Cfsu allows tracking of this development, from an initial estimate of the functional size of the requirements to an estimate of the functional size of the delivered system in a way that is possible without, but would be labor-intensive.

5.1.6 Conclusion

For a properly specified system using UML, a complete set of use cases and their associated sequence diagrams facilitates the simple estimation of the software size using the COSMIC FFP method. Provided certain conventions are followed in drawing the sequence diagrams, the counting process can be automated, thus removing human error from this part of the size estimation. This size estimate can be produced at various stages of development and give both an early estimate based on specification and a later estimate based on the developed system. With a suitable tool, the estimate can easily be recalculated as modifications are made to the specification.

5.2 Verification and Validation of a Knowledge-Based System

Jean-Marc Desharnais, Alain Abran, Julien Vilz, François Gruselin, and Naji Habra

5.2.1 Introduction

There are verification and validation (V&V) problems in a KBS related to the considerable number of references in its construction:

- The knowledge of the expert (even if considerable) is not necessarily well defined. The user requirements for a KBS are then ill-defined (Hayes et al. 1998).
- A text approach is sometimes the only way to express the knowledge of the expert; it is then difficult to verify the consistency of each text, when there are many, within others in the KBS.
- There are many links to consider between different parts of the knowledge system.

There are a number of publications on V&V for knowledge-based systems, such as Preece (2001; Preece and Decker 2002) and Meseguer et al. (1995). Related research includes testing by Ayel (1991), a rule-based system by Knauf et al. (1999, 2002), case-based reasoning by Klaus-Dieter (1997), and the database issue for expert systems by Coenen (1998). The terminology used by these authors is somewhat ambiguous, in that the same terms are used often, but in different contexts. They all agree, however, on Barry Boehm's definition of verification (doing the system right) and validation (doing the right system), even though the techniques they used are different (Boehm et al. 2000).

Verification and validation of the KBS is fairly new as a research topic. In 2001, Preece (2001) noted that it is still difficult to draw conclusions about the efficiency of different verification and validation techniques because of a lack of available data. Information on knowledge-based systems is often textual and of a semantic nature, and as such, it is recognized that manual inspection can detect anomalies related to the quality of knowledge, formal methods not yet proving to be convenient for most V&V projects. Under a set of conditions, automated support tools for detecting anomalies should be useful, provided that the data are structured enough to allow some level of automation. Hayes et al. (1998) have worked on CBR (Case Based Reasoning) using XML, but their approach is not directly related to the verification and validation process. Instead, they were looking "to extend the incremental CBR approach to network applications, to examine the distributed architecture to such a system and to situate the first two strands as part of a process of creating open standards for case-based network computing" (Desharnais 2000, p. 1).

An overview of the KBS is presented in Section 5.2.2, and the key features of the first and second prototypes of COSMICXpert in Section 5.2.3. Transitioning between the two prototypes and the design of verification and validation plans are presented in Section 5.2.4. Execution of the verification and validation plans is presented in Sections 5.2.5 and 5.2.6, respectively. Lessons learned are presented in Section 5.2.7.

5.2.2 Overview of the Selected Hybrid KBS Approach

One of the steps suggested by Van Heijst et al. (1997) for building a knowledge model[*] is to construct a task model. Figure 5.10 shows the different steps in the task model used in the design of COSMICXpert, a hybrid KBS developed to improve the measurement accuracy and repeatability of measurers using ISO 19761:2003—COSMIC FFP functional size measurement method.

Figure 5.12 shows the dynamics of the role of the measurer performing each task. The square boxes show where the measurer needs to interact with the KBS system (entering a keyword, choosing topological concepts, choosing case problems, responding to the themes using facts).

---

[*] In our project, the way we use van Heijst's approach is more specific than proposed by him.

The first part is like CBR, because all the tasks contribute to finding a case similar to the one the measurer has to measure. The second part is rule based, because all the tasks contribute to solving the case. In Figure 5.10, the heuristics formulas are represented by a pentagon (giving priority to topological concepts, giving priority to case problems, interpreting the answers, assessing the results).

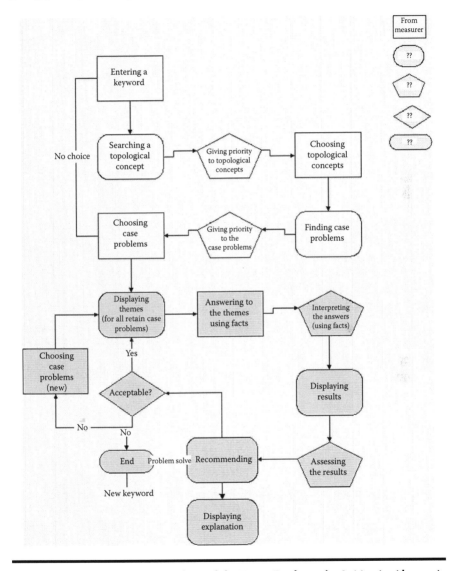

Figure 5.10 COSMICXpert task model. (From Desharnais, J.-M., A. Abran, A. Mayers, and T. Küssing. 2002. Design of a diagnostic tool to improve the quality of functional measurement. *Software Measurement and Estimation*. ed. R. R. Dumke et al., 52–60. Aachen, Germany. Shaker Publishers. With Permission.)

Some of them used certainty theory formulas proposed in MYCIN (Durkin 1994). Table 5.1 lists and describes each task (Abran et al. 1998, 2004).

5.2.3 Description of the First and Second Prototypes

Two prototypes of the COSMICXpert tool were built initially. The functionality and the design of both prototypes are similar from the point of view of the COSMIC FFP measurer (Figure 5.11). What changed is the technology used: Microsoft Visual Basic 6 (language) and Microsoft Access (database) for the first prototype, and a Web approach with XML structure for the second prototype.

The design of the KBS for both prototypes is composed of classes, use cases, and scenarios. Examples of a class diagram, a use case diagram, and one scenario are presented in this paper. The full, detailed design appears in Desharnais (2004). A class is "a description of a set of objects that share the same attributes, operations, methods, relationships, and semantics. A class may use a set of interfaces to specify collections of operations it provides to its environment" (Rational 1997, p. 32). There are a number of classes in our class diagram in Figure 5.11 ("diagram that shows a collection of declarative—static—model elements, such as classes, types, and their contents and relationships") (Rational 1997, p. 34).

A use case (Figure 5.12) is "the specification of a sequence of actions, including variants that a system (or other entity) can perform, interactions with actors of the system" (Rational 1997, p. 33). The use case diagram (diagram that shows the relationships among actors and use cases within a system) of COSMICXpert is presented in Figure 5.12 with three actors (or agents): the measurer, the expert, and the administrator. An actor is "a coherent set of roles that users of use cases play when interacting with these use cases. An actor has one role for each use case with which it communicates" (Rational 1997, p. 37).

A scenario is "a specific sequence of actions that illustrates behaviors." (Rational Software Corporation 1997, p. 35) As already mentioned, there are many scenarios in our KBS. The scenario in Table 5.2 describes the registration of a measurer in a session.

The interfaces (expert, measurer) evolved considerably from prototype 1 to prototype 2. The first prototype includes two interfaces:

Table 5.1   Task List of the KBS Tool for Functional Size Measurement

NO.	TASK	DESCRIPTION
1.	Entering a keyword	The measurer will enter a keyword that will help the tool find the topological concepts related to the case problem
2.	Searching a topological concept	The tool will present the topological concepts to the measurer

Table 5.1 Task List of the KBS Tool for Functional Size Measurement (Continued)

NO.	TASK	DESCRIPTION
3.	Giving priority to topological concepts	The tool will present the topological concepts to the measurer in order of priority
4.	Choosing a topological concept	The measurer chooses one or multiple topological concepts
5.	Finding a case problem	The tool will find the case problems related to the topological concepts chosen by the measurer
6.	Giving priority to case problems	The tool will present the case problems to the measurer in order of priority
7.	Choosing case problems	The measurer will choose the case problems corresponding with his/her interpretation of the problem
8.	Displaying themes	The tool will show all the themes related to the case problems to the measurer
9.	Responding to? themes	The measurer will find facts for each theme
10.	Rating facts	An algorithm will rate the fact chosen
11.	Displaying results	The percentage will be presented to the measurer
12.	Assessing the results	The tool will assess the results based on heuristics
13.	Recommending	The tool will recommend a solution to each case problem, another case problem and/or an explanation as to why the case problem was not solved
14.	Displaying other case problems	The tool will suggest one or more new case problems to the user
15.	Displaying an explanation	The tool will give an explanation about the solution if necessary
16.	Acceptable	The measurer will decide if the recommendation is acceptable
17.	Choosing case problems (new)	The measurer will choose another case problem, either one already suggested by the tool or his own.

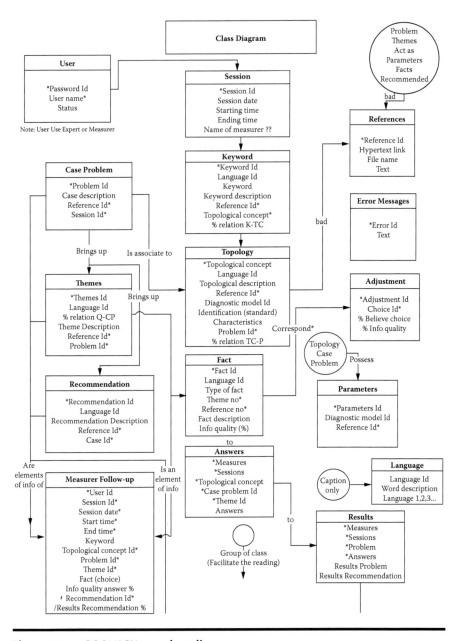

Figure 5.11   COSMICXpert class diagram.

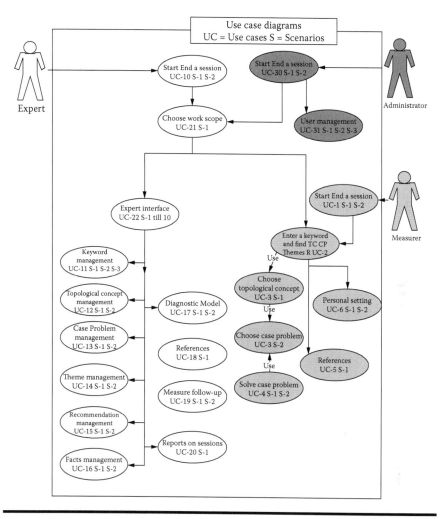

Figure 5.12 Use case diagram of COSMICXpert.

■ An interface for the expert who must put into the diagnostic tool the knowledge required for the establishment of diagnostics, and who must maintain it
■ An interface for the measurer to support him in his measurements tasks

The measurer interface is built in accordance with the task model presented in Figure 5.11. An example of this initial interface is presented in Figure 5.13.

In the second prototype, the measurer interface is Web based, and the expert interface has been replaced by a single input (XMLSpy 2002) for both the administrator and the expert (Figure 5.14).

Table 5.2 Example of a Scenario

Use case 1: Measurer registration in a session
Scenario 1: Session registration
<u>Description</u>: A screen permitting entry of the identification of the measurer and the password Primary education actor: Measurer Secondary actor: No Pre-condition: No <u>Short description</u>: The measurer enters his name (recognized by the software) and his password. The identification of the session is created automatically by the software. <u>Exception</u>: If the name and the password do not correspond to the content of the class password, there is an error message. Post-condition (rules of termination) Access to the software <u>Classes used</u>: Session, measurer <u>Data exchanged</u>: Identification of the measurer, password, identification of the session User interface: see Table 5.1.
Calculation: Yes: No: X

5.2.4 Transitioning and V&V processes

5.2.4.1 Transitioning

The first prototype required the input of more than a hundred case problems, which produced nearly eight hundred files, each from half a page to three pages in length (for a total of more than a thousand pages). In the KBS of that protoype, the knowledge is stored in multiple types of documents (see Figure 5.15); depending on the type of document, the structure and the content vary.

It can be observed from Figure 5.15 that some parts of the various types of documents are repetitive within each type of document (e.g., definitions). The number of files for each document type is presented in Table 5.3, for a total of 779 files.

5.2.4.2 Verification Process

Verification must be carried out on the whole KBS, including all 779 files. A key verification challenge is to ensure that each concept (definition, principles, context, rules, etc.) used in one specific document is used exactly the same way in all the document types. We also need to verify that all the links are used. Table 5.4 presents the verification plan of the first prototype.

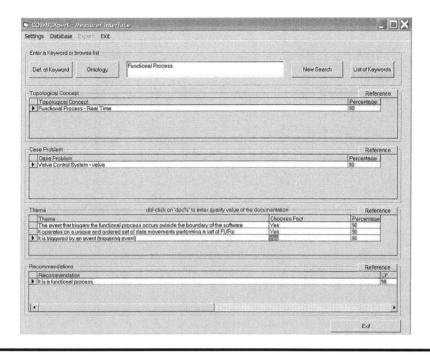

Figure 5.13   Measurer interface prototype 1.

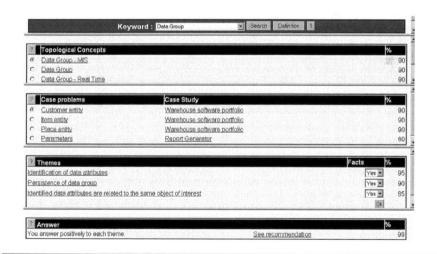

Figure 5.14   Measurer interface prototype 2.

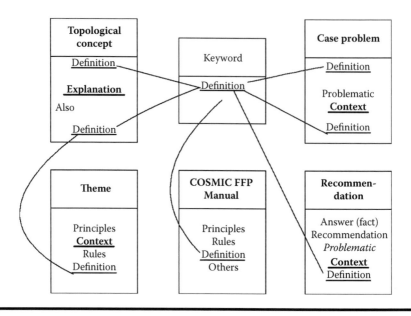

Figure 5.15   Types of documents (prototype 2).

A detailed verification process was designed for each verification criterion. In this paper, we present the detailed process for arriving at the coherency criteria, as well as the verification results for each criterion.

5.2.4.3   Validation Process

The validation process for this KBS consists of analyzing whether or not the issued recommendations are appropriate. We applied the validation process to the recommendations, validation being related to the user results. This implies that the

Table 5.3   Number of Files by Document Type

Document type	Number of files
Generic definition	6
Keywords	30
Topological concepts	15
Themes	250
Case problems	82
Recommendations	402
Total	779

Table 5.4 Verification Plan

Criteria	Techniques	Execution
Coherency	Inspection	Creating XML files matching determined XML schemas (XSD)
Redundancy, reusability	Static verification	XML schema (with XSD) and XSL (reusing part of several XML files in an output)
Completeness	Check the following links: Do we have all the links? Do we have all the recommendations? Production of: • Links between topological concepts and case problems • Links between keywords and topological concepts • Links between case problems and themes • Links between themes and recommendations • Overall links	Automate with a tool to ensure that all links are present (We used ROBOT from Rational Software.)

validation process is not as sensitive to the technology used. However, there is a relation between the verification and the validation. If there is an effective verification process, it is easier to execute the validation process. For example, if the KBS is not working well because many links are missing, it will not be possible to validate all the recommendations. Table 5.5 shows the validation plan, which can be applied independently for both prototypes.

5.2.5   Execution of the Verification Plan

5.2.5.1   Coherency Detail Process

For Craig et al. (1973), "Coherency is related to the compatibility and interconnection of the different elements within a configuration. For example, within a dialog the *coherency* generally means that utterances are connected to each other in some understandable, orderly and meaningful way."

To ensure the coherency of the structure when creating a specific structure, the use of a standard is recommended for all the elements of a configuration.

Table 5.5   Validation Plan

Validation Criteria	Validation Techniques	Validation Execution
1 Correctness (to ensure that all the recommendations are correct based on the different possibilities)	Decision tree Inspection	Generate, from all the case problems, all the recommendations
2 Correctness (check that the %s linking criteria to the various concepts are correct)	Decision tree Inspection	Generate a report of the various concepts with all associated percentages
3 Reliability (check that the context of each case problem described was related to the case study)	Manual inspection by an expert Automation not yet possible. Was carried out by a Ph.D. student using UML.	Generate HTML files (through XSL) that use information on the context

The files were therefore created with the Extensible Markup Language (XML) using a predefined structure for each type of file. To verify this structure, an XML Schema Definition (XSD) was created using XMLSpy software. To create a specific XML file from an RTF file, the following steps, shown in Table 5.6, were required:

- Definition of a minimal XML structure using a formal description syntax (XML Declaration Syntax, or XSD)
- Identification of the various RTF files that need to be converted
- Conversion of the RTF file into an HTML file using a filter that is partly manual: Judgment of individuals who decide which information is useful based on a checklist
- Partly automated: Using Filter Tool 2.0 from Microsoft after converting the RTF file in an HTML file with Microsoft Word
- Filter Tool 2.0 to keep the graphics in Graphic Interchange Format (GIF)
- Creation of XML files matching an XML schema and reusing parts of converted RTF files
- For the last step, a schema approach was used. Below is an example of a schema for a concept within COSMICXpert.

Table 5.6   Schema Approach

```
<?xml version="1.0" encoding="UTF-8"?>

<!-- edited with XMLSPY v5 U (http://www.xmlspy.com) by Jean-Marc
Desharnais (Université du Québec) -->

<xs:schema xmlns:xs="http://www.w3.org/2001/XMLSchema"
elementFormDefault="qualified" attributeFormDefault="unqualified">
        <xs:include schemaLocation="C:\COSMICXpert\XML\textHTML.
xsd"/>
        <xs:element name="Concept">
                <xs:annotation>
                        <xs:documentation>Definition of concept used
within COSMIC-Xpert</xs:documentation>
                </xs:annotation>
                <xs:complexType>
                        <xs:complexContent>
                                <xs:extension base="TextHTML">
                                        <xs:attribute name="Name"
type="xs:string" use="required"/>
                                        <xs:attribute name="Ref"
type="xs:string" use="optional"/>
                                </xs:extension>
                        </xs:complexContent>
                </xs:complexType>
        </xs:element>
</xs:schema>
```

Defining a syntax for each XML reference file made it possible to verify whether or not each file follows the syntax. It is possible then to transform the XML file into HTML format, which will make it easier for the reader to read the text. The presentation of the HTML text is possible through an XSL language or a transformation language. Via the XSL language, the programmer decides how to present the document to the user. The following example was used to define a concept within COSMIC-Xpert:

```
<?xml version="1.0" encoding="UTF-8"?>

<!-- edited with XMLSPY v5 U (http://www.xmlspy.com) by Jean-Marc
Desharnais (Université du Québec) -->

<?xml-stylesheet type="text/xsl" href="C:\COSMIC-Xpert\XML\Concept.xslt"?>
```

Continued

Table 5.6   Schema Approach (Continued)

```
<Concept          xmlns:xsi="http://www.w3.org/2001/XMLSchema-instance" xsi
:noNamespaceSchemaLocation="C:\COSMIC-Xpert\XML\Concept.xsd"
Name="Ontology" Ref="Uschold M., Jasper R., Ontologies for

Knowledge Management, in Knowledge Management - A Micro Level
Approach ed.

Rajkumar Roy, Verlag, 570 pages 1st edition, January 2001">
        <p>This is the vocabulary and the structure
of the development process (SWEBOK) and COSMIC-FFP. </p>
        <p>Uschold and Jasper wrote about the
ontology definition: &quot;In the artificial intelligence community, ontology
is generally presumed to consist of set of terms with formal axioms that define
each term's meaning. More recently, the word has been much more widely
used to include
sets of terms, the terms of which may have neither explicit definitions nor
carefully defined
relationships among them. An ontology may take a variety of forms, but
necessarily includes a vocabulary of terms, and some indication of what the
terms mean&quot;.</p>
</Concept>
```

5.2.5.2   Quantitative Outcomes

There are a number of outcomes for each type of verification criterion:

- Conformity with the structural standard (including statistics on the number of user documents that did not conform to the standard before the transformation process from RTF to XML)
- Conformity with the ontology concept definition of COSMIC FFP within each document
- Uniformity of the syntax and grammar of each document (user document)

Finally, applying a structural standard using verification criteria significantly reduced the number of documents (from nearly 800 to 150), which could help reduce the maintenance work on the system.

5.2.5.3   Conformity with the Structural Standard

The verification outcomes of each of the five types of XML documents (COSMIC manual is not included) are presented next (Table 5.7):

Table 5.7 Outcomes of the Verification of Concepts

Keyword	• 1 deleted
	• 2 added
	• modification to 7 keywords
	• modification or addition of 7 references to the definitions
Topological concept	Addition of an example for one of the themes versus topological concepts (what does this mean?)
	• the relations between those 2 concepts were modified for 12% of the cases
Themes	• 9 themes modified
	• 5 references added
	1 to 4 definitions added to 30 different themes
Recommendations	1 to 4 definitions added to 288 recommendations out of the over 500 verified.

- Keywords: Deletion of one keyword, addition of two others, and modifications to the definitions of seven distinct keywords. We also had to modify or add seven references to the definition.
- Topological concept: We added five bibliographical references.
- Themes: Nine themes were modified, but only very slightly.
- Themes: Four definitions were added to thirty different themes.
- Recommendations: More than five hundred recommendations were verified. We added one to four definitions for 288 recommendations.

Using XML format gives us the opportunity to find many errors (most of them small) that would be untraceable using the RTF format for the documents. The number of definitions added to many documents was possible because all the definitions are in one file and each definition could be used as a specific reference within each document.

5.2.5.4 Conformity with the Ontological Definitions

All the definitions were verified through keywords. The verification outcomes were:

- Modification to the names of two definitions, removal of one definition (not used by another concept), and addition of two definitions
- Modification of the content of six definitions (cosmetic)
- Addition or clarification to the references for eight definitions

Using of a well-defined structure provided the opportunity to identify a keyword not used by other concepts (orphan keyword). The content and the references of a number of definitions were also improved.

5.2.5.5 Syntax and Grammar for All the User Documents

The syntax and grammar correction was performed manually via the Word Grammar tool. Since the number of documents was reduced significantly, it was possible to spend more time on each document to verify the syntax and grammar.

5.2.6 Execution of the Validation Plan

Two different validation approaches were used for the execution of the validation plan, one for each of the two prototypes. For prototype 1, the validation was carried out by four COSMIC FFP experts, while a single COSMIC FFP expert executed the validation plan for prototype 2. For prototype 1, only criteria 2 and 4 were validated.

5.2.6.1 Validation Outcomes for Prototype 1

Four experts from different countries executed the validation process. They were asked to use the prototype and execute different case problems to determine whether or not they agreed with the recommendations (they did not; however, check the completeness of the recommendations and the percents that link the various concepts). The experts provided comments when they did not agree. They all looked at the same thirty-four case problems. Only two validating criteria were used (see 2 and 3 in Table 5.5).

Table 5.8 presents the validation outcomes on criterion 2: agreement, disagreement, and don't know. On the basis of the experts' comments, the disagreement and don't know responses were related to a misunderstanding of the case problems, mainly because they were ambiguous or ill-defined (criterion 4).

For the majority of the case problems (80%), the experts agreed with the recommendations. The range of variation between the experts is low for the agreements (between 79 and 85%), and higher for the disagreements and don't know.

5.2.6.2 Validations Outcomes for Prototype 2

The validation plan was executed by a single expert for prototype 2. The same four validation criteria were used as for verification (see Table 5.5). Essentially, the expert agreed with the recommendations for the 104 case problems (criterion 2), but proposed some changes in the content of many of the recommendations (for example, he proposed adding definitions to 120 recommendations) (criterion 4). He also established the maximum number of recommendations (1,480) and

Table 5.8   Validation Outcomes—Prototype 1 (Criteria 2 and 4)

Type of answer	Expert 1	Expert 2	Expert 3	Expert 4	Average
% who agree	82%	79%	85%	85%	83%
% who disagree	15%	18%	3%	9%	11%
% who don't know	3%	3%	12%	6%	6%

suggested using only a subset (545) of these, because many recommendations were very similar (criterion 1). He also checked that the percents linking to the various concepts were correct. There was no modification. Because there was only one expert, the recommendations should be cross-validated by additional experts.

5.2.7   Benefits and Lessons Learned

The main benefits are:

- The number of anomalies in our KBS were reduced considerably.
- The KBS will be easier to maintain in the future, not only because the number of files are reduced, but also because there is a structural link between the different parts of the KBS.
- The information in the KBS is consistent because there is only one source of information.
- The information in the KBS is nonredundant for the same reason.
- We know that the expert agrees with the recommendations.

In summary, the verification and validation of the same KBS, but constructed with two different techniques, made it possible to demonstrate the efficiency of one technique over the other one. Our research is in sync with the emergence of using XML in the CBRS (Case-Based Reasoning Service) domain (Hayes et al. 1998).

5.3   Survey of Automation Tools Supporting COSMIC FFP–ISO 19761

Anabel Stambollian and Alain Abran

5.3.1   Introduction

ISO 14143-1:1998 (ISO 1998, p. 24) defines the functional size of a software as the size "derived by quantifying the functional user requirements." Also specified in this

ISO standard is the fact that the functional user requirements (FURs) represent "user practices and procedures that the software must perform to fulfil the user's needs. They exclude quality requirements and any technical requirements" (Desharnais 2004, p. 19).

The functional size measurement (FSM) methods based on FURs can be used at any phase of the software life cycle. At the end of the development phase, for example, FSM results can be used to derive productivity ratios and to develop estimation models. When used in the beginning of the life cycle phase, at the requirements phase, for example, the measurement results can be used in estimation models to forecast software project effort. The software size information can then provide valuable information for requirements control, project estimation, and project productivity analyses.

Four FSM methods are now recognized as ISO standards:

- ISO 19761: COSMIC-FFP (ISO 2003a)
- ISO 20926: Function Point Analysis (FPA) (e.g., IFPUG 4.1, Unadjusted Function Points Only) (ISO 2003b)
- ISO 20968: Mk II (ISO 2002)
- ISO 24570: NESMA (ISO 2005) (a Dutch interpretation of FPA, version 4.1)

The first generation of FSM was designed by Alan Albrecht of IBM in 1979 (Albrecht 1979) and is referred to as function point analysis (FPA); it is now supported by the International Function Point Users Group (IFPUG 1994). The FPA, Mark II, and NESMA methods were primarily designed to measure business application software.

COSMIC FFP is referred to as a second generation of FSM and is designed to handle other types of software as well, such as real-time, telecommunications, and infrastructure software. The evolution of this method is managed by an international advisory committee of functional size measurement experts from fourteen countries.

All the steps and procedures prescribed by the FSM methods to measure the functional size of a software product are initially performed manually by a measurer. This makes the use of FSM methods time-consuming and prone to errors, especially if performed by inexperienced measurers.

There have been numerous attempts to automate FSM methods, in particular for the first generation of these methods. In 1996, Mendes et al. (1996a) proposed a framework to classify the functions that could be automated in the measurement of functional size.

On the market today, we see the emergence of such software support tools, which have been developed for second-generation measurement methods to help make the COSMIC FFP method easier to use.

This paper presents a survey of COSMIC FFP-related tools and a list of related resources available. The tools identified here have been grouped into two sets: those that are already available on the market and those still under development in the research community. Finally, a gap analysis of functions that tool vendors have not yet addressed is presented.

The paper is organized as follows: Section 5.3.2 presents a classification framework of functions that can benefit from automated support. Section 5.3.3 presents an overview of the COSMIC FFP method framework and fundamentals. Section 5.3.4 presents the results of the April 2006 survey of COSMIC FFP support tools available in the marketplace. Section 5.3.5 presents a survey of research prototypes. Finally, Section 5.3.6 identifies gaps and suggests future research directions.

5.3.2   *FSM Tool Classification Framework*

All the FSM methods are described as ways to manually assess software functions and to manually calculate their size. In order to make the measurement procedure easier and to reduce the margin of error in manual measurement, a variety of support tools have been developed.

A classification framework for FSM support tools can help vendors, prospective tool buyers, and measurers to position these tools by:

- Identifying key dimensions of FSM
- Proposing a comprehensive, full-cycle FSM framework
- Identifying major tool categories
- Identifying category functions and characteristics
- Classifying the existing FSM tools in the identified categories

Mendes et al. (1996b) developed such a classification framework, which they call the FSM general framework (Figure 5.16). It includes ten tool categories and addresses the following four key dimensions (Table 5.9):

1. Measurement support (documentation and training)
2. Measurement (manual or automated)
3. Storage (repository of measurement results)
4. Utilization (project planning, sizing, estimation and prediction, management, productivity modeling, baselining, and benchmarking)

This tool classification framework is useful to identify the coverage of functions included in each FSM support tool, as well as to develop an understanding of the type of support the market offers (Table 5.10).

This classification framework was initially used in 1996 for a survey of FPA-related support tools (Mendes et al. 1996a); of course, in 1996, the COSMIC FFP method did not yet exist and was not included in that survey. This paper now addresses this market segment of support tools.

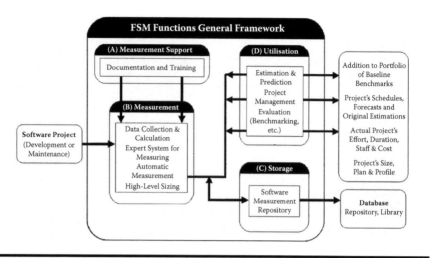

Figure 5.16 FSM Functions - General Framework. (Adapted from Mendes, O., A. Abran, and P. Bourque. 1996. FP Tool Classification Framework and Market Survey.)

5.3.3 COSMIC FFP Fundamentals

COSMIC FFP was designed to measure the functional size of both business application software and real-time software (including embedded, infrastructure, communications, avionics, etc.) (Mendes et al. 1996a) and has been successfully tested. To help classify related support tools, an overview of the COSMIC FFP method is presented next.

Table 5.9 FSM Categories and Key Dimensions

FSM Key Dimensions (4)	Tool Categories (10)
• A) Measurement Support	• Documentation • Training
• B) Measurement	• Data Collection & Calculation • Expert System for Measuring • Automatic Measurement • High-Level Sizing
• C) Storage	• Software Measurement Repository
• D) Ultilization	• Estimation & Prediction • Project Management • Evaluation (Benchmarking, etc.)

Table 5.10 Classification of COSMIC FFP–ISO 19761 Software Support Tools

FSM Key Dimensions (4)	Tool Categories (10)	COSMIC Xpert	ISBSG	MeterIT-Cosmic MeterIT-Project PredictIT	Experience Pro	Knowledge Plan	SIESTA
A) Measurement Support	Documentation	X		X			
	Training	X		X			
B) Measurement	Data Collection & Calculation			X	X	X	X
	Expert System for Measuring	X					
	Automatic Measurement						
	High-Level Sizing			X	X	X	X
C) Storage	Software Measurement Repository		X	X	X	X	
D) Utilization	Estimation & Prediction			X	X	X	X
	Project Management			X	X	X	X
	Evaluation (Benchmarking, etc.)		X	X	X	X	

The method uses only the functional user requirements (FURs) (of a software project) as inputs to the COSMIC FFP measurement process. The process has two phases (Figure 5.17). The first is the mapping phase, where a COSMIC FFP model is generated from the software's FURs that are suitable and necessary as inputs to the measurement process. The second, the measurement phase, is where the COSMIC FFP measurement rules are applied to the FUR model, in order to derive sizes based on the ISO standard of COSMIC FFP (ISO/IEC 19761; ISO 2003a). The COSMIC FFP method takes into account the fact that the software's FURs can be broken down into a set of functional processes. Each of these functional processes can have a unique set of subprocesses that perform either data movements or data manipulations. This decomposition represents the basis of functional size measurement of the COSMIC FFP software model (Figure 5.18). This software model distinguishes four different types of data movements: entry, exit, read, and write (Figure 5.19). For any of the types of movement mentioned, COSMIC FFP considers that a data movement moves exactly one data group (for example, an object in OO software). An entry type data movement distinguishes the data that move from the user (outside the software boundary) across the boundary (through the external software interface) to the inside of the functional process (inside the software boundary). In contrast, the exit type data movement only considers the data group that moves from the inside of the functional process, across the boundary, to the user. The read and write type movements are characterized by the data that are moved from, and to, a persistent data storage (for example, a database). It is from these data movements

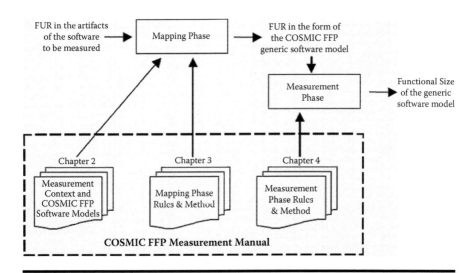

Figure 5.17 COSMIC FFP measurement process model. (Adapted from ISO. 2003. ISO/IEC 19761:2003. Software engineering -COSMIC FFP—A functional size measurement method. International Organization for Standardization. Geneva, Switzerland. ISO Publication.)

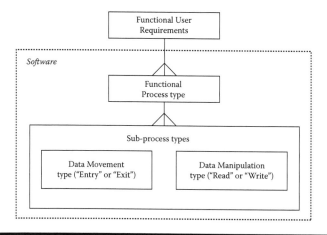

Figure 5.18 COSMIC FFP measurement process model. (Adapted from ISO. 2003. ISO/IEC 19761:2003. Software engineering -COSMIC FFP—A functional size measurement method. International Organization for Standardization. Geneva, Switzerland. ISO Publication.)

that the functional size of a software product is determined in the COSMIC FFP method. To each data movement identified in the software product being measured, a single unit of measure is assigned, which is, by convention, equal to 1 COSMIC functional size unit (Cfsu). Therefore, the total functional size of a measured software product corresponds exactly to the sum of all the assessed data group movements. For detailed measurement rules, see Abran et al. (2003).

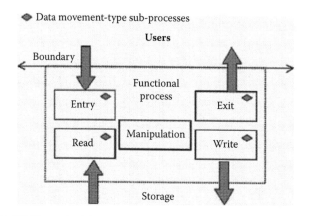

Figure 5.19 COSMIC FFP sub-process types and some of their relationships. (Adapted from ISO. 2003. ISO/IEC 19761:2003. Software engineering -COSMIC FFP—A functional size measurement method. International Organization for Standardization. Geneva, Switzerland. ISO Publication.)

5.3.4 2006 Market Survey Results

A number of support tools are available on the market for COSMIC FFP that help make the method easier to use. In terms of FPA support, COSMIC FFP support tools vary considerably from one to another. The survey has shown that they cover different aspects of the method itself, the method's phases, and the method's outputs for different purposes. Table 5.10 gives a high-level overview of the functions of the seven tools surveyed. For each of these tools, an X fills the cell where a tool addresses (partially or fully) a specific tool category. The tools are presented in Table 5.10 in decreasing order of their number of functions. If two tools have the same number of Xs, no particular order was used. The seven tools surveyed are:

- COSMICXpert
- ISBSG
- MeterIT-Cosmic, MeterIT-Project, PredictIT
- ExperiencePro
- KnowledgePlan
- SIESTA

All the tools mentioned above address more than one of the four key FSM tool dimensions (presented above: measurement support, measurement, storage, and utilization). These tools openly specialize in their respective chosen key dimensions, as they do not purport to do more than they are designed to do, nor do they plan to (see Table 5.10). All the tools included in this survey are briefly described next, based mostly on information provided by their suppliers.

5.3.4.1 COSMICXpert

COSMICXpert is a Web-based expert system that helps practitioners understand COSMIC FFP rules, apply them correctly, and make correct decisions when measuring software. Developed by Desharnais (2000, 2004) in 2004, this tool offers functionalities that help practitioners find the correct measurement answers (solutions) to address the following issue: "How do I interpret my software artifacts in relation to COSMIC FFP rules, in order to derive the correct functional size?" Desharnais (2004) has identified four distinct steps that measurement practitioners must go through when measuring functional size on the basis of FURs. These steps are (in order of execution): understand, interpret, use, and solve (e.g., find the correct measurement result).

When a practitioner enters a keyword,[*] COSMICXpert presents the lists of concepts associated with that keyword, followed by a number of "problem cases"[†] associated

---

[*] The term *keyword*, as used here, comes from the software engineering domain and the COSMIC FFP method terminology. Keywords are used and retained to help a measurer close in on the environment of his problem.

[†] COSMICXpert's knowledge base contains more than one hundred problem cases (Desharnais 2004).

with the concepts on the lists. Finally, it reveals the various topics that correspond to the topological concepts on those lists. The practitioner can then reduce the number of problem cases proposed by COSMICXpert by eliminating the topological concepts that he considers not to be relevant to him. He can also reduce the number of topics by eliminating the nonrelevant problem cases iteratively, until only one problem case remains (interpretation). Lastly, the practitioner can propose a response to the various topics (use) and find the appropriate recommendation (solution). He can also consult the references related to all the COSMICXpert concepts, such as the keywords, the topological concepts, the problem cases, the topics, and the recommendations.

COSMICXpert can be used free of charge, and is available at http://cosmicxpert. ele.etsmtl.ca.

5.3.4.2 ISBSG Release 9

The International Software Benchmarking Standards Group (ISBSG) recently marketed its release 9 (ISBSG 2004), which includes a repository of over three thousand software projects and two software tools: ISBSG Estimation Reality Checker Tool release 3, and ISBSG Comparative Estimation Tool release 5.

The ISBSG Estimation Reality Checker Tool release 3 was designed for the most part for two purposes:

1. To compare software project estimates that have already been calculated against the project history of the ISBSG release 9 CD data (to obtain a reality check)
2. To obtain an initial ballpark estimate for a particular project, again based on the project history of the ISBSG release 9 CD data

The other tool, the ISBSG Comparative Estimating Tool release 5, is an automated MS Excel-based tool designed for early software project life cycle estimation and software project benchmarking. It is used to generate estimates of software project effort, delivery rate, duration, and speed of delivery. The tool provides a number of parameters to select similar projects from the ISBSG release 9 CD data and derived ranges of estimates.

At first, it could not be determined whether this tool's estimating equations (or those of the ISBSG Estimation Reality Checker Tool release 3) were based on projects measured with COSMIC FFP alone or on alternate sizing methods, including COSMIC FFP. But further investigation of the ISBSG Repository release 9 (extract) (ISBSG project data, extracted and implemented in both tools) reveals that the function points seem to include only those measured with the IFPUG method, even though ISBSG release 9 CD data do include software projects sized using the COSMIC FFP method.

Nevertheless, software benchmarking and estimating with COSMIC FFP projects can be performed with ISBSG's latest release, either manually or by using other automated COSMIC FFP support tools.

ISBSG release 9 is commercially available at this address: www.isbsg.org. The ISBSG website[*] also mentions third-party support tools that can be used with the ISBSG release 9 CD data, such as ExperiencePro (www.sttf.fi) and KnowledgePlan (www.spr.com). These third-party support tools are described later in this paper, as they support the COSMIC FFP method.

5.3.4.3 MeterIT Tool Suite

The tool suite consisting of MeterIT-Cosmic, MeterIT-Project, and PredictIT is distributed by Telmaco (www.telmaco.com). It supports users in measuring software, measuring projects, and estimating projects.

The latest version of MeterIT-Cosmic (v1.5, March 2006) (Telmaco 2006) is the main tool considered in this section. It delivers software sizes to the MeterIT-Project tool (project measurement and software benchmarking tool), which in turn provides calibration information to the PredictIT tool (project estimation tool). Table 5.10 does, however, consider the complete tool suite, since it offers, as a whole, functionalities that cover more key dimensions and tool categories than MeterIT-Cosmic alone.

MeterIT-Cosmic is a stand-alone tool that allows practitioners to size existing software products, as well as to estimate software product size (early or late in the software life cycle). Estimation of software size is made possible in MeterIT-Cosmic by making it possible to maintain and quantify, throughout the software life cycle, software requirements as they evolve, and by updating the estimates as the process goes on.

MeterIT-Cosmic accepts a variety of product architectures, such as stand-alone applications, large distributed software products, and hosted, embedded, or real-time applications. It also accepts different product types, such as new software or developments, as well as baseline or enhancement software projects (as does the COSMIC FFP method). The tool offers a product-wide measurement environment that enables a practitioner to measure a piece of software within its product context. This means that a practitioner who wants to measure a complex software product using MeterIT-Cosmic is offered the choice of including the software product's whole system, layers of it, or other items in it. There is even the option of measuring a stand-alone software item without having to include the overall software system's overhead.

According to the product manufacturer's description (Telmaco 2006), the Telmaco tool also offers a means to maintain the COSMIC FFP components, a feature that can be useful for the more experienced practitioner. This means that each of the standard measurement components (such as system, layer, software item, user, triggering event, object of interest, data group, functional process, and data movement) can be created, updated, or deleted in a controlled fashion, so that any software product structure can be modeled and measured according to the practitioner's needs

---

[*] www.isbsg.org.

and wishes. MeterIT-Cosmic also offers functionalities that enable the practitioner to automatically create and upgrade a measurement database.

MeterIT-Project provides reports of the detailed sizing information of software items and aggregated sizing information of software products, and delivers this information to the tool when needed. It also includes a tutorial.

Telmaco offers a thirty-day free trial of MeterIT-Cosmic at http://www.telmaco.com.

5.3.4.4   ExperiencePro 3.1

ExperiencePro is a commercially distributed, stand-alone software tool, developed by Software Technology Transfer Finland (STTF). This tool was designed to help practitioners with software scope management, project estimation and control, change management, software measurement, and data collection (Forselius 2006).

ExperiencePro can use ISBSG project data (see the ISBSG release 9 description presented earlier), as well as the data collected by STTF. STTF (2005) identifies roles for practitioners using ExperiencePro, which are the project manager, the project customer representative, the project office people of the ExperiencePro user company, the database administrator of STTF, the ExperiencePro tool, and lastly, the service provider.

The tool is based on recognized measurement methods (including COSMIC FFP), and it offers functionalities that support software assessment and software measurement and estimation throughout the software life cycle (from early estimation, useful in the earliest life cycle phases, to final reviews, useful in the latest phases).

In addition to supporting project manager needs, ExperiencePro offers several features for project benchmarking and research activities, including (Forselius 2006):

■ Early estimation
■ Improved estimates
■ Progress control
■ Advanced scope management
■ Change management
■ Version comparison reports
■ Project closure and postmortem analysis
■ Project portfolio management and integration facilities

The tool also provides interfaces to other related systems and tools. It enables data transfers from ExperiencePro to other project management tools, such as MS Project, Niku Portfolio Manager, and Artemis, or even MS Excel for statistical studies. ExperiencePro also supports data collection from other project data sources, such as the ISBSG, or the most popular, which are Gartner and Compass (STTF 2005).

ExperiencePro 3.1 is commercially available at www.sttf.fi.

5.3.4.5   KnowledgePlan 4.2

Software Productivity Research (SPR) developed KnowledgePlan 4.2, which offers features to help in tracking milestones, schedules, resources, actual work effort, and the defects found in a software project (SPR 2006b). The SPR website* also mentions that KnowledgePlan can provide a rational view of trade-offs among features, schedules, quality, and costs. The cost and value implications of additional resources, languages, development tools, methods, and technical changes can also be explored with the help of this tool.

KnowledgePlan also provides interfaces to project management applications to create integrated, full software life cycle solutions by enabling practitioners to export and import project data to and from MS Project and other software project management tools (SPR 2006a). In addition, reports and output tables can also be exported for analysis and extended reporting. Some of the project management functions (such as critical path scheduling) are also offered.

According to SPR (2006b), KnowledgePlan is a stand-alone tool that offers a base of historical project data where project sizes were measured using the IFPUG and COSMIC FFP methods. KnowledgePlan also uses this project data knowledge base of functional metrics to derive predictive and analytical productivity rates, given a large number of known (or assumed) parameters. The project data contained in the tool are derived from software projects that have been collected by SPR. It also offers modules to create and calibrate other sets of benchmarking data (such as ISBSG, for example).

KnowledgePlan is a parametric model, with a project data knowledge base as its source of information. There are four primary inputs to the KnowledgePlan model (SPR 2006b). The first is size, which is the key scaling factor and central to the model. The other three inputs revolve around this key factor, and pertain to configurable variables that can alter the model's final outputs, which are the complexity and tools used for the software project, the capability and risk associated with the software project, and finally, the work processes that will be used to complete the software project.

The outputs of the model are deliverable size, assignment scope, production rate, resources, predecessors, work, cost, duration, and defects.

KnowledgePlan 4.2 is commercially available by contacting SPR (www.spr.com).

5.3.4.6   SIESTA Version 1.2.3

SIESTA (Sizing and Estimating Application) is a tool developed by Sogeti (The Netherlands) that supports sizing, estimation, and control. Sogeti now offers this automated tool commercially. SIESTA's functionalities focus on software sizing to support the most widely used methods of software functional sizing, such as FPA and COSMIC

---

* http://www.spr.com/products/knowledge.shtm.

FFP. Variants of these measurement methods have also been implemented in the tool, in order to enable estimation and budget planning early in the software life cycle.

In addition, maintenance variants of both methods have been implemented in SIESTA to estimate what Sogeti calls functional maintenance. As SIESTA's user manual specifies (Sogeti 2003), the tool integrates more than what is proposed in the COSMIC FFP model. The difference is that SIESTA adds estimation functionalities based on Sogeti's measurement model components, which address the maintenance aspect of a software product. The measurement of maintenance, using COSMIC FFP, is very similar to the measurement of new development (Koppenberg and Dekkers 2004). SIESTA differs from COSMIC FFP only in that the modified data movements are calculated and specific situations are considered, such as deleting, replacing, and retesting unmodified functionalities. More precisely, the following three cases are addressed in the SIESTA tool:

1. Functionality deletion: The normal COSMIC FFP size of that functionality is calculated and then multiplied by 0.1.
2. Functionality replacement: The size of the functionality to be replaced is calculated and multiplied by 1.1 (1.0 for new development and 0.1 for deletion of that functionality).
3. Unmodified functionality retesting: The sizes of the functionalities to be retested are calculated (using the COSMIC FFP method) and multiplied by 0.1.

The latest version of SIESTA has been developed considering different types of practitioners. This has been achieved by assigning specific tool features to specific roles, the analyst and the estimator. The tool offers features to enable the *analyst* to name and determine the value of the components of the project being sized, and features to enable the *estimator* to define the budget information by means of which the size of the project can be translated into effort (in hours). According to Sogeti (2003), SIESTA can only be used in one role at a time; however, during project size definition or estimation, one can switch between these two roles.

Sogeti (2003) stipulates that, based on product delivery rates per environment (hours/units) and influences (risks and opportunities), the tool can calculate the expected effort automatically. With respect to the estimation process, the historical project data have to be entered manually.

SIESTA is commercially available by contacting Sogeti (www.sogeti.nl).

5.3.5 Research Prototypes

5.3.5.1 XForms-Format

Inspired by the COSMIC FFP measurement method, Li et al. (2003; Li 2003) propose a functional size metric for interactive software using the user interface (UI) specifications, which, according to these authors (Li et al. 2003), have proved to be effective for effort estimation in the requirements analysis phase (first phase of the software life cycle). It is a noncommercial support system and is still under development at this time. The above-mentioned study reports that an automated measurement support system has been developed, based on the XForms-Format UI specifications, which will facilitate the process of measuring the functional size of interactive software.

Related studies (Li 2003) demonstrate several extensions to the current W3C XForms (XForms is the next generation of Web forms) for its application in FSM, and propose an XForms-Format UI specification that is capable of describing the abstract semantics of user-computer interactions for FSM. It also presents details with regard to the automation of the measurement procedure for measuring standard functional size based on XForms-Format UI specifications. Moreover, it describes the architecture of the support system, as well as the conversion and measurement tools incorporated in that system.

In addition, the tool offers a custom software design environment and a set of measurement tools based on the MS Visio platform. According to Li (2003), this system supports the automatic generation of XForms-Format UI specifications and enables quick FSM for such specifications. The results outputted by this system have been validated systematically in Li's study, to ensure their correctness and completeness.

In summary, the system provides a UI specification format applicable to FSM, and it is one that enables a description of the abstract semantics of user–computer interaction and XForms. The system also enables automatic measurement based on the proposed UI specification format. The former manual measurement procedure is mapped to an automatic version, making the proposed format useful. Finally, the study stipulates that the system integrates an easy-to-use visual diagramming and measurement tool. This environment facilitates both the generation of UI specifications and automatic measurement to better assist in the measurement process.

A prototype version of this tool is available by contacting Zhen Li (see Li 2003).

5.3.5.2 μcROSE, ROOM

μcROSE* is a support tool (still in the research stage) that is being designed to automatically measure the functional size of software (as defined by the COSMIC FFP method) for Rational Rose RealTime (RRRT) models. According to Diab et al. (2004) μcROSE's goal is to streamline the measurement process, ensuring repeatability and consistency in measurement, while eliminating measurement costs. μcROSE was originally developed to be integrated into the RRRT tool set, a CASE tool for designing embedded, real-time, and distributed systems. The authors' (Diab et al. 2004) main motivation for selecting RRRT as the first target for COSMIC FFP measurement automation was its market penetration and close correspondence with COSMIC FFP.

---

* Pronounced "McROSE."

First, the tool enables the automation of software measurement: once the practitioner has identified the subsets of the system to be measured, μcROSE handles all the analyses and calculations based on the COSMIC FFP model by processing the RRRT model. Second, it removes measurement variances and ensures repeatability, tasks that are ensured by the completely automated measurement algorithm. This algorithm is based on the Diab et al. (2004) interpretation of the COSMIC FFP definitions and has been validated by experts who participated in defining the COSMIC FFP method. This interpretation has been formalized in a mathematical definition that is publicly available, and has been implemented in μcROSE.

It is said in Diab et al. (2004) that μcROSE can assist in building a database of completed development projects (containing actual COSMIC FFP size, actual cost, and other measures) to build cost estimation and defect prediction models and to manage software maintenance and outsourcing, all of which are based on functional software size.

The tool accepts software requirements of any size written in the RRRT notation, and then calculates their functional size. A practitioner can select any collection of capsules included in an RRRT model or obtain measurement data with a small number of interactions.

More precisely, the main functionalities offered by μcROSE are (Diab et al. 2004):

1. Visual support of the COSMIC FFP measurement process
2. Generation of an RRRT model in XML format
3. Extraction of RRRT entities required in the measurement process
4. Analysis of C++ code included in the RRRT model
5. Identification of functional processes, data groups, and data movements
6. Calculation of COSMIC FFP and representation of the functional size
7. Aggregation and reporting of measurement results

The initial prototype was originally developed in 2001, but none are currently available for the latest version of RRRT. For more information on this study, contact the authors of this paper.

5.3.5.3 COSMIC RUP

The COSMIC RUP prototype was developed by Azouz (2003) to establish a direct mapping between COSMIC FFP and UML concepts and notation. The objective of this research project was to demonstrate the feasibility of the approach. The prototype's goal and foundation was to extract Rational Rose artifacts to proceed to the software project measurement process. This goal included calculation of the software's functional sizes (once all the specifications had been established, by using RUP early in the life cycle) and provision of early size indicators when only high-level information was available (earlier in the software life cycle, in the requirements phase, for example).

Various artifacts for a software product can be extracted using RUP, and each can correspond to a different level of detail in the software requirements description. Azouz et al. (2004) identified three levels of measurement, where each has its own level of granularity and its own unit of measurement:

1. At the business modeling and requirements analysis level: The use case diagrams are used as artifacts from which the functional size can be calculated. The size unit at this level is referred to as a use case functional size unit (Ufsu).
2. At the analysis level: The scenario diagrams are used as artifacts from which the functional size can be calculated. The size unit at this level is referred to as a scenario functional size unit (Sfsu).
3. At the analysis (and sometimes design) level: The detailed scenario diagrams are used as artifacts from which the functional size can be calculated. The size unit at this level corresponds exactly to the ISO 19761 COSMIC functional size unit (Cfsu).

COSMIC RUP also offers other features that help with estimation, such as an MS Access database, designed to contain a history of project measurements for all three levels of measurement results (Ufsu, Sfsu, and Cfsu). Also, outputted data (measurement results) can either be displayed or sent to an MS Excel worksheet, where they can then be arranged, saved, or printed.

For more details on the 2003 initial prototype, see Azouz (2003).

5.3.5.4 Ontological Formalization

Bévo et al. (2003) proposed an ontological formalization of the COSMIC FFP method, in order to eventually design a tool for software FSM. It is based on the identification of all the concepts handled in the COSMIC FFP method's measurement procedure, as well as the relationships between these concepts (domain ontology). Second, it is based on the identification of all the tasks associated with the method's measurement procedure, as well as the links between those tasks (task ontology).

Bévo et al. (2003) provide the foundations for an ontological formalization of the procedure. These ontologies can easily be used for the design of measurement tools where the tasks and concepts can be described according to the CommonKADS methodology (the leading methodology that supports structured knowledge engineering).*

The authors stipulate in Bévo et al. (1999) that an XML, followed by XMI translation of this ontology, is to be produced for the development of measurement results analysis and documentation tools, as well as some aspects of measurement

---

* http://www.commonkads.uva.nl/frameset-commonkads.html.

result validation. Since XML is appropriate for document exchange, historical databases on projects could also be extended to store more detailed data pertaining to FSM. In that perspective, it is said that the ISBSG could store its project data in either XML or XMI format. This study could also be helpful for data exchange between different FSM tools (in the case where several measurement tools are used for the same FSM method).

The authors stipulate that, eventually, an ontology-oriented approach will be introduced for the complete or partial automation of a method's measurement procedure, because the work on automation is based on the implementation of ontologies. For information about this prototype, contact Valéry Bévo (Bévo et al. 2003).

5.3.6 Observations and Future Work

5.3.6.1 Observations

A survey of the COSMIC FFP support tools has been presented here, and they have been grouped into either commercially available tools or research prototypes. This concise classification of COSMIC FFP–ISO 19761 software support tools makes it possible to perform a gap analysis of them, as well as to identify the functions that have not yet been addressed up to now.

Table 5.10 shows that COSMIC FFP support tools vary considerably, as they cover different aspects of the method or method phase. These tools support one or more of the Mendes et al. (1996b) FSM life cycle phases, but none of them yet fully support automation of the "measurement" key function.

The initial version of COSMIC FFP was published in 1999, and its latest version was released in 2003, the same year it was adopted as an ISO standard. Vendors have therefore only recently started to design tools to facilitate use of the method. This domain of activity is clearly growing rapidly, since almost half the COSMIC FFP support tools assessed only support that method in their newest versions. It has also been shown that one particular tool category has not been addressed by the functions of the tools assessed: "automatic measurement." However, it has also been revealed that an attempt is being made in all the tools being studied at this time to fully automate this particular activity of the COSMIC FFP method's process.

5.3.6.2 Future Work

One step would be to test and evaluate all these tools, and to test each of their features and functionalities to better establish their true usefulness as COSMIC FFP support tools.

It would also be useful to survey the support tools that have not been addressed here, thereby covering, and complying with, the other standardized FSM methods (IFPUG, Mk II FPA, and NESMA).

From Table 5.10, it is possible to evaluate the shortfalls of each of these tools on the one hand, and, on the other, to evaluate the shortfalls inherent in combining all of them, in order to better identify the deficiencies of the market in automating the COSMIC FFP method's process.

In fact, a tool designed to acquire final FSM results that offers full automation of FSM measurement is viewed by the authors of this paper as not requiring the practitioner's low-level input. For example, a tool that requires inputs such as the number of data movements for one software functionality (for the software being measured) actually requires the practitioner to manually count those data movements. This manual count still demands that the practitioner be an expert in the COSMIC FFP method for counting, and does not yet significantly reduce the time taken in performing this activity. Ideally, once the requirements (of the software to be measured) are established and documented in some way (early in the software life cycle phase), automatic measurement would consider the related artifacts as FUR inputs to the support tool, without the need for direct inputs on the part of the practitioner.

This clearly reflects a market shortcoming of COSMIC FFP support tools, although an attempt is being made with the COSMIC FFP support tools currently under study to bridge that gap (see Section 5.3.4).

Acknowledgments

The opinions expressed in this report are solely those of the authors. Special thanks are due to all the tool vendors who responded to our inquiries.

References

Abran, A., J.-M. Desharnais, S. Oligny, D. St.-Pierre, and C. Symons. 2003. *Measurement manual COSMIC full function points 2.2, the COSMIC implementation guide for ISO/IEC 19761*. Montréal: École de technologie supérieure, Université du Québec, University Press.

Abran, A., J.-P. Jacquet, and R. Dupuis. 1998. *Une analyse structurée des méthodes de validation des métriques*. Montreal: Laboratoire de recherche en gestion des logiciels, Département d'informatique Montreal, UQAM Press.

Abran, A., J. W. Moore, P. Bourque, R. Dupuis, and L. Trip. 2004. *Guide to the software engineering body of knowledge*. Los Alamitos, CA: IEEE Computer Society Press.

Albrecht, A. J. 1979. Measuring application development productivity. In *Proceedings of the IBM Applications Development Symposium*, ed. K. Gibson et al., 34–43. Monterey, CA: IBM Corp. Publ.

Ayel, M. 1991. *Validation, verification and testing of knowledge based systems*. Cichester, UK: John Wiley & Sons.

Azouz, S. 2003. Calcul avec ISO 19761 de la taille fonctionnelle des logiciels développés avec Rational Unified Process. Master degree thesis report, Department of Computer Sciences, Université du Québec à Montréal, Canada.

Azouz, S., and A. Abran. 2004. A proposed measurement role in the rational unified process and its implementation with ISO 19761: COSMIC-FFP. In *Proceedings of Software Measurement European Forum 2004 (SMEF2004)*, ed. R. Meli et al., 403–15. Rome, Italy: DPO Publ.

Bévo, V., G. Lévesque, and A. Abran. 1999. Application de la Mèthode FFP à partir d'une spécification selon la notation UML: compte rendu des premiers essais d'application et questions. Paper presented at the International Workshop on Software Measurement (IWSM99). http://www.lrgl.uqam.ca/iwsm99/index2.html (accessed January 31, 2010).

Bévo, V., G. Lévesque, and J.-G. Meunier. 2003. Toward an ontological formalization for a software functional size measurement methods' application process: The COSMIC-FFP case. In *Investigations in software measurement*, ed. R. R. Dumke and A. Abran, 186–203. Aachen, Germany: Shaker Publ.

Boehm, B. W., et al. 2000. *Software cost estimation with COCOMO II*. Englewood Cliffs, NJ: Prentice-Hall.

Coenen, F. 1998. Verification and validation issues in expert and database systems: The expert systems perspective. In *Proceedings of the Ninth International Workshop on Database and Expert Systems Applications (DEXA 98)*, ed. R. R. Wagner, 16–21. Vienna, Austria: University Press.

Craig, C. E., and R. C. Harris. 1973. Total productivity measurement at the firm level. *Sloan Management Review* 14(1):13–29.

Desharnais, J.-M. 2000. *Description sommaire de Help CPR et Help FFP*. ETS Montreal: Université du Québec, University Press.

Desharnais, J.-M. 2004. *Application de la Mesure Fonctionnelle COSMICFFP: une Approche cognitive*. Internal report. Montréal: Université du Québec à Montréal, University Press.

Desharnais, J.-M., A. Abran, A. Mayers, and T. Küssing. 2002. Design of a diagnostic tool to improve the quality of functional measurement. In *Software measurement and estimation*, ed. R. R. Dumke et al., 52–60. Aachen, Germany: Shaker Publ.

Diab, H., F. Koukane, M. Frappier, and R. St.-Denis. 2004. μcROSE: Automated measurement of COSMIC-FFP for Rational Rose Real Time. Internal report. Université de Sherbrooke, Canada. www.dmi.usherb.ca/~frappier/Frappier/Papers/McRose-IST.pdf (accessed January 31, 2010).

Durkin, J. 1994. *Expert system: Design and development*. New York: Prentice Hall.

Eriksson, H.-E., and M. Penker. 1998. *UML toolkit*. Chichester, UK: John Wiley & Sons.

Forselius, P. 2006. *The most important features of ExperiencePro 3—Memo*. Technical report. Tampere, Finland: University Press.

Hayes, C., P. Cunningham, and M. Doyle. 1998. *Distributed CBR using XML*. Technical report. Dublin: Department of Computer Science, Trinity College, University Press.

IFPUG. 1994. *Function point counting practices manual*. Release 4.0. Westerville, OH: International Function Point User Group (IFPUG) Publ.

ISBSG. 2004. *ISBSG estimating, benchmarking and research*. Suite R9. Hawthorn, Victoria, Australia: ISBSG Press.

ISO. 1998. *Information technology—Software measurement—Functional size measurement—Definition of concepts.* ISO/IEC 14143-1:1998(e). Geneva, Switzerland: International Organization for Standardization (ISO) Publ.

ISO. 2002. *Software engineering. MkII function point analysis—Counting practices manual.* ISO/IEC IS 20968. International Organization for Standardization. http://www.iso.org (accessed January 31, 2010).

ISO. 2003a. *Software engineering—COSMIC-FFP—A functional size measurement method.* ISO/IEC 19761:2003. Geneva, Switzerland: International Organization for Standardization (ISO) Publ.

ISO. 2003b. *Software engineering—IFPUG 4.1 unadjusted functional size measurement method—Counting practices manual.* ISO/IEC 20926:2003. International Organization for Standardization. http://www.iso.org (accessed January 31, 2010).

ISO. 2005. *Software engineering—NESMA functional size measurement method version 2.1—Definitions and counting guidelines for the application of function point analysis.* ISO/IEC 24570:2005. Geneva, Switzerland: International Standardization Organization (ISO) Publ.

Jenner, M. S. 2001. COSMIC FFP 2.0 and UML: Estimation of the size of a system specified in UML—Problems of granularity. In *Proceedings of FESMA-DASMA*, ed. M. Bundschuh et al., 173–84. Heidelberg, Germany: FESMA Publ.

Klaus-Dieter, A. 1997. *Validation of CASE-BASED REASONING systems.* Kaiserslautern, Germany: Fraunhofer Institute for Experimental Software Engineering, IESE Publ.

Knauf, R., A. J. Gonzalez, and T. Abel. 2002. A framework for validation of rule-based systems. *IEEE Transactions on Systems, Man and Cybernetics* 32(3):281–95.

Knauf, R., A. J. Gonzalez, and K. P. Jantke. 1999. Validating rule-based systems: A complete methodology. In *IEEE SMC '99 Conference Proceedings*, ed. F. Harashima, 744–49. Los Alamitos, CA: IEEE Computer Society Press.

Koppenberg, T., and T. Dekkers. 2004. Estimating maintenance projects using COSMIC-FFP. In *Software measurement—Research and application*, ed. A. Abran et al., 165–74. Aachen, Germany: Shaker Publ.

Li, Z. 2003. Measuring functional size of interactive software: A measurement support system basing on XForms-Format user interface specifications. Master thesis, Waseda University, Japan.

Li, Z., M. Nonaka, A. Kakurai, and M. Azuma. 2003. Measuring functional size of interactive software: A support system based on XForms-Format user interface specifications. Paper presented at the Third International Conference on Quality Software (QSIC'03). http://doi.ieeecomputersociety.org/10.1109/QSIC.2003.1319123 (accessed January 31, 2010).

Mendes, O., A. Abran, and P. Bourque. 1996a. *Function point tool market survey.* Working Paper. Montréal: Université du Québec à Montréal LRGL, University Press.

Mendes, O., A. Abran, and P. Bourque. 1996b. FP tool classification framework and market survey. Paper presented at the SEMRL, IFPUG Fall Conference. www.gelog.etsmtl.ca/publications/pdf/83.pdf (accessed January 31, 2010).

Meseguer, P., and A. Preece. 1995. Verification and validation of knowledge-based systems. *Knowledge Engineering Review* 10(4):234–48.

Muller, P.-A. 1997. *Instant UML.* Birmingham, UK: Wrox Press.

Preece, A. 2001. Evaluating verification and validation methods in knowledge engineering. In *Micro-level knowledge management*, ed. R. Roy, 123–45. San Francisco: Morgan Kaufman Publ.

Preece, A., and S. Decker. 2002. Intelligent web services. *IEEE Intelligent Systems* 17(1):15–17.

Rational Software Corporation. 1997. *UML semantics*. Appendix M1-UML: Glossary. http://www.ibm.com/developerworks/rational/ (accessed January 31, 2010).

Rule, P. G. 2001. Using measures to understand requirements. In *Proceedings of the ESCOM 2001*. http://www.gifpa.co.uk/library/Papers/Rule/20010404_escom_pgr/v1a.html (accessed January 31, 2010).

Sogeti Nederland B.V. 2003. *SIESTA: User manual*. PW de Meern, Netherlands: Sogeti Press.

SPR. 2006a. *SPR KnowledgePLAN version 4.2 specifications*. Product specification sheet. Hendersonville, NC: Software Productivity Research (SPR) Press.

SPR. 2006b. *SPR KnowledgePLAN version 4 advertisement*. Product brochure. Hendersonville, NC: Software Productivity Research (SPR) Press.

STTF. 2005. *Product description of the ExperiencePro tool*. Software Technology Transfer Finland. http://www.sttf.fi/eng/products/experience/ExperienceSisalto/ExperienceTool.htm (accessed January 31, 2010).

Telmaco. 2006. Product description, MeterIT-COSMIC Software measurement tool. http://www.telmaco.com/pdmetco15e.pdf (accessed January 31, 2010).

Van Heijst, G., A. T. Schreiber, and A. Wielinga. 1997. *Using explicit ontologies in KBS development*. Internal report. Amsterdam: Department of Social Science Informatics, University of Amsterdam Press.

XMLSpy. 2002. Enterprise edition. Alcova. http://www.altova.com (accessed January 31, 2010).

Index

Printed and bound by CPI Group (UK) Ltd, Croydon, CR0 4YY

23/10/2024

01777673-0014